KATYN KILLINGS:
IN THE RECORD

by
John H. Lauck

The Kingston Press Inc.

ISBN: 0-940670-30-5

LC: 88-80479

Published by

The Kingston Press, Inc.
P.O. Box 2759
Clifton, N.J. 07015

Printed in the United States of America

Contents

Maps

Photographs

Appendices

Requiescat in Pace
(Rest in Peace)

A memorial dedicated to the Polish prisoners of war who disappeared during World War II (1940) on Russian soil, without leaving a trace of evidence as to what happened, except for the facts provided herein and in other analyses. May their bereaved families be consoled by the Lord's Beatitude: "Blessed are the poor in spirit; the kingdom of heaven is theirs."

Acknowledgements

Gratitude is expressed to two special authors whose books on the Katyn atrocity motivated this writer to research his interest in the incident: Joseph Mackiewicz (THE KATYN WOODS MURDERS—1951), who recorded one of the eyewitness accounts of Katyn; and Josef Czapski (THE INHUMAN LAND—1951), a Polish officer who chronicled his survival of prisoner of war status at Starobielsk. Both Journalist Mackiewicz and Major Czapski appeared as witnesses at the Hearings of the Select Committee composed of members of the United States House of Representatives. The printed record of these Hearings contributed substantially to the factual data researched by the writer. Another significant contribution was that of the Polish Cultural Foundation (THE CRIME OF KATYN—published in Polish, 1945, and in English, 1965).

Other authors, including a considerable number of Europeans, who wrote versions and eyewitness accounts of the harsh life, hope for survival, and desire for escape from prisoner of war camps are recognized, also. (See BIBLIOGRAPHY.) One classic example of prisoner of war perseverance in the face of overwhelming odds was chronicled by Edgar D. Whitcomb (ESCAPE FROM CORREGIDOR—1958), an American prisoner of war who became a Governor of Indiana.

Special appreciation is extended to many individuals who provided the writer with encouragement, support, and/or expertise. Professor Z. C. Szkopiak, Undersecretary of State, Republic of Poland, Government-in-Exile, London, made the Polish library available. Brigadier General Edward Simmons, USMC, Retired, Director of the Marine Corps Museum and History, gave organizational counsel and provided considerable direction. Colonel Verle E. Ludwig, USMC, Retired, presented succinct policy suggestions. Dr. James Koch, President, University of Montana and formerly Provost and Vice President for Academic Affairs, Ball State University, provided motivation and support. Marie Fraser, Director of Public Relations, Ball State University, assisted with publication advice. Gail Winsmore and her hard working staff at the Indiana State Library, Indianapolis, assisted and located invaluable research sources. Timothy Mulligan and the Military Reference Branch, Military Archives Division, National Archives, Washington, D.C., aided in the research process. Professor Emeritus C. Jane Whelan, Ball State University, did an indispensable task of editing.

Thomas M. Brown, M.D., a United States Naval Surgeon in the Pacific Theater of Operations in World War II (Iwo Jima, Japan, etc.), corroborated the accuracy of the forensic medicine research. Dr. James E. Walters, Ball State University, reacted with dialogue on technical points of organizational strategy and support. The staff of Bracken Library, Ball State University, gave aid in the use of this primary resource center. The Publications and Intellectual Properties Committee of Ball State University has offered support, loyalty, and encouragement.

Special acknowledgement for her encouragement goes to my wife, the eternal dreamer, who gives meaning to the Marine Corps motto, SEMPER FIDELIS—"Always Faithful."

Introduction

History is approaching the 50th Anniversary of the tragic atrocity referred to as the Katyn Forest Massacre. Should the killings that occurred at Katyn Forest remain an unsolved murder mystery? If blame is to be established, would justice eventually prevail? Has the time arrived to reflect on governmental conscience as it prevailed then, and as it prevails now? Are attitudes toward justice different today; or could an atrocity in similar form, or of even greater magnitude, be repeated without blame or censure?

Accounts state that approximately 15,000 Polish officers disappeared into the U.S.S.R. early in World War II; yet approximately only 4,253 bodies could be found and exhumed. What happened to the other 10,000 plus leaders, still missing in action? Actually, no evidence of the whereabouts of these victims has ever been found.

None of these missing persons were political prisoners, or criminals; they were predominately officers of the Polish army who were condemned to be prisoners of a war which was never formally declared to be a war by the Russian government. In fact, fighting had ended eight months earlier at the time these prisoners of war were captured; too, supposedly, it was peacetime! Can their souls *Requiescat in Pace* (Rest in Peace)—meaning "Peace in Death" in the Christian world—when the country responsible for their victimization has never been specifically identified?

History confirms that mass murder as government policy has been around for a long time. Though the Katyn killings were not of the magnitude of Hitler's extermination of the Jews before and during World War II, Stalin's starvation of the Ukranians in 1932–33, or Mao's induced famine that resulted in starvation of the Chinese between 1957 and 1962, even as a microcosm the Katyn atrocity punctuates the fact that the policy of mass murder does not serve justice.

In accord with this premise, the writer concentrated on the two opposing reference areas relative to the Katyn data: first, the German account of its investigation; second, the Russian posture for its position; finally, then, that research was used to make a comparative correlation of facts for use in identifying evidential conclusions. This in-depth analysis required the development of a basic strategy. Paramount in the writer's reference-frame was an understanding of the significance of the political policies in effect at that time. Both pre- and immediate post-World War II data, as well as the forensic medicine techniques of the time, were researched. Also, newspaper releases, maps showing boundary changes, dictionary revisions, dated atlases, etc., were used to visualize the war theater and political arena of that era. Anticipating that government techniques and policies that encourage and violate the concepts of human rights do reoccur, the writer then correlated the significance-value placed on past actions with the possible import such actions could have within present and future timeframes.

Because both governments proffered information that led to contrary findings, a stalemate of identity continues to exist: the German government still blames the Russians for committing the Katyn atrocity; the Russian government claims the Germans were the culprits. From the writer's findings where would you place the blame?

PART I

KATYN KILLINGS

Chapter 1

WORLD WAR II ERUPTS IN EUROPE

According to the peace terms established by the Treaty of Versailles (1919), formally ending World War I, Poland included Russian Poland, parts of East Prussia, Upper Silesia, Galicia, Prosen, and Lithuania; and its borders touched the Baltic Sea, Lithuania, Latvia, the Soviet Union, Romania, Czechoslovakia, and Germany. Its best known product exports were coal, petroleum, iron and steel, zinc, timber, grains, and animal products. The country covered an area of 149,915 square miles (1937) and accommodated a total population of 34,220,000.[1] Warsaw, its capital, (often identified as Warsazawa in Europe) had in this timeframe the largest Polish population in the world—mostly Slavs and Jews; Chicago, Illinois, some 4,000 miles away, housed the second largest number of Poles. The primary religion was Catholic.

Prior to the peace terms that formally ended World War I and established "modern Poland" (1919), the "partition (division into parts[2]) of Poland" had become a common expression; in fact, earlier Poland had endured three partitions.[3] The first partition occurred when Frederick the Great of Prussia, who wanted to prevent Austria from weakening his political strength, entered into an agreement with Catherine of Russia (1772). Catherine took the country east of the Duna and Dnieper Rivers; Frederick took West Prussia, except Danzig and Thorn, and thereby linked old Brandenburg and Prussia; and Austria received Galicia and the city of Cracow (Krakow). The second partition followed (1793) when Russia took additional territory. Two years later (1795) Austria joined Russia and Prussia to partition Poland for the third time. Austria took the upper valley of the Vistual; Prussia the lower valley, including Warsaw; and Russia acquired the remainder, by far the largest portion. True, Poland was the victim of other partitions, but these occurred years later.[4]

During this earlier period Poland's political situation could have been easily thwarted. But the country suffered from four predicaments: a lack of natural boundaries; a heterogeneous population composed of nobles and peasants that lacked the presence of an influential middle class; a diversification of

3

religions; and an ineffective government administered by an elective king who was a puppet of a Diet which could not enact laws without unanimous agreement (liberum veto), including assent of the European powers.

After World War I Marshal Joseph Pilsudski emerged as head of state and commander of the Polish army. His goal was not only to retrocede (to 1795) Poland's freedom as a country, but also to return (to 1772) its frontiers to the boundaries encompassed before its first partition. Since Russia was in the throes of a Civil War which the communists were winning, Marshal Pilsudski launched his first attack, gaining the element of surprise, against the Russians (April 25, 1920). Although there had been some fighting earlier, this surprise attack carried the Poles all the way to Kiev (May 7, 1920). The Russians counterattacked (May 15) with a numerically superior force that pushed the Polish army back until Marshal Pilsudski held a defensive line that protected Warsaw, Lublin, and Lwow until mid-August.

The budding communist government of Russia believed that all Europe was ready for a revolution and if its army could beat the Poles and get beyond Warsaw, the resultant victory would rally its cause in the countries of central and eastern Europe. In truth, this Russian government was committed to imperialistic expansion that would lead to the domination of Europe and eventually the world, for the dismemberment of the German and Austro-Hungarian empires after World War I had left no significant military power east of France that could contain the Soviets. The Marxists (then, so-called) already controlled Hungary and parts of Germany (Bavaria and Berlin) and they were aware that their future impact in Europe depended upon the outcome of the fight between the Soviets and the Poles for Warsaw.

Between May and August of 1920 the Russians had pushed the Polish army from Kiev back to Warsaw. There, in a daring military maneuver (later known as the Battle of Warsaw), Marshal Pilsudski's Polish army moved to the offensive, attacked the Soviet army in the center of its line and breeched the Russian positions at a time and place least expected. Then, within five days, (by August 21, 1920), the Polish army moved north and defeated Russia's right flank. Victory for the Poles was within their grasp, for General Sikorski and his units had held the Polish southern (right) flank with a minimum of troops then had moved to the offensive and succeeded in forcing the army to retreat. By now the armies of both Poland and Russia were so depleted and debilitated the governments agreed to an armistice (October 10, 1920), which was formalized in the Treaty of Riga, (March 18, 1921), that established the line of Poland's eastern border. This line was maintained until broken by the intervention of the German and Russian armies at the outset of World War II (September, 1939).

In passing it should be noted that Poland, almost twenty years before the outbreak of hostilities of World War II, standing alone, temporarily thwarted communism militarily and deterred direct aggression by Russia against other countries; a Polish victory the Soviets would not forget.

Lebensraum, (the concept of living space), had become the "core" word in the strategy being developed in Germany prior to World War II. Adolf Hitler let the world know throughout the pages of his book, Mein Kampf, (My Battle),[5] that Germany would ultimately become the world's leading political and military power with him as its leader, and that the peaceful policies of industrialization espoused by the Second Reich[6] (the Kaiser's government) would lower Germany to the level of a colony. He considered overseas trade to be a "monumental folly" because trade depended on peaceful co-existence which could portend only one conclusion: the nullification of all hope for an effective policy of government. The categorical opponents of his "master race" were pinpointed as Marxism and Judaism because their philosophy of commerce and peace would only divide the German nation; therefore, he proposed that Marxists and Jews must be ruthlessly exterminated. Because "nature reserves land and soil for that people which has the energy to take it and the industry to cultivate it" Hitler contended that expansion by Germany on the European continent was but a natural law.[7] Where, then, he countered but in the Old World would be found the Lebensraum which would be required for a vibrant, dynamic, vital German nation to exist; thereby establishing as his special mission the conquest of all lands to the east, and the destruction of the bolshevist civilization of the Union of Soviet Socialist Republics (U.S.S.R.).

Deviously, efficiently and without haste, Hitler set his plan in motion to become the world's "peaceful" conqueror. The Nazi Party was organized (1921), then, the SA (storm troops) were formed (1922), followed by the SS (elite troops) and the Gestapo (secret police). The strength of this consolidated Nazi power was evidenced immediately after the fire of the Reichstag building (February 27, 1933). On the day following the fire Hitler obtained a decree from the aged and ailing President von Hindenburg of the Weimar Republic that any constitutional guarantees of civil liberties would be suspended, which foretold that secret arrests and indefinite detention would be made without charges, without evidence, and without counsel.[8] Since the Nazi strategy of bloodless victories identified no line between war and peace, so-called "peace" became simply a "broadened strategy" of society that involved economic, psychological, and other non-military tactics. All of which inferred that the Nazi armed forces of the Third Reich would be used as a German war machine only when unavoidable and as a last resort.

Hitler believed in following a well-developed policy of chopping away, of destroying one small state after another. As a consequence far-reaching political changes were being made without bloodshed and without the use of troops as instruments of combat, but at all times Hitler maintained the threat of war by

5

keeping Germany's overwhelming military capabilities visibly exposed. As examples of these tactics recall the logic of intervention in Spain, the military alliance with Italy (1939), the campaign to recover the Saar, the re-occupation of the Rhineland (March 7, 1936), the seizure of Czechoslovakia (March 13, 1939), the occupation of Sudetenland (October, 1938), the invasion and annexation of Austria (March 13, 1938), the construction of the west wall, the non-aggression pact with the Soviet Union (1939), and the planned partition of Poland (1939). Usually, Hitler would warn his next victim of Germany's aggression by renouncing an earlier non-aggression pact, such as his agreement with Poland (1934) and the Naval Treaty with Great Britain (1935). But, finally, Great Britain and France became alerted by the seizure of Czechoslovakia by Germany that the ambitions of the Axis countries had become insatiable. Both countries promised armed support to Turkey, Greece, Romania, and Poland if the Axis nations initiated an attack.

Because of the ill feeling that had developed in both western and eastern European nations against Russia's system of government the Soviets could not form any common front against the Axis powers. In fact, Russia attempted to assure its own safety and survival by assuming an attitude of isolation. The Soviets perceived Munich (the agreement between Adolf Hitler and Great Britain's Prime Minister Neville Chamberlain regarding Czechoslovakia) as a vehicle the English and French were using to seek peace for themselves by encouraging Hitler to expand to the east. As a result Russia made the trade agreement with Germany (August 23, 1939) followed by the non-aggression pact that pledged both countries to settle all disputes by peaceful consultation for a period of ten years.

Poland's isolation had become almost complete! Although Great Britain and France had made pledges to help, neither country offered any substantial military support. But Poland, weak and ill-equipped for war, prepared to fight. The Polish army was fully aware of the danger involved in armed conflict against Germany, for Poland's top-rated intelligence network had been functioning at peak efficiency. They were cognizant that Germany appeared to have two exclusive advantages; by joining in the pact with Russia, Hitler had assured himself that (1) neither France nor Great Britain would become a Soviet ally, and that (2) he would not have to fight on two fronts at the same time. Hitler's mighty German army that he had used in the past as a part of his "war of nerves" was going to have to fight to conquer Poland.

Germany now needed a military victory, and Poland was to become Hitler's first victim (September 1, 1939) in the war that Hitler anticipated would lead to his ultimate conquest of Europe. Militarily, Hitler employed the blitzkrieg tactics, defined as a penetration for paralysis aroused by lightning armored columns, supported by tactical air, exploited by firepower of infantry and artillery, and all other supporting arms that assured mobility and shock action.[9]

Although Great Britain and France, as a fulfillment of their pledge to defend Polish independence, declared war on the Third Reich, (September 3, 1939), neither country was prepared to launch a "second front" to take the pressure off Poland.

The German "blitz" of Poland ended summarily on September 18, 1939, when the government of Poland collapsed. The Poles had fought valiantly to protect their western areas between the German border and their capital— Warsaw. In fact, their plan had been to maintain a general reserve of troops in the vicinity of Warsaw. The tanks of the German army had reached the capital city by September 8, but the Poles held it until September 27. When the Polish government fled on September 17, the Germans already had claimed almost 700,000 Poles as prisoners of war. However, some 80,000 Poles had made border escapes.

Blitzkrieg, this tactical success of the Germans, now became known world-wide as the use of mobile warfare that combined strong armored columns with tactical air forces and supported by artillery units. The blitzkrieg theory had been tested earlier in Great Britain where it had been described as "lightning," but the German-Polish clash had provided conclusive proof that its operational use would be successful.

Because the flat, open plains of western Poland had been ideally suited for an invasion by mobile forces a critic[10] will observe occasionally that the Polish army would have been better positioned had it been assembled farther eastward behind the broad beds of the Vistula and San Rivers. Doing so, however, would have made the most valuable portions of Poland's western country more vulnerable to attack, including its Silesian coal fields and great industrial zone. Too, Poland had to consider its economic (or business) argument for trying to keep intact its industrial heartland, an argument reinforced by a strong sense of national pride and confidence, as well as the hope its western allies would come to its assistance. The Poles' plan was to be offensive-minded and ready to counterattack and not be tied down to a main line of resistance that could be penetrated easily. Their intent was good but their ability to move quickly was hindered, for redeployment of troops was virtually impossible when the Germans were attacking the railroad and road networks by air. In short, though the Polish army fought bravely against great odds, the consequences of a lack of mechanized capability as well as not being completely mobile and fully prepared ultimately brought about the collapse of the government.

History is less specific about what was developing along Poland's eastern frontier. The Hitler-Stalin pact (summer, 1939) had planned for Germany to seize the western one half of Poland and Russia the eastern. Militarily, the Soviets seemed slow to respond, perhaps because the Russian propaganda system was transmitting radio messages into Poland suggesting the Russians were coming to the aid of the Poles. The Polish Ambassador to Moscow (Grzybowski) found out the propaganda was false when he was called to the Deputy Soviet Commissar for Foreign Affairs' (Potemkin) office at 3:00 A.M. (September 17, 1939) to have read to him and then receive the "note" which officially notified the Poles that the Russians were overtly entering Poland from her eastern borders. Polish Ambassador Grzybowski refused to receive the note.[11]

The Russian attack (September 17, 1939) from the east came on the day Poland's government fled from Warsaw. Even though the Germans had gained the upper hand over Poland, there appeared to be some information that the army of the Third Reich could have overextended itself, and if the intelligence data were correct and the German attack slackened, the Poles might have continued their fight had Russia not attacked their eastern border. Also, the French had promised to attack Germany's western border on that same day but cancelled after Russia's attack on Poland. Excerpts from two governmental documents confirm Poland's plight. First, the statement from the British Ministry of Information (September 18, 1939):

> The British Government has considered the situation created by the attack upon Poland ordered by the Soviet Government. This attack made upon Great Britain's ally at a moment when she is prostrate in the face of overwhelming forces brought against her by Germany cannot, in view of His Majesty's Government, be justified by the arguments put forward by the Soviet Government. The full implication of this is not yet apparent, but His Majesty's Government takes the opportunity of stating that nothing has occurred that can make any difference to the determination of His Majesty's Government, with full support of the country, to fulfill their obligation to Poland and prosecute the war with all the energy until their objectives have been achieved.

Second, the joint statement made by the German and Russian governments (September 28, 1939), just ten days after the statement of Great Britain:

> The Government of the Third Reich and the Government of the USSR having, by means of the treaty signed today, definitely settled the problems of the disintegration of the Polish state and having thereby created a firm foundation for a lasting peace in Eastern Europe, they mutually express their conviction that it would serve the true interest of all peoples to put an end to the state of war existing between Germany on the one side and England and France on the other. Both Governments will therefore direct their common efforts, jointly with other friendly powers if occasion arises, toward attaining this goal as soon as possible.
>
> Should, however, the efforts of the two Governments remain fruitless, this would demonstrate the fact that England and France were responsible for the continuation of the war; in which case the Governments of Germany

and the USSR shall engage in mutual consultation with regard to necessary measures.

Obviously, the second document points out the fact that Russia did invade Poland from the east for the benefit of the U.S.S.R.; that Russia entered Poland in a clear act of aggression that had been well planned before Hitler attacked Poland.

The German and Russian forces met along the line that extended from East Prussia south past Bialystok, Brest-Litovsk, and Lwow to the Carpathians. They welcomed each other as friends, as well as military and political partners ready to consummate another partition of Poland. Germany took the western one half of Poland, including Warsaw; Russia the eastern one half. The Ribbentrop-Molotov Line, so-named for the foreign ministers who had formulated the non-aggression pact between the two countries (August 23, 1939), became the line of demarcation.

Captured Polish soldiers were now prisoners of war of either Germany or Russia. Russia's style of prisoner of war assignments was to quickly separate military officers, especially senior officers, from the enlisted men. The Soviets used the time-tested theory of political action propaganda to get opposing soldiers to surrender. Russia was aware it could use the troops of Poland advantageously, provided they could be converted to the Soviets' doctrine. For example, one item of propaganda disseminated by the Russians to the Polish soldiers told them "the leaders of the Polish state, together with their inept generals, plunged the country into war with Germany, but they soon failed."[12]

Often propaganda leaflets would be transmitted by dropping them from an aircraft or including them in artillery shells. Shortly after the Red Army had invaded Poland, General S. Timoshenko, Commander in Chief of the Ukranian Front, prodded the Polish soldiers to turn against their leaders and surrender to the Russians. The following message, directed to the Poles, is a sample:

> In the last few days the Polish Army has been finally defeated. The soldiers of the towns of Tarnopol, Halicz, Rowne, Dubno, over 60,000 of them voluntarily came over to our side.
>
> Soldiers, what is left for you? What are you fighting for? Against whom are you fighting? Why do you risk your lives? Your resistance is useless. Your officers are light-heartedly driving you to slaughter. They hate you and your families. They shot your negotiators whom you sent to us with a proposal of surrender.
>
> Do not trust your officers! Your officers and generals are your enemies. They wish you death. Soldiers, turn on your officers and generals. Do not submit to the orders of your officers. Drive them out from your soil. Come to us boldly, to your brothers, to the Red Army. Here you will be cared for, here you will be respected.

> Remember that only the Red Army will liberate the Polish people from
> the fatal war and after that you will be able to begin a new life.
> Believe us, the Red Army of the Soviet Union is your friend.[13]

The Poles now faced the lot of a defeated nation. Their military forces found themselves unsuccessful in the defense of the nation's freedom, and, in effect, the military organization was disbanded. Some men were able to depart from their military assignments and make their way home, there to anticipate their future in a defeated country. Most Polish soldiers were seized by the Russian army wherever they were found and made prisoner of war captives.

As prisoners of war of Russia, the captured Poles were "gathered up" and transported on long arduous trips to Russian POW camps. Before being moved these prisoners would be segregated according to rank or rate in the military service; in effect, leaders were separated from followers. This technique was one of the psychological weapons Russia used to deny Polish officers the responsibility and direction for the enlisted men assigned to their leadership.[14] The Soviets made on-the-spot capture assignments as more and more Poles came under their control. Perhaps a few individuals would be taken here, a squad or platoon there, a larger unit somewhere else—and this practice was not relegated to just the military; any Polish army remnants, such as border or frontier guards, received equal "heinous kindness."

The Polish military structure was being dismembered. Approximately 14,920 Polish leaders—officers (regular and reserve), cadet officers, military policemen, frontier guards, etc.—were sent to three primary Russian POW camps: Kozielsk, Ostashkov, and Starobielsk.[15] These three camps had been religious monasteries many years earlier but had not been used since religious orders had been outlawed in Russia. Any amenities of livability were zero due to the state of disrepair of the buildings. The camps became classical examples of demoralization and deprivation.[16] Non-leaders, by the same Soviet standards, were herded together in a series of other POW camps deep inside the Soviet Union.

Within the leader camps an endeavor quickly evolved to organize some type of internal self-management. These prisoners of war hoped for an early release and return to Poland. Instead, their interrogation sessions by the Russians were begun immediately. In these one-on-one meetings a skilled NKVD (Soviet secret police) interrogator would question a Polish officer. The session could be either long or short, depending upon the discretion of the Russian and in this inquisition-like atmosphere the mood could change quickly from an attempt at friendliness to one of hostility. The Russians hoped to glean some crumbs of military intelligence data from the sessions, but the obvious purpose of each interrogation was to determine whether that Polish officer could be cultivated into the communist mold, either on an individual or group basis. The ones "selected" could be used later to promote the tenets of the Communist Party back in Poland, after being schooled sufficiently by the NKVD and with direct control from Moscow.

The strong will, moral fiber, and loyal patriotism of the Polish officers was exceedingly commendable, for few Poles filtered into being of any resource value to the Russians. Those "selectees" usually were gifted individuals—such as artists, painters, authors, scholars, creative individuals, etc.—because their value in the future to Russia could be anticipated even though they made no commitment to be "communized."[17]

After the German army invaded Poland (1939), both Great Britain and France knew their conclusions of Hitler's goals were correct. The temperament of appeasement had simply made Adolf Hitler bolder and Germany gained the Saar, Rhineland, Austria, Sudetenland, and Czechoslovakia. Even though Hitler's aggression brought about a declaration of war against Germany by both countries, fulfilling their pledge by militarily defending Polish independence was not compatible with their capabilities. Neither nation was prepared to engage in full scale war activities or to immediately send military support.

France made a limited attack on the Saar Basin after mobilizing its army along the Maginot Line, whose defensive positions had been built before World War II at a cost of approximately two million dollars a mile. The winter for the French government was spent primarily in war-preparedness measures, such as the building of tanks, planes, etc. No major effort to open a second front to relieve the pressure on the Polish army by the Germans was developed by France, though the French were aware the Polish military was fighting for the survival of the Polish Republic.

After a month Great Britain sent a small expeditionary force to assist the French in their defensive role. No air raids were initiated against the Germans by either government perhaps because both countries feared a swift reprisal by the Germans knowing the large number of planes in the German air force. As an alternative, the two countries followed the example of defensive measures used in World War I and began to enhance industrial bases where military armaments could be produced for use wherever and whenever the army of the Third Reich might attack.

Without providing troops being involved in major military engagements, Great Britain and France made the war appear as "a phony" to countries outside of Europe (winter, 1939–40). The military capability of Germany had become known as "blitzkrieg" (lightning war) and the British and French response as "sitzkrieg" (sitting war). No credit was given to Great Britain and France for declaring war on Germany when the latter attacked Poland, and for refusing to accept Hitler's offer of peace (October, 1939) after Poland had been

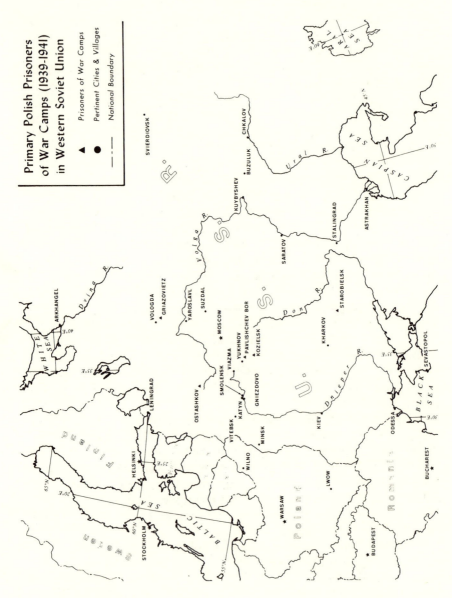

Primary Polish Prisoners
of War Camps (1939-1941)
in Western Soviet Union

▲   Prisoners of War Camps
●   Pertinent Cities & Villages
---   National Boundary

conquered, unless freedom was restored to Czechoslovakia and Poland. The assumption prevailed that Germany could not retain the spoils of war without overcoming Great Britain and France.

The British government was so aroused when Germany claimed Denmark and Norway that it replaced Prime Minister Neville Chamberlain with Winston Churchill. The latter changed from "peace in our time" (Chamberlain's Munich remark) to "Our only aim is victory, for without victory there is no survival!" and that success would require "blood, toil, tears, and sweat," the words used in the acceptance remarks of now Prime Minister Churchill.

The Nazi blitzkrieg that roared across the border of Holland, Belgium, and Luxembourg was designed to make a swift advance into France and gain a quick victory. It did! France fell in one month (May, 1940). The German army made a lightning-like attack, coordinated its tank advances with aviation support, bypassed the frontal assault the French were hoping for, and swept around the left flank of France's Maginot Line. France's government was already diffused with many internal problems and its plight as a nation divided made its downfall imminent.

Germany's military success in France caused Great Britain to order the commencing of a withdrawal of troops from Dunkirk. The Germany's Army of the Third Reich breeched the Allies' defensive line with a penetration of sixty miles (May 17) and reached the sea (May 20), thereby splitting the allies. The British barely escaped defeat at Dunkirk, for the Belgian army had capitulated (May 28) and left the British army in a small pocket some twenty three miles in width. From this tight defensive area the British successfully evacuated approximately 337,000 personnel in over 880 ships of all types in one of the more noteworthy retrograde achievements in military annals. Even so, Britain was committed to a declaration of war against Germany over the issue of Poland.

Germany began its final phase of the campaign against France (June 5) by penetrating almost to Rethel (June 9). The invaders crossed the Seine River (June 11), entered Paris (June 14), and reached the Swiss frontier (June 17), a move that closed the Maginot Line. Marshal Henri Petain, provisional head of the French government, was forced to ask for an armistice (signed, June 25). It was a military defeat that humiliated France internationally. Other immediate losses were later sustained by France, such as its colonial empire, including French Indo China. The seat of government was moved to Vichy, in southern France. Paris was occupied by the Germans.

During this final German conquest of France, Benito Mussolini had sent his Italian Alpine troops into southern France (June 10), thereby fulfilling his agreement with Germany to be an Axis partner. President Roosevelt succinctly described this attack in one sentence: "The hand that held the dagger has struck it into the back of its neighbor."

These early defeats of Poland's allies, including the withdrawal of

Great Britain and the capitulation of France and Belgium, foretold its demise on the continent.

The high command of the German army knew that Britain might not be prepared for amphibious landings. Their plan was to pulverize Britain by having the German air force of some 2,750 aircraft start the so-called "Battle of Britain" by destroying the British air force. Then Germany would use its navy to complete an amphibious landing that would overcome the strength of the Royal Navy. The air attacks by the Germans went far beyond military targets, such as air fields (July, August, 1940). During the summer cities (especially London, beginning September 6) suffered heavy bombings intended by Germany to demoralize the civilian population and destroy logistical support targets, such as food supplies. The British suffered a high toll but the will to resist was strengthened, not weakened, by these air attacks. Although Great Britain was incapable of returning combat forces to Europe, it had sought and been given material support from the United States which was a country at peace and one that would not become actively engaged militarily until the next year after Japan committed its dastardly attack on Pearl Harbor.

Adolf Hitler would have preferred to have defeated Great Britain, or to have accomplished a negotiated peace, but neither of these alternatives was presently available and his military operations were beginning to stalemate. He issued a secret order (December 18, 1940) to his Chiefs of Service to plan to overwhelm the Soviet Union in a single, lightning-like campaign (later called operation BARBAROSSA). His non-aggression pact with the Soviets (1939) had been only a ruse to prevent having to fight on two fronts. He announced and justified this conquest to the German people on the premise "Russia was getting read to proceed against me." His utopia of Lebensraum was going to have to be accomplished by moving troops eastward into Russia while keeping Great Britain on the defensive with air attacks. An invasion of the U.S.S.R. would be a gigantic task for the Third Reich. Soviet territory covered some 8,500,000 square miles—one sixth of the land mass of the globe—approximately three times the area of the United States.

Hitler planned to advance on Leningrad and Moscow, to overwhelm the Russian forces defending these cities, and to execute this military maneuver before any outside forces could become involved. This German blitzkrieg, (operation BARBAROSSA), was unleashed (June 21, 1941) from the Bug River, and the encircling movements (called "pincer movements") used by veteran soldiers of the Third Reich gathered territory, cities, towns, and Russian prisoners (323,000 at Minsk alone) under the German umbrella. Also, targeted for attacks were Kiev, Kharkov, Rostov, Stalingrad, and the Caucasian oil fields. But the initial goal was to render Moscow inoperable before the 1941–42 winter set in. If Russia did not accept Germany's terms, Caucasia would be seized the following year. Because Germany had been the only ally Finland ever had, an ancillary operation would be affected by that country. In addition, an offensive operation from the upper Pruth was planned with the Romanians.

All of the German army groups (northern, central, and southern) enjoyed initial successes, but this continuation will include only data about the central army group that utilized the primary route to Moscow because one of its objectives was Smolensk.

Smolensk was a vital railroad and communication center located only 250 miles from Moscow. The German army reached its outskirts (July 16) and initiated a tank battle of great magnitude that lasted three weeks (to August 7). Reports from the media indicated the Russians fought hard and suffered large casualties because they did not want to give up this city and its nearby villages and woods. The German central army group prevailed even though heavy casualties and material losses disrupted their Moscow timetable. As a matter of fact, they remained on the defensive until another battle could be initiated (October 2). The combined groups of German troops[18] had opened a 2,000 mile front that would ultimately facilitate penetration of some 600 miles into the heart of the Soviet Union.

In the meantime the families and friends of the Polish prisoners of war at the three Russian prisoners of war camps (Kozielsk, Ostashkov, and Starobielsk) had received no communication from those incarcerated since March, 1940. Concerned families who inquired about their whereabouts were told by the Soviet authorities that the camps had been "closed." Since it would be absurd to assume any public facility (prison, jail, hospital, etc.), operated by a governmental agency would be "closed" when the country was not under seige, the question of where these POWs literally had disappeared to, required an answer.

Tolstoy, in "Stalin's Secret War,"[19] explained, in detail, the Soviet system of "closing" incarceration locations in times of emergency. When the contingency was anticipated, prisoners would be transported to another location by a lorry (the "black raven"), a bus-like vehicle designed with a narrow center aisle from which doors opened into cage-like compartments. If the evacuation were on short notice, an emergency basis, the prisoners simply would be shot to death and left behind as the remaining guards fled. In other words, when there was a possibility a prison would be overrun by an approaching enemy, Stalin dictated prisoners would be subjected to the lowest abyss of inhumanity, a massacre. Rationalizing such an action, Kravchenko described how the fear of a prison outbreak could be a retaliation on the leaders of the Soviet system: "perhaps in a nightmare (the Communist leaders) saw twenty million slaves suddenly crushing through prison walls and barbed wire enclosures in a multitudinous stampede of hatred and vengeance, in a flood tide of destruction. . . ."[20] When the Germans attacked (June 21), an order was sent from NKVD headquarters to all Gulag administrators with these instructions: "All camps threatened by the German advance would be evacuated eastward. If impossible, all the inmates were to be executed."[21] Some few prisoners did escape the slaughter, but no record was found as to which prison they were from or how they gained their freedom.

Without question, the NKVD efficiently carried out Stalin's order, for the remains of wholesale slaughters were sighted by the German army in every city along the conquest trail. Prisons within the Soviet Union were visibly "closed." The German soldiers could attest to the fact that the Soviets, when confronted with a significant military engagement, slaughtered their prisoners unconscionably.[22]

The nearer the German army came to Moscow, the greater the panic reflected by the Soviet government. The NKVD were busy "closing" prisons. The files of the Lubianka prison, the principal Moscow jail, were burned. A state of havoc broke out in Moscow when there was no police protection available (October 16, 17, and 18) and stores, shops, storage buildings, as well as the empty Embassy of Great Britain were broken into and looted by vandals. On the day (October 18) the Russian military position stabilized, Premier Stalin issued a special decree that the NKVD was to round up and shoot all anti-Russian suspects.[23]

Included in this style of "closing" of Soviet prisons had been the three Russian prisoner of war camps (Kozielsk, Ostashkov, and Starobielsk) holding approximately 14,920 Polish leaders. All communication from these captives had ceased (March, 1940), and inquiries to Russian authorities had proven unproductive. Of the two exceptions, the first included the majority of approximately 448 Polish survivors who had been separated from the main body of Polish captives at the three camps and would ultimately be sent to Pavlishchev Bor, and fewer to Griazovietz. These surviving prisoners of war would join the Polish army in Russia, starting in September, 1941. The second related to the victims found at Katyn.

Because the Russian losses in the early stages of fighting were so staggering, a secret decree (September, 1941) ordered each Russian soldier to commit suicide rather than be captured.[24] An oft-quoted comment made by Deputy Foreign Minister Vyshinsky at a social gathering was that the German Wehrmacht had already taken 3,800,000 Russian prisoners of war, a number higher than the number of soldiers in the invading German army.[25]

Some familiarity with known statements about Katyn could possibly portend some logic to the events that followed which comprised the Katyn atrocity. It should be recognized here the later breech between the opinions of Josef Stalin and Nikita Khrushchev[26] about the secret police chief, Lavrenti P. Beria.[27] Years later, when Khrushchev followed the deceased Stalin (and others) as premier, he called the secret police chief "arrogant, sinister, two-faced, treacherous, scheming, and vain." Such traits as arrogance and vanity frequently are evident in individuals who are reluctant to ask questions when they do not understand instructions or directions given to them. These persons could be embarrassed to request a clarification of the connotation of a word being used by a superior. For example, the word "liquidate."[28] To a business or legal mind the word could mean "the settling of affairs of a corporation or estate, . . . with the purpose of closing," or "to gradually extinguish, as the obligation of a bankrupt."[29] In these definitions the meaning of closing or ending for "liquidate" is clear. If the order from the Premier of the Soviet Union, Josef Stalin, instructed the secret police chief, Beria, to "liquidate" the Polish POW camps, apparently to Beria it could have only one meaning: to close out or "liquidate" the lives of the Polish prisoners of war. Yet, Premier Stalin could have intended for Beria to "liquidate" the camps by moving the POWs to other camps, to a location deeper within the country, or to a place farther away from the possibility of a German attack. Perhaps Beria was "arrogant" or "vain" or simply believed it would have been disrespectful to question an order from his Premier.[30] Although the final responsibility for action would rest with Stalin, there could have been an error on the part of Beria himself, which was not without possibility or precedent.[31]

In the final analysis, perhaps Nikita Khrushchev, as Premier of the U.S.S.R., best summarized Beria's worth in a secret speech delivered in a closed session of the 20th Congress of the Communist Party (February 27, 1956):

> Beria, who gained such a position in the Party and the State, so as to become the First Deputy Chairman of the Council of Ministers of the Soviet Union and a member of the Central Committee Political Bureau . . . had climbed up the government ladder over an untold number of corpses.

Chapter 2

KATYN

Hard fighting continued! Kiev fell to the Germans and the Russians lost 500,000 in the struggle, but the victory cost the Germans 100,000 lives. After the Germans made the siege on Leningrad it continued into the winter of 1943.

This time frame was unique. From the invasion of the U.S.S.R. until the spring of 1943, almost a two-year period, other changes occurred in the restructuring of the Allies. The Russians were pressed militarily and politically, and were desperately in need of assistance. In July, 1941, both Great Britain and a defeated France signed a mutual aid pact with the Soviets making them an ally.[1] On July 31, 1941, the U.S.S.R. signed a pact with Poland, the nation which the Soviets had attacked without provocation or warning on September 17, 1939, less than two years before. The terms included the release of the civilian prisoners who had been deported to Russia; also, a Polish Army in Russia was to be reconstituted through the release of all military prisoners of war held in the Soviet Union, including all soldiers and officers.

General Wladyslaw Anders, whose title would be Commander in Chief of the Polish Forces in the U.S.S.R. was released from the Lubianka Prison in Moscow on August 4, 1941. Twelve days later, on August 16, 1941, General Anders met with the Soviet military authorities (General Panfilov, U.S.S.R., and General Zhukov, U.S.S.R.), at which time the Russians estimated they held 1,000 officers and 20,000 other Polish military personnel. Inquiries were made to the Soviet military authorities by General Anders regarding the missing Polish officers. The Soviets would make no response to such inquiries at this or any of the five successive meetings. Also, Ambassador Stanislaw Kot of Poland and Deputy Commissar of Foreign Affairs Andrei Vyshinsky of the U.S.S.R. met many times, but no information was ever given by the Soviets regarding the missing officers.[2]

Ambassador Kot met with Foreign Minister Molotov on November 1, 1941; then on November 14, 1941, with Premier Josef Stalin and Molotov. Again the missing officers were discussed. General Sikorski, the Polish Prime

Minister and Commander in Chief, and General Anders met with Stalin
Molotov at the Kremlin on December 3, 1941, but received the same ev
answers. Stalin said perhaps the prisoners had "escaped." When asked
they would go, he said, "to Manchuria." General Anders met with Pr
Josef Stalin again on March 18, 1942. At all the meetings for almost a tw
period—in fact, from the time the pact was signed on July 31, 1941—the
leaders asked about the missing Poles from Kozielsk, Ostashkov, and Star
without hearing of their whereabouts. Where had the missing Polish priso
war been impounded?

The Russian Army had fought so hard to keep Smolensk out of
hands that the Germans had sustained a delay in their time schedule: bu
July, 1941, Smolensk fell, and the German attack toward Moscow cont

The railway station of Gniezdovo, west of Smolensk, was abou
kilometers, then another three kilometers west was Katyn (Ka' teen)
large woods with a road to Smolensk and the Dnieper River flowing th
At the end of a dirt road and near the river was a dacha, called the
Castle, which the local inhabitants said was a rest home for membe
NKVD. The elevation, or slight hill in Katyn Forest was known as K
(sometimes Kosigori, or Kose Gory), meaning "Goat Woods" because
times it was said goats grazed there.

Taking a closer look at the immediate vicinity means leaving
and going westward toward Vitebsk, the first wood seen is eight kilom
of Smolensk and called Krasny Bor. Next is the little town of Gniezdo
railroad station. Still farther west the road crosses the railroad track
more woods extending several kilometers along the road. The fore
section of approximately one kilometer fenced in. However, the for
tends on for some distance south of the road. The road is of aspha
cally running east-west. This part of the forest is limited on the s
Dnieper River. As one turns off the Smolensk Road entering Katyn
is going south on the very narrow dirt road running north-south
"Dnieper Castle." Some front line fighting had taken place in the
forest to the west of the little dirt road leading to the dacha was no
the forest on the east side of the road. Eyewitnesses would com
feature. In an "after the fact" analysis, the graves had been on the
the small fir trees planted over the graves gave the appearance of a
compared to the other side of the road. The east-west road reviev
westward to Katyn Forest then continues to the railroad station of
to the town of Katyn which is on the opposite side of the Dnieper
no importance to the analysis, other than providing the name, r
famy. Farther to the east is the railroad station of Vyazma, hence
asphalt road, the Smolensk-Vyazma Highway.

In summary, the distance from Smolensk to Gniezdo

19

mately twelve kilometers (about seven and one half miles) and Gniezdovo to Katyn Forest approximately three kilometers (almost two miles). The total would be Smolensk to Katyn Forest approximately fifteen kilometers (about nine and one half miles).

The entire area from Smolensk to Katyn is a valley of the Dnieper River (and its tributary, the Olsha), which is wooded and known as the Katyn Forest, in its entirety. However, different portions of the forest had different names, i.e., Tshorny Bor (Black Forest), Krasny Bor (Red Forest), etc. All this in addition to the already introduced Kosy Gory, which provides an elevation which starts north of the Smolensk Highway sloping gradually to the south toward the Dnieper River.

Facts relating to the extinction of the Polish officers began to filter through a variety of sources. For example, some Polish workers, used as laborers by the German army, learned that the Katyn Forest while it belonged to the NKVD had been used as an execution location for many years. The woods were off limits to the Russian peasants who lived nearby, but they would go there to pick mushrooms even though "keep out" signs were posted and often security soldiers were present, sometimes with guard dogs. With the Russians retreating and the Germans in control of Smolensk and the immediate vicinity, the local inhabitants became more talkative about the "location for executions" story.

The Polish laborers asked a peasant to guide them to the site of the graves. When shown the exact spot they found some bodies in a very shallow grave. But thirty months of significant weather changes had caused extensive body decomposition; for three summers and winters had taken a toll. The few bodies exposed were not in German or Russian uniforms; in fact, they were identified as uniforms of Polish officers. Of course, the Polish laborers made the logical assumption that the deceased were Polish officers, so they covered the bodies and placed two small "rugged crosses" fashioned from tree limbs at the grave site.[3] Ultimately, this early discovery would prove beneficial for the Germans, although at this modest beginning no one could possibly know the extent of the discovery. At this point it might have been felt these were only a few isolated graves, for there was no time for an extensive research to be conducted. Later some studies indicated that the Polish laborers had learned "execution acts" as early as the summer of 1941, but no follow up was pursued as they moved on with the German army. Even so, the execution stories about the Poles being the victims had persisted.

Another example was the story of how railway cars filled with Polish officers were taken to the Gniezdovo Station, then transported by lorry (the Russian "Black Raven") to a destination along the Smolensk-Katyn Highway, which seemingly had to be the Katyn Forest.

The Germans were "hot on the intelligence trail" during the winter of 1942–43. Information leads were followed, and the Germans confirmed the

presence of the cadavers in uniforms of Polish officers; but the severity of the winter weather mitigated any major exhumation effort. Meantime, preparations were made for a massive and intensive search, and when the harsh, cold temperatures finally moderated, the Germans attacked this problem with typical intensity and thoroughness by conducting exhumations on a large scale. Their vigor, perseverance, and enthusiasm were rewarded.

The date of April 13, 1943, will live forever in infamy for the nation of Poland. On that day, Dr. Joseph Goebbels, the German Minister of Propaganda, released a news media coup d'etat to the continent of Europe and the international community. The (2:15 P.M. London time) announcement by Radio Berlin reported the German army in Russia had discovered a large common grave site in Katyn Forest that contained the bodies of Polish officers. Individual corpses were being identified, and it was anticipated that the total number to be exhumed would be 10,000 Polish officers[4] who had been murdered by the "Soviet secret state police." The grisly message in its entirety read:

A report has reached us from Smolensk to the effect that the local inhabitants have mentioned to the German authorities the existence of a place where mass executions had been carried out by the Bolsheviks and where 10,000 Polish officers had been murdered by the BPU.[5] The German authorities accordingly went to a place called Kozy Gory, (i.e. "Goats Hill"— a small forested hill inside Katyn), a Soviet health resort situated twelve kilometers west of Smolensk, where a terrible discovery was made. A ditch was found, 28 meters long and 16 meters wide, in which the bodies of 3,000 Polish officers were piled up in twelve layers. They were fully dressed in military uniforms, some were bound, and all had pistol shot wounds in the back of their heads. There will be no difficulty in identifying the bodies as, owing to the nature of the ground, they were in a state of mummification and the Russians had left on the bodies their personal documents. It has been stated today, that General Smorinwinski from Lublin has been found amongst other murdered officers. Previously these officers were in a camp at Kozielsk near Orel and in February and March, 1940, were brought in "cattle" freight cars to Smolensk. Hence they were taken in lorries (trucks) to Kozy Gory and were murdered there by the Bolsheviks. The search for further pits is in progress. New layers may be found under those already discovered. It is estimated that the total number of officers killed amounts to 10,000, which would correspond to the entire cadre of Polish officers taken by the Russians. The correspondents of Norwegian newspapers, who were on the spot and were able to obtain direct evidence of the crime, immediately sent their dispatches to their papers in Oslo.

At the time the German radio announcement was released, thousands of murdered Polish officers, who had been prisoners of war of the Russians at

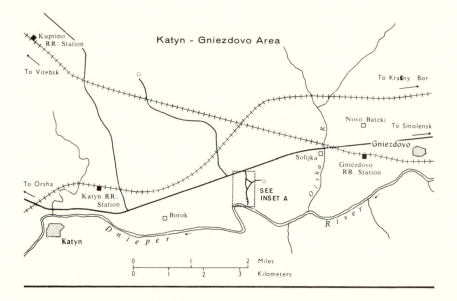

Katyn - Gniezdovo Area

Kuprino RR. Station

To Vitebsk

To Krasny Bor

Novo Bateki

To Smolensk

Gniezdovo

Sofijka

Gniezdovo RR. Station

Olsha R.

To Orsha

Katyn RR. Station

SEE INSET A

Borok

River

Dnieper

Katyn

0   1   2   Miles
0   1   2   3   Kilometers

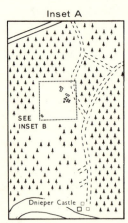

Inset A

SEE INSET B

Dnieper Castle

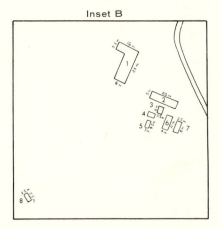

Inset B

1

2

3

4

5

6

7

8

the Kozielsk camp, had already been found interned in mass graves at Katyn Forest.

The bullet which entered the back of the skull of each victim was of German origin, and many spent bullets were in evidence; in fact, some were seen protruding from the frontal bone (forehead) of the victim. Some spent cartridge (shell) casings were also recovered. These spent casings were found inside the gravesite between the bodies; sometimes between the upturned collar of the greatcoat and the victim's neck, and sometimes about the area near the graves. The caliber of the bullets was 7.65 mm. This ammunition was of German origin and could be traced to its manufacturer, Genschow. Sales of this ammunition were made to both Poland and Russia before World War II. One analysis stated that the ammunition in Polish arsenals was taken over by the Russians when they occupied eastern Poland.

Some of the bodies had their hands tied behind their backs with a plain cord which was of equal length with all the cords used to tie other victims, an indication the cords had been precut to a standard size. Some bodies had their greatcoats pulled up over their heads and bound and others had their mouths filled with sawdust; probably because they had resisted the executioners in some way, possibly by screaming and shouting. Bodies with broken jaws and arms were disinterred, again suggesting the captives had resisted their executioners. Some of the victims had resisted the movement to the gravesite, they had been bayoneted; and of course, many had resisted. The bayonet wounds bore the telltale "plus sign" (+), a mark of the Russian rifle bayonet only for other governments had adopted the smooth blade with the bleeders on the side.[6]

The bodies of the deceased Polish officers were clothed in winter underwear and well-fitted uniforms, including insignia.[7] Their outside garments, including military greatcoats, suggested their deaths occurred in cold weather. Their military boots, including wooden pull-over "clogs" made in the POW camps, indicated they went to the grave during the winter. Some victims were wearing leather or fur jerkins, pullovers, and sweaters; all indications of frigid temperatures. Most officers were in possession of their identification papers and documents, including designations of awards for meritorious service or citations for bravery. Most insignia of rank was either worn on the uniform of the deceased or found in a pocket of his uniform. Also, many had personal possessions with them; such as newspaper articles, letters and postcards from home, diaries, etc., with dates thereon. Documents found on bodies in graves numbers one through seven were dated up through March and April, but in grave number eight the dates ran from late April into the first week of May, 1940. The reasoning for such variation was that considerable time would be required to execute and bury so many Polish POWs; therefore, dates on documents would probably coincide with the time of internment.

The ground at the grave site was described as yellow colored sand that had turned into soil of a thick, hard substance—probably caused from the reaction of body chemicals emitted in the decomposition stages—which literally entombed the cadavers within an air-tight seal. The bodies were stacked so closely and tightly together, sometimes piled twelve layers (bodies) deep, that a natural vacuum atmosphere was developed that greatly retarded the normal putrification process. Too, the cold weather slowed down the decomposition of the bodies considerably and caused the skin to be hard and leather-like. "Mummified" was a word used by some eyewitnesses to describe the appearance of the cadavers.

One could try to equate what happened during the decomposition and putrification process within the entombment of the Polish POWs in their sand and clay-like burial vaults at Katyn Forest by using historic examples. The early Egyptians developed primitive but effective embalming techniques which included wrapping dead bodies (after evisceration) so no air could come in contact with the deceased. The Babylonians covered the bodies of their dead with honey; then later immersed them in honey. All air was excluded and some delay in the process of putrification accrued; however, nothing beyond a temporary preservation was possible. The Scythians coated the bodies of their dead with wax; thereby temporarily shutting out the atmosphere.

The bayonets, already introduced, were of Russian origin with fluted edges which left the tell tale marks in the flesh and clothing of the victims and were still recognizable after three years of burial because of the condition of the bodies.

New small trees had been planted over the mass grave site so it would not look like an open field, a normal mass grave consideration. This was intended to make Katyn look more like the woods it was before the killings.

The statements of local residents—those who lived near Katyn Forest, those who worked near the road between Katyn and Gniezdovo Station, and those who had worked or had occasion to be near the railway terminal at Gniezdovo—confirmed with statements concerning the increased people-transportation activity in the early part of 1940. They identified the railroad passengers as "Polish officers" who were moved by train to Gniezdovo Station, then by lorries to Katyn.

Two reports made by Germans provide a summation of finding about the Katyn killings to date and corroborate the facts stated in this chapter. The first was the final report, dated June 10, 1943, prepared by Lieutenant Ludwig Voss, Secretary of the German Field Police.[9] The second report reflects the professional medical opinion of Dr. Gerhard Buhtz, Professor of Forensic Medicine and Criminology at Breslau University, who was the senior medical officer in charge of the German forensic medicine investigation.[10]

In summary, a CAPSTONE of the research data presents these circumstances and conditions surrounding the Katyn Killings that are known to date:

1. The Katyn Forest, near Smolensk, was a Russian possession until the invasion of Russia by the German Army.
2. Germany made the first announcement about the location of the graves of the missing Polish officers because it knew the Germans had not committed the atrocity.
3. The Germans could confirm easily such details as the location of the ammunitions manufacturer who supplied the ammunition used in the execution of the Polish POWs; the ammunition used was of German origin, and the sale and shipping of quantities to eastern Poland, which could have been captured by the Russians.
4. Germany could verify that ammunition was shipped directly to the U.S.S.R. in pre-World War II days, then assume that ultimately some of it could have been used to execute the Polish prisoners of war.
5. The evidence indicated that many of the executions occurred outside the burial pits; however, the forensic medicine representatives noted that some stray bullets had lodged near the outside skin of some bodies. Pathologists could deduce that some of the executions took place in the burial pit, and that the death bullet which passed from the back of the skull where it entered to the front where it exited then struck an already murdered victim and lodged in the second victim's body near the surface of the skin.
6. The medical report of the German doctor stated the death of each victim was the result of a gunshot wound fired from an immediate proximity, for evidence showed that the bullet had entered the back of the head or back of the neck ("nape of the neck" or "Nackenschuss" in German).
7. The 7.65 mm weapon that fired each projectile from back to front would shatter a skull if the explosive action of the round fired was at close range. Two vital parts of the human brain are medulla oblongata and pons cerebri, and destruction of either would cause death instantaneously.
8. Powder burns were found on many of the skulls; thereby confirming the close proximity of the muzzle of the weapon to the target.
9. Apparently, the intent of the killer was to shoot the bullet into the rear of the head, have it exit at the root of the nose, and thus destroy the medulla simultaneously.
10. The medical findings indicated the complete absence of insects in the burial pits or on the bodies of the deceased.
11. The traditional time when there is an obvious absence of insects is winter; therefore, the executions had to be conducted in a very cold weather atmosphere.
12. Since the location of the burial pits required clearing away of a considerable area of trees so that graves could be dug, replacement planting of trees obviously occurred after the executions were completed.
13. Experts in forestry noted the small trees were five years old, and

stunted in growth due to the fact that they were in the shade of older, more mature trees.

14. Also, these experts in forestry estimated the time the trees had been planted over the grave sites as three years earlier; another indication that the executions occurred in April and May, 1940.

Russian Prisoner-Of-War Camp at Kozielsk

Aerial View of Katyn Forest in Vicinity of Dnieper Castle

Railroad Station at Gniezdovo, Russia

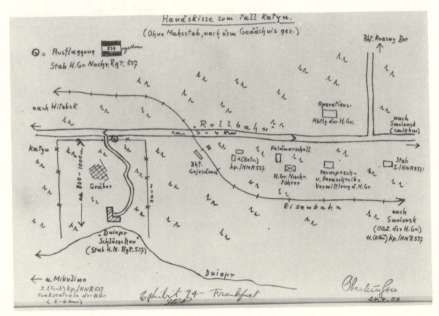

Sketch Map of Katyn Forest

Site of Mass Graves as Exumations Commence

Victims at Katyn Buried in Mass Graves

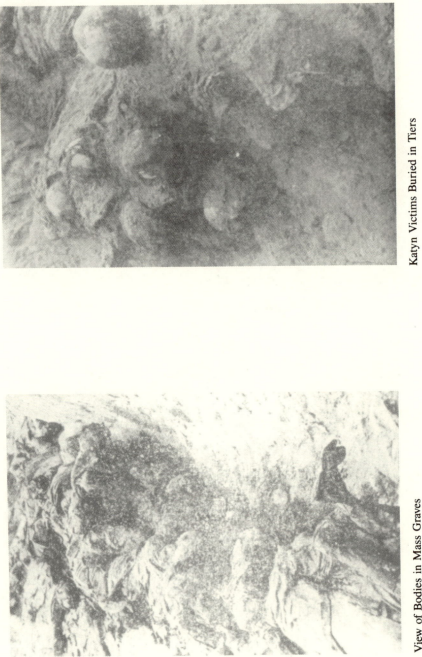

Katyn Victims Buried in Tiers

View of Bodies in Mass Graves

Rows of Exhumed Bodies at Katyn

Exhumed Bodies of Polish Victims at Katyn

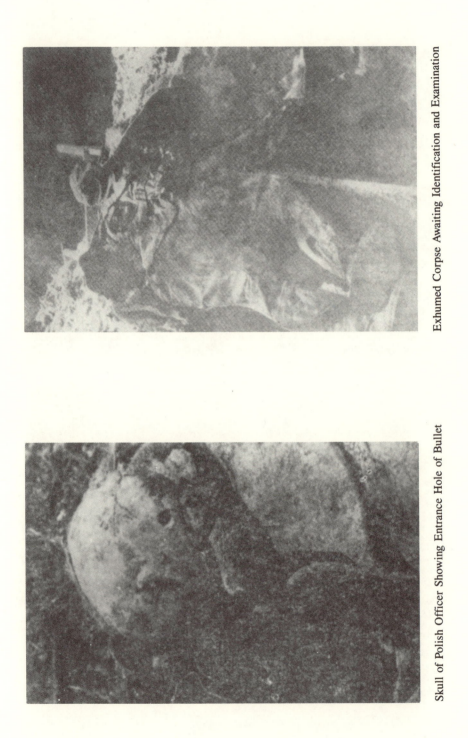

Exhumed Corpse Awaiting Identification and Examination

Skull of Polish Officer Showing Entrance Hole of Bullet

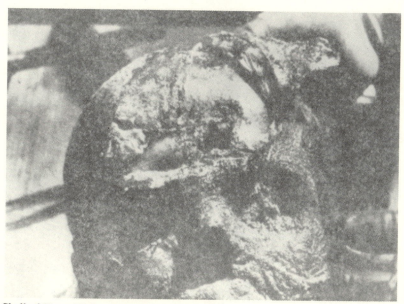

Skull of Katyn Victim with Exiting Bullet Visible

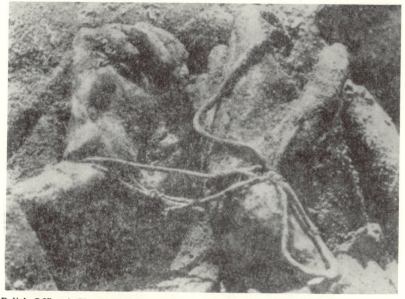

Polish Officer's Hands Tied Behind Back With Cord

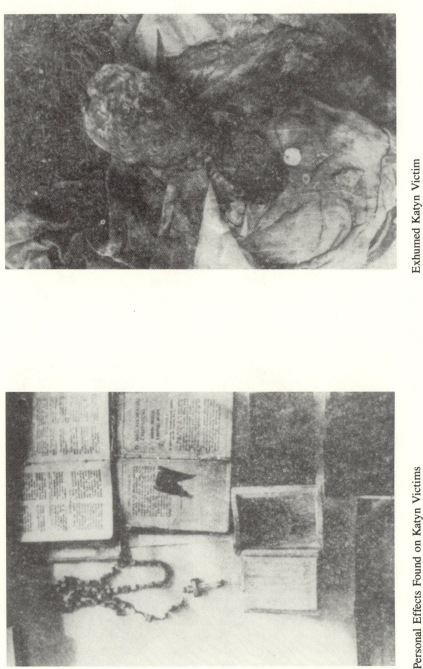

Exhumed Katyn Victim

Personal Effects Found on Katyn Victims

Katyn Victim's Diary, Date Visible as April 19

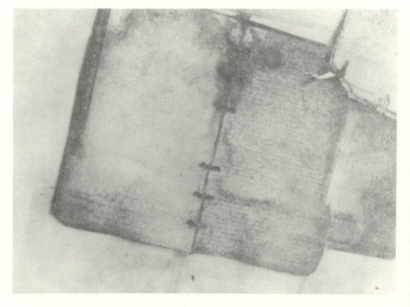

Murdered Polish Officer's Diary

Roll Call List of Officers with Notation "Kozielsk, 12 April 1940"

Personal Belongings of a Polish General

Page of a Polish Officer's Pay Book (A Chaplain, Rev. Jan Ziolkowski)

Stamp Collection of a Polish Victim

Polish Zloty (Currency) Found on Body of Katyn Victim

Dnieper Castle

Members of International Medical Commission Walking Past Dnieper Castle in Katyn Woods

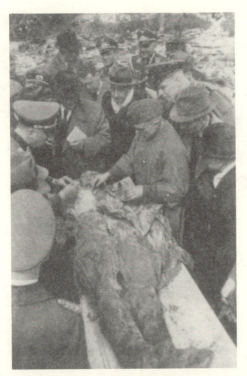

Professor Buhtz (on Left) in Presence of International Medical Commission Removing
Identification Papers from Body

Dr. Buhtz (on Left) and International Medical Commission Members Examining One of
the Exhumed Bodies

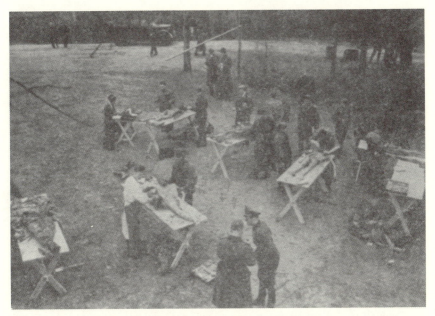

View of Autopsy Tables Showing Members of International Medical Commission at Work

Laboratory in German Institute at Smolensk. Professor Miloslavich Holding Skull

Dr. Orsos (Hungary) and Professor Saxen (Finland) Examining Exhumed Katyn Corpse

Dr. Orsos Explains Theory of Calcification In Brain Pulp to the Members of the Commission

Professor Frantisek Hajek (Czechoslovakia) Removing Boot of Katyn Dead

Professor Hajek Holding Arm of Katyn Victim

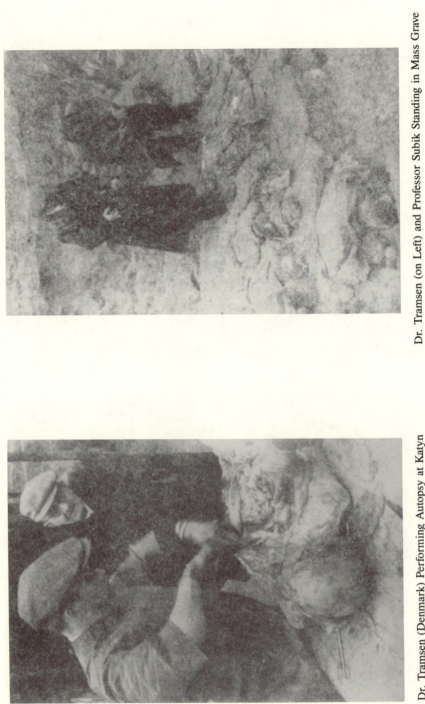

Dr. Tramsen (on Left) and Professor Subik Standing in Mass Grave

Dr. Tramsen (Denmark) Performing Autopsy at Katyn

Professor Miloslavich Examining Identification Paper of Katyn Victim as Dr. Tramsen Watches

Conversation Between Members of the International Medical Commission and a Russian Native

Exhumation of Katyn Victim—Watching at Edge of Pit is Dr. Orsos (Hungary) and Others

Final Meeting of Commission at the Institute in Smolensk. Dr. Buhtz, German Professor, Standing

International Medical Commission Signing Protocol

Protocol Signatures

German Foresters Making Laboratory Tests of Trees from Katyn Forest

Russian Worker with Polish Red Cross Director Skarzynski and Others

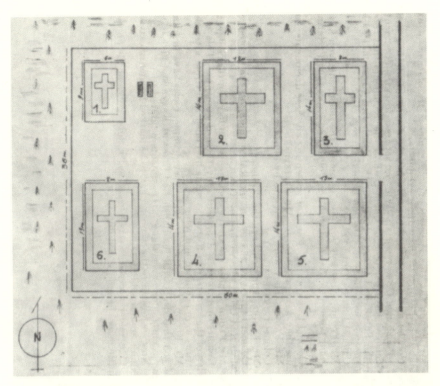

Sketch of Reburial Site

Reburial Location for Polish Murdered

Body of Russian Woman Found in Another Mass Grave, Not with Polish Officers

Chapter 3

KATYN—
INTERNATIONAL MEDICAL
COMMISSION

The German announcement concerning the finding of the mass graves at Katyn dominated the news scene of April 13, 1943. Even though the occupation of Warsaw and western Poland by the Germans had been just as harsh and cruel, the Third Reich authorities wanted to propagandize the alleged Katyn killings as being Soviet atrocities. The German high command had kept its own atrocities very secret. However, information leaks had filtered into the media concerning their concentration camps or death camps; therefore, if the German strategists could embarrass the Russians by blaming them for the massacre at Katyn, with their usual meticulous and thorough "logic" they could place the responsibility for this "crime without parallel"[1] on the Soviets.

Within a brief forty-eight hours after this initial German announcement regarding the discovery of Katyn, the Russians delivered a scathing blast via Moscow radio (April 15, 1943) which claimed the Russians were innocent of the crime and the murders had been perpetrated by the Germans after the Army of the Third Reich invaded the Soviet Union on June 21, 1941, and uncovered or captured Smolensk late in July, 1941. The Russian newscaster stated:

> In the past two or three days Goebbels slanderers have been spreading vile fabrications alleging that the Soviet authorities carried out a mass shooting of Polish officers in the spring of 1940, in the Smolensk area. In launching this monstrous invention the German-Fascist scoundrels did not hesitate to spread the most unscrupulous and base lie, in their attempts to cover up crimes which, as has now become evident, were perpetrated by themselves.
>
> The German-Fascist report on this subject leaves no doubt as to the tragic fate of the former Polish prisoners of war who in 1941 were engaged in construction work in areas west of the Smolensk region and who fell into

51

the hands of the German-Fascist hangmen in the summer of 1941, after the withdrawal of the Soviet troops from the Smolensk area.

Beyond doubt Goebbels slanderers are now trying with lies and calumnies to cover up the bloody crimes of the Hitlerite gangsters. In their clumsily concocted fabrication about the numerous graves which the Germans allegedly discovered near Smolensk, the Hitlerite liars mention the village of Gniezdovo. But, like the swindlers they are, they remain silent about the fact that it was near the village of Gniezdovo that the archaeological excavations of the historic 'Gniezdovo burial place' were made.

The statement of the Tass News Agency, speaking for the U.S.S.R., said with a news release dated April 15, 1943:

> The Polish prisoners in question were interned in the vicinity of Smolensk, in special camps and were employed in road construction. It was impossible to evacuate them at the time of the approach of the German troops, and as a result they fell into their hands. If therefore they have been found murdered, it means that they have been murdered by the Germans, who, for reasons of provocation, claim now that the crime has been committed by the Soviet authorities.[2]

In addition to conducting an extensive military campaign by the German army, on March 20, 1943, the Germans started a massive exhumation operation in the Katyn woods that required employment not only of an administrative organization but also of a large record keeping staff to supervise its myriad logistical details. The German high command recognized the significance of the Katyn Forest massacre and therefore brought to the grave site its most qualified specialists in forensic medicine. The administration of this task "fell" on the able shoulders of Dr. Gerhard Buhtz, a physician who before the war was Professor of Forensic Medicine and Criminology at Breslau (Wroclau) University, and who was regarded as prominent criminologist and legal expert in forensic medicine. A reference to his report was included in the previous chapter.

Dr. Buhtz's job was to pinpoint the time of death of each victim; an issue of overwhelming importance. The Germans knew such information was critical to their propaganda efforts; for if capable forensic medical professionals could confirm that death occurred to the Polish POWs on Russian soil during the time they were captives of the NKVD, then the blame for the Katyn Killings would rest unequivocally with the U.S.S.R.

The German investigators used these findings as a basis for concluding that the Katyn Killings occurred during April or May, 1940:

1. No letters, postcards, newspaper clippings, diaries, personal possessions, etc., found on the bodies were dated after March, April, and May, 1940.

2. Because of the vacuum type seal of the grave site due to the ground composition, the bodies of the victims were, all things considered, in good condition. A single unembalmed body thrown into a single grave goes quickly through the stages of putrification and decomposition until decay of tissue is complete. In the mass graves at Katyn the murdered captives were packed so tightly together (either dead or dying) and sealed over with copious quantities of solid soil, that the putrification process was slowed considerably. For example, in the "L" shaped grave (see map following p. 21) the initial interment was estimated to be almost 3,000 bodies. These bodies were packed together so tightly that decaying and decomposing fluids of each body penetrated, imbibed, and infiltrated other dead bodies within the grave. In effect, the grave held one huge body which could be recognized as single bodies primarily because the heads were protruding.

3. The skin, tissue, bones, etc., could be easily examined by the German doctors and experts. Within this atmosphere a skilled pathologist working in forensic medicine conditions would be looking on each body for the presence of adipocere, the formation of a fatty, waxy substance similar to soap known as the process of saponification. If the human body had decayed in an atmosphere, environment, soil, and earth which is humid or contains water (both were present at Katyn), then a waxy adipocere would form. The presence of adipocere is not, of itself, conclusive evidence for determining the exact time of burial, for under some conditions it could develop within a single year. For example, if incisions had been made in a muscle (a musculature study), a person skilled in forensic medicine could determine if the muscle did contain adipocere which would appear in the muscle as soon as decay was complete. Microscopically, the muscle in which adipocere has formed would have been completely destroyed in the saponification process (no muscle fibers; no striation of muscle substance).

4. The most compelling reason for concluding the bodies had been buried for three years was the medical finding of chrystalus deposits in the skull cavities of a random sampling of bodies examined during the exhumations. Chrystalus deposits have the overall appearance of a crust, and are formed by decay into a necrotic structure of uniform clay around the surface of the brain. The experts concluded that bodies which had been in graves less than three years would not expose this condition; but unembalmed bodies buried for three years or more would show it. Since many of the skulls examined had such a chrystalus crust on the brain, then the time of execution of the Katyn victims had to be about April or May, 1940. At this time the German army had not invaded Russia, and Smolensk and the Katyn Forest belonged to the Soviets; also, this timeframe was after the Russians had invaded the eastern one-half of Poland

and captured many members of the Polish military forces and held them as prisoners of war.

Three days after the German high command made the first public announcement of the discovery at Katyn Forest, the German Red Cross sent to the International Red Cross at Geneva a request for an investigation of the situation to determine the authenticity of the German findings. The request stated:

> Reference the news published on the discovery of thousands of bodies of Polish officers in Katyn Forest near Smolensk. In view of the international importance of the affair we regard the participation of the International Red Cross as very desirable, particularly in view of the many cases of disappearance of persons in the U.S.S.R. reported by the German Red Cross, the Polish Red Cross and other bodies. According to information obtained by the German Red Cross all facilities will be given to the representatives of the Committee to enable them to proceed forthwith to the place to take part in the investigations.
>
> (Signed) Grawitz.

On the next day, April 17, 1943, the Polish Government in London sent to the Polish Red Cross delegate a similar request at the International Red Cross in Geneva asking that an investigation by neutral representatives, to be selected by the International Red Cross, be conducted of the Katyn Forest massacre of thousands of Polish prisoners of war.

The International Red Cross had been requested to make the investigation by two interested parties: Germany and Poland, but could not send a delegation to Russia unless all parties involved participated. The Soviets would not extend the invitation to the International Red Cross and would not be a party to the neutral investigation. The IRC actually scheduled a meeting for April 20, 1943, to discuss the formation of the delegation, but the meeting was not held because of the Russian opposition. The outcome was the International Red Cross was unable to act at all, no matter how impressive the humanitarian consideration; for the enabling agreement of September 12, 1939, would not allow participation of an IRC neutral investigation unless there was agreement by all interested parties. The German and Polish governments were notified of the situation by the International Red Cross, who suggested the two governments approach the U.S.S.R. through some other governmental body to gain Soviet approval. The Polish government in exile, had already decided to make this request direct to the U.S.S.R. at its cabinet meeting on April 17, 1943, which was done by a letter to the Soviet Ambassador dated April 20, 1943. An excerpt from the letter follows:

. . . to communicate the Polish Government detailed and precise information as to the fate of the prisoners of war and civilians previously detained in the camps at Kozielsk, Starobielsk and Ostashkov.

Public opinion in Poland and throughout the world has quite rightly been so deeply shocked, that only irrefutable facts can outweigh the numerous and detailed German statements concerning the discovery of the bodies of many thousands of Polish officers murdered near Smolensk in the spring of 1940.

This request by Poland not only went unanswered, but also, along with the Polish government's request to the International Red Cross for an impartial investigation of Katyn, probably provided the U.S.S.R. with a reason for severing relations with Poland. The break was official with the person-to-person delivery of the Minister of Foreign Affairs Molotov's letter dated April 25, 1943 (Easter Sunday), to Poland's Ambassador Romer at 12:15 A.M. on April 26, 1943, after the Ambassador had been called to Mr. Molotov's office on a one-hour notice. Mr. Romer refused acceptance, but the letter was delivered to him at his quarters shortly thereafter by an official from the Soviet Foreign Office. Mr. Romer responded on April 26, 1943, and his letter was sent to Mr. Molotov the same day. Both messages are included in Appendices 2 and 3.

The International Red Cross, with a world-wide reputation at stake, sent the following message to all belligerent nations April 23, 1943:

The German Red Cross and the Polish Government in London have approached the International Red Cross with a request for its participation in the identification of bodies which, according to German reports, have been discovered near Smolensk.

In both instances the International Red Cross replied that in principle it is prepared to offer assistance by selecting experts, on condition that similar appeals are received from all other parties interested in this question. This is in accordance with the memorandum sent by the International Red Cross, on September 12, 1939, to all belligerent nations, defining the principles on the basis of which the International Red Cross may participate in this kind of investigation.

With the opportunity for a neutral investigation thwarted by the U.S.S.R., the German government began to form its own investigative body. The Germans already had sent the reputable Dr. Gerhard Buhtz and his colleagues to Katyn as experts in forensic medicine, and planned at a later time to send another delegation of the best doctors from the University Institute of Forensic Medicine in Berlin, led by their chief, Dr. Mueller-Hesse.

In the meantime a suggestion to form an International Medical Commission came from Dr. Wilhelm Zietz, the Deputy Chief of Public Health Service whose immediate superior was Dr. Conti, the Reich Leader of Public Health Service and Secretary of State. Dr. Zietz was a personal friend of Dr. Buhtz, the expert already at Katyn conducting the autopsies. Dr. Zietz called Dr. Buhtz the first or second week in April, 1943, to ask if a committee of international scientists could assist in the investigation process and thereby support the findings of Dr. Buhtz and his colleagues. The approval of the plan by Dr. Conti was complete, and Dr. Zietz gained further support from the Foreign Office, including the approval of Foreign Minister Ribbentrop.

A call went out from the Foreign Office for experts in forensic medicine to form an International Medical Commission that would go to Katyn to corroborate the findings of the German experts. Invitations were extended, and these dedicated, interested professionals became committed to the rules of the commission protocol:

1. Belgium: Dr. Speleers, Professor in Ordinary of Ophthalmology at the University of Ghent
2. Bulgaria: Dr. Markov, lecturer in Medical Jurisprudence and Criminology at the University of Sofia
3. Denmark: Dr. Tramsen, Prosecutor at the Institute of Medical Jurisprudence of Copenhagen
4. Finland: Dr. Saxen, Professor in Ordinary of Pathological Anatomy at the University of Helsinki
5. Italy: Dr. Palmieri, Professor in Ordinary of Medical Jurisprudence and Criminology at the University of Naples.
6. Croatia (a province of Yugoslavia): Dr. Miloslavich, Professor in Ordinary of Medical Jurisprudence and Criminology at the University of Agram
7. Netherlands: Dr. de Burlet, Professor in Ordinary of Anatomy at the University of Groningen.
8. Protectorate of Bohemia and Moravia: Dr. Hajek, Professor in Ordinary of Medical Jurisprudence and Criminology at Prague
9. Roumania: Dr. Birkle, Medico-legal Adviser to the Roumanian Ministry of Justice and First Assistant at the Institute of Medical Jurisprudence and Criminology in Bucharest
10. Switzerland: Dr. Naville, Professor in Ordinary of Medical Jurisprudence at the University of Geneva
11. Slovakia: Dr. Subik, Professor in Ordinary of Pathological Anatomy at the University of Bratislava, Head of the Public Health Department of Slovakia
12. Hungary: Dr. Orsos, Professor in Ordinary of Medical Jurisprudence and Criminology at the University of Budapest

The International Medical Commission members assembled in Berlin and traveled by air to Smolensk, making one stop enroute at Warsaw. Individually, and as a group, they were ready to probe into the investigative findings in progress at Katyn Forest.

In Smolensk the group was greeted by a general surgeon, Dr. Holm, who was their host, and Dr. Buhtz, the senior medical officer at Katyn. At this initial meeting the commission members got acquainted with one another, and Doctors Holm and Buhtz, who expressed a concern that each of the International Medical Commission members gain an independent opinion about the Katyn Killings. Little mention was made about the grave site during that first evening in Smolensk.

The next morning the commission members were taken to the Katyn woods. Doctors Holm and Buhtz had made meticulous preparations for the medical task at hand. Highly qualified interpreters and secretaries from the Institute of Forensic Medicine in Smolensk (moved there from Breslau) had been brought to the grave site to assist the commission members. Also available were medics to remove the bodies from mass graves, non-commissioned officers from the army to conduct the identification process, and Polish and Russian laborers to transport the bodies to the reburial location.

About 10 A.M. on April 29, 1943, as the commission members entered the Katyn woods they were greeted with the "terrible smell of decay," and commented on the sparseness of the woods area on the west side of the dirt road. In a side lane the visitors observed that bodies already exhumed had been placed in long rows (about 20 rows with about 15 cadavers in each row). They were informed that seven pits containing bodies had already been opened—in some, the bodies had been placed in neat stacks; in others, thrown in "like cord wood" sometimes twelve layers high and fifteen bodies from pit-side to pit-side.

A body was chosen and placed on a wooden table for Dr. Buhtz to use in his post-mortem demonstration. First, the body was identified from the personal papers and letters found in the pockets of the uniform jacket. As the post-mortem progressed other evidence was reviewed: such as, the bullet holes, entry and exit; the proximity of the murder weapon to the back of the skull; the condition and fit of the uniform and boots; et al.

The commission members decided that the nine pathologists should conduct an autopsy individually. Each pathologist went through the entire investigation process; from choosing the body, completing the identification, noting the condition of the clothing, etc., to conducting the post-mortem.

The protocol report of the International Medical Commission, dated Smolensk, April 30, 1943, was both succinct and complete. A summary of their investigative findings follows:

STATISTICS of BACKGROUND DATA. From the mass graves of Polish officers, 782 had been disinterred and 70 per cent had been identified.

Seven graves had been opened and the number of bodies found in the largest was estimated to be 2,500.

IDENTIFICATION of POWS. In addition to letters and documents, such items as pay books, mobilization notices, newspaper clippings, postcards, etc., were found on the bodies. Nothing of value was found; however, many of the documents issued at Kozielsk were dated April, 1940, or earlier. At least three murdered clergymen were identified.

CONDITION of CLOTHING. The uniforms were well-fitted and buttoned. Many of the dead wore overcoats, sweaters, woolly pullovers, thick scarfs, and two kinds of underwear. Because the clothing had been on the bodies for a long time it was compacted to the skin and had to be cut open to conduct the search for identification items.

CONDITION of BODIES. Most of the bodies observed had their hands tied behind their backs and were "mummified" in an "extraordinary kind of decay." This condition was attributed to the pressure of tons of yellow, sandy soil with which the bodies had been covered.

CAUSE of DEATH. Death occurred instantly from a bullet which entered the back of the skull (nape of the neck) and exited at the hair line in the front of the skull. Bullets that did not completely exit would be trapped between the skin and the frontal bone (forehead). A few bodies were found that had a bullet elsewhere in their bodies, usually near the surface of the skin which suggested these were spent bullets that had passed through the skull of one victim and then lodged near the surface of the skin of a second victim. The commission members estimated the size of the bullet to be less than eight millimeters.

DIAGNOSIS of BULLET TRAJECTORY. As pathologists removed the soft tissue at the back of the neck the commission members could observe that the bullet wound in the occipital bone at the rear of the head was perfectly round. By cutting through the bone the pathologists could show that the same hole inside the head was larger because the back of the skull has an outside and an inside layer with cells in between. Also, at the point of entry of the bullet in the soft tissue, there were markings where black gunpowder had been pushed into the skin by the muzzle of the handgun. The powder burns on the skin (often referred to as tattooing) were caused by gunpowder, an indication the weapon was fired at a proximity so close that it could cause a blast effect, including long lines of fracture. The point of exit on most bodies was along the line of the hair border at the level of the right or left temple; in only one body was it below the eye level, and in only one was there more than a single entry and exit. Concerning the results of the bullet in the back of the head, Dr. Tramsen, one of the pathologists, when asked about the mortal impact on the body upon which he had conducted an autopsy responded, "The direction of the bullet in that skull was such as it couldn't possibly have avoided a lesion, a serious lesion, of the bottom of the brain and the so-called medulla oblongata, the nerve center of respiration, with an absolutely deadly effect."[3]

COMPONENTS of other MATERIAL EVIDENCE. In addition to the seven mass graves already opened up, to and including the time the International Medical Commission was at Katyn, other graves were being found which did not contain murdered Polish prisoners of war. These graves contained bodies—apparently enemies of the state—that had been executed before World War II began; in come cases, long before. Some were individual graves; others were mass graves, called *fraternal graves* (because the bodies included both men and women). One of these bodies was dug out while the commission members were present: the body of a woman with a hood, a "sort of sacking," tied in place over her head; then an extension of the same cord-like material down her back that bound her hands behind her back. Another similarity to bodies being exhumed for investigative purposes was that the cause of death was identical; the shot through the head from back to front. The condition of the body, however, indicated that this particular body had been in its grave much, much longer than the Polish officers.

The commission pathologists noted that some of the shell cases of the ammunition used for the executions were found in the pits. They were informed that the ammunition had been manufactured in Germany, but that large quantities had been exported to Russia and Poland before the war. The commission members also noted the bayonet wounds on some of the victims that resulted in a wound identified as either square (four-sided) or triangular (three-sided) because some wounds were hard to judge, but none were identified as being flat surfaced.

The commission members not only had the cadavers of the autopsies they personally performed, but also they had other skulls, viscera, tissue, etc., which they had removed, or that had been removed earlier and taken to Smolensk for a more thorough laboratory examination. The pathologists wanted a further examination made to locate in the brains of the cadavers a pulp, similar to heavily compressed clay, that usually appeared in a body after it had been buried for at least two years.

OBSERVATIONS of ENVIRONMENTAL FACTORS. The commission members noted no insects, mites, eggs, or ants, were found in the graves, which suggested the burials took place during cold weather. This theory was supported by the fact that the bodies lacked evidence of original decay.

The commission members noted the presence of the small fir trees, estimated to be one-and one-half to three feet in height, that had been removed from the grave site over which obviously they had been planted. The rings of the trees were analyzed microscopically. As a tree is known to add a ring each year, a diagonal cut would permit an observer to calculate its age. The microscopic inspection indicated these trees had been transplanted three years earlier, and that previously they had grown somewhere else for two years. Because these trees were five years old, their growth had been stunted because of the transplanting, a phenomenon that occurred as the trees adjusted to the new soil.

The commission members interrogated local peasants while at Katyn;

some of whom could not speak Russian, others of whom could. For example, Dr. Orsos had been in a Russian prisoner of war camp in World War I for four years and spoke fluent Russian. The peasants recalled their experiences in the spring of 1940, such as seeing Polish prisoners of war taken from the prison trains to Gniezdovo and driven by lorry to Katyn Forest, hearing shooting, especially in the early morning hours, and seeing the woods being guarded by Russian soldiers for a lengthy period of time when no peasants would be allowed within a specified portion.

The last two paragraphs of the commission's report summarized the foregoing findings.

In the Katyn wood, mass graves of Polish officers were examined by the Commission, seven of which have so far been opened. From these 782 corpses have so far been recovered, examined, partly dissected and 70 per cent identified.

The corpses show exclusively that death was due to shots in the nape of the neck. From the statements of witnesses, letters, diaries, newspapers, etc., found on corpses, it is concluded that the shootings took place in the months of March and April, 1940.[4]

Germany needed a medical analysis such as the one provided by the International Medical Commission. Any data reported by Dr. Buhtz and his colleagues, no matter how professional, could be challenged as something less than objective; but an outside medical analysis by a body of physicians of the stature of those included in the membership of the International Medical Commission taken to Katyn from April 28 to 30, 1943, would support the German findings that the execution of the Polish prisoners of war occurred in March and April, 1940, thereby placing the guilt for their disappearance on Russia. At that time, the Soviets were not at war with the Germans; actually, it would be a year and one-quarter before Germany invaded the U.S.S.R. In fact, Russia was not formally at war with Poland since no declaration had been made, and was allied closely with Germany in the war with Poland. When the International Medical Commission concluded the deaths occurred in March and April, 1940, the full force of guilt resided within the Kremlin, and consequently made Russia responsible for almost 15,000 captured Poles who had disappeared on Russian soil in peacetime. Since a country in which concentration camps, extermination camps, death camps, etc., were located would be held responsible for their control, the same logic would prevail for any POW holocaust engendered within like boundaries. In March and April, 1940, when the criminal killings were perpetrated, the country that held the area in and around Smolensk, about fifteen kilometers from Katyn, would be the guilty country.

When the German message of Russian guilt for the Katyn killings reached the continent of Europe and the international scene in 1943, it was Germany's intent to drive a wedge between the U.S.S.R. and her Allies: Great Britain, France, the United States, and especially Poland. The Germans, in spite of their harsh treatment of occupied Poland and its citizens, were trying to make the world believe there were other totalitarian systems as bad as, or worse than, their own. The Germans went out of their way to include in the delegations taken to Katyn top Polish journalists and other Poles of influence. The Polish Red Cross representatives were among the first to be shown the grave site in the Katyn woods. Some of them stayed, later augmented by others, to form an organization involved in exhumations, research, identification, and reburial. The Polish Red Cross compiled lists of those executed and notified government authorities, individual journalists, news media in general, and the underground. Also, the Germans invited Polish physicians and clergymen to Katyn because they were trying to reach the Polish people on a peer-group or grass-roots level. Polish workers were taken to the grave site not only to work at exhuming the bodies but also to form an honor guard for the deceased. Initially, it had been a group of Polish workers traveling with the attacking German army who had searched out and found the Katyn grave site. Now, it was Germany's intent to attain the widest possible dissemination of information so the full measure of guilt for the Katyn atrocity would be directed to the Russians.

Perhaps a more theoretical approach toward German logic would be to consider that the German high command was being confronted with the discovery of the Katyn killings during the winter of 1942–43. At the highest level of command it was known the Germans had not committed this specific crime. Obviously, knowing they were not the violating party, the conclusion that Russia was responsible provided them with a made-to-order public relations bonanza. They could embarrass the Russians by exposing them as the merciless butchers they had been known to be in their violations of human rights;[5] which could shake the loyalty to Russia of the Allies including Great Britain, France, the United States, and more keenly the relationship between the U.S.S.R. and Poland. In reverse, (in this theoretical approach) if the German High Command could envision losing the war in the winter of 1942–43, the full force of blame for the Katyn killings could easily accrue to them because for a time they held the Katyn Forest. To engender some practical application into this theoretical analysis, the Soviets did place the blame on the Germans in 1943 and 1944 with a Russian investigation and report, then again in 1945 and 1946 at the Nuremberg Tribunal; however, the logic of the Soviet effort was proven suspect in both attempts.

The public relations agency of the Soviets that answered the German announcement of April 13, 1943, with a news release on April 15, 1943, that told how the Polish prisoners of war doing construction work near Smolensk had been captured by the Germans might have had little or no knowledge of top-level decisions made earlier by the Russian government and the efficient NKVD. As a result the Soviet logic and reasoning was assailed successfully, for the public relations personnel apparently did not know of the pleas of Ambassador Kot, General Anders, General Sikorski, etc., to Deputy Commissioner of Foreign Affairs Vyshinsky, Foreign Minister Molotov, and Premier Stalin, in the summer, fall, and winter of 1941, into the spring of 1942, and beyond. This was long after Germany had invaded Russia but before, long before, the mass graves at Katyn had been discovered.

A personnel accounting method may explain the computation of the numbers of Polish prisoners of war who literally disappeared. These approximations were based on handwritten personal records, and from the memory of people who witnessed soldiers dying enroute to prisoners of war camps, etc. When World War II was nearing an end, the prewar country of Poland was occupied in its entirety by the Red Army of the U.S.S.R.; hence, what chance would there be for Polish records to be released if they embarrassed the Soviets?

The personnel audit balance sheet showed how the Russians computed the distribution of the 14,920 Polish prisoners of war they captured. These 14,920 POWs included Polish officers, reserve officers, cadet officers, policemen and military policemen, frontier guards, etc. Many were reserve officers, activated by the wartime emergency, who were pursuing careers in diverse professions such as the clergy, teaching, industrial inventions, art, writing, painting, law, etc., and were referred to as Poland's intelligentsia. In any case, their value as leaders of the future of Poland was obvious.

From this approximation of 14,920 Polish POWs, 448 were "selected" by the NKVD, Russia's secret police, for transfer to Pavlishchev Bor for NKVD "training." From this group even fewer were sent shortly to Griazovietz, where the survivors were permitted to join the reactivated Polish army in September, 1941. The only living eye witnesses able to report on their appalling ordeals were from the survivors who escaped the NKVD camp closings. Not all POWs sent to Pavlishchev Bor were present at Griazovietz to join the Polish army in September, 1941, one and one-half years later. Attrition had been high before leaving Pavlishchev Bor and after reaching Griazovietz.

According to the Voss report of June 10, 1943, the Buhtz report, et al., the number of Polish POWs remaining in each camp was reported, and from Kozielsk 4,255 had been sent via Gniezdovo to Katyn. From the first seven grave sites (numbers one through seven) at Katyn some 4,143 cadavers were removed. When the exhumations of these first seven graves were almost over, another grave site (number eight) was found on June 1, 1943, and exhumations were begun. It was estimated that another 200 bodies would be located in the new grave, but only 100 (or perhaps 110) cadavers actually were seen. On June 2, 1943, the exhumation operation was halted by the Germans for reasons of health and sanitation. As a result, some sources added the 200 estimated to be in grave number eight, to the 4,143 already exhumed from graves numbers one through seven, making an overall total of 4,343. Later sources added the 100 (or perhaps 110) cadavers actually seen in grave number eight to the 4,143 already exhumed from graves one through seven, making an overall total of 4,243 (or 4,253). Since the last figure closely approximated the total number of Polish prisoners of war sent from Kozielsk, via Gniezdovo, to Katyn, (4,255) the logical total of record would be 4,253.

Finally, regardless of total used, the exhumations at Katyn Forest by the German authorities were the only cadavers of Polish prisoners of war actually located. The mystery remains as to what happened to the POWs from Ostashkov, totaling 6,376, and Starobielsk, totaling 3,841. No trace has ever been found of these 10,217 missing prisoners of war. The total of POWs at Ostashkov (6,376), plus those at Starobielsk (3,841) and the estimated total from Katyn (4,253) make an overall total of 14,470 missing Polish prisoners of war. The two others reported "missing in action" on the Balance Sheet audit (14,472) could be the difference between those who departed Kozielsk (5,255) and the estimated number of cadavers found there (5,253).

Or, stated another way, of the 14,920 Polish prisoners of war in the camps at Kozielsk, Ostashkov and Starobielsk some 448 survived to Pavlishchev Bor, and even fewer were still alive to join the Polish Army. The survival rate to Pavlishchev Bor is a scant three per cent.[6]

Personnel Audit Balance Sheet (Approximations)

Kozielsk (officers, reserve officers, cadet
    officers)   4,500
    Less 245 "selected," some of whom
    later succeeded in joining the Polish
    Army   245
    Remainder sent, via Gniezdovo, to
    Katyn   4,255
Polish POWs found at Katyn   4,253

Ostashkov (officers, policemen and
    military policemen, frontier guards)   6,500
    Less 124 "selected," some of whom
    later succeeded in joining the Polish
    Army   124
Remainder sent via Viazma to ?   6,376

Starobielsk (officers, reserve officers, cadet officers)	3,920		
Less 79 "selected," some of whom later succeeded in joining the Polish Army		79	
Remainder sent via Kharkov to ?			3,841
Total captured	14,920		
Survivors sent to Pavlishchev Bor		448	
Missing in action			14,472
Found murdered at Katyn			4,253

Chapter 4

FIGHTING INTENSIFIES—
RUSSIAN INVESTIGATION

When the Germans first attacked Russia, the fighting around Smolensk was severe. On July 16, 1941, the advanced units of the German army were on the outskirts of Smolensk, only 250 miles from Moscow; however, the Russian communiques indicated Smolensk was still in Soviet hands on July 25, 1941. A significant tank battle lasted until August 7, 1941, and German losses were great. The Army of the Third Reich remained in defensive positions until October 2, 1941; then the German attack commenced again. Analysts agree that fighting was particularly hard, and that Russia was defending Smolensk and the outlying regions with savage tenacity because it was important to them for other than military reasons. A similar experience could be related about the fighting around Kharkov.

By September 20, 1941, the German armored forces had entered the Crimea; and by November 11 had occupied Rostov. Germany had completed its southern campaign. On October 2, 1941, the major offensive against Moscow commenced once more. Mozhaisk, a town just sixty-five miles west of the Soviet capital, was taken on October 15. But winter came three weeks early and operations slowed because the tanks had problems with mud; in addition, the forests, swamps, and poor roads were impassable. On December 5, 1941, the Germans made their last major offensive toward Moscow for the year, but it stalled just thirty-five miles from the city. On the very next day Russia's Marshal Zhukov, who had replaced Marshal Timoshenko, started a counterattack; in the meantime, however, the Germans had encircled the city of Leningrad to the north.

All of the initial German attacks had been successful. Now, adverse and severe weather, formidable terrain, and lack of support due to the great distances to be traversed were operating against them, factors which made the shifting of units more costly. For example, the Sixth Panzer Division had been leading the way toward Leningrad, and in three weeks it had traveled 500 miles and was within sight of the city. Then, 600 miles to the south the center army group needed to be reinforced in leading the attack on Moscow, and the Sixth Panzer Division was the logical unit to be moved. So as units moved back and forth, offensive and defensive actions shifted from north to center and from center to south between Germany and Russia.

Hitler had prepared for a short war. His military intelligence people had not anticipated the problems or obstacles to be encountered in the launching of an attack on Russia. Their belief that a political upheaval of great magnitude would result merely through the threat of attack indicated a lack of appreciation of the Russian political system; hence the Germans found Russia's resistance stronger than anticipated. Research indicated that the initial harsh attitude and treatment of the Russian soldiers and civilians captured by the Germans prompted these Russians, who might have been inclined to abandon the controlled society of communism, to develop a spirit of nationalism and to become staunch supporters of the U.S.S.R. This lack of strategic planning was a German psychological warfare blunder of some magnitude.

Unanticipated delays were encountered everywhere. Rutted roads were further aggravated by the overall bad weather. The railroad system in Russia was of little help to the Germans, which complicated the transportation problems and congested the road networks. Even though movement of tanks was not tied to the roads, their supply columns were. The German advantage in the air was obvious, and it took a big toll on the Russian air capability until the quality performance became a quantity advantage. The opposition performance improvement by the Russians in the air was offset, however, by the extension of the German air cover as its army pushed deeper into the heartland of the Soviet Union.

While Hitler was concentrating on an attempt to defeat the Russians in the last six months of 1941, an opportunity was provided to Great Britain to recover military strength, and to Egypt who would no longer be faced with the threat of a two-front war. In other words, the occupied countries had an opportunity to assess their strengths and weaknesses. As Russian guerilla activity increased in German occupied areas, the Army of the Third Reich lost some of its strength and attacking spirit which it never fully recovered. Also, changes were occurring in the German high command.

Even though the Russians had been severely and strongly handled, they certainly were not destroyed. Leningrad, although encircled, had not been taken. The Caucasian oil fields had not been lost and were still a considerable distance from the Germans. The Russians had yielded vast stretches of their country before the German attack, such as the Minsk pocket (250 miles deep and twice as wide) and the Kiev pocket (120 miles in length).

The campaigns ground on and on—attacks, defenses, and counterattacks. The Germans' hedgehog defenses held well in early winter but occasionally showed weaknesses. The Russian people and soldiers tended more and more to support the Soviet system with a renewed spirit of nationalism and thereby gained strength in the knowledge that their military units were holding the Germans. Obviously such circumstances would lead to a war of attrition. There would be successful campaigns of the Germans such as the one of 1942, but each time distance, obstacles, weather, etc., would work against them.

The winter of 1942–43 was a costly one for the Germans. Hitler demanded that Stalingrad be taken in spite of the military recommendation that it would overextend the front; hence the German Sixth Army was entrapped because Hitler ignored the advice of his generals. After Stalingrad the initiative passed to the Russians, and in their typical style of a slow but effective advance, they pushed the Germans back in the summer and autumn campaigns of 1943. Hitler assumed supreme direction of the war in 1943 and tried to hold the Russians back while striving for local tactical victories that became "Pyrrhic victories" either for one side or the other. The German withdrawal was methodical during the winter of 1943 and into the spring of 1944, with the Germans yielding but extracting a great price from the Russians. By the summer of 1944 military supplies and equipment from the United States had provided a significant and favorable advantage to the Russian fighting capability. Some of the quantities that had been shipped to the U.S.S.R. were staggering: 7,800 planes, 4,700 tanks, 170,000 trucks, 6,000.000 pairs of boots, 200,000 field telephones, 740,000 tons of aviation gas, 1,350,000 tons of steel, and 2,500,000 tons of foodstuffs; a total value approaching five billion dollars.

The war of attrition that pitted the German manpower (about 1,500,000 men in about 200 divisions) against the Russians (some 300 divisions consisting of 4,500,000 men) became a war of exhaustion that took a huge toll from both sides. Military authors pointed out that Hitler had intended, and started, a classic war of annihilation; not a war of attrition. Hitler seemed to have no clear long-range plan of action; and his poor use of psychological warfare prompted the Russian peasants to remain loyal to the Soviet Union even though they would have received more favorable treatment by the Germans, especially the early prisoners, that could have been turned into an advantage of significant worth. Poor military intelligence might be blamed for the miscalculations of the climate and terrain conditions under which the Russian invasion would be fought, but Hitler's strategic mistake was his rule which forbade withdrawals. Sometimes even a modest need to withdrawal to shorten lines or readjust lines would be summarily rejected by him. His objective was to penetrate deeper and deeper into Russian territory even though that tactical approach exhausted his troops. A wiser withdrawal policy would have been to exhaust the enemy, then to launch counterattacks; but his field commanders were denied the alternative of executing even a well-planned withdrawal policy.

Germany had yielded Smolensk back to Russia during the summer and autumn campaigns of 1943. The city itself had been captured on September 25, 1943, and soon thereafter all the outlying areas, including Katyn Forest, fell to the Russians. Immediately the Russian "information" system started announcements anew about the Katyn Forest massacres being perpetrated by the Germans in August and September, 1941, shortly after the Army of the Third Reich attacked the Soviet Union. The U.S.S.R. used their press announcement of April 15, 1943, as the guide. The subject had been dormant, but now that they held Smolensk and the Katyn Forest, the subject was renewed by their news media. An announcement was made on November 2, 1943, by decree of the Supreme Soviet that an investigation body (called "The Extraordinary State Commission of Ascertaining and Investigating the Crimes Committed by the German Fascist Invaders and their Associates") would go to Katyn and conduct a scientific study of the facts. The final report of a "Special Commission for Ascertaining and Investigating the Circumstances of the Shooting of Polish Officer Prisoners by the German Fascist Invaders in the Katyn Wood" was dated January 24, 1944. The term, "Special Commission" was never mentioned until this final report was published, at which time its all-Russian membership was made public. (See Appendix 6)

Immediately after the city's return to Russia, their Special Commission proceeded to visit Smolensk. The introductory paragraphs of its final report asserted, from an organizational point of view, how it "was set up upon the decision of the Extraordinary State Committee," and provided additional background information about membership of the Special Commission and the method with which the investigation would take place. After some seven paragraphs the report introduced Katyn Forest with this opening statement:

> The Katyn Forest had for a long time been the favorite resort of Smolensk people, where they used to rest on holidays. The population of the neighborhood grazed cattle and gathered fuel in the Katyn Forest. Access to the Katyn Forest was not banned or restricted in any way. This situation prevailed in the Katyn Forest up to the outbreak of war. Even in the summer of 1941 there was a Young Pioneers' Camp of the Industrial Insurance Board in this forest, which was not disbanded until July, 1941.[1]

In summary, the report of the Special Commission stated the "graves in which are the Polish war prisoners shot by the German occupationists were buried." The total number of bodies, "as calculated by the medico-legal experts, is 11,000."[2] The report further indicated the time of death as "autumn, 1941," a particular point of interest because earlier estimates consistently stated the time of death as August-September, 1941, and each stipulation by witnesses was dated in August-September, 1941. The August-September, 1941, dates continued through the visit to Katyn by foreign correspondents in January, 1944; however, these correspondents reported later, that during the returning train trip to Moscow the Russian guides asked if the correspondents had been convinced that the Germans committed the Katyn crimes. Questions from the visiting correspondents evolved from the fact the bodies were dressed in winter clothing, which was unusual for August or September in Russia. There has been a strong feeling that because of this apparent weakness in the logic, the Soviets changed the timeframe from August-September, 1941, to autumn, 1941, so the death dates would appear within a little cooler weather period. No other part of the report was altered and all statements and testimony of each witness remained as recorded at August-September, 1941. This discrepancy, along with other factors, has put a cloud of doubt over the Russian investigation. (Incidentally, most foreign correspondents reported only that they had been taken to the gravesite at Katyn and had seen the bodies. They avoided making any conclusions.)[3]

Witnesses under oath addressed themselves to this Russian investigation in some detail during the Hearings; however, some relevant comments would be appropriate. When the exhumations at Katyn were being conducted with Dr. Buhtz in charge, the eyewitnesses reported the investigation was being conducted in a professional and objective atmosphere. During his tenure, an inspection and identification of bodies was made by a most efficient Polish Red Cross team, numerous journalists and viewers were permitted to visit the grave site, and members of the International Medical Commission were able to select personally a cadaver and follow it through the identification and search for a pay card, personal papers, a diary, a roster, any mementos, etc.; then photographs of many of these items were published on a world-wide basis. The cadavers themselves were post mortemed in a very public and professional manner by forensic medicine experts who were members of the Commission.

In contrast, Russia's Special Commission was composed entirely of Russian legal-medical representatives who spent very little time in explaining to the few visitors who were permitted to view the grave site any details relating to how the bodies were interred and identified. (General N. N. Burdenko, the chairman, might be an exception, for many foreign correspondents said he was courteous.) A few letters and documents were "on display", but no objective eyewitnesses were permitted to watch the evidence actually being removed from the bodies of the dead Polish officers.

When the Germans opened grave number eight, exhumations were not completed for health and sanitation reasons, then their work was stopped on June 2, 1943. The German plan to exhume more bodies in the autumn never materialized because the Russians recaptured Smolensk on September 25, 1943, and started their own investigation. The Russians claimed 11,000 Polish officers were buried in Katyn; the Germans could account for the 4,143 exhumed and

69

make an estimate of the bodies in grave number eight. Much more forensic medicine and identification work needed to be done by Russians at Katyn before a realistic approach to an accurate accounting of the massacre could be credible.

Theoretically, the Russians could have basked in world-wide public relations had their claim that 11,000 bodies were found been proved to be truthful; a claim that could have been verified if they had extended an invitation to the Polish Red Cross to return to Katyn Forest and continue their identification of bodies. Russia claimed that the Germans had found only one-third the number of bodies (11,000) the Russians had located. Even though Warsaw was still occupied by the Germans, they might have been so sure of their claim that they would have allowed the Polish Red Cross to continue its humanitarian work in order to contest the Russian claim; or the Soviets could have requested the International Red Cross to prove the truthfulness of their claim. Any attempt by the Russians to gain some international recognition for their investigation would have given it some credibility.

Another unbelievable Russian "truth" was that they reported finding letters, receipts, and an icon which, when added together, documented a total of nine items found among the bodies of 11,000 Polish officers. The Germans had reported finding pay books by the thousands among the 4,143 exhumed bodies. If those 4,143 bodies had not been touched by the Russian investigators, the remaining almost 7,000 bodies claimed to have been found should have produced thousands of pay books, letters, photographs, diaries, rosters, etc.; yet only nine pieces of documentary evidence were found on six numbered bodies: Numbers 4, 92, 53, 46 [three documents], 101, and 71. Also listing bodies by number instead of by name and rank shortened the possibility for the audit to be of much value insofar as further research is concerned.

The Russian report tried to make a case by stating that the Polish prisoners of war had actually been sent from Russia's camps at Kozielsk, Ostashkov, and Starobielsk to Smolensk in the spring of 1940. These prisoners had disembarked at the Gniezdovo station and had been incarcerated at three "special camps": Camp No. 1 O.N., Camp No. 2 O.N., and Camp No. 3 O.N., which were spread out from twenty-five to forty-five kilometers (roughly fifteen to twenty-eight miles) west of Smolensk. In view of the accuracy demanded with personnel records and numerous roll calls before Kozielsk, Ostashkov, and Starobielsk were closed, why did not the Russian report give the number of prisoners in each of these new camps, a total of all POWs in camps in this region, or the rank and name of each prisoner, or the specific location of each camp instead of "twenty-five to forty-five kilometers" west of Smolensk? This last question is important, for if the camps were spread out from fifteen to twenty-eight miles west of Smolensk, why were the prisoners all off-loaded at Gniezdovo? Obviously some prisoners (perhaps one-third) would have detrained at Gniezdovo; but why not detrain others (perhaps one-third) farther west than

Gniezdovo, and off-load the last group (perhaps one-third) still farther west? Why were these three camps called "special"? Why were the prisoners in camps numbered 1, 2, and 3 "building and repairing" roads (a fact not mentioned in the German studies or reported by Russian witnesses earlier) when the Poles imprisoned at Griazovietz were exempt from forced labor? Why were the prisoners in these camps never heard from through correspondence with their families and friends when during the same year and one-half (April, 1940, through autumn, 1941) the prisoners at Griazovietz were able to send and receive correspondence regularly?

Why would senior officers including generals, and handicapped individuals with artificial limbs be sent to the special road work camps when younger, healthier junior officers were sent to Griazovietz where they did no "repair work"? How can it be feasible to have the first camp only thirteen miles from the third camp; a camp spread of fifteen to twenty-eight miles west of Smolensk? Could 11,000 Polish prisoners of war be repairing thirteen miles of road (an average of almost 1,000 workers per mile)? How much security would be required if 11,000 Poles were working on thirteen miles of road? Stories of prisoners of war escaping were legend; yet how could a single Pole not escape from such an apparently extended work detail?

In actuality, the Russian report by the Special Commission leaves more questions unanswered than answered.

Chapter 5

THE YALTA CONFERENCE: ITS DISREGARD FOR THE KATYN DATA

On February 12, 1945, the first public announcement was made of the conclusion of an eight-day conference at Yalta on the Crimean Peninsula between Winston Churchill, Prime Minister of Great Britain, Franklin Roosevelt, President of the United States of America, and Josef Stalin, Premier of the Union of Soviet Socialist Republics. Among these "Big Three" and their staffs the final plan for the defeat of Germany was formulated, and agreement was readied on policies and plans for enforcing the unconditional surrender terms (to assure that no ally would make a separate peace treaty). The separate zones of occupation of each country were agreed upon;[1] an announcement of a conference in San Francisco on April 25, 1945, to draw up a charter for a United Nations security plan was made; the agreements concerning the control of liberated areas and Poland were reached;[2] and the inducements for an entrance by Russia into the world war conflict against the Japanese were formulated.

The concessions made by Great Britain and the United States of America to the Russian Government at Yalta can be measured by the fact that Poland's pre-World War II total area of 149,915 square miles (1937) was reduced to 119,800 square miles (the post-war estimate), and the population of 34,2200,000 (1937) was decreased to 32,390,000 (the post-war estimate).[3] The agreement of the "Big Three" (Churchill, Roosevelt, and Stalin) at Yalta gave Russia all of the territory from eastern Poland that extended to the Curzon Line. As a compensation to the Polish government the seaport city of Danzig (which earlier had been a part of East Prussia) and parts of eastern Germany were provisionally awarded to Poland.

A map-study will assist in understanding the significant and profound geographic impact of the Yalta meeting results on Poland when comparing pre-war and post-war boundaries.[4] On a pre-World War II map cities and town in the eastern extremities of Poland have the Polish names of locations mentioned in early news releases of World War II; e.g. common radio reports of "fighting in and around the Polish cities of Grodno, Brest, and Lvov." A post-World War II map-study would show these same three cities to be located in the Union of Soviet Socialist Republics.[5] Other maps show changes in boundaries that move these three (and many other) cities from eastern Poland (indicating they were in pre-war Poland) to western Russia (indicating they were moved to the Soviet Union).[6]

Also of significance were the Russian propaganda invitations by radio and leaflet to the Polish soldiers that started when the German invasion began and continued until Russia attacked the eastern border of Poland. The soldiers were told they could either "go home" or go south "into Romania," the country that bordered on the south, along with Czechoslovakia. In the post-World War II "readjustment" of map boundaries, a Polish soldier who tried to "go south" into Romania would find the country to the south was now part of U.S.S.R. and Czechoslovakia. For example, in the pre-World War II timeframe (or before September 1, 1939) a Polish soldier would travel south through the Polish city of Kolomyya just before crossing the border into Romania; in post-World War II that Polish soldier would go through the Russian city of Kolomyya to reach the border of Romania, only after traveling approximately 200 kilometers (about 130 miles) from the "readjusted" southern border of Poland.

In retrospect an evaluation of the Yalta agreements made in February, 1945, would depend upon the allegiance of the evaluator. The Soviets considered the Yalta Conference a great success because it brought legitimacy to their imperialistic goals. The British and the Americans could conjecture that either they gave up more than they gained or their gains were less than their losses. An objective appraisal of the value of the Yalta Conference could be made only by an observer who was there in 1945 and who knew the "then current" thinking of the "Big Three." The war had been dragging on for almost four and one-half years; the United States had been directly involved for over three years—in fact, since the Japanese sneak attack on Pearl Harbor on December 7, 1941. Although Winston Churchill was clearly aware of the dangers of Soviet expansionism into central Europe, he was also sensitive to the impact of four and one-half years of warfare on Great Britain; he knew the suffering of its people had been immense and its resources were about expended. The British were weary of the war and tended to be supportive of the Soviets, their Ally. Since their initial landings on June 6, 1944, to open a "second front" in Europe, the Americans had fought through a cold and bloody winter (1944–45) which included the battles of the Bulge and Bastogne. The Russians had been involved in fighting since September 17, 1939, when they supported Hitler in the invasion of Poland; and later the same year when they invaded Finland, again as an ally of Germany. When Hitler attacked Russia in June, 1941, both sides suffered hor-

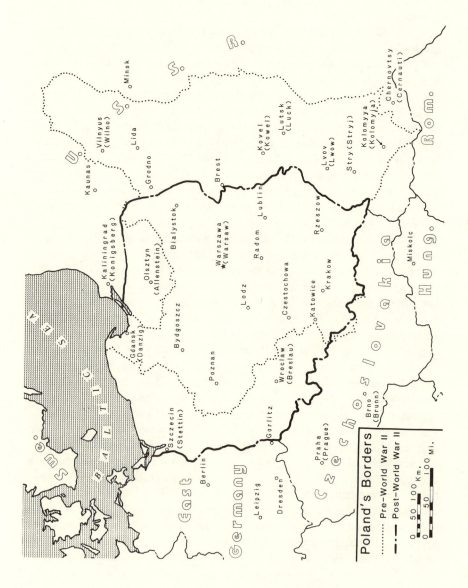

Poland's Borders

.... Pre-World War II
—··— Post-World War II

0 50 100 Km.
0 50 100 Mi.

rendous casualties. Although the German success had been very costly to the Russians both in troops and artillery, the Soviet losses mounted when Russia counterattacked and fought on German soil with Berlin as its goal.

Even though the military commanders of Great Britain and the United States were sensitive to their own casualties, they were also aware of the high casualties the Russians were absorbing by fighting the Germans on the eastern front. The Allied commanders wanted to favor the Russians and keep them on the Allied side because of the constant and open threat from Moscow having to do with a separate peace with the Germans (as happened in World War I) that would leave the British and Americans fighting a one-front war against Hitler's Germany. (The Allies could never forget the August 23, 1939, agreement and pact between Adolf Hitler and Josef Stalin.)

Winston Churchill was a skilled negotiator. His efforts to save Poland were noteworthy, but he could not do it alone. He needed the active support of Franklin Roosevelt. To this end, Mr. Churchill proposed a pre-Yalta conference to consolidate "Anglo-American strategy," thereby offering a unified Churchill-Roosevelt policy at Yalta. But Mr. Roosevelt did not want to give the impression the combined British-American effort was trying to "gang up" on Stalin. Mr. Roosevelt's rejection of Mr. Churchill's suggestion indicated he wanted to treat both Prime Minister Churchill and Premier Stalin on a level of moral equality. Josef Stalin was aware of this intention and therefore drove a wedge between Churchill and Roosevelt who had worked together since the Atlantic Charter (August, 1941). Prime Minister Churchill was trying to help the eastern European nations; primarily Poland, Britain's Ally, for whom the latter had gone to war in the first place. The conclusion of most observers was that while Mr. Churchill supported Mr. Roosevelt, Mr. Roosevelt placated Mr. Stalin. Some author[7] quote Anthony Eden, England's Foreign Minister, who concluded that Josef Stalin was the only one of the "Big Three" who knew what he wanted at Yalta and went for it with single-mindedness, determination, perseverance and tenacity. Stalin got what he wanted, which was "Soviet military, political and economic paramountcy in all Europe east of the Elbe."

Obviously, the key strategy at Yalta rotated around the critical issue of the Soviet system of government in Poland. Because the Poles hated the Soviets, any free election in Poland would have returned to power a very strong anti-Russian government and ended the Russian outcome of success at Yalta. Mr. Churchill insisted upon a Polish election system supervised by international agencies. Mr. Roosevelt, by failing to support Mr. Churchill on this vital issue, passed the control of the Polish elections directly to Mr. Stalin with the vague, unresponsive, and unenforceable commitment to sustain "the right of all people to choose the form of government under which they will live." Mr. Roosevelt had Mr. Stalin agree to "unsupervised elections in which all democratic and Anti-Nazi parties shall have the right to take part." Yalta analysts note that

Premier Stalin won complete control of Poland for the U.S.S.R. at that conference.[8] Mr. Jimmy Byrnes, personal advisor to the president, who later became
Secretary of State, pointed out that "at Yalta, Mr. Roosevelt, instead of being an
advocate of the Polish cause was an arbiter trying to settle the dispute by giving
away what we had little right to give."[9]

In return, Premier Stalin openly and vocally proceeded to recant on
each one of the promises he made at Yalta. On March 23, 1945, barely six
weeks after Yalta, Josef Stalin announced that communist style elections would
be held in Poland. This decree, when heard by the ailing President Roosevelt,
prompted him to note: "Stalin has broken *every* one of the promises he made at
Yalta. We cannot do business with him." President Roosevelt died at Warm
Springs, Georgia, three weeks later, on April 12, 1945. He tried to play the role
of a good Ally, including trying to accept the Russian version of the Katyn
Forest massacre. But near the end of his life Franklin Roosevelt recognized the
sham of Stalin's promises.

Many analysts of the Yalta Conference stated the President of the
United States and the Prime Minister of Great Britain were "too easy" or "too
soft" on Stalin in granting his wishes on so many points; such as boundaries for
Poland, elections for Poland, etc. These critical analysts suggested that the
President and Prime Minister could/should have used the knowledge they had of
the Katyn Forest murders[10] as a wedge to counter Stalin at the bargaining table;
or, if that failed, to alert the rest of the "free world" to recognize that the
Russian system of being an "Ally" was no more morally responsible than the
"enemy" of Germany was morally responsible for its conduct. At the time of
Yalta (February, 1945) both the President and Prime Minister had much information concerning the atrocities at Katyn, but they (specifically, the President
more so than the Prime Minister) chose the keep trying to work with Premier
Stalin so he would not abandon the Allies and make a separate peace pact with
Hitler; also, they were trying to induce the Soviets to join in the fight against
Japan. Both goals were accomplished; however, the latter, the involvement
against the Japanese, benefited the U.S.S.R. much more than anyone could
foresee at the time.

Even so, the results of Yalta could have been even more disastrous.
President Roosevelt had indicated to the other Allies (including Stalin) that the
United States troops hopefully would be out of Europe within two years. In that
event within twenty-four months of the termination of hostilities in the European
conflict, which could be foreseen at Yalta, the withdrawal of such a formidable
military force as the United States Army, Navy, etc., would have left the western
European nations exceedingly vulnerable. An impatient Premier Stalin so intim-
idated the other Allies during the balance of 1945 that when President Roosevelt
died, his successor, President Harry Truman, was alerted to the dangers to
western Europe, as were the other Allies. A wave of resistance to the expansion-

ist concepts of the U.S.S.R. resulted. It was determined that only two alternatives were available: to abandon western Europe, or to resist further Soviet expansion. The decision to select the latter set the stage for differences of opinion and potential clashes for the next one-half century, at least.

The losses of Poland and other "satellite countries" was a big price to pay for becoming alerted to the dangers of communism and the Russian policy of expansionism in the post-World War II period. The North Atlantic Treaty Organization became the foundation for the destiny of western European countries to maintain concepts of democracy west of the "iron curtain," which led to military preparedness, economic stability, business prosperity, and political hope. The price was the loss of eastern European countries; a loss most keenly felt within the eastern European countries themselves because of the loss of whatever freedom they had—the loss of Poland being especially tragic and significant.

When in mid-March, 1945, President Roosevelt went to Capitol Hill to report to the United States Congress on the Yalta Conference, as he was waiting to make his presentation information reached him that one-half a world away, Admiral Nimitz, Commander in Chief, Pacific, had declared the island of Iwo Jima "secured." The former Japanese possession in the Volcano Island had been attacked in amphibious assault by three Marine Divisions; and while much fighting was still going on, a brief five-minute ceremony ran up the United States flag at the base of Mount Suribachi, and at the same time lowered the "stars and stripes" on the top of the mountain where the historic flag-raising picture had been taken four days after the initial landing by the Marines on February 19, 1945.

The news of Iwo Jima being secured on this date was so encouraging that it prompted President Roosevelt to add it to his remarks (after he detailed the agreements reached by Winston Churchill, Josef Stalin, and himself to finish the war in Europe) by stating; "The Japanese warlords know they are not being overlooked. They have felt the force of our B-29s and our carrier planes. They have felt the naval might of the United States and do not appear very anxious to come out and try again. . . . The Japs know what it means that 'The Marines have landed.' And I think I may add, having Iwo Jima in mind, that the situation is well in hand."[11] The quiet listeners packed into the House chamber broke into a roaring, shouting, applauding audience, as the Commander in Chief acknowledged their support. President Roosevelt had given his last report to the Congress of the United States.

Chapter 6

NUREMBERG[1] TRIBUNAL: A KATYN "INCIDENT" INVOLVEMENT

While World War II was in progress, a number of heads of state of the Allied nations had commented that "war criminals" should be punished. The United States Department of Justice, under the wartime leadership of Attorney General Francis Biddle,[2] conducted a series of planning sessions on the subject. In attendance were cabinet ranking members and other government leaders, including President Franklin Roosevelt. The three ranking cabinet members and their departments—Justice, State, and War—came to an agreement that a "fair trial" for "war criminals" could and should be conducted. The recognized parameters were that a trial should not be a sham in which guilt would be assumed before the "war criminals" entered the court room, nor should it provide a base from which the German leaders would have an unexcelled opportunity for propaganda. This plan was approved by President Roosevelt; in fact, he took the preliminary proposal with him to the Yalta Conference in February, 1945, but for unspecified reasons no opportunity became available to discuss it with Prime Minister Winston Churchill of Great Britain or Premier Josef Stalin of the Union of Soviet Socialist Republics. President Roosevelt assigned the task of implementation to Judge Samuel I. Rosenman upon returning to Washington. After President Roosevelt's death, his successor, President Harry Truman, asked Judge Rosenman to discuss the project with the other members of the "Big Four" at the San Francisco Conference scheduled for April, 1945. At the San Francisco Conference details were worked out and on August 8, 1945, the London Agreement and Charter providing for international trials was signed by the United States, Great Britain, the U.S.S.R., and the Provisional Government of France; thereby creating the International Military Tribunal for the purpose of trying German "war criminals." Associate Justice of the United States Supreme Court Robert Jackson was designated by President Truman to act as chief prosecutor for the United States.[3]

The initial membership of the International Military Tribunal was composed of these personages: GREAT BRITAIN: Mr. Justice Geoffrey Lawrence, a member of the Court of Appeals, who was ultimately elected president of the Tribunal; and Sir Norman Birkett, his alternate (non-voting member), a member of the Court of King's Bench. FRANCE: M. Donnedieu de Vabres, a professor from the Ecole de Droits in Paris; and Robert Falco,[4] his alternate, a member of the Cour de Cassation, the highest court in France. U.S.S.R.: Major General I. T. Nikitchenko, vice chairman of the Supreme Court of the U.S.S.R.; and Lieutenant Colonel A. F. Volchkov, his alternate, a member of the Soviet District Court. UNITED STATES: Francis J. Biddle, wartime Attorney General of the United States; and John J. Parker, his alternate, Judge of the United States Circuit Court of Appeals for the Fourth Circuit.

Nuremberg, Germany, located in American occupied territory was selected as the location for the trials because of its available courthouse and prison. The "crimes" were segregated into four categories with responsibility for prosecution being delegated to specific Allied nations, as follows:

COUNT I: *Conspiracy,* and COUNT II: *Crimes Against Peace:* delegated to the United States and Great Britain.
COUNT III: *War Crimes,* and COUNT IV: *Crimes Against Humanity:* delegated to France for western Europe and Russia for eastern Europe, which included Poland, Yugoslavia, Bulgaria, and Czechoslovakia.

The trials began formally on November 20, 1945, with a brief statement by the tribunal president, Geoffrey Lawrence, the British member.

Inevitably, the Katyn Forest "incident" would be brought before the International Military Tribunal since the Russians were responsible for crimes in eastern Europe. This Russian presentation would be the last official chance for the Soviets to place the full blame for the Katyn Forest killings on the Germans. The U.S.S.R. had not wavered from the position of no responsibility established by its communique of April 15, 1943; but immediately after the Russians recaptured Smolensk on July 25, 1943, they started to exhume for a second time the bodies of the Polish prisoners of war.

The Soviet investigative organization, the "Extraordinary State Commission of Ascertaining and Investigating the Crimes Committed by the German Fascist Invaders and their Associates," had only Russians as members. The announcement of the formation of this commission was made on November 2, 1943, and its final report was published on January 24, 1944. When this dated "final report" was issued, "Special Commission" appeared for the first time in the formal title, which was "Report of the Special Commission for Ascertaining and Investigating the Circumstances of the Shooting of Polish Officer Prisoners by the German-Fascist Invaders in the Katyn Forest."

The strategy of the U.S.S.R. at Nuremberg was to place the blame, finally and formally, on the Germans so that from that time forward the history of World War II would record the Katyn killings as a German crime. The Russian chief prosecutor, General R. A. Rudenko, pursued this indictment with enthusiasm, although the "so-called" defendant was not remotely connected with the killings. Even the American prosecutor, Robert Jackson, attempted to persuade the Russian prosecutor, General Rudenko, to omit the charge; but Rudenko could not be dissuaded and did include the allegation that the Germans were responsible for the Katyn killings. Considering the standards of late 1945, the issue was controversial. The Soviet Special Commission submitted its 1944 report, which included the testimonies by three German witnesses during one week. The Russian prosecutor made a concerted effort to assure beyond a reasonable doubt the Germans were the Katyn "war criminals." The charges were leveled against Marshal Hermann Goring because he was considered the highest ranking individual of the German defendants.

After the Soviets had completed their prosecution, the German defense asked for time to produce its own witnesses. The Russian prosecutor opposed allowing the Germans to petition for leave to produce three witnesses. Although General Rudenko spoke lengthily against the Germans being allowed to produce any defense witnesses, the judgment of the high tribunal was that the Russian prosecutor had been allowed to introduce in his final report hearsay evidence, backed up by a Soviet version of eye witnesses; therefore a fairness to the defendant, German witnesses must be allowed to present their defense. The judges knew the Germans would present the documented data of the International Medical Commission in which no German membership had been included.

When the announcement was made of the tribunal's decision to allow the German defense to produce witnesses, the Russian prosecutor filed a petition for a rehearing, which turned out to be the only single petition for a reargument the judges received in the course of the entire trial. The language used by Rudenko was coarse and offensive. He not only challenged the court's interpretation of the charter which founded the tribunal but also stated his opinion strongly that the court had violated its duty and responsibility. After the verbal attack by the Russian prosecutor, and the refiling of the rehearing petition, the tribunal proposed during private deliberations that the prosecutor be cited for contempt and perhaps sent to prison since there was no defense for his unjustifiable attack on the integrity of the court. The proposal was approved by a vote of three to one. (The Russian judge dissented.)

After considerable "negotiating" and "compromising," the Russian prosecutor was not cited for contempt, not arrested, not imprisoned, nor his opinion openly mentioned in court; in fact, no information leaked to the press regarding the internal private discussion of the court members. The motion was simply denied—formally—during the next session.

Then a specific identification of the charge as printed in the indictment was made, which read: "In September, 1941, 11,000 Polish officers were killed in the Katyn Forest near Smolensk."[5] The first evidence had been submitted as early as February, 1946, by the Russian prosecutor, who cited the Russian Investigation Report of January, 1944. Members of the prosecution team from other countries proposed using witnesses only for the Katyn portion of the indictment, but the Russian prosecutor protested vigorously by stating ". . . the prosecution of the Soviet Union categorically protests against witnesses. . . ."[6] If the defense wants two witnesses, we, the Russians, want ten witnesses."[7] Ultimately, the presiding judge allowed three witnesses for each member nation. The three witnesses called by the Germans did such a credible job for the defense that the prosecutors for the Russians who vehemently cross-examined the witnesses could not enhance their case.

After the witnesses for the Germans completed their testimony for the defense, nothing more was heard about Katyn Forest from the Russian prosecutors for the balance of the trial.

In the final statements, July 6, 1946, the German defense attorney, Dr. Stahmer, had made a strong plea of innocence for Hermann Goring, the senior defendant; also, a plea that there was "no proof" of guilt on the part of Germany for the Katyn killings. On July 29, 1946, the Russian prosecutor made his final statement and never used the word "Katyn." Moreover, the court did not mention "Katyn" nor was the "incident" addressed by the International Military Tribunal when the final judgment was delivered on October 2, 1946. As a result the case of identity for the Katyn Forest massacre was left, and remains, undecided.

But the paradox of the Katyn forest massacre remained an enigma because it was cited by the Russian prosecutors at the International Military Tribunal as a German crime; then when the charge, in effect, was "dropped" by the Soviets, the loss for the U.S.S.R. became significant because if the Germans were not guilty, who was? The irony was that the unfortunate Polish prisoners of war who were slaughtered at Katyn Forest never had a formal International Court of Justice or United Nations judicial system establish guilt for this crime.

On April 24, 1952,[8] the Select Committee of the United States House of Representatives, at a meeting in Frankfurt, Germany, examined some of the strategies and "infighting" that unfolded at the Nuremberg Trial by calling on witnesses to express before the Committee their interpretation of the trial's events. Dr. Robert Kempner, assistant prosecutor to Justice Robert H. Jackson, the senior prosecutor for the United States, was the first witness to testify. Justice Jackson was on loan from the Supreme Court; Dr. Kempner from the War Department. Dr. Kempner, initially assigned to Nuremberg for thirty days, remained there four years and four months—from July, 1945, until October, 1949. Dr. Kempner's interpretation of how the trial involved Katyn pertained to all four categorial "counts" of war crimes.

In relation to Count III and IV, the French were spokesmen for themselves, the Dutch, the Belgians, and other German occupied territories; the Russians for themselves, the Polish, the Yugoslavs, the Czechoslovakians and other German occupied territories.

The Select Committee asked Dr. Kempner why other governments did not prefer charges for other violations than those established in the Categorical Counts. For example, if the subject material included plans of conspiracy and crimes against peace, war crimes and crimes against humanity, why did not the tribunal at Nuremberg prefer charges for acts of aggression such as Russia attacking Finland, or Latvia, or Estonia, or Lithuania, or Poland? Dr. Kempner answered that the only charges of aggression to be considered by the Tribunal were those which had been committed by the Germans.

A solid witness before the Select Committee was Dr. Otto Stahmer, the defense counsel for Reichmarshal Hermann Goring at Nuremberg who discussed the indictment in the charge: "In September, 1941, 11,000 Polish officers were killed in the Katyn Forest near Smolensk."[9] Dr. Stahmer testified he had another German defense attorney (for General Jodl) accompany him to a meeting with Colonel Prochownik of the U.S.S.R. Colonel Prochownik proposed to shorten the Nuremberg proceedings by not hearing witnesses but by submitting affidavits instead of testimony, and stated this procedural change would be in compliance with the wishes of the chairman, Judge Lawrence. Dr. Stahmer refused the suggestion because he wanted the German witnesses— Colonel Ahrens, General Oberhaeuser and First Lieutenant Von Eichborn—to be heard. The Russian witnesses were the former Buergermeister of Smolensk; a Bulgarian professor and signer of the Protocol of the International Medical Commission, Dr. Markov, whose country was occupied by the Russians; and a professor of anatomy who had worked at Smolensk and Katyn and had been evacuated by the Germans.

Dr. Stahmer's summary was brisk and vigorous and his arguments rotated around the testimonies of Ahrens, Oberhaeuser, and Von Eichborn. He proved, he thought, by beginning his summary with the conclusive statement that the crime could not have been perpetrated by the German Wehrmacht in the timeframe it had occurred; therefore, the Germans were innocent of the crime of Katyn. Favorable comments indicated that Dr. Stahmer had made an eloquent and persuasive argument for the honor of the German Army. He had no way of knowing that the prosecuting counsel for the Russians who followed him would make absolutely no mention of Katyn. He testified the Russians did not ask that the charge of Katyn be dropped from the indictment; they simply never referred to it again—not even in their closing arguments. The tribunal had picked up this omission quickly and had made no mention or reference at all to Katyn in its conclusions. Dr. Stahmer indicated that since his job as defense counsel was to prove the German army and its officers who had been accused were not guilty, the tribunal had determined their innocence with the court's adjudication; in other words, Dr. Stahmer felt he had succeeded in his defense effort.

The Select Commission asked Dr. Stahmer why he had not gone beyond the indictment to try to establish guilt on someone else, thereby showing the innocence of the Germans regarding the crime. The defense counsel stated, "In my opinion, I had fulfilled my task of proving that the Germans were not the perpetrators of the crime."[10] When the Select Committee persisted in asking why the defense counsel was not concerned with trying to find out who was guilty, Dr. Stahmer gave this opinion:

> I believe that the court would have objected to that, in view of the fact that the Russians were not the accused. We had this experience on several occasions, when we ventured to point out that the other side had occasionally sinned, that it was immediately pointed out to us that the other side was not sitting on the bench of the accused.[11]

Almost one-half century has elapsed with Poland's eternal hope for justice being an unfulfilled dream. Do the people of Poland have an opinion about the Katyn "incident?" Can anyone hear their voices? If Russia could not prove the guilt of the Germans at Nuremberg, would the Soviets become the only primary suspect for Katyn? Did the International Medical Commission successfully prove Germany's innocence for the horrendous massacre? Can the Russians produce similar evidence of their innocence? Why was the Katyn Massacre not placed "in the record" of World War II historical atrocities along with other violations of justice of the Hague Convention, the Geneva Convention, etc.?

PART II

IN THE RECORD

Chapter 7

UNITED STATES HOUSE OF REPRESENTATIVES: SELECT COMMITTEE ORGANIZED FOR HEARINGS ON KATYN MASSACRE

The Katyn Forest killings were brought to the attention of the American public specifically, and to the public of the world at large, during 1951 and 1952 by a committee of the United States House of Representatives who conducted research to investigate the authenticity of the data and place "in the record" the Katyn "incident" testimony. This special committee was unanimously authorized by Congress on September 18, 1951. The members of this Select Committee to Conduct an Investigation and Study the Facts, Evidence and Circumstances of the Katyn Forest Massacre were appointed by the Speaker of the House of Representatives: four Democrats and three Republicans.[1] In line with the procedural style of such committee operations, hearings were held in numerous locations, including Washington and Chicago, the latter of which boasts of a large Polish population. Unusual, however, were the overseas hearings in London, Frankfurt, and Naples. Testimonies were received from eighty-one witnesses, and over one hundred depositions were received from additional witnesses who were unable to appear for various reasons; also, 183 exhibits were studied and made a part of the record. Two reports were submitted: an interim report,[2] and a final report.[3]

The committee, after exhaustive efforts, published its findings in a report that the membership of the committee

> unanimously agrees that evidence dealing with the first phase of its investigation proves conclusively and irrevocably the Soviet NKVD (Peoples Commissariat of Internal Affairs) committed the massacre of Polish Army officers in the Katyn Forest near Smolensk, Russia, not later than the spring of 1940.

87

This Committee further concludes that the Soviets had plotted this criminal extermination of Poland's intellectual leadership as early as fall of 1939—shortly after Russia's treacherous invasion of the Polish nation's borders. There can be no doubt this massacre was a calculated plot to eliminate all Polish leaders who subsequently would have opposed the Soviets' plans for communizing Poland.[4]

The vigor and enthusiasm with which the Select Committee approached its duties was commendable. The members were motivated by the mood of the American people who had concluded, and correctly so, the German Government had been the "enemy" during World War II; however, the people sensed the Russians, in the immediate post-World War II period, had not only abandoned their "favored nation" role of "Ally" but also reverted to an aggressive, totalitarian role of expansionism. Clearly, the committee could see a mandate from the American people to make some logical assessment of the Russian government's conduct of possible corrupted morality and violation of human rights after the war;[5] therefore, the committee's immediate task was to determine whether this attitude had been present during the war as well. The killing of captive Polish prisoners of war at Katyn Forest was selected as the subject material upon which the Select Committee would base its judgment of Russia's guilt, and the people in America awaited the findings!

Only places, dates, and circumstances of each hearing held by the Select Committee will be included in this portion of the precis; samplings of testimonies of witnesses will follow in succeeding chapters.

The committee began Part I of the Hearings on October 11, 1951, in Washington, D.C., with the testimony of an American eyewitness, Lieutenant Colonel Donald B. Stewart, U.S.A., who was captured in North Africa on February 15, 1943, and ordered to go to the Katyn Forest grave site by the Germans. Likewise, his senior American officer, Colonel John H. Van Vliet, U.S.A., was similarly captured in mid-February, 1943, and ordered to Katyn Forest. Both American officers refused to go lest they become a part of a German propaganda plot, but the Germans gave them written orders. Colonel Van Vliet's testimony was related in Part 2 of the Hearings, conducted on February 4, 5, 6, and 7, 1952.

The committee moved to Chicago, Illinois, and held Part 3 of the Hearings on March 13 and 14, 1952. Historically, key witnesses provide more pertinent information to a Congressional committee that will go wherever the most succinct information is available that ultimately will help committee members arrive at meaningful conclusions and fulfill their responsibility of keeping the American public informed.

Part 4 of the Hearings convened in London, England, on April 16 and continued through April 19. Here the members of the Select Committee heard numerous witnesses testify who otherwise might not have been provided the opportunity except for the mobility of the Committee.

Frankfurt, Germany, was the site for Part 5 of the Hearings from April 21 through 26, 1952. Again eyewitnesses were provided opportunity to testify before the Select Committee, and these witnesses were either Poles or Germans. In Part 5 the testimony taken on April 27, 1952, in Naples, Italy, of a member of the International Medical Commission, Dr. Palmieri, who was unable to journey to Frankfurt, was included.

Part 6 of the Hearings related to the Polish White Paper, etc., that had been referred to in London by the Polish Government in Exile. Because of its voluminous proportions this paper was made a separate part of the Hearings. The Polish Government in Exile became an outstanding data-gathering source for the Congressional Select Committee.

The "pulling together" of all loose ends of the committee's work, including addressing itself to internal matters, was incorporated in Part 7 of the Hearings, which began on June 3 and 4, 1952, and concluded after the elections of November, 1952 with witnesses testifying November 11, 12, 13 and 14, 1952. The final report of the Select Committee was presented at a news conference on December 22, 1952.

Chapter 8

SELECT COMMITTEE HEARINGS: WASHINGTON

A sampling of selective testimonies of Katyn witnesses, presented under oath at the Select Committee Hearings held in Washington, D.C., beginning on October 11, 1951, follows:

The testimony of Lieutenant Colonel Donald B. Stewart, U.S.A.,[1] indicated the German prisoners of war party of Allied officers included two American officers: Colonel (then Lieutenant Colonel) John H. Van Vliet, U.S.A., and Lieutenant Colonel (then Captain) Stewart, U.S.A.; also, Lieutenant Colonel Stevenson, British South Africa Forces (senior officer present), and Captain Gilder of the British Medical Corps. In addition to these four there were three British enlisted men and a British civilian, whose names could be neither remembered nor determined because Lieutenant Colonel Stewart's small notebook with written details had been taken away from him later in the war by a German prison guard. This visiting Allied POW party consisted of these eight men; plus guards, civilians from the Propaganda Ministry, some German officers, and an interpreter—a total of about twenty people aboard a small transport aircraft that landed at Smolensk, approximately forty miles behind the front lines. The "meager" supper provided them consisted of a piece of cheese and a slice of rye bread, and tea. After spending the night in Smolensk, the Allied group was taken to Katyn Forest on Thursday, May 13, 1943, by car. Three graves had been opened at that time (probably Numbers 1, 2, and 3: the first being the "L" shaped grave). The

> bodies were laid out in rows across the narrow dimensions of the grave. Practically all bodies were face down. There were layer after layer, they were practically all "headed" the same way. It was obvious they had not been tossed into the graves from the banks, they had been apparently thrown down in there after they were killed, and then packed in very tightly.
>
> The grave in which we walked, the officers were mostly dressed in overcoats of heavy material, a little darker and longer than our own. . . .[2]

In response to questions, Lieutenant Colonel Stewart estimated that according to the number of bodies in each row "there must have been about nine or ten thousand men in those graves."[3]

Lieutenant Colonel Stewart's testimony confirmed that the bodies were "packed very, very tightly, like cigars." Also, he stated that at the autopsy tables where the bodies were being examined and identified before reburial, the bodies viewed had

their hands tied behind their backs, with strings, the equivalent of binder cord, sunk into the flesh so that it was obvious that it had been put on when they were alive; it was not a recent addition. . . .

and

they had on black boots, of very good leather.

You can look at a piece of leather and you can tell whether it is good or not. Those boots were good. They had leather heels on their boots, and the leather heels were not worn down; the heels were in good shape.

Most of them were in breeches of elastic material similar to our own prewar Army officer breeches. That material was of very good quality and showed practically no wear.

The blouses were darker. Now when I say they showed no wear, the material was not worn, and the boots were not worn. The clothing fitted: they looked like they were tailor made clothes.[4]

Lieutenant Colonel Stewart further testified that the Allied representatives were made to select a body at random upon which the next autopsy would be conducted. One of the purposes was to determine the cause of death. With the flesh of the scalp removed surgically the small bullet hole showed in the back of the head, the larger bullet hole in the front; in other words, the exit hole was larger than the hole where the bullet entered. Dr. Buhtz, the senior German medical officer in charge, performed the autopsy.

The body was searched for identification, and the clothing, including boots, was removed to look for concealed objects. The body looked "as if it were mummified. The flesh was black and hard, pressed to the bone. . . ."[5]

The Allied prisoners of war group was told no papers or documents dated later than April or May, 1940 had been found on the deceased. Also, clothing material examined showed bayonet wound marks with a fluted blade imprint, which in the cloth being examined appeared to be "a sort of triangular hole in it, not a straight cut as our present bayonet makes, not a knife cut."[6]

"My decision was that those men were killed by the Russians while they were prisoners of the Russians."[7]

Congress adjourned shortly after the first witness appeared before the

Select Committee and by the time it reconvened on February 4, 1952, the Committee had met in executive session and had briefed President Harry Truman regarding its activities to date. He heartily supported the purpose of the Hearings and issued instructions to all departments of the government to cooperate "100 per cent" in supplying files and evidence to the committee.

The second witness to appear before the Select Committee was the senior American member of the Allied prisoners of war group ordered by the Germans to be sent to Katyn Forest as an observer, Colonel (then Lieutenant Colonel) John H. Van Vliet, Jr., U.S.A.[8] Colonel Van Vliet was captured in Tunisia in mid-February, 1943, and as a prisoner of war was sent to the German camp at Rotenburg, where he arrived in mid-March, 1943. The camp was primarily for British officers—about 300 to 350 were incarcerated there; along with approximately 125 American officers. The first word on the subject of Katyn came to this group via the German press in the last week of April, 1943. The German authorities announced that one or two British officers and one or two American officers would be sent as a part of a committee to investigate the circumstances of the alleged murder of many thousands of Polish officers. The senior Allied officers protested that they should not be sent lest they fall into a propaganda trap set for the benefit of the Germans. The protest was put into writing, with copies furnished the Germans and the Swiss protecting power; but the Germans ordered, in writing, two British and two American officers to go to Katyn.

The testimony of Colonel Van Vliet confirmed the earlier remarks of Lieutenant Colonel Stewart concerning the background of the trip to Katyn, the estimates of distances, and the descriptions of the bodies and related data. The review of the grave site coincided with Lieutenant Colonel Stewart's testimony; such as the three grave sites being opened at that time, the required observation of one autopsy after selecting the body, the search for identification and personal possessions, and the reburial in the "new grave which had been recently dug"[9] within one hundred yards of the grave from which the body had been selected for autopsy. Also, Colonel Van Vliet confirmed Lieutenant Colonel Stewart's estimated number of murdered Polish prisoners of war, for his conclusion was "that the Russians had killed 10,000 Polish officers, or thereabouts."[10]

Colonel Van Vliet further testified that after the German prisoner of war camp was overrun by the Russian army and after experiencing many problems and much turmoil, he reached the American lines on May 5, 1945, and promptly notified the intelligence function of the local American unit (104th Infantry Division) that he had a matter to be discussed with either the War Department or the State Department because of its political significance. He testified he was transported to Paris and flown to Washington, D.C., where he reported to the Pentagon; then on May 22, 1945, he spoke privately with Major General Bissell, U.S.A., who was Assistant Chief of Staff, G-2, of the War

Department. General Bissell asked him to dictate his report which he accomplished, then signed it. Colonel Van Vliet mentioned he had sought the guidance of the G-2 about possible political implications of his forced Katyn visit, and that General Bissell had verbally directed him neither to mention nor to discuss it with anyone in or out of the military service without specific approval in writing from the War Department. Colonel Van Vliet said he asked for this guidance so that he could not be badgered into any discussions about the incident. He adhered to this guidance to the degree that he ignored a telephone call about the loss of his original report; but later he received a letter, dated April 26, 1950, from the Chief of Information, Major General F. L. Parks, U.S.A., that could not be ignored. The letter notified Colonel Van Vliet that the original report which he had dictated, signed, and hand delivered to Major General Bissell on May 22, 1945, could not be found, stated that a search was continuing within the various intelligence agencies, and "requested that another report on your experience with the Katyn case be prepared."[11] Colonel Van Vliet said he was released from the silence directed in General Bissell's original guidance for this one particular report, and he responded with an eight-page report dated May 11, 1950,[12] by personally typing, which he mailed "return receipt requested" from Fort Lewis, Washington, to Major General Parks in Washington, D.C.

The testimonies of both Colonel Van Vliet and Lieutenant Colonel Stewart further indicated that one of their conclusions, which was neither included in the briefing nor pointed out to them by the Germans, was that the uniforms of the murdered Polish prisoners of war were not worn or tattered in any way. Both men had observed that the clothing was well fitted, well tailored, and of fine quality; in fact, it gave no sign of previously being worn. Moreover, the shoes and boots of the victims showed no wear either on the heels or anywhere else. The attention to detail by the American officers who were eyewitnesses at Katyn contributed to their conclusion that the Polish officers were executed soon after their capture, or early in 1940 (March, April, May) when the Russians were in control in Smolensk and the U.S.S.R. was at peace and had not yet been invaded by the Germans. (The German invasion occurred in June, 1941.) This conclusion contradicted the Russian version of Katyn, which stated the Polish officers were working on roads in the vicinity of Smolensk when captured by the Germans and were executed in August and September of 1941. The final conclusion of Colonel Van Vliet and Lieutenant Colonel Stewart, both prisoners of war who would be knowledgable on serviceability and appearance of military uniforms under captivity conditions, was that the Russians were guilty of the Katyn massacre.

Another witness who gave corroborating evidence concerning the good condition of the boots was Marion (Mike) Gwiak who was perhaps the youngest of the prisoners of war to survive. He was a Polish military cadet who found himself pressed into front-line service with an artillery unit against the Germans in September, 1939. He was sent to Kozielsk about November, 1939, and turned out to be one of the survivors of that ill-fated POW camp. He was among the last remaining prisoners of war (one of 245) at Kozielsk who left that camp after the victims had been moved 150 to 200 at a time to Gniezdovo and finally to Katyn. He was transported to Pavlishchev Bor (one of approximately 448 Poles), then to Griezovietz where the survivors (some 400 or less) remained until allowed to join the Polish Army in Russia after Germany's attack on the U.S.S.R.

In his testimony Mr. Gwiak confirmed the prisoners attempted to take good care of their boots because they did not know how long they would be in captivity. Some evidence indicated wooden "clogs" had been worn to save "wear and tear" on the boots—Mr. Gwiak used the term "wooden shoes." The emphasis on the quality of the boots and their non use made a portion of Mr. Gwiak's testimony important to the Hearings.

> In the camp we didn't use our boots. We realized that maybe we would be stuck there for a long period. I am talking now about precautions. We had something like wooden shoes instead of using our own military shoes. I had them, too. We used to use our wooden shoes or rags or something like that. If we could save our uniforms we were proud. Everybody was proud of his army uniform. We didn't wear them. That is the reason at the time the transport started we had everything in good condition.[13]

The next testimony in Part 2 of the Select Committee Hearings was given by former Polish Ambassador to Moscow Thadeusz Romer, who was appointed to Russia in August, 1942, while on assignment in Africa. (Ambassador Kot had departed from the Soviet Union in July, 1942.) After his re-assignment, Ambassador Romer proceeded through Egypt into Iran and on into Russia. He assumed his ambassadorial duties there in November, 1942. One of the individuals to whom Ambassador Romer spoke in Teheran, while enroute to Russia, was former Ambassador Kot who turned over his files and archives to the new ambassador; including the lists of Polish prisoners of war who were missing, as well as other refugees who were unaccounted for but were somewhere within the Soviet Union. Also, former Ambassador Kot provided Ambassador Romer with minutes of all conversations and interventions with the Russian authorities during his tour of duty. Ambassador Romer met with General Anders, who expressed his concern about the missing officers and described his own experiences with the Soviet leaders. The new ambassador also spent time with Josef Czapski, who had been assigned the responsibility for ascertaining the location of the missing Poles. One of Ambassador Romer's personal observations was that "at the time of the German-Soviet friendship, some sort of liquidation of these leading groups of Polish intelligentsia was agreed upon by the two totalitarian partners, whose final aim was the definite destruction of the Polish nation."

Ambassador Romer never excluded the possibility that the Nazis would be capable of committing such a mass murder, for he knew only too well their retaliatory methods in occupied Poland and elsewhere; however, there was sufficient evidence from the Polish underground in German-occupied Poland for him to be certain there had been no mass exchange of prisoners (or even individual escapes) into German-occupied Poland. "I came to the evident conclusion that the responsibility for the fate of these 15,000 men lay on the Russian side."[14]

Finally, Mr. Romer noted the circumstances under which he was awakened on the night of Easter Sunday, April 25, 1943, at 11 P.M. and told that Foreign Minister Molotov wanted to see him. The Polish Ambassador arrived by midnight and Mr. Molotov saw him fifteen minutes later, or on April 26, 1943. Ambassador Romer was given a note severing relations between the U.S.S.R. and the Polish Government in Exile in London. Mr. Romer would not accept the note after debate, but it was delivered to him within an hour after he returned to his hotel.[15] (The contents of the note and the response by the Polish Ambassador are included as Appendices 2 and 3.)

Colonel George Grobicki of the Polish army (since November, 1918) had been captured by the Russians on September 26, 1939, and as a prisoner of war at Kozielsk testified as a witness before the Select Committee on February 7, 1952. He stated that his life had been threatened a number of times, especially immediately after he was captured; also, that he had been seriously ill and was in the prison hospital when his name was called to be on a mid-April "transport list" to depart from Kozielsk (for Katyn), but the Russian medical officer would not allow him to go. By the time he was dismissed from the hospital his name appeared again on the "transport list." On May 1, 1940, he was sent to Pavlishchev Bor rather than Katyn, then on to Griazovietz "by accident."

Colonel Grobicki was a mature, experienced officer whose value as a witness was appreciated by the members of the committee. He confirmed the testimony of earlier witnesses and responded well to questions asked by members and counsels. One response was his identification of a Russian handgun, a revolver (Nagant), used by Russian troops. He noted that for a time these weapons had been issued to the surviving Poles for training purposes as they formed a Polish army on Russian soil in the late summer and early fall of 1941. The ammunition for this weapon had been described to them by a Soviet ammunition officer, who was schooling them during target practice, as being made in Russia, in Belgium, and in Germany. The Russian ammunition officer stated the Belgian and German types were less accurate than the Russian type.[16]

Colonel Grobicki offered an opinion that the Russians were practicing genocide on the Polish nation by destroying its leadership; present and future. He stated this was already being witnessed in the Baltic States of Estonia, Latvia, and Lithuania; also in Bulgaria, Hungary, Czechoslovakia, and Albania. He alleged that the killing of Polish intelligentsia, "the brains of the nation,"[17] was the Russians' goal.

When asked why any were spared death, he responded that there had been reasons why the last "transports" were sent to Pavlishchev Bor. One reason had been to show some specimens of Polish officers if it were ever necessary to display them outside of Russia. Another reason was to fulfill the Soviet goal of organizing Polish communist army. (This reason dovetails with comments made later about the speed of the German attack against France in the spring of 1940, at which time Russia might have felt a need for this "in-Russia" Polish Army to be available.) The final reason pertained to the delay of the train in which Colonel Grobicki was travelling. When the train stopped at Babenino, it was detained amidst great confusion among the train guards; likewise, upon departure from Kozielsk and arrival at Pavlishchev Bor. At the last stop two sets of guards were away while the train was being detained, which could have suggested a great decision had been made—perhaps at the highest level in Moscow—and the Russians wanted this adjustment period to be witnessed by the Polish officer captives detained at Babenino who instead of proceeding to Katyn, had been diverted to Pavlishchev Bor.[18]

An American Catholic priest, Father Leopold Braun, Augustinian of the Assumption, served as chaplain to the American Catholics in the Soviet Union for an "uninterrupted twelve-year period, from March 1, 1934 until December 27, 1945." He had been allowed entrance into the U.S.S.R. as a clergyman because of a religious protocol signed by President Roosevelt and Maxim Maximovich Litvinov at the time of recognition of the Soviet Government by the United States of America on November 16, 1933. The protocol stated

> We will expect that religious groups or congregations composed of nationals of the United States of America in the territory of the Union of Soviet Socialist Republics will be given the right to have their spiritual needs ministered to by clergymen, priests, rabbis, or other ecclesiastical functionaries who are nationals of the United States of America.[19]

Father Braun was a solid witness who presented succinct, factual data in a methodical and logical approach and reviewed the deportation from Poland to Russia of some 1,750,000 civilian Poles in addition to the military prisoners of war. He identified the Allied press correspondents who were taken to the graves at Katyn during the time of the Russians investigation. These civilians, including doctors, professors, clergy, etc., had been sent to a number of points, many to Siberia and Kazakhstan bordering on the Caspian and Black Seas.

Father Braun noted the location of his church across the street from the NKVD prison called Malay, Lubianka—the name of the street. Interned in this prison were General Anders, who was separated from all other Polish prisoners incarcerated there, and a hand-picked group of Polish officers, who were later released (August, 1941) to form the Polish army in Russia. He also discussed with the Select Committee his conversations with Ambassador Stanislaus Kot and their intense search for the missing Polish prisoners of war; the same search that was being conducted by Josef (Jan) Czapski after he was released from Griazovietz. Father Braun also identified the American Ambassadors sent to Moscow: Lawrence A. Steinhardt was ambassador when the Germans struck in 1941; next, Admiral William Harrison Standley, U.S.N., who had been Chief of Naval Operation; followed by Averell Harriman. His review of the NKVD helped the American people to understand the direction and purpose of that Russian governmental security agency regarding genocide. Father Braun re-called the oft-quoted remark by General Beria and General Merkulov in response to a question about the Polish survivors who were thought to be ame-nable toward communism. The question concerned whether the Polish officers from Starobielsk and Kozielsk could be included in the Polish army in Russia. "No, not those men, we have made a great blunder with them."[20]

The final witness to testify was Mr. Henry Clarence Cassidy, who had served in Moscow as Associated Press (AP) correspondent from August 3, 1940 to August 3, 1944. He had been the bureau chief for Associated Press and also a newscaster for the National Broadcasting Company (NBC). Mr. Cassidy was a member of the group of Allied press correspondents who were taken to what the Russians called "Goat Hill," a name the Soviets used instead of Katyn Forest. The group left by train in January, 1944, on a "well-organized" trip that in-cluded the city of Smolensk. The correspondents saw open graves and watched work being done on the exhumed bodies; then they were taken back into town for a meeting with the Soviet Atrocities commission investigating the Katyn Forest massacre. The Allied correspondents viewed documents, buttons, per-sonal possessions, and letters—especially one letter to which the Russians at-tached great importance. This unmailed letter was dated in late summer of 1941 when the Germans occupied the territory; or so the Soviets claimed. Also, the attention of the correspondents was directed to a diary and some newspapers the Russians said were dated in August and September, 1941 that were on exhibit in glass display cases. The correspondents did not see any documents removed from the bodies of the POWs but rather were permitted to review them in this "after-the-fact" manner. This procedure, plus other events, prompted Mr. Cas-sidy to testify thus: "The performance that we saw was entirely staged."[21] On their return trip the Allied correspondents told the Russian guides that they had not proven their point. In the Hearings record the statement of the correspondents was so printed: "Among the American correspondents, we came back with the feeling that the Russians had not proven their case."[22]

Mr. Cassidy indicated the Allied correspondents had been shown about 400 bodies by the Russians who estimated there were approximately 11,000 bodies in all. The press release by the reporters offered no personal conclusions; rather, they reported simply two points: the journalists had seen some of the graves and viewed some of the bodies; and they were told by the Russians that the Germans committed the Katyn crime.

On February 7, 1952, Parts 1 and 2 of the Hearings of the Select Committee, held in Washington, D.C., were concluded.

Chapter 9

SELECT COMMITTEE HEARINGS: CHICAGO

Part 3 of the Select Committee Hearings convened in Chicago, Illinois, on Thursday, March 13, 1952.[1] The initial testimony was provided by Dr. Edward Lucas Miloslavich,[2] an American, living in St. Louis, Missouri, who appeared under subpena. After completing his medical education in Europe, he had returned to the United States, his native country; then later, in 1934, he accepted a position at the University of Zagreb, Croatia, (now a part of Yugoslavia) to form an Institute of Legal Medicine and Criminology.

Dr. Miloslavich was in Croatia, then occupied by the Germans, when the German announcement about Katyn was made on April 13, 1943. Professional curiosity prompted his desire to examine the graves at Katyn and, after permission was granted by the Germans, paid his own expenses for the trip. The International Medical Commission made him a member so he could participate in the autopsies; in fact, he conducted one himself with a personally selected cadaver (April 29, 1943). Dr. Buhtz, the German medical officer in charge at Katyn, and the other forensic experts, discussed the medical issues with him. Moreover, along with the other members, he signed the medical findings (Protocol) of the International Medical Commission, dated April 30, 1943.

The availability of Dr. Miloslavich was advantageous for the Select Committee because he was a medical expert of international repute, and his speciality was forensic challenges of a military nature. His experience included examination of atrocities in military engagements in other parts of the globe, eyewitness participation at the Katyn exhumations by the Germans, and membership on the International Medical Commission. His testimony was interesting because he could articulate and present technical data in lay language.

The next witness to testify on March 13, 1952, was Mrs. Irene Hajduk Metelica,[3] a resident of Chicago, whose father, Major Pawel Hajduk, an infantry officer in the Polish army, had been one of the victims discovered at Katyn. Mrs. Metelica was deported from Poland to Russia, along with her mother, as a family member of a Polish officer. Her father's name appeared on the list of victims provided to the Select Committee, which was attached as a 317-page appendix to the testimony of Part 3 of the Hearings. The lengthy roster included names of the dead who were identified at Katyn, and listed the Polish prisoners of war who had been interned at each of these camps: Kozielsk, Ostashkov, and Starobliesk. The series of rosters had been prepared by Adam Moszynski[4] who was interned at Starobliesk, and who had been among the approximately 448 survivors of the three camps to be sent to Pavlishchev Bor.

The third witness to testify was Bronislaw Mylnarski,[5] of Los Angeles, California. He had been a member of the Polish Army Reserve and was called to active duty in Warsaw two days after the Germans invaded Poland. Having been on active duty during the Russo-Polish War of 1920, and being 39-years old, he served as an engineer (sapper) and a staff officer with the rank of major. As the senior level headquarters fell back from the advancing Germans, the Poles moved eastward, toward the direction the Russians came from starting on September 17, 1939. Major Mylnarski reported that when the first identifiable Russian airplanes were seen, they thought the Soviets had put away the three-centuries-old differences and the "two Slavic nations would come together to fight the Teutonic foe."[6] By radio broadcast they heard the correct answer within hours; the Red Army had crossed the border in great strength with no indication of friendship. The Polish soldiers tried to go south between the German and Soviet lines, but they were captured on September 19, 1939, two days after the Russians had invaded Poland's eastern border, and sixteen days after Major Mylnarski had been called to active duty as a reserve officer. He was with the first group interned at Starobielsk on September 30, 1939, and was among the sixty-eight personnel remaining who left when the camp was closed on May 12, 1940. They were transferred to Pavlishchev Bor for twenty-eight days before moving on to Griazovietz. Finally, in September, 1941 this group was permitted to join the Polish army being formed in the U.S.S.R.

Dr. Mieczyslaw Srokowski[7] of Chicago, Illinois testified he had been chief surgeon of the Polish Red Cross Hospital in Warsaw when he was mobilized as a reserve officer in the Polish army. By the time the war was over he had attained the rank of major. While attending Polish wounded on the very day the Russians invaded, September 17, 1939, he was captured and selected to help a Russian woman physician care for the sick in the small hospital at Kozielsk. Dr. Srokowski estimated about 500 Polish physicians were at Kozielsk. In response to a question as to why he had not been taken to Katyn to be killed, Dr. Srokowski offered the opinion that his wife was French and had departed for her native country the day before the Germans invaded. Since the two had exchanged letters, he reasoned that someone "Might later be asking about me." Another opinion about him being spared was that he had been of valuable assistance to the resident Russian woman physician.

Traditionally, if a witness did not want his/her identity known to the general public because of a fear of personal safety for himself/herself, his/her family or relatives, he/she could request the Select Committee to keep the identity confidential. The committee members would meet these individuals privately; then, if the Select Committee thought the testimony was valuable and the witness credible, a "John Doe," or witness known only to the committee would be approved. Such a "John Doe"[8] was the next witness to appear before the Select Committee.

This "John Doe" witness had been a Catholic priest/chaplain in the Polish Army who had been captured by the Germans, held in one of their prisoner of war camps, and later transferred to a German Displaced Persons Camp for Poles. This "John Doe" witness and Major Gruber, a Polish officer who served with the British as a liaison officer had interrogated a Russian eyewitness who had reported what seemed to be an authentic account concerning the events that occurred at Katyn. In a two-hour interview, this Russian peasant had confirmed that his home had adjoined the Katyn Forest, that heavy guard had been posted to ban entrance to the forest, that, being caught, in the area after this warning meant immediate death, and that a construction project of some magnitude appeared to be commencing near the end of 1939 or early in 1940.

When the "John Doe" witness and Major Gruber asked the Russian peasant about the stories that began circulating among the natives in the spring of 1940 regarding the way Russian trucks would arrive at Katyn in the late night hours and depart in early morning, the Russian explained how he would hide beside the road undetected so he could listen to the voices coming from the trucks, then observe the next morning how the empty trucks would leave with the tail-gates open. Although this Russian said he could not understand the language being spoken by the people on the trucks entering the forest, he had stated no voices at all could be heard as the trucks exited. Too, he said that as he crawled deeper into the forest, he could get close enough to the scene to see Russian soldiers moving people out of the trucks, forming them into columns, and marching them under guard a considerable distance away; however, he could not observe whether they were NKVD or regular soldiers. The Russian told his interviewer that he heard shouts, screams, and revolver shots, in addition to voices swearing in Russian; that he could see the people removed from the trucks were not civilians because they were wearing military clothing; and that after several hours the shouts would subside and the Russians would go back to their trucks and leave the area.

Since the local population knew there were camps where Poles were being held, the Russian stated he began to suspect the victims were the inmates of the Polish camps. Even though all of this activity stopped in the spring of 1940, the area had been kept heavily guarded and trespassing was forbidden;

and the only daytime activity seen by the Russian had been the planting of trees; young saplings.

The situation remained unchanged until the Germans invaded the area at which time the Russian peasant told the Germans of his observations. The Third Reich officers investigated the area, made notes and sketches, but did not activate a search until 1943 when the mass exhumations began. The Russian told Major Gruber and the "John Doe" witness that after he had been a key witness for the Germans, he feared for his life; therefore, he had asked for, and received, protection from the Germans who sent him to Berlin and later to Verdun.

The "John Doe" witness told the Select Committee that Major Gruber had reported this story to the Polish Government in Exile in London without response; but when Major Gruber had related the story to British Intelligence, a car had been sent to pick up the Russian eyewitness and one friend within an hour. The "John Doe" witness advised the committee members that this potential eyewitness could probably be found in England, that both the Polish Government in Exile and Major Gruber could probably help locate him.

The pattern of circumstances in the Katyn Forest massacre emerged in the testimonies given on the first day of Hearings in Chicago, March 13, 1952. Note the testimony of Dr. Miloslavich corroborated the search made for forensic medical evidence as related in Chapters 2 and 3. The approval by Dr. Miloslavich of the techniques and conclusions of the International Medical Commission was all the testimony the Select Committee required from him, for his confirmation of the Commission's specifics would be what any forensic medical expert would search for at Katyn.

At the morning session on Friday, March 14, 1952, in Chicago, the Select Committee first heard Vasili Ershov,[9] a former Soviet citizen who worked as a civilian manager in a Russian meat processing plant until June 22, 1941. When the Germans invaded Russia, he was called to duty in the Red Army and began working with the quartermaster of general supplies of a Russian military division in Leningrad. He remained on active duty after the war until 1949 when he asked the British forces for asylum and was taken by airplane along with his wife and child. As deputy quartermaster, Mr. Ershov supplied the unit with food, clothing, footwear, ordnance, gasoline, technical equipment, etc. He testified the NKVD detachments had about 25 or 30 men in each Soviet division and that this organization was not under the control of the commanding officer or the commissar but of Beria, the Minister of National Security, who issued orders directly from Moscow. These units were called "smersh,"[10] a combination or corruption of the words "death to spies." The commandant of the "smersh" unit in this division was Captain Borisov, a man who had boasted about the executions he had conducted, and who was particularly talkative while he was drinking heavily, usually vodka. On several occasions, when only Borisov and

Ershov were present and Borisov was heavily inebriated, he would boast of being a part of the execution teams who "destroyed or shot over 400 Polish officers at Katyn."[11] Also, the witness testified of hearing about similar references to Katyn from other "smersh" unit members.

Mr. Casimer Starzynski,[12] a resident of Calgary, Alberta, Canada, was the next witness. For fifteen years before the war he had been the vice president of the Polish Pulp and Paper Company, Ltd. When the Germans occupied the country, Mr. Starzynski and the entire board of directors were fired because the plants were taken over as private property by the Third Reich. Mr. Starzynski volunteered for duty with the Polish Red Cross and had accepted the responsibility of being its general secretary.

In January, 1940, the Germans notified the Red Cross to be prepared to receive Polish officers who were supposed to come back from internment at camps in Kozielsk, Ostashkov, and Starobielsk in Soviet Russia. The news electrified the nation of Poland, especially the families of the Polish officers. The Polish Red Cross hastened to send doctors, nurses, and supplies to refugee camps being organized at Terespol. In April or May, 1940, the German authorities rescinded the January, 1940, order with a verbal order to the Polish Red Cross that the "officers won't come back."[13]

Before the German announcement on April 13, 1943, concerning the discovery of the mass graves at Katyn, the Propaganda Ministry in Berlin had sent representatives to Warsaw to invite the Polish Red Cross to send some of its personnel to Katyn. Mr. Starzynski testified that he, along with two other Red Cross administrators from Krakow and three Red Cross workers, had flown on a German airplane from Warsaw to Smolensk on April 14 and 15, 1943. The witness stated that on April 16, 1943, he had been taken on a tour of approximately six hours through the Katyn grave site and had viewed about three hundred bodies, including the remains of two generals: Smorawinski and Bohaterowicz. This witness confirmed again that all the victims had been shot through the base of the cranium and that some had their hands tied behind them with rope. Also, he stated the bodies were wearing winter clothing and some had an overcoat up over the head tied in place with a rope. Mr. Starzynski said he had been permitted to speak with some Russian peasants and to visit the police station about one and one-half miles distant from Katyn Forest to view the documents, possessions, personal effects, etc., of the victims. He observed that none had dates after the months of April and May, 1940.

As the representative in charge for the Polish Red Cross, Mr. Starzynski had assigned the three-man team of Red Cross workers the responsibility of working with the German army to identify the murdered Polish officers. When the witness returned to Warsaw the night of April 16 and reported to the Polish Red Cross the next day, he was asked for a report from the German Red Cross supervisor. Finally, Mr. Starzynski was able to report to the Polish underground his findings at Katyn, and to make a brief but effective report to the Polish Red Cross. (See Appendix 9.)

Mr. Starzynski noted that nine members had been added to the original three, for a total of twelve and told how the team operated in identifying the cadavers, searching the bodies, reburying the victims, collecting the possessions of letters, diaries, newspaper clippings, etc. He commended the cooperation of the German medical representative, Dr. Buhtz, and other occupation military members from Germany. He told of the seven mass graves that had been opened, mentioned the finding of other graves predating the start of World War II that contained murdered "enemies of the state," and gave an account of the excitement on June 1, 1943, when grave number eight was located.[14] Mr. Starzynski testified this grave had not been emptied because just as exhumations began on June 2, 1943, the work was halted when Lieutenant Slovenczyk announced the weather was becoming too hot to continue exhumation work due to poor sanitation conditions, which mitigated further exhumations; therefore, grave number eight was recovered and exhumations at Katyn Forest ceased. (See progress report of Technical Commission, Appendix 10.)

Mr. Starzynski further noted the documents recovered from the cadavers had been stored in nine large boxes[15] for return to Poland where they had been kept under German control and moved from place to place. His final testimony related how the Russians had surrounded Breslau on three sides and how the German SS troops had swept into Breslau University to escape with these nine large boxes, leaving their whereabouts and, more importantly, their contents to remain a mystery.

Colonel Henry I. Szymanski,[16] of the U.S. Army, was the last witness. He had been ordered as a military intelligence officer to the assignment of assistant military attache, Cairo, Egypt; specifically, as the liaison officer to the Polish and Czechoslovakian forces in the Middle East. He had traveled to Cairo, Egypt; Rehovot, Palestine; Mosul and Khanaquin, Iraq; Teheran, Iran; etc.; and had spoken to General Anders, General Sikorski, and President Raczkiewicz. He had interrogated hundreds of Polish prisoners of war and refugees who had been released in accordance with the Russian-Polish Pact of July 30, 1941, and had been present to see the miserable condition of the Polish refugees coming from internment in the Soviet Union. He testified that the first 80,000 left a particularly and singularly unfavorable impact on him because of the physical suffering these civilians and children had endured. His personal report had been delivered to the Assistant Chief of Staff, G-2, in Washington, D.C., in November, 1942, after the had returned from the Middle East.

In April, 1943, after he was back in Cairo, Colonel Szymanski had received a directive from Washington that had been sent his commanding general ordering him to investigate the Katyn affair. He testified he had proceeded to Iraq where he talked to General Anders who made all records available and provided much data and support. Also two Polish Captains, Czapski and Mylnarski, both survivors of captive status as Polish prisoners of war in the U.S.S.R. had been of special assistance, because they had been working on the missing officer problem since their own release from internment. Colonel Szymanski soon had a gold mine of valuable information to forward to Washington, and had sent nine enclosures with his covering letter of May 29, 1943, to Major General Strong, Assistant Chief of Staff, G-2, Military Intelligence Service, Washington, D.C. All of these documents were included as exhibits in the Hearings of the Select Committee. A wide range of subjects had been covered by these data; including the search for the missing Polish officers after Germany attacked Russia by General Sikorski, General Anders, Ambassador Kot, and Captain Czapski. The reported data of these four men had been lengthy, detailed, and thorough. On November 22, 1942, Lieutenant Colonel Szymanski concluded his earlier investigation by submitting a multi-page report, a copy of which was provided the Select Committee as he concluded his testimony on March 14, 1952. This report included pictures of starving Polish children and an analysis of past, present, and future Polish-Russian relations: such as the plight of the Polish refugees; a comparison of the Russian communist system with the "four freedoms" of President Roosevelt—freedoms of speech and worship, and freedoms from want and terrorism; comments on communistic imperialism; etc., and this summary statement: "The choice in Europe is not merely Democracy versus Hitler, as so many Americans seem to think it is."[17]

After two days (March 13 and 14, 1952) of listening to recriminating testimonies, the Select committee adjourned its Hearings in the Chicago, Illinois, area.

Chapter 10

SELECT COMMITTEE HEARINGS: LONDON

Upon completion of the Hearings in Washington, D.C. and Chicago, Illinois, the Select Committee was ready to start Part 4 of the Hearings by beginning its overseas commitment. Private meetings were held, invitations were extended, witnesses were scheduled, and miscellaneous preparations completed. The first overseas Hearings were conducted in London, England, on April 16, 1952,[1] in Room 111, Kensington Palace Hotel, with the Honorable Ray J. Madden presiding. In addition to Chairman Madden, the committee members present included Congressmen Flood, Machrowicz, Dondero, and O'Konski. Congressmen Furcolo and Sheehan were unable to attend. The record of proceedings started with the Select Committee's announcement of the invitation of March 18, 1952,[2] to the Ambassador of Poland to extend to the Polish government in Warsaw an opportunity to participate in the investigation. Congressman Madden, as Chairman, had signed the invitation on behalf of the U.S. House of Representatives. Next to be included in the record was the strongly worded response of March 31, 1952,[3] to the U.S. Department of State declining the invitation to participate in the Hearings by the Polish Government in Warsaw. (See Appendix 11 for Mr. Madden's invitation on behalf of the Select Committee, and Appendix 12 for the response by the Polish Government in Warsaw.)

The first witness to testify was Wladyslaw Jan Furteck[4] who resided in London but had been in the Polish armed forces since September 30, 1938. When the war broke out, he was a cadet officer in the Polish Cadet Officers School at Komorowo; then, on September 18, 1939, he was captured in Tarnopol. After spending time in a series of transient camps, he was told he would be sent home; instead, he had been sent to the mines in the iron basin of Kriwoj Rog. When he refused to work in the mines, he had been interned in prisons as punishment. Finally, he arrived at the camp at Kozielsk about the middle of January, 1940, where he was placed in strict confinement for about seven days before he was allowed to join the other prisoners of war. He described Kozielsk as a very old monastery with its churches and chapels all in deplorable condition, and estimated that between 4,500 to 5,000 Polish prisoners of war were interned there.

The first time the political commissars told the prisoners, "You are going home. You will be exchanged at the border,"[5] was about April 3, 1940; a date which coincided with the first railroad transports of Polish POWs to depart in groups of 150 to 200. After the commissars read the names and the group formations had been assembled, a thorough search of the prisoners resulted in the removal of many of their personal effects and belongings. Such groups were being formed and transported in a continual succession.

Mr. Furtek had departed on April 26, 1940, with a group of approximately 107 "lucky" prisoners. As Mr. Furtek was going into the cellar where the search of prisoners was being conducted, he heard the Soviet political commissar of the camp say, "Well, you got away with it!"[6] Although at the time no one knew the significance of the remark, Mr. Furtek felt the discovery of the Katyn graves three years later clarified its meaning, for his group had been sent to Pavlishchev Bor instead of Katyn; then later to Griazovietz and eventually to join General Anders and the Polish Army being formed in Russia. Obviously, the Soviet political commissar knew this group had escaped the Katyn massacre, which had been the reasoning for his remark; however, the POWs were unaware at the time that going from one prisoner of war camp to another would be such an advantage.

On the train enroute to Pavlishchev Bor, the captives found on the walls and ceilings of the railroad prison cars messages or inscriptions written in Polish, with dates, that told the current passengers where preceding passengers had gone and that they had disembarked "two stations past Smolensk." One of the survivors, Colonel Prokop, indicated his friend, Lieutenant Colonel Kutyba, had agreed to leave message if he could, and the name of Josef Kutyba was found on the list of murdered victims at Katyn.

Another significant event occurred as Mr. Furtek's group was about to entrain from Kozielsk. One of the Polish officers, Lieutenant Abramski, noted the inscription "Gniezdovo" on the outside wall of the railroad train and pointed it out to another officer, Dr. Skotlewski, a dental surgeon, who said, "Look we are going to Gniezdovo." A Russian guard standing nearby said in his native tongue, "They found out!" Both Poles were immediately surrounded by Soviet NKVD soldiers and Lieutenant Abramski was asked, "How did you find out?"[7] The answer was to point to the name on the side of the railroad prison carriage. The incident was over; however, three years later when Dr. Goebbels announced the discovery of the site of the Katyn massacre, these survivors could well remember "two stations past Smolensk" and "Gniezdovo" inscribed on the railroad cars that had taken them to Pavlishchev Bor; and survival. Also, there were two other facts that convinced Mr. Furtek the Russians had committed the murders: first, the names of the deceased were bunched together on the Katyn lists the same way they had been bunched together on the departure lists from Kozielsk; second, the winter clothing the POWs were wearing when departing the camp had been the same as the winter clothing they were found to be wearing when exhumed at Katyn.

As with the anonymous "John Doe" witness in Chicago, the next witness in London was known simply as Mr. W,[8] although the Select Committee had his name and address on record. Mr. W arrived at Kozielsk either November 1 or 2, 1939, and later had been assigned to the kitchen as a stoker. His testimony confirmed that rumors had been spread that POWs were going to be moved even before the lists of names and movement to the transports began on April 3, 1940. Because of the crowded conditions at Kozielsk it seemed obvious the spring weather would bring health concerns and perhaps epidemics among the prisoners. The witness stated that three rumors had persisted as to where the Poles would be sent: to Germany, to Poland, or to another camp in Russia. He further testified the Soviet staff members often tried to mislead the prisoners by their remarks. Mr. W's date of departure from Kozielsk had been April 26, 1940; the same date Mr. Furtek had departed. Both of the witnesses had been in the group of 107 survivors which also included General Wolkowicki. Their testimonies were identical concerning the writings on the walls and ceilings of the railroad cars, which had been typical prisoner transports with bars on the windows and grated doors. Mr. W mentioned that one of the messages in his railroad car read "We are getting off at Gniezdovo."[9] His testimony reestablished the evidence that the same railroad prison cars had taken some POWs to Katyn to die; others to Pavlishchev Bor to live.

Mr. W stated that another very sensitive grapevine related to whether a POW had been among men known for their communist activities in the camps. He said that in his group he knew that at least two, Kukulinski and Berling, were communists, and that both were sent later to "the villa" for further indoctrination. In the meantime the entire group had to travel together for two days before arriving at Babenino; then by lorry for another two hours before getting to Pavlishchev Bor.

Mr. W testified that several days later sixty-three Poles—officers, candidate officers, and civilians—came to Pavlishchev Bor from Starobielsk; and, after another group arrived from Ostashkov, well over 400 people were in that camp. The witness, who still worked in the kitchen, remembered the numbers of people because of food preparation requirements. Ultimately, most of these prisoners of war were moved to Griazovietz in the identical railroad "prison wagons" used previously, and remained there until September, 1941, when they joined the Polish army in Russia under General Anders.

The witness testified he knew the names of the POWs on the Katyn "death list" because these men had been segregated before the group had left Kozielsk together. He remarked that he had been told the Katyn victims had been found in the same winter clothing they had on when they departed Kozielsk, and that their insignia of rank were in good condition, as were their uniforms and boots when their bodies had been exhumed. He knew that many of the Katyn victims had been recently activated, and that they had been issued new uniforms which they had taken care of very well; also, that even in camp the prisoners had tried to preserve their boots by shining them with fat in the hope they would last longer, for prisoners were sensitive to the fact that it would be difficult to get new shoes in a prison camp.

Mr. W recalled that the captives who were taken to Griazovietz had been allowed to exchange letters with their families and to receive numerous queries from other families concerning their own husbands, sons, brothers, and friends. Also, he commented about the difference in the atmosphere among the group departing from Kozielsk—where rumors abounded, imaginations stirred, and uncertainty prevailed—as compared to the group that departed from Pavlishchev Bor. The witness testified that prior to the latter departure from Pavlishchev Bor, the Soviets had given the prisoners clear-cut information about going to another camp where they would be better off; and he concluded by saying that was the only time "the bolsheviks told us the truth."[10]

Witness A,[11] a "John Doe" with relatives remaining in Poland, was the third witness. He declined to give his name for the record but his identity was known to the Select Committee. He testified that as a major he was wounded and taken prisoner on October 1, 1939, and had been interned at Starobielsk from October 11, 1939, until April 25, 1940. From the time he had been interned until December, 1939, he had been aware that a lengthy selection process by interrogation of prisoners was being conducted by NKVD representatives. Present were officers from the Polish army, (primarily the Second Division of General Langner of Lvov), military police and border guards and chaplains of all faiths, judges, and legal prosecutors. Rumors flourished among the POWs: One was that the Russians had stated the prisoners would be taken to a neutral country. This story which coincided with the large scale evacuation of the camp, had begun at Starobliesk on April 5, 1940. Witness A testified the departures were well organized. Bread and herring were given to the departing prisoners who left in groups of 250 to 360 officers via specially prepared railroad prison cars.

On the day of the departure of Witness A, sixty-five other prisoners boarded the railroad cars with him. This group of Poles found messages written on the ceilings and walls of the prison cars that were identical with the examples found in the Kozielsk to Katyn trains, such as messages about getting off at "Gniezdovo" and "two stations beyond Smolensk;" but these survivors from Starobielsk also found messages written by the non-survivors on the walls of the prison trains, e. g., "We are being removed or unloaded in Kharkov."[12] The non-survivors from Starobliesk who left those messages had to be considered "victims" since they were never heard from again. Also, while the railroad prison cars were disconnected at Kharkov to await further movement to Pavlishchev Bor, a porter who came to clean out the car said to the prisoners in Russian, "Your people previously had been unloaded here."[13] During his internment Witness A had prepared a roster of the approximately 400-plus survivors who had been sent from Kozielsk, Ostashkov and Starobliesk to Pavlishchev Bor, and he asked that it be included in the record.

Early in October, 1940, Witness A was one of seven taken to the "Villa of Bliss," in Moscow (two colonels, four lieutenant colonels, and one major) for further indoctrination. Although Witness A later was sent first to the prison at Butyrki, then to Lubianka where more interrogations were held, he spoke to two high ranking NKVD officials named Jygorov and Merkulov while in Moscow. In one of their discussions concerning the possibility of forming an artillery brigade, witness A asked if some artillery officers could be received from Kozielsk or Starobielsk, and Merkulov's answer was, "We have committed an error. These men are not available. We will give you others."[14] Witness A testified he was an eyewitness to this answer: he was not a participant in a similar conversation between three of the seven Poles and Beria, the Minister of the NKVD, at another time in October, 1940, when Lieutenant Colonel Berling, Colonel Gorczynski, and Lieutenant Colonel Tyszynski were invited to Beria's office, then to dinner. Within three hours of their return to the "Villa," Colonel Gorczynski summarized for Witness A the discussion between the three Polish officers and Beria regarding the formulation of a Polish Panzer division:

> Beria said he wants to form or organize a Panzer fist. To this Berling asked or inquired; 'And where will we get officers? I would want to have my officers from Starobielsk and from Kozielsk.' Ostashkov did not enter into the conversation because Ostashkov had primarily border police and guards. To this Beria replied—in Russian, of course—that, 'We have committed a great blunder;' and he repeated it twice, 'We have made a great mistake; we have made a great mistake.'[15]

While this testimony was being presented by Witness A, a series of documents in the custody of Colonel Jerzy Lunkiewicz[16] was presented to the Select Committee that fulfilled the stipulation for documentation of a written "hearing of a witness," when stated in the speaker's identical terms; such as Beria's statement, "We made a mistake." Thus, the documentation entered in the record by Colonel Lunkiewicz was complimentary and supportive of Witness A's testimony.

Colonel Jerzy Lunkiewicz was called as a witness the next day: Friday, April 18, 1952. As custodian of the Polish Archives of Documents and Files, he presented an array of exhibits; such as statements of "Facts and Documents About Polish Prisoners of War in the U.S.S.R.," "supplementary reports on the facts and documents concerning the Katyn Forest Massacre," "additional information and documentation concerning prison camps," "question of discovery of the Commission of Polish Red Cross in the Kriwoserczew case," "the diplomatic documents," "Proclamation of Timoshenko," "instruction of How to Deport the Civilian Population from Lithuania, Estonia and Latvia," "Report of the Villa of Bliss—the Komarnicki Report," "Plan of the Cemetery in Katyn as made by Polish Red Cross after the Victims were Exhumed and Reburied," etc. During other testimonies Colonel Lunkiewicz would be recalled to present additional documentation from the archives, such as the letter of the Polish journalist, Mr. Goetel, who was one of the very first to visit Katyn about April 10, 1943.

Another document included by Colonel Lunkiewicz was the report of Mrs. Ostromecka concerning the body of her sister, Lieutenant Janina (Doxbor-Musnicka) Lewandowski, whose airplane was shot down while on a reconnaissance flight over eastern Poland. Mrs. Ostromecka reported her sister had been taken prisoner by the Red Army and sent to Kozielsk and ultimately to Katyn, where her body was found, bound, and shot "like the others." Lieutenant Janina Lewandowski had been the only woman Polish officer in the Kozielsk camp, and the only woman found among the 4,143 bodies exhumed from the first seven graves.

"John Doe" Witness B[17] testified he had been captured with his unit by the Russians on September 28, 1939, and arrived at Kozielsk on November 2, 1939. His estimate of the number of prisoners there was between four to five thousand, with people coming and going all the time. He had departed from Kozielsk with a group of about 300 on April 29, 1940, after the general liquidation of the camp started on April 3, 1940. Prior to departure each prisoner had been searched before being taken to waiting prison cars at the railroad station. The first stop had been Smolensk; then the train stopped again after traveling about thirty minutes (about ten miles or fifteen kilometers) in a northwesterly direction. Early in the morning a column of NKVD soldiers entered his prison car and called out his name; then they locked him in a compartment in an empty "wagon" of the train from which the prisoners in that compartment had already departed. He climbed to the top bunk to peer through a small slit below the ceiling. From there he observed that the train had been parked away from the station itself, and that it was surrounded by large numbers of NKVD guards carrying rifles with fixed bayonets. He could see that two vehicles, one auto bus and one prison vehicle with windows, were moving prisoners from the prison cars. For some hours the procedure followed by the auto bus would be to back up to the train doors where about thirty prisoners would debark from the train and enter directly into the bus via its back doors; then, once full, the auto bus would depart and return empty in about thirty minutes.

Much later the NKVD colonel came back and removed Witness B from the train and turned him over to the NKVD captain who was accompanied by approximately five guards. Finally, he was taken to a special NKVD prison in Smolensk where he was incarcerated in a separate cell in the basement for about one week. He was visited daily by the head of the prison who brought him books and talked with him for thirty to forty-five minutes. He was not treated badly; in fact, he was allowed to buy things from the prison shop. No reason was ever given for the separation from his comrades, but at the end of the week he was taken from Smolensk to Moscow and held in the Lubianka prison for the next ten months.

In response to questions by the committee members as to why he had been separated (and ultimately survived), Witness B had two reasons: first, as a professor of economics at a university in Poland, he had been head of a group doing research on the Russian economy, which included working with German research institutes that were studying eastern economic problems; second, his publications and books were known in Moscow and perhaps the Russians thought he could advise them about organizations of anti-Soviet intelligence. In addition, in the Soviet court proceedings in 1937 when dissenters had been tried and sentenced, one accused person had referred to writings authored by Witness B in his defense. It appeared the Russian authorities were now planning to accuse Witness B of being an enemy of the state and he was issued an indictment. In response to his question as to what happened to his comrades, he was told, " 'The fate of your comrades in very nice. They are being sent home to their families.' but they told me that because I conducted anti-Soviet spying, I have to stay in prison."[18]

Witness B testified he could recall the names of three officers who were with him on that train from Kozielsk to a station west of Smolensk and all three were on the list of officers killed by Katyn. He also recalled that the prisoners on that trip, beginning April 29, 1940, were wearing overcoats and boots because it was at a time when the weather was cold and snow was lying on the ground.

The sixth witness was Colonel Stanislaw Lubodziecki,[19] who had been promoted to that rank in 1919 and had retired in 1931, but who was back in uniform when the war broke out because he had made himself available for active duty. This witness testified he had been taken prisoner by the Russians "near the village of Zbaraza on September 17, 1939," then, on November 3, 1939, he was transferred to Kozielsk where he remained until March 8, 1940. He estimated there were 4,000 prisoners at Kozielsk at that time.

Colonel Lubodziecki left Kozielsk with a small group—fifteen Polish officers and civilians—who were taken to Smolensk. This group had been splintered away after the addition of one other officer, Captain Leopold Lichnowski, with whom he was transferred to Kharkov; then to Kiev. Of the fourteen who left Kozielsk with him on March 8, 1940, he found five names he recognized on the list of murdered prisoners of war at Katyn. While still at Kozielsk, in addition to the stories of being transferred from the camp, one NKVD officer, Lieutenant Urbanowicz had said that if the prisoners "knew where they would be evacuated to, their eyes would virtually pop out."[20]

Mr. Zygmunt Luszczynski,[21] the seventh witness, had been a captain in the Polish army. Before the outbreak of hostilities in 1939, he had been the Chief of Police in the province of Palesia, Brzesc. On September 24, 1939, he had been captured wearing civilian clothing, held in Brzesc for three days, then sent to Ostashkov by train—a journey lasting three weeks, with arrival about the middle of October, 1939. He had remained at Ostashkov until April 24, 1940, when he departed with approximately 300 other POWs who had been crowded into a train consisting of only seven cars. He watched these prisoners being beaten as they boarded their assigned cars for transportation to Wiasma, where the cars sat on a railroad siding for three days; then, six of the seven cars were disconnected and taken in another direction. The car with Mr. Luszczynski was taken to Babenino, then to Pavlishchev Bor, where he met officers from Starobliesk and Kozielsk. Nothing was ever heard again about the people on the six-car train detached at Wiasma.

Mr. Luszczynski described Ostashkov as a large camp situated on an island that imprisoned Polish police (about 2,000), border guards (about 300), jail and prison guards (about 200), military police and officers, and noncommissioned officers. Also, incarcerated there were civilians, clergymen (priests, rabbis and Protestant ministers—about 200 in all), lawyers and district attorneys, businessmen, landowners, professors, public officials, and members of the courts. In all, the witness estimated approximately 6,500 POWs were interned at Ostashkov. Interrogations were being held constantly, but only single individuals had been evacuated from the camp from mid-October, 1939, until April 1, 1940. On that date a steady stream of evacuations started that totaled two to three hundred prisoners daily. Then, about mid-April, 1940, another train from Ostashkov brought approximately one hundred more Poles to Pavlishchev Bor.

After the amnesty in 1941, Mr. Luszczynski became one of the individuals by order of General Anders who provided information to Captain Josef Czapski in his effort to find the missing prisoners of war. The witness served as chief of intelligence of the Sixth Division of the Polish army and, as such, was in communication with NKVD officers. The Russian liaison officer, Colonel Gulakewicz, assured him that the search for the missing Polish POWs was being continued by the central headquarters of the NKVD. The Polish search was

113

tireless: each lead was traced, and stories that the missing comrades might have been taken to the Saint Francis Islands in the northern part of the U.S.S.R. were followed up; but not a story or a rumor produced a single missing prisoner. In response to the question as to who committed the murders, Mr. Luszczynski's unequivocal answer was, "Unquestionably Russia. There is no question about it. I have observed the tactics of the NKVD from the borderlands of Poland for the last twenty years, and I am well familiar with their tactics."[22]

The brief testimony of witness number eight, Mrs. Janine Knopp,[23] established that her husband, a Lieutenant Colonel in the Polish army and a commanding officer of a regiment, was taken to Starobielsk on October 1, 1939. They exchanged mail, and his last card to her was dated April 6, 1940. Mrs. Knopp had been removed from her mother-in-law's home in Lvov by the Soviets and sent to Russia where the mail was forwarded. Lieutenant Colonel Knopp also had written to his mother, and his last message to her, written from Starobielsk about the time of his April 6, 1940, message to his wife, indicated he was being transferred. He was never heard from again.

The exchange between the next witness, Mr. Tadeusz Felsztyn,[24] and the Select Committee members became significant because the witness was an ammunition expert and a member of the Institute of Armament Research when the war broke out. Since 1914 he had been with the Armed Forces and the Polish Legion. On September 17, 1939, he had been taken prisoner near Mizoch, ultimately had arrived at Kozielsk on November 1, 1939, and was with the group that departed from there on April 26, 1940. The prison train on which this group was placed first went to Sukienniczc, then on to Pavlishchev Bor, and after twenty-eight days, finally to Griazovietz. The witness testified "inscriptions" were written on the walls of the train, and messages had been pencilled in by previous prisoners who had departed from Kozielsk earlier. One such message stated, "We were unloaded two stations west of Smolensk." Included too, were some signatures.

As an expert in ammunition, Mr. Felsztyn also had served in other capabilities, such as a lieutenant of ballistics at Warsaw University for ten years, and at the Military Institute of Research. The committee had asked him this question: "How could Russia use the 7.65 German ammunition?" for shells or casings of this caliber of ammunition had been found in the graves at Katyn. The witness reported that large quantities of the German Geco ammunition were available in Poland, for it was identified as a good quality ammunition. Because not much ammunition was produced in Poland, this ammunition was imported for such reasons as private shooting, sports shooting, and the Polish officers' weapons.

The Russians had one revolver, the 7.62 caliber Nagant which would not fire the 7.65 ammunition; however, the Soviet Tokarew pistol would fire this 7.65 ammunition. Mr. Felsztyn testified he had seen this latter type of pistol carried by members of the Soviet armed forces. He summarized that the Geco ammunition from Germany was often used in the Russian Tokarew pistol, especially since this pistol was "easier to shoot" than the Russian Nagant revolver, that had "a very hard trigger" and a tiring one if "you have to shoot much."

Another incident occurred at Kozielsk about February, 1940, when the Polish General Minkiewicz, who was aware of the "psychological seesaw in our camp with plenty of rumors," asked Comrade Zarubin, the NKVD general, what the Russians intended to do with the Polish prisoners. The reply from Comrade Zarubin was

> I do not think it would be right. Let us suppose we have decided to keep you to the end of the war. It could last five or six years. You would get mad if I told you. I assure you it would be inhuman. I assure you General, it is better for you not to know what we want to do to you.[25]

Again, when the transports were departing Kozielsk, General Minkiewicz asked Captain Alexandrowicz, the camp commander, "Where are the transports going?" The answer was

> You are going to the transit camps where you will have to decide. Do you want to be given back to the Germans or do you ask to remain in Russia? Those of you who will have a very strong will can perhaps go to a new country.[26]

Mr. Felsztyn confirmed that Comrade Zarubin, the NKVD general who supervised interrogations at Kozielsk, was the U.S.S.R. Ambassador to Great Britain in London at the time of the Hearings.

Major Jan Kaczkowski,[27] who had been a reserve officer in the Polish army, was called as the tenth witness on April 18, 1952. He spoke of the special bureau established by General Anders in November, 1941, to deal with the families of the Polish officers who had been incarcerated in the three prisoner of war camps: Kozielsk, Ostashkov, and Starobielsk. The mission of the bureau had been to find the missing soldiers, bring them into the Polish army, and give material assistance to their families. The overall responsibility had been Mr. Czapski's but when he had been sent into Russia to make an effort to locate the missing Poles, the duty had been assigned to this witness, Mr. Kaczkowski, who testified thousands of letters had been received from families asking about sons, husbands, brothers, fathers, and friends. He stated that included in these inquiries had been postcards received from prisoners, most of which had dates of February, March, or April of 1940, with none dated later than the middle of April.

Major Kaczkowski told one story of a wife who (officer husband, Dr. Drapalski, a Polish lieutenant, and veterinarian), had been sent to Siberia. Daily she visited the chief of the NKVD asking for the location of her husband. Later it appeared this Russian NKVD officer became interested in the wife, who was very young, and told her: "You should seek another husband, because it is not possible that you can find your husband in your life."[28] The woman knew something was wrong. She survived and was living in London at the time of the Hearings. Her husband was listed among the victims murdered at Katyn: "Drapalski, Erazm, Second Lieutenant, Veterinary doctor."

Major Jan Kaczkowski was recalled to appear at the Hearings the next day, April 19, 1952, in order to present the two-volume series listing names of the missing Poles arranged alphabetically (Volume 1—A to L, Volume 2—M to Z); with 9,989 names listed in the two volumes.

Captain Eugeniusz Lubomirski[29] and Captain Roman Voit[30] testified they had worked closely with Major Kaczkowski in the search for the missing Polish officers. Both substantiated the testimony of the previous witness; in fact, Captain Lubomirski submitted one written statement concerning former Polish prisoners in Russia which had been prepared earlier for the archives. Captain Lubomirski also had served as interpreter for General Anders and spoke about the numerous times the fate of the missing officers would be included as a subject for discussion.

The only surviving general from any of the three prisoner of war camps was the thirteenth witness called by the Select Committee: Major General Jerzy Wolkowicki,[31] who had been promoted to the rank of general in 1927. He had been a division commander before he was captured by the Russians on September 26, 1939, and incarcerated at Kozielsk at the beginning of November, 1939, along with four other Polish generals. A departing group of ninety-six in which he was a member, left Kozielsk on April 26, 1940, for Pavlishchev Bor, and latter continued to Griazovietz. Three of the officers with the rank of "General" had departed before General Wolkowicki, and one after; so none of the officers in this rank were with him on the transport. The names of those four were found listed "in the record" of victims murdered at Katyn: General Minkiewicz, General Smorawinski, General Bohaterewicz, and Admiral Czernicki.

Although correspondence to the NKVD was forbidden, General Wolkowicki wrote to the Griazovietz prisoner of war authorities on September 9, 1940, complaining about the lack of information regarding the fate of the other officers. After this communication the Polish prisoners had been permitted to write families and friends, and to receive answers; however, up to this time only two letters had been sent, and no answers had ever been received. The responses to the prisoners' correspondence indicated many families had not heard from any of their sons, husbands, brothers, etc., for many months, General Wolkowicki initiated a series of meetings with the NKVD Captain Wasilewsky, during which the Polish general inquired why the prisoners at Griazovietz were receiving so many letters asking about missing comrades. The NKVD captain offered a number of positions; such as the possibility the Polish prisoners had not wanted to write, no correspondence had been sent to the headquarters of the NKVD from General Wolkowicki providing a list of prisoners' names from whom nothing had been heard, no instruction by the Polish officers to their families about how to communicate with them, etc. This interchange took place through the fall, winter, and spring of 1940–41; in fact, up to the time the Germans had invaded Russia.

The obvious question asked by the Select Committee was why General Wolkowicki had been the only officer with that rank permitted to survive the Kozielsk prisoner of war camp. The sixty-nine-year-old general responded that before Poland was formed as a country in 1919, he had been a Russian naval officer long before World War I. When he had served aboard ship in the Battle of Tsushima (Russo-Japanese War of 1904–05), he had been on a ship surrendered by the Russian admiral to the Japanese. Perhaps the Soviets took an interest in him to the point of permitting his survival because he had been the only officer who opposed the surrender of his ship.

Finally, a part of the documentation provided by General Wolkowicki was his own certificate of an inoculation against typhus which was dated December 6, 1939. Each Pole so inoculated for typhoid fever and paratyphoid had been given the certificate after being given the "shot" by Russian medical personnel, but he had been permitted to retain this document during the last intense search before leaving Kozielsk. Every other paper had been taken from him; even his personal letters. The point being made for the Select Committee and the record by the General was that inoculation certificates (a means of identification) had been found on many bodies of murdered Polish POWs at Katyn.

Then, the General was asked the classic question: "Who committed the massacre at Katyn?" General Wolkowicki responded: "On the basis of my own personal observations, it is my belief that the massacre at Katyn was perpetrated by the Russians.[32]

The next testimony was given by Adam Moszynski[33] who had prepared the list of prisoners of war interned in the three camps at Kozielsk, Ostashkov, and Starobielsk. This was the same list that had been submitted to the Select Committee during the Chicago Hearings; therefore, it was already in the Hearings record. The witness testified the compilation of his list had been based on the German white book on Katyn that had been published in Berlin in 1943 (which included the names of those POWs exhumed), and on lists prepared by the Polish Red Cross and Major Kaczkowski who had been with the Polish army in Russia. The witness reviewed the problems in coordinating so many lists (German, Polish Red Cross, and Polish army) in view of the wartime atmo-

117

sphere; as well as personal problems such as one officer taking another's bank book which had been left behind in the hope it would be returned later. Because of these problems the list was constantly being updated by Mr. Moszynski by publishing suggestions for corrections in the weekly newspaper, "White Eagle;" then later publishing a revised list in the Polish newspaper, "White Eagle."

The Russians, who claimed the Germans shot the Poles at Katyn, neither prepared nor publicly published such a list. Mr. Moszynski's assignment had been to estimate the number of prisoners missing from the three POW camps. He told this story about Kozielsk: After it had been closed down, or "liquidated," in the spring of 1940, it had been reopened as Kozielsk Number 2. A Polish policeman who was interned there told that he found an inscription in the kitchen carved in the wall in Polish: "There are 5,000 of us Polish officers here."[34]

The known fate of the prisoners of war from Kozielsk had been Katyn; but in response to the question concerning how he accounted for the Poles incarcerated at Ostashkov and Starobielsk, Mr. Moszynski replied: "I am sure there are three Katyns in the world. One Katyn is in the Katyn Forest near Gniezdovo (Smolensk); the second Katyn, of Starobielsk, could be near Kharkov; and the prisoners of Ostashkov, near the White Sea."[35]

The drownings story surfaced again: a tale that concluded with prisoners of Ostashkov being placed on two very old barges which were towed out into the White Sea and destroyed by Russian artillery fire. It was estimated that over 5,000 Polish prisoners of war perished in that incident. The logic of the Starobliesk prisoners being killed near Kharkov was so reasonable because the survivors who had been sent to Pavlishchev Bor and Griazovietz found inscriptions on the railroad prison trains that mentioned Kharkov, including Mr. Moszynski when he was transported with nineteen other POWs on May 12, 1940. At that time only eleven Polish officers were survivors out of an overall total of 3,920 who had been previously imprisoned at Starobliesk. Mr. Moszynski had been an eyewitness to this inscription: "We arrived at the station in Kharkov. Most probably we will be unloaded or removed from the train."[36]

The second day of the London Hearings began on Thursday, April 17, 1952, with the testimony of the fifteenth witness: Lieutenant General Zygmunt Peter Bogusz-Szyszko,[37] who had been the first chief of the Polish military mission in Moscow after Poland and the U.S.S.R. reestablished diplomatic relations in 1941. His tour had been from August 1, 1941, to December 31, 1941, and his appointment had been from General Sikorski, the Prime Minister of the Polish Government in Exile. Professor Stanislaw Kot had been the first Polish Ambassador to Moscow, arriving on September 1, 1941. General Bogusz-Szyszko explained to the Select Committee how the Polish military mission had been organized, and how he and General Anders, who was released from the Lubianka prison and nominated to be commander-in-chief of the Polish army, were to be the two spokesmen for Poland. The Russian Government had been represented by General Zhukov who, as chief of the security division of the Russian army, had the title of Plenipotentiary of the Soviet Government, a position comparable to that of a general. The Russian army had been represented by Major General Panfilov.

At the initial meeting of the military missions in mid-August a request was made for a list of all the Polish officers who were being held in Russia. So far, the only data available had been from a speech made by Molotov in 1939 when he announced the Russians had imprisoned over 250,000 Polish soldiers and over 10,000 Polish officers. Two meetings later the list of officers from Griazovietz was provided; a roster that consisted of 1,100 Polish officers, 300 non-commissioned officers and police officers, and a few civilians. The absence of high ranking officers was immediately noted; only three generals—Wolkowicki, Przezdziecki, and Jarnuskiewicz—and a few colonels and lieutenant colonels were listed. The Polish representatives asked, "Where are the rest of the Polish officers and when will their names be furnished?" General Zhukov replied that their names would be furnished later. A total of six conferences were held. Whenever the missing Polish prisoner-of-war issue was brought up, the atmosphere became unpleasant and the Russians became "very much disturbed and rattled." At one social occasion General Bogusz-Szyszko asked General Zhukov about two of the missing Polish prisoners of war who were close personal friends. General Zhukov replied very bluntly; "Please do not ask about these men, because in this particular case I cannot help you."[38]

During the second phase of conversations the Russians no longer produced any POW lists; however, the Polish representatives were continually preparing lists. As each new Pole was released from a Russian POW camp to enlist in the Polish army in Russia he was asked to remember the names of the officers in this specific camp; so, ultimately, lengthy lists were compiled. When the Russians at the negotiating table would ask, "Who specifically are you looking for?" "Who do you believe should be in Russia?"; these rosters had served a purpose and had become a basis for the official list used in diplomatic intervention by the Polish Ambassador in Russia, Stanislaw Kot. Later, when General Sikorski, as Prime Minister of the Polish Government in Exile in London, met with the Soviet Premier, Josef Stalin, on December 3, 1941, he handed a copy of the official list to Premier Stalin.

When the diplomatic channel was no longer effective, the military route was continued in two ways: First, through the official channel—General Anders would provide formal letters of authorization to Major Czapski who would contact the top Soviet military command of the NKVD and request information of the whereabouts of the missing Polish officers. Second, unofficially—at the same time, Polish representatives were sent to the various locations and camps where Polish officers might still be held captive; including the Far North from which no information was gained. Very few of these secret agents ever returned, and those that did brought no additional information. All through 1942 the Polish attempts to gather data were completely without success.

In 1943, at the time of the German broadcast concerning Katyn, the entire Polish Army was out of Russia and in the Middle East. Within forty-eight hours after the broadcast the Russians were stating, "The Germans did it." Not only were the Poles shocked by that report but also they were surprised and disturbed by the Russian version. They asked themselves this question: "Why did not the Russians tell us where these men were if they had known that they were there during our entire negotiations?"[39] Why would the Soviets not say the prisoners of war were in labor details in Smolensk and the Germans had taken them prisoner? To the last inevitable question regarding responsibility for the atrocity, General Bogusz-Szyszko responded: "There is no doubt or misunderstanding in my mind. I am certain that this could have been done only be the Russians."[40]

Edward Raczynski,[41] the sixteenth witness, was appointed Polish Ambassador to London and remained in that capacity until the recognition of the Polish government was withdrawn in July, 1945; therefore, he served as Ambassador for eleven years which included the World War II years. His testimony related primarily to organizational and personnel matters. During his tenure as Ambassador for Poland, Mr. Myski was Ambassador of the Soviet Government in London, and Mr. Bogomolow was the Soviet Ambassador to the Polish Government in London. Mr. Raczynski spoke of the efforts by the Polish government in London to learn the whereabout of the missing prisoners of war, especially after Germany attacked Russia in June, 1941. He told how this effort was increased in intensity with requests in writing and in person by Mr. Kot, Polish Ambassador to Moscow, to the Deputy Foreign Minister A. Vyshinsky; also, in person by General Sikorski, Polish Prime Minister, to Premier Stalin at their meeting on December 3, 1941. Specifically, the witness addressed himself to his letter of January 28, 1942, to Ambassador Bogomolow requesting the U.S.S.R. to note that the Soviet decree of August 12, 1941, giving all Polish military and civilians amnesty had not been carried out. This letter, dispatched through diplomatic channels, mentioned the fact that the prisoners of war from Kozielsk, Ostashkov, and Starobielsk had not yet been accounted for; neither were they present in occupied Poland nor in prisoners of war camps in Germany. His firm but tactful letter was answered by the letter of March 13, 1942, from Soviet Ambassador to the Polish government which stated, "The amnesty of Polish citizens had been strictly carried out."[42] The witness referred to the formal character of the response and stated repeated requests in personal communications and conversations had brought the same negative results. Since all requests were always answered in the same "purely and entirely formal" style, it became evident Soviet representatives had been given instructions to use stereotyped answers, and to make no deviation lest a slip or mistake be included; so the formal wording remained the same again and again.

Mr. Raczynski also reviewed the impact of the German announcement of the finding of the murdered Polish officers at Katyn on April 13, 1943, and the Russian response of April 15, 1943. Because of the appearance of authenticity of the German announcements the Polish government, through its Council of Ministers' meeting on April 15, 1943, decided that a strong Polish reaction was necessary. The hope was that the German information could be impartially verified; therefore, the best source of authenticity of this discovery was considered to be the International Red Cross at Geneva. At the Council of Ministers' meeting on April 17, 1943, it was decided to make one final attempt to appeal to the Soviet Government for information about the POWs; so another letter was delivered to the Soviet Ambassador on April 20, 1943. This letter was cautiously worded, but it reminded the Russian government of the numerous attempts by the military leaders, the diplomatic representatives, and the Head of State, General Sikorski, to gain some information about the missing Polish officers.

At the same meeting the Council of Ministers dispatched a request to the International Red Cross in Geneva to take action through the Polish representative in Switzerland. It was hoped this body could provide an impartial investigation of the crime at Katyn "in order to establish the truth." The International Red Cross responded by saying all interested parties had to make the same invitation or request, meaning Germany and Russia would have to make similar requests. The German government made its request, including a promise of collaboration, to the International Red Cross for an objective judgment of what happened at Katyn on April 16, 1943. The Polish Council of Ministers had reached its decision on April 15 and its request to the International Red Cross was dated April 17, 1943. That same day the Polish government in London requested assistance from the International Red Cross and forwarded with its request a Statement of the Polish Government Concerning the Discovery of the Graves of Polish Officers near Katyn.

Mr. Raczynski then added a final note to his testimony:

> Because I think it is the proper place for me to do it. It had occurred to me that one important element point to the responsibility of the Soviet Government, and the authorship of the Soviets of the crime, has not been sufficiently underlined so far, and that is this: Although the Soviet Government had not signed the Geneva Convention relating to war prisoners, it has nonetheless generally pretended to have observed that convention. In this case the Soviet Government, caught in its own mesh of fiction, had declared to the world that it had actually employed thousands of Polish officers including more than one hundred generals, admirals and colonels advanced in age, in breaking stones on the road near Smolensk. I think that this kind of

employment, this kind of occupation, for senior officers is scandalous in itself, and I may go one step further and say that so far as I am aware from all available evidence, this has not been done by the Soviet Government. They have been cruel to the prisoners; they have for a time kept them in very primitive conditions; they have deprived them, for instance, of non-commissioned officers as aides at certain stages of their detention, but the Soviet Government had certainly not sent senior officers of the rank of general or admiral to break stones. This has not been done by any of the belligerents anywhere in the great war, and would be, as I say, scandalous in itself, but to my mind it is additional evidence showing that having been caught in their own tissue of stories, they did not know how to explain this fact away, and I think that this should be underlined as an additional point of circumstantial evidence showing the responsibility for the crime.[43]

The seventeenth witness was Zbigniew Rowinski,[44] a Polish Air Force officer and an attorney who served as a prosecuting attorney before he was called to active duty from his reserve status in 1939. He was captured by the Germans and taken to the German prisoner of war camp at Woldenberg where he was interned. When the Katyn Forest massacre was first announced, quite by accident Mr. Rowinski was included in a list of officers provided by the Polish authorities within the camp when the administrators asked for names. It was called an "accident" because the German representatives would not accept the initial names provided by the Poles. By the time the groups from various prisoner of war camps were assembled to fly from Berlin to Smolensk, via Warsaw, eight Polish officers were included. Colonel Mosser, who spoke Russian, was in charge. In Smolensk the group was quartered under guard because the officers would not give a parole (meaning the POWs would not try to escape). Their flight was on April 16, 1943, and in their quarters that evening a German officer provided photographs and statements of what had occurred at Katyn since the beginning of the exhumations. The Polish officers concluded, privately, that it might be a German propaganda effort. They doubted the Germans exhumed the high number of bodies estimated to be at Katyn (12,000); however, they concurred the photographs and the savings bankbooks looked genuine.

On the next day the group was taken by car to the gravesite, which was a twenty-minute ride. the witness stated that Katyn was about one-and-one-half kilometers beyond the railroad station at Gniezdovo. First, they were introduced to Professor Buhtz. Mr. Rowinski asked Dr. Buhtz some questions about a book on traffic accidents which the latter had written and which Mr. Rowinski had used while acting as a prosecutor in Poland. The attitude of Dr. Buhtz and all the Germans at Katyn was one of cooperation. The group observed that the grave which was to be the largest was being excavated at about five different places. The grave the group visited had bodies interred with the hands bound with cord. The witness produced a length of cord which Professor Buhtz, in Mr.

Rowinski's presence, had cut from the hands of a victim. The witness confirmed the victims had been shot in the back of the skull with the bullet usually exiting through the front of the skull. Some had been hooded and tied, and some had sawdust in the mouth.

Mr. Rowinski concluded these were indeed bodies of Polish officers; in fact, testified one was the body of an acquaintance, Captain Sidor. Moreover, the witness stated he observed the uniforms had Polish stamps of different manufacturers on the shirts and underwear. Too, he decided these were the original Polish uniforms that had been on the bodies when they were put in the grave because the uniforms were pasted to the skin, and the many folds stuck together; an indication the bodies must have still been warm when placed in the grave. Some victims were wearing overcoats; some were not. The boots on the bodies were in very good condition, and had "something like a wooden sole (a clog) in order to protect the leather. The officers probably did (made) them in the camps."[45]

Professor Buhtz allowed the group to choose any body and have it extracted from the grave for search, identification, and autopsy. They selected a body about four tiers from the top; one with its stomach region depressed upon the head of the cadaver below it. The conclusion of the group was that this body must have been lying in the same position for at least two years. Mr. Rowinski estimated there were thirteen layers of bodies pressed together, making a total of 8,000 bodies; not the 12,000 estimated by the Germans.

The witness stated that Colonel Mosser went across the small dirt road leading into the grave site to a place where the Germans had removed bodies of civilians, all of whom wore boots and civilian clothes. These cadavers had been buried perhaps six to eight years longer than the POWs, meaning they had been there since 1937 or earlier. The hands of these cadavers were tied in the same fashion behind the back as the POWs but these individuals were Russians who had been executed at Katyn.

Since the documents found on the bodies were of great interest to the Poles, a visit was made by the group to the small house not far from the gravesite where the Germans had collected the documents. In examining the documents placed at their disposal, the group made the following notations:

1. The dates on the documents included the months of March and April, 1940.
2. One diary noted the prison train had arrived at Gniezdovo, the small station near Katyn Forest.
3. The calendar diary of Second Lieutenant Jan Bartys had this notation on March 15, 1940: "We have just arrived at the Gniezdovo station, and I see NKVD people standing from the railway station up to the woods."[46] All the pages beyond that date were intact but blank.

Mr. Rowinski testified he was at Katyn shortly after exhumations had begun, for approximately only 160 bodies had been exhumed. He described the soil as sandy with a yellowish color, and mentioned that due to a slight gradient to the ground water was standing in one place. He observed the surrounding area was a woods, but stated that in the part of the forest where the bodies were located there were only a few big fir trees interspersed among small fir trees.

Because they feared the Germans would use their findings for propaganda purposes the group of visiting Polish officers did not offer any conclusions regarding responsibility in their report (sometimes referred to as Colonel Mosser's Report). They were required to file a report with the Germans and the Poles dutifully reported what they had seen, including the estimated dates of death as March and April, 1940. The witness provided his detailed notes for the committee to include in the record since his notes had been the basis of the formal report submitted to the Germans. Privately, the eight Polish officers who visited the gravesite unanimously concluded the crime was "done by the Russians."

The eighteenth witness, Lieutenant General Tadeusz Bor-Komorowski,[47] explained he had remained in Poland after its defeat by the Germans. As one of the organizers of the Polish Home Army, he ultimately became its commander in chief when General Roweski was arrested. After the Warsaw uprising of 1944 he was captured and interned in a German prisoners of war camp until liberated by the United States Army in May, 1945. He testified that when the protocol between the Soviet and Polish governments went into effect in 1941, all Polish prisoners were to be released. General Sikorski, the Prime Minister of Poland in London, sent an order to the Polish underground to look for the missing prisoners of war in Germany and in areas occupied by the Germans, including Russia. General Sikorski was aware that many Polish officers had written letters from Kozielsk, Ostashkov, and Starobliesk, that had been received with dates through April, 1940. After that month letters sent to the prisoners were returned stamped: "Retour-Parti"—"Return to Sender; Addressee Gone Away." These questions arose: If the prisoners were moved, why wasn't the mail forwarded to them? Where could they have gone? General Sikorski knew over 8,000 Polish officers had been captured by the Russians and after the signing of the Russo-Polish agreement approximately only 400 were known to be at Griazovietz. An intense search using clandestine liaison within the German prisoner of war camps brought no results. Not a single Polish officer of the 8,000 captured by the Russians was found; neither in the German camps nor on Soviet territory occupied by the Germans.

Early in April, 1943, the German Ministry of Propaganda from Berlin held meetings in three selected cities in Poland: Warsaw, Krakow, and Lublin. These Poles were organized into delegations; then were told to prepare for a long journey by plane, for they were to be eyewitnesses to the discovery of mass graves of victims of Soviet terrorism near Smolensk. On April 10, 1943, three days before the actual announcement of the findings of the graves by Dr. Goebbels, the first contingent departed, followed very shortly by a second group. Included in the delegation was an observer, a trustworthy man of the underground, who was given specific instructions as to what to look for. From this time on specific data were collected by General Roweski and the witness, General Komorowski, of the Home Army; then forwarded to General Sikorski in London. Copies of these reports were given to the Select Committee by the witness.

The witness testified that the observer reported the German estimate of 10,000 corpses was exaggerated because the seven graves that had been opened would contain about 4,000 bodies. As the observer worked among those men doing the exhumations, he removed from uniform pockets notebooks, diaries, letters, memoirs, and pre-war zloty bank notes. In his opinion, his most significant find was the diary of Major Adam Solski, with entries telling of departing from Kozielsk, then Jelnia, then Smolensk, then the departure by "lorries fitted with cells; terrible. Taken to forest somewhere, something like a summer resort. Very thorough search of our belongings. They took my watch which showed time as 6:30—asked about my ring, which was taken, main belt, penknife."[48] This diary, like the others, ended after recording the trip from Kozielsk to Katyn in April, 1940. An expert compared the writing in one diary with other handwriting samples of the writer and confirmed they were written by the same person. After his visit to Katyn the observer gave copies of fifteen diaries to General Komorowski, who forwarded them to London by courier. Copies of other diaries were hidden and buried in different places in Poland.

The witness reported that the refusal by the U.S.S.R. to permit the International Red Cross to investigate the Katyn Forest massacre caused much embarrassment to the Polish communists who openly stated that "Polish reactionaries" had been liquidated. Warsaw communists started rumors reporting a mutiny had broken out in one of the camps and some officers had been executed. Finally, the observer brought a cord that had been cut from the bound hands of one of the murdered victims. The cord was examined by an expert who stated the material was not known in Poland or western Europe.

Numerous documents, transcripts of messages to London, and copies of the diaries (ten of the fifteen) were formally introduced in the record of the Select Committee by General Komorowski. He stated that initially when the Katyn announcement was made, he thought it was a German trick because the Poles knew how many crimes the Germans had committed. Not until he heard the report of his observer and personally received the diaries was he convinced the crimes had been committed by the Russians.

The climax of this testimony was the exchange between Mr. O'Konski of the committee and General Komorowski which highlighted the Warsaw uprising of August and September, 1944, when approximately 100,000 Polish citizens were killed. (The Germans said 200,000 were killed; the Russian propaganda system said 250,000 to 300,000 Poles died.) When the uprising started, the Russian army was only about fifteen miles from Warsaw. Within six weeks it was just across the Vistula River and could be seen by the Poles, but the Russians refused assistance to the Home Army and would not cross the river. The feeling persisted in Poland that the resistance groups were to be "massacred and liquidated." Mr. O'Konski inferred the strategy of the Russians in not aiding the Home Army was the same; which was "to destroy the national elements of Poles."[49] The strategy was logical! the Russian estimate of Polish Home Army Civilians killed in action in the Warsaw uprising was 250,000 to 300,000, all of whom would have been possible future leaders for Poland; likewise, at Katyn and elsewhere 15,000 Polish officers had been murdered. If these Polish patriots had been allowed to survive, they would have been capable of forming resistance groups, fighting any kind of dictatorship, and providing leadership for the Polish government; also, both groups would have been foes of communism. Even after the Russian army entered Warsaw, some 50,000 of the Home Army soldiers were arrested and departed to the Soviet Union, the intent being to liquidate the Polish leadership of the future.

The nineteenth witness at the London hearings was Lieutenant General Marian Kukiel[50] who had served before in the Polish legion before the Polish army and been reconstituted in 1918. At the time of the Katyn announcement by the German government, General Kukiel was the Minister of National Defense of the Polish Government in London. He began his testimony by telling of the Russian violation of the convention of Lvov. This agreement between the Poles and Russians stipulated that when the local military forces capitulated on the agreed-to date of September 22, 1939, the Poles would be permitted the right of free movement to leave Poland and fight on against the Germans. Instead the agreement was violated by the Russians, for after their surrender the Poles were marched eastward. The three Polish officers that escaped made they way to General Sikorski's headquarters in Paris and reported as of January, 1940; the prisoners of war were starving, freezing, being deprived of medical help, etc. The witness stated that escape was probably effected before the Poles were split into the three principal officer camps. General Sikorski directly sought intervention from the western powers, including the United States. The American Ambassador to London, Mr. Biddle, was sympathetic and promised to appeal to the President of the United States, Mr. Roosevelt, for intervention. General Sikorski envisioned that over one million Poles could be deported to Russia in 1940 and 1941 to live in the same appalling conditions as the war prisoners already in Soviet hands. The impact of this realization on General Sikorski hastened his agreeing to the terms of the July, 1941, amnesty accords with the Soviet Union. Although he could have perhaps driven a harder bargain by waiting, he did not;

for as he said, "I had the impression of hearing the voices of masses of people who were begging me: 'Hurry, do not wait; we are perishing.' "[51]

General Kukiel, as Minister of Defense and Military Affairs, was an eyewitness to the Sikorski/Anders meeting with Stalin/Molotov in Moscow on December 3, 1941. Premier Stalin, when asked by the General to release the missing Polish officers, said that they probably had escaped "to Manchuria." General Kukiel said,

> I got a very disagreeable impression; it sounded like mockery, like a quite sinister joke. At that time—it was still before Teheran—we did not realize that kind of humor was peculiar to Mr. Stalin. At Teheran there was a memorable scene when Stalin, at dinner with Mr. Roosevelt and Mr. Churchill, proposed a toast to the 40,000 to 50,000 German officers who must be shot.[52]

General Kukiel had been appointed Minister of Military Affairs at the end of September, 1942. On October 12, 1942, he was invited to lunch with Ambassador Bogomolow of the U.S.S.R. Directly after the almost three-hour luncheon session, General Kukiel prepared a memorandum for the record and forwarded it to General Sikorski the same day. He reported the luncheon included only Ambassador Bogomolow and himself; however, Colonel Sizov of the Soviet Embassy joined them later. In his brief but complete recording of the discussion, the General emphasized he kept trying to bring the Ambassador back to the subject of the missing Polish officers. During the latter stages of the discussion General Kukiel described Ambassador Bogomolow as being "depressed and—I should even say—alarmingly helpless, completely exhausted," etc. The General testified that he had tried to be sincere and straightforward in expressing the attitude of Poland toward Russia. The end of his report to his superior, General Sikorski, was equally straightforward: "I have come to the conclusion that in the case of our 8,000 officers, unfortunately, all hope should be abandoned, and that Bogomolow knows that they have perished."[53]

General Kukiel had been instructed by General Sikorski to request information about the missing Polish officers, for their absence was presenting a problem in continuing to recruit Poles into the Polish armed forces while they were still being held in Russia, even though General Anders and the Polish army had departed the Soviet Union. When these points were first brought up by General Kukiel, the Soviet ambassador explained that personnel lists would be provided, for the missing men must be somewhere, since they were not with the Germans, etc. When the requests were repeated, the response by the Soviet ambassador changed from a position of the prisoners being released to being dispersed elsewhere, or being in German hands, etc. When the Ambassador spoke of the matter being in the past and that the two countries of Poland and

Russia should look to the future, General Kukiel countered with statements such as the missing officers of the past would be the future leaders of Poland, perhaps possible internment locations could be suggested, etc. At this point the Ambassador became upset and his change in attitude was noted. While the two men were still on friendly terms, the conversation broke abruptly. General Kukiel then drew the conclusion that "our officers were no more alive."[54]

The balance of General Kukiel's testimony related to the Polish memorandum of April 17, 1943, concerning the fate of the Polish prisoners of war, the correspondence attempting to gain the approval of the International Red Cross to investigate the Katyn massacre, the Russian claim that the Germans did it, and the publication of the official Polish position regarding Katyn to all its commanders. The Polish Government in Exile did not yet know the circumstances of the murders; however, it did know about the captivity of its POWs by the Russians and their disappearance, and was aware that neither the German version nor the Russian version of their whereabouts could be accepted until a final investigation was completed. The witness also provided testimony of a military nature; relating to the outbreak of war, the number of Polish divisions, their defensive plans, the mobilization of 1.2 million soldiers, the estimate that the Germans had only a ten-to-fifteen days supply of ammunition, and the fact the Polish Army could have resisted much longer if the Russians had not attacked on September 17, 1939. The General concluded by saying that the army's resistance capability would have been stronger in eastern and southern Poland, especially at the so-called Romanian Bridgehead adjacent to the common frontier with Romania, had not the Russians perpetrated an attack.

Mr. Ferdinand Goetel,[55] the twentieth witness, was a writer residing in Warsaw in April, 1943. He was invited to be briefed on the discovery of the graves at Katyn by Dr. Grundman of the German Propaganda Office, and was asked to be among the members of the first Polish group to visit the gravesite on the 8th or 9th of April, 1943. A delegation of foreign journalists had been the only group to precede the Polish group to Katyn. During the briefing of the Polish group by Lieutenant Slovenczyk the Polish visitors were asked about Kozielsk since the name had appeared on so many documents found on the exhumed bodies. This witness believed the Germans did not know about the Polish POW camp in Russia called Kozielsk, or about its significance, until this delegation of Poles told them.

Exhumations had begun shortly before this delegation arrived. The visitors were given full freedom to talk to the peasants. These people described the planting of small fir trees after the gravesite had been filled in by the Russians, some of which were still there; the trajectory of the bullet which ended the life of each victim; the nature of the ground as sandy lime, very dry, and yellow in color; and the large number of Russian newspapers, or portions of newspapers, found with the victims, none of which were dated after April,

1940. The delegations observed that the uniforms on the victims were in excellent condition, as were the boots. Mr. Goetel recognized the remains of General Bohaterowicz, but not the body of General Smorawinski; however, the documents on the cadavers identified both, as did their uniforms and insignia of rank. The apparent significance of the small trees to Mr. Goetel was that they were strong and appeared to have been in that location for two or three years.

The old Russian peasant Kisselev lived the closest to the forest and was the most vocal; the other peasant Kriwozercew was more quiet. Kisselev told of hearing shots and people crying in April, 1940. It was he who first showed the gravesite to the Germans, including the graves marked with small and large crosses.

Mr. Goetel traveled from Germany to meet Kriwozercew in Italy in 1945, so he could make a record about what happened at Katyn. As a public relations officer with General Anders, Mr. Goetel stayed with Kriwozercew for two weeks at the Villa Barducci in Ancona to record the peasant's long story. To summarize: Kriwozercew's father, a kulak or landowner, had been murdered by the bolsheviks. In April, 1940, Kriwozercew was working near Katyn (close to Gniezdovo). He observed a train, consisting of four cars, coming from the direction of Smolensk. Kriwozercew knew that Katyn was a place of execution so he assumed these were Finnish officers because the U.S.S.R. was at war with Finland. The next day he was told they were not Finns but Polish officers. Every day he saw the trains coming from Smolensk. The main train consisted of about eight cars; four cars would be left behind and the other four would be taken to Gniezdovo. When the empty four cars were brought back to Smolensk, the four full cars would be taken on to Gniezdovo. A point that had not been brought out before was that the small siding at Gniezdovo could hold only four cars, so the first four prison cars would go on to Gniezdovo in the morning, the prisoners would be unloaded and taken to Katyn to be executed. The four empty cars would be returned to Smolensk where the four cars full of prisoners had been held; then the operation would be repeated in the afternoon. Kriwozercew reported this procedure continued until the 20th or 21st of April, 1940. He indicated smaller groups of Poles could have been executed after that date but the primary effort had been completed by April 25, 1940.

Mr. Goetel testified he had not signed any documents for the Germans; but when he returned to Warsaw, he filed an open report with General Roweski, the leader of the underground army. Almost everyone in Poland believed it was the Germans who committed the massacre but Mr. Goetel had maintained all along that it was the Russians; a point he emphasized to the Select Committee. After he returned from Katyn, Mr. Goetel recommended the Polish Red Cross become involved, and this group was represented in the second delegation sent to Katyn and did complete the identifications and reburials of the bodies of the victims.

Finally, in June, 1945, after the Russians had occupied all of Poland, Mr. Goetel, who was hiding in a cloister in Krakow, found out he was wanted by the Soviets. When he inquired of Mr. Sawicki of the Red Cross in Warsaw why he was wanted, this answer came back:

> Oh, we have nothing against Mr. Goetel, who is a famous writer, but if he signs a statement that he was kept by force at Katyn and that his main impression at Katyn was that the massacre was done by Germans. Oh, we have nothing; he can live here and write books and so on.[56]

The Select Committee made a comparison of the pressure asserted on Mr. Goetel with the pressure exerted on Dr. Markov, a member of the International Medical Commission who remained in Bulgaria even after the Russians occupied the country, and who later changed his story.

On Friday, April 18, 1952, the Select Committee continued its hearings with its twenty-first witness, Adam Sawczynski,[57] who had been a colonel in the Polish army when the war began, and had been captured by the Germans and incarcerated at the prisoner of war camp at Arnswalde in Western Pomerania. In several discussions with Colonel Loebecke, the German camp commander, concerning prisoner exchanges between Germany and Russia, Colonel Sawczynski, senior commander of a Polish prisoner battalion, had occasion to discuss the fate of Polish officers who were in Russian hands. He testified that no one went from Germany to Russia, but some enlisted men (and officers, disguised as enlisted men) did come from Russia to Germany, including some who arrived at the camp where Colonel Sawczynski was interned. In one of the discussions Colonel Loebecke, who could not understand why any Poles would consider being transferred to Russia, said: "Why, they are murdering your people; they are murdering you."[58]

Colonel Sawczynski related one more story of a personal friend and former aide, Lieutenant Alfons Koehler, who had left the Polish army in order to work as an intelligence officer in a Lithuanian Intelligence Department, and who had asked to be transferred to a German prisoner of war camp because he believed the Russians were taking over Lithuania and the Lithuanian prisoner of war camps. Lieutenant Koehler was transferred to the same camp at Arnswalde where his former superior, Colonel Sawczynski, was located. Lieutenant Koehler related a story heard about July, 1940, from conversations with Lithuanian Intelligence Department officers who reported, "Why those in the camp at Kozielsk had been murdered!" When Lieutenant Koehler challenged this statement as impossible because of the thousands of people interned there, the Lithuanian intelligence officer replied, "Whether this is true or not, I don't know, but that is the information we have."[59]

Next to testify was Jerzy Lewszecki,[60] the twenty second witness, who

130

had been a first lieutenant in the Polish army when taken prisoner and interned in the German prisoner of war camp at Lubeck. Among the Russian prisoners in the same camp was the eldest son of Josef Stalin and his first wife, Senior Lieutenant Jacob Dzhugashvili. (Stalin is the literal translation of the name "Dzhugashvili" from Georgian into Russian.) Three ranks of lieutenant existed in the Russian army and Stalin was in a special room with a window. Too, he had a register to sign in to see him and a guard was present constantly. Because Stalin had arrived very sick and undernourished the other prisoners would bring him food packages, thereby hoping the restore him to good health.

Lieutenant Lewszecki, who spoke fluent Russian, showed Stalin letters from Poland inquiring about friends who had disappeared from the three officer prisoner of war camps. At first Stalin appeared shocked, but later he recalled a reported uprising at a camp near Smolensk that had been suppressed. During one conversation Stalin remarked that during the collectivization of the Ukraine some three million Russians were murdered, so, "Why are you surprised that your people should be murdered, also?"[61]

At another time Stalin remarked that the Poles were the intelligentsia, an element not easily converted to communism; whereas younger people were capable of being converted. He reassured Lieutenant Lewszecki that the "murders must have been committed with a humanitarian method, unlike the brutal tactics of the Germans."[62] In summary, his message was that the intelligentsia had to be destroyed, removed—that was a national and governmental necessity.

Following next was witness number twenty three, Josef Garlinski,[63] who had been a reserve officer in the Polish army and had been arrested by the Gestapo in Warsaw on April 20, 1943. He was sent to a prison camp called Pawiak inside the Jewish ghetto of Warsaw, later to the camp at Oswiecim (Auschwitz), and still later to Wittenberg, Germany. About 400 internees, mostly Russians, had been sent to this small camp to work in a factory. Mr. Garlinski became acquainted with a person of Greek background, although the person had been born in Russia. The Greek told of being near Kharkov in the spring of 1940 when the Russians started building a tall wood fence. The people were told not to go near the wall or try to see what was going on beyond it. Later, when the Germans came, they discovered people had been killed there and placed in a mass grave, like Katyn. The Germans had brought Russian citizens from nearby to the gravesite at Kharkov in order to identify relatives whom the bolsheviks had killed. Mr. Garlinski's father had been a prisoner at Starobliesk, the nearest camp to Kharkov; hence, this information was of personal value to this witness. Mr. Garlinski was freed by the American Armed Forces in May, 1945, and emigrated to England in November, 1945. When he arrived in Great Britain, he told his story to the Polish Government in Exile in London. Mr. Garlinski's father had been a major in the reserves of the Polish army when he was captured by the Russians. For some time Mr. Garlinski's wife, and his mother were together in Warsaw; then later the two wives remained together after the arrest and incarceration of Mr. Garlinski. His mother had received a post card from his father indicating he was at Starobielsk; another card came in January or February, 1940; and the last message, a telegram or Happy Namesday wishes was received on March 25, 1940. The Polish custom was to honor a Saint's Day or names' day; in this case Saint Mary's Day because the mother's name was Maria.

The committee asked the wife of the witness to continue the testimony and Mrs. Eileen Frances Garlinska confirmed the receipt of two cards and the telegram on Saint's Day, or names' day, on March 25, 1940. This telegram from Major Garlinski to his wife, sent from Starobielsk, was the last message she received from him.

The committee's twenty fourth witness was Mr. Janus Prawdzic Szlaski,[64] who in 1944 was commanding officer of an underground unit in the district of Nowogrodek. This Polish Home Underground Army, as it was best known and remembered, as it participated in the Warsaw uprising in August and September, 1944. When the Russians fell back from the German attack in 1941, many Russian officers and NKVD officers transferred their allegiances to the German Gestapo. These Russians, now in the employ of the Germans, began an intensive campaign to collect the intelligentsia of the area for surrender to the Gestapo. Their purpose was to eliminate the loyal pro-Polish element.

In one classic example, an agreement was reached wherein the Russians were to participate in an underground meeting; however, at the December 1, 1943, meeting, the armed Russians attacked the underground members, captured them, and deported them to the U.S.S.R. As a result of this incident the underground army found itself fighting the Russian partisans. In one confrontation when the underground army killed a Russian officer, the papers found on him included an order from the Russian commanding officer to destroy the Polish underground battalions, and particularly to select the officers and non-commissioned officers for execution.

The witness compared the Russian killing of the leaders of the underground movement to the Russian killing of the leaders at Katyn. The Soviet policy was to wipe out Polish leadership and Polish intelligentsia; thereby removing possible Polish resistance to their Soviet communist goals.

Mr. C[65] appeared anonymously as witness number twenty five because of the presence of relatives behind the iron curtain. Mr. C first enlisted in the Polish Armed Forces on September 7, 1919, and joined the border guards as a staff sergeant in 1922. When the war broke out, he was taken back into the army. He was arrested by the Russians on October 25, 1939, when he registered in order to move from eastern to western Poland, and remained their prisoner until August 24, 1941, in keeping with the Polish-Russian Pact. He was first interned at Ostashkov on February 11, 1940, where approximately 7,000 Poles were incarcerated; including policemen, border guards, civilians, priests, lawyers, and others. He was in the second to the last group of seventy which departed the very next day. The rest of the camp had been evacuated in groups of seventy to one hundred thirty, starting on April 4, 1940. The procedure followed for each departing group was to turn in the camp equipment (such as mattress and blankets), go directly to a thorough search location, and finally gather inside a ring of guards to be marched away.

One of the first rumors was that the first one thousand prisoners who left Ostashkov were put on ships (barges) which were pulled out into the White Sea and there sunk by artillery fire on or about May 1, 1940. When this witness departed the camp on May 13, he was sent by prison train to Pavlishchev Bor.

While testifying, M. C referred to small boards which were the staves from his knapsack. He wrote notes and dates on pieces of paper or on the boards themselves so he could remember each incident. He believed the prisoners at Ostashkov and Starobliesk were not killed at Katyn but elsewhere, for he stated there were other and "More Katyns in Russia."

Mr. Joseph Mackiewicz,[66] a recognized journalist and author, and an eyewitness at Katyn, was the twenty sixth witness. He was encouraged by his colleagues to write his 1951 book, THE KATYN WOOD MURDERS; an astute addition to the common body of knowledge about the Katyn incident. The committee wanted to determine the authenticity of the statements in the Russian Commission Report; hence, that report was introduced into the testimony for the witness to critique.

Mr. Mackiewicz noted such initial discrepancies as the Russians claimed the Germans committed the Katyn crimes in 1941 when the Germans had already claimed the Russians committed them in 1940. He testified that as the Russians retreated they committed many murders and mass atrocities; e. g. Provienka (Lithuania), Berzewez, Willejka, and Lvov. He stated fierce violations of human rights had been inflicted by the Russians prior to 1940; but the Germans had not made a big propaganda issue of the crimes when they were committed. Actually, the Germans could have published that the Katyn deaths occurred in the summer of 1941; but, being very competent in methods of brutality themselves, they knew that an early disclosure of the truth would be effective in placing guilt on the Russians for commission of the crimes in March and April, 1940. Moreover, it was known the German did not commit atrocities against entire POW camps. Why, the, would they make an exception here? Also, why would they murder prisoners held by the Russian? Another key point was that at Ostashkov, a camp of about 6,500 people, many policemen were there dressed in uniforms different than those worn by the Polish soldiers. When the Germans invaded Poland, not only did they retain the Polish police force, but also they continued to search for additional Polish soldiers and recruits to be used as policemen to maintain order. Why would the Germans want to kill some 5,000 policemen and others who were bitterly opposed to communism?

Next the witness considered the number of bodies involved: The Russians claimed that they found 11,000 bodies at Katyn after the Germans departed, but only slightly more than 4,000 bodies were exhumed by the Germans. If the Russian report was correct, where were the other 7,000 bodies? If one assumed the Germans killed the 4,000 they exhumed, which was the Russians' claim, what happened to the rest? How about the Russians'c claim that they found nine documents or bits of evidence that indicated death of the POWs had occurred about August or September of 1941 at the hands of the Germans? If this were true, wouldn't the families of these POWs in Poland have been receiving and writing letters to the captives? As potential witnesses in Poland, these families would have defended the Russian point of view; a number that could be in the tens of thousands if each of the 11,000 captives had been alive and writing to friends and relatives.

Another factor was that the citizens of Poland hated the Germans and were looking for reasons to believe the Russian story, but it was too "full of holes" to be believable. Also, a German lie would have spread quickly through the country, and the Germans knew that only the truth would hold up. Regarding the question of the Jews, the world knew the Germans were conducting an intense anti-Semitic action; yet they did not jeopardize the truth of the Katyn Massacre when they found many Jews there who were victims of the Russians.

The next discrepancy in the Russian report was a statement that the Poles were brought to Gniezdovo in 1940 and placed in three camps spread out twenty-five to forty-five miles west of Smolenski, and that during the German attack these captives fell into the hands of the Germans. In actuality, no records existed of the "three camps;" there were no witnesses who saw the camps, no stories by peasants and no citing of specific locations. How easy it would have been for the Russians, if the camps really existed, to have so notified Ambassador Kot, General Sikorski, General Anders, and Mr. Czapski; officials who were constantly inquiring as to the whereabouts of the Polish prisoners of war. Also, the Russian report stated the Poles to be interned in the three alleged camps were to be unloaded or detrained at Gniezdovo in the spring of 1940. The report did not explain why these POWs were unloaded at Gniezdovo and then transported by some method for another fifteen to thirty miles when they could just as easily have been kept on the train for the entire journey. The witness maintained there were no "three camps" or this fact would have come out in discussions with the peasants; in fact, Mr. Mackiewicz posed this question specifically to the old peasant, Kriwozercew, who stated he knew nothing about such camps.

Conversely, the Russian commander of alleged Camp Number 1, Major Wietosznikow of the NKVD, stated that as the Germans approached Smolensk, he asked the commanding officer of transport forces, Iwannov, for rail transportation to evacuate the Polish prisoners. When the transportation was not available, the claim was made that the Poles fell into the hands of the Germans and Wietosznikow fell back with the Russians. If Wietosznikow, the person responsible for Russian security forces, knew of the Poles' presence, why did not Stalin, Molotov, and Vyshinsky know about them since their presence was almost within the shadow of Moscow? Why should they pretend they did not know the whereabouts of the Polish prisoners? If Major Wietosznikow had reported to his NKVD superiors what was supposed to have happened to the Poles, the NKVD officials should have notified Czapski the Poles had been captured by the Germans. Finally, when Iwannov did not provide rail transportation for Wietosznikow as requested on July 12, 1941, the prisoners could have moved by foot to Smolensk because during the war the Russians maintained they still held Smolensk on July 23, 1941. Wietosznikow could have notified his superiors he could not get rail transportation; then they would have known the fate of the Poles as early as July, 1941.

The report stated Major Wietosznikow failed to return to camp but joined in the retreat of the Russians. If there were any elements of truth to the Russian report, would the Russians have abandoned perhaps 11,000 Polish prisoners of war without any guards? Would that many captives have done nothing until recaptured by the Germans? With no control over the camps, most prisoners would have seized the opportunity to escape. They would have fled, scattered, made a run to freedom; and many would have lived to bear witness to the story.

The witness testified the German blitzkrieg operated by thrusting the Army of the Third Reich ahead, thereby leaving vast areas completely unguarded and unoccupied; e. g. at Wilno the German attack was so penetrating that large numbers of Russian units were left behind and unguarded in a woods called Rudnicki. How absurd to think the Germans would stop to guard unarmed Polish POWs when whole armies of Russians had been bypassed. Surely, many Polish prisoners would have escaped under such circumstances—left with no guards in a devastated no-man's land created by the German attack.

The full-time duty for some enemies of the Germans was to try to discredit any German version of war events as reported. Mr. Mackiewicz cited an instance that occurred while he was at Katyn. Two Portuguese correspondents had stated the bodies of exhumed Polish officers were actually Jews dressed in Polish uniforms; a fabrication greater than the lie about the "three camps," in the opinion of Mr. Mackiewicz.

A letter, attributed to a Pole named Stanislaw Kuczynski, dated June 20, 1941, had been mentioned in the Russian report. Even though the letter could have been written, the witness cited the fact that Kuczynski, who once had been incarcerated at Starobielsk, had been removed from the camp in December, 1939, and had never been heard from again; in fact, had not been at Kozielsk and his remains were not found at Katyn. The Germans had exhumed 4,143 bodies at Katyn and had found thereupon some 3,940 documents, letters, and other writing. How then, if the Russians had found another 7,000 bodies of Poles, as they claimed, could they not find more than nine pieces of correspondence?

Mr. Mackiewicz testified he had spent three days at Katyn, starting about May 20, 1943, and he had seen countless bits of newspapers blowing about the forest; none of which were dated later than April, 1940. Exhumations had been going on for about two months when he arrived. He testified the woods was sparsely covered with small fir trees, small bushes, and other small trees; and the soil was sandy and yellow. Seven graves had been exhumed; later an eighth grave was found. The witness stated it had been reported the soil was more like clay at the eighth gravesite.

In the Russian report there were other questionable issues; e. g. all the Russian witnesses claimed the Germans committed the crimes in August and September, 1941; whereas a number of witnesses had testified the German atrocities were over by the middle of September, 1941. Not a single witness said any executions took place in October or November, 1941. The Russian report also claimed the murders took place between September and December, 1941; thereby establishing a discrepancy between the dates cited by the witnesses and the report. Unquestionably, no one would wear winter clothing in August or September, and all witnesses had reported the cadavers had been dressed in cold-weather clothing; therefore, the September-December time frame would correlate with the clothing found on the exhumed bodies. It appeared the Russians must have recorded the testimony of the final report after the fact.

The committee asked the inevitable last question: who do you believe was responsible for the Katyn murders? Mr. Mackiewicz answered, "I am convinced that the crimes were committed by the bolsheviks."[67] Unquestionably, this witness presented a superb analytical and theoretical approach to his critique of the Russians Commission Report.

The Select Committee reconvened at 7:40 P.M. to hear testimony in its first evening session. Ambassador Stanislaw Kot[68] was its twenty seventh witness. He gave the members of the committee a summary of his notes for the meetings with Russian officials held in Kuibyshev. The governmental agencies had moved there from Moscow because the Third Reich Army was getting close to Moscow.

Ambassador Kot reported that in addition to the usual introductory diplomatic sessions, his first meeting with Deputy Commissar for Foreign Affairs, A. J. Vyshinsky had been on September 20, 1941. Their next meeting was on October 6, 1941. At this meeting the fact that of 9,500 missing Polish officers only 2,000 had been accounted for, leaving the fate of the other 7,500 in doubt, had been brought to Vyshinsky's attention. Prior to this meeting the Ambassador had sent Vyshinsky a note on September 27, 1941, inquiring about the whereabouts of the missing Poles promised by the Russians had not yet been received. Later (October 14, 1941) the two men held another conference at which the Ambassador announced General Sikorski would be coming to Moscow as soon as possible. Also, General Sikorski sent a note of confirmation to Ambassador Bogomolow at the Soviet Embassy in London the same day.

Ambassador Kot had an appointment with Commissar of Foreign Affairs V. Molotov on October 22, 1941. The Ambassador wanted to have all the Polish officers released before General Sikorski arrived for his meeting with Premier Stalin. At the meeting Dr. Kot gave the names of specific officers to be released to Commissar Molotov (Major Jan Furman, and two outstanding general officers: Generals Orlik Lukowski and Kmicic Skrzynski). On November 1, 1941, a note was sent to Commissar Molotov telling him the amnesty agreement was not being fulfilled by the Russians and informing him that General Sikorski should not come to Moscow prior to receipt of the list. On November 2, 1941, Ambassador Kot met once more with Deputy Commissar Vyshinsky, at which meeting the Polish position was challenged by the Russians with a statement to the effect the number of prisoners claimed to be missing was exaggerated.

In the meantime, Dr. Kot had asked British Ambassador Cripps to support the Polish position, which he did by intervening with Mr. Molotov. On November 8, 1941, a Russian note saying all the Polish prisoners had been released by the terms of the amnesty agreement was received; an indication that the intervention of Ambassador Cripps had not been effective. Future Ambassador Harriman of the United States sent a telegram to Premier Stalin on November 11, 1941, asking the Russians to concur with the Poles' request. Then, on November 12, 1941, Ambassador Kot met with Deputy Commissar Vyshinsky again. The Commissar was pleasant and asked Ambassador Kot if he wanted to explain to Premier Stalin why General Sikorski should not come to Moscow. Vyshinsky told Kot he was convinced the Polish officers had been released but their whereabouts had not been determined. He assured Kot he had the list of Polish officers, as had Molotov earlier. The committee members noted for the record the interned Poles had been murdered over one-and-one-half years earlier and the Soviets were still making promises to get lists.

On November 14, 1941, Ambassador Kot (with his translator First Secretary W. Arlet) met with Premier Stalin and Minister of Foreign Affairs Molotov (and their translator) at the Kremlin in Moscow. Molotov made only one observation—the meeting was called because of the Polish Ambassador's resistance to General Sikorski's visit. The conversation was carried on by Stalin and Kot. (General Sikorski was already in Cairo and would not indicate to the press if he was going to Moscow or back to London.) Ambassador Kot had cautioned that General Sikorski's visit would be exploited for the Soviets' own purposes rather than for the release of the imprisoned Poles. It was apparent Stalin wanted the Polish Prime Minister to visit him. At first Premier Stalin spoke of the character of the Polish people and the future of Poland. The Ambassador countered with the fact that Russia would not want a large Polish army formed in Russia now that army rations had been reduced to the point where 14,000 military volunteers had to be turned down. Finally, the conversation included the missing Polish officers from Starobielsk, then Kozielsk, then Ostashkov; all of whom had been sent away in April and May, 1940. Stalin brought up General Langner of Lvov who escaped and suggested the other officers might have done the same. He also asked if the Poles had accurate lists of the missing officers. The Polish Ambassador reminded Stalin the prisoners had rosters and the NKVD had interrogated each officer; yet not a single officer of the staff of General Anders' command in Poland had been released. Stalin was on his feet now, walking around the table, lighting a cigarette, listening intently, and answering questions. He walked to the telephone and placed a call to the NKVD (with Molotov's help). Stalin spoke:

> This is Stalin. Have all the Poles already been released from jail? (There is a moment of quiet while he is listening to an answer.) For the Polish Ambassador is here in my office and he tells me that not all. (Again he listens to the answer and then puts the telephone aside. He returns to the conference table.) And shortly thereafter, (Stalin arises from his seat when the telephone rings and is listening most probably to the answer to the question which he gave a few minutes ago regarding the release of the Poles. He puts aside the receiver and returns, not saying one word.)[69] That was then end of the conversation on that subject.

Ambassador Kot saw Mr. Molotov immediately thereafter and presented him with a pro-memoria asking for complete amnesty for the people for whom the Ambassador was searching. Mr. Molotov sent a reply dated November 19, 1941, stressing the completeness of the amnesty and the fact that everybody had been released. When Dr. Kot returned to Kuibyshev on November 17, 1941, he wanted a list prepared of all the missing officers. He enlisted the aid of General Anders, and Major Czapski who, with additional help, had already started the list of missing, and was delegated to complete the project.

Premier Stalin personally had wanted a visit by General Sikorski. Ambassador Kot accompanied the Polish Prime Minister and General Anders to Moscow. Their meeting with Premier Stalin, and Commissar Molotov, and their translator, took place in the Kremlin on December 3, 1941. General Sikorski was accompanied by Ambassador Kot and General Anders, the latter translating for the Poles. The meeting lasted two-and one-half hours and was non-productive insofar as information about the missing officers of Kozielsk, Os-tashkov, and Starobielsk was concerned. General Sikorski did gain the approval of Premier Stalin to transfer the Polish army to Iran to recover its strength and be ready to fight. Stalin was irritated and retorted they would never return. General Sikorski said he would bring them back personally if necessary. Stalin regained his composure and calmly discussed where in the south the Poles could go to avoid the freezing Russian weather. During this same meeting, Sikorski brought up the question of the missing Polish prisoners of war and presented the list to Stalin. At that point Stalin stated the missing officers had escaped. When General Anders asked where they could have escaped to, Stalin responded, "Manchuria."[70]

Ambassador Kot presented another pro-memoria to Mr. Molotov immediately after that meeting because he had received no answer to his previous pro-memoria of November 19, 1941, and he did not want the Foreign Minister's note to go unanswered. Again on January 9, 1942, the Soviets replied to the last note of December 3, 1941, but by now both sides had polarized and were maintaining or repeating the same points.

On December 4, 1941, General Sikorski spoke on the radio "to the whole world." Later that evening there was a large reception at Premier Stalin's residence in honor of General Sikorski, which lasted from 8 to 2 A.M. Many toasts were offered for a future Poland and for the brave Polish officers, etc., by Premier Stalin and Commissar Molotov. Premier Stalin and General Sikorski talked briefly together then they signed a declaration of friendly cooperation.

At the meeting with Stalin, General Sikorski gained approval and permission to tour the various Polish army camps and to take a Russian confidante with him. Vyshinsky was assigned. While the Poles became better acquainted with the Deputy Commissar of Foreign Affairs and his aides, the issue of the missing officers was not brought up because other matters were being settled.

During May and June, 1942, Ambassador Kot visited the new British Ambassador Carr and the United States Ambassador, Admiral Standley to intercede for the Poles about the problem of the missing officers. Neither Carr nor Standley had any fruitful suggestions. General Sikorski wanted the Ambassador to renew his conversations with the Russians. Ambassador Kot sent a memorandum to Mr. Vyshinsky on May 19, 1942, referring to forty-two different notes sent to Russian diplomats and administrators on the missing officers; followed by another note on June 13, 1942. Finally, when Ambassador Kot was preparing to leave Russia, he brought up the subject again on his farewell visit to Vyshinsky on July 8, 1942. A summary of their discussion—a very strongly worded review about the missing Polish officers and the failure of the Soviet government to respond in any meaningful way—was submitted to the committee in its entirety. Ambassador Kot and his translator, a legal aide named Sokolnicki, were as forceful as they could be in such diplomatic matters. Some of Vyshinsky's responses were: "I see a tendency of considering our replies to you as purely formal." "We have no lists." "Maybe these people are beyond the borders of the U.S.S.R.; maybe a part of them have died; some of them have been released before the war with the Germans."[71]

Two more comments by Ambassador Kot have relevance to his testimony: First, when the German announcement of Katyn's discovery was made on April 13, 1943, and Dr. Kot was Minister of Information in London, he had been visited by a high dignitary of the Soviet Embassy who stated he was there under instructions from the Kremlin to ask Dr. Kot to make a public announcement that the Poles had been murdered by the Germans. This visit had occurred about April 16, 1943. Dr. Kot had refused. Second, in response to the question concerning responsibility for the massacre at Katyn, the Ambassador indicated it was the Russians, who committed the crimes.

The last day of the London hearings began on Saturday, April 19, 1952, with General Wladyslaw Anders[72] as the twenty-eighth witness. Under urging by the committee, the modest and able General Anders briefly reviewed his distinguished career. Born hear Warsaw, under Russian domination, he served as a soldier and later as an officer, so that when World War I began he spent all of his time on the German front serving as a Russian officer. After the Russian Revolution he became a member of the Polish army, usually assigned to his specialty of cavalry. He fought against the Germans in 1919 and later transferred to the east where he participated in the Russo-Polish War in 1919 and 1920 until the peace treaty was signed. After being assigned to numerous duties in and out of Poland, he was transferred from eastern to western Poland in March 1939, when war seemed obvious. He had fought against the Germans as commander in chief of the group in very heavy fighting, including encirclement as the Polish army moved, under orders, from Warsaw toward Lublin. He had been ordered to the south and had fought successfully against the Germans through the morning of September 24, 1939, but by 4 P.M. his Poles were fighting the Russians. There had been no declaration of war by the Russians. General Anders stated he had been wounded once by the Germans and twice by the Russians who captured him. Because of his serious wounds he had been transferred to a hospital in Lvov. His military plan had been to move his army group across the border and into Hungary. When asked whether it was the Russians or Germans blocking the roads, he stated: "Whoever got in my way, that was the one I fought with or against."[73]

The witness stated the intent of the Russians had been to block the way to Hungary and Romania; also, that information was then being received that Poles were being murdered and deported. General Anders said he had been arrested in Lvov and taken from hospital to jail in December, 1939. He was interned there until February, 1940, when he was transferred to the Lubianka prison in Moscow (sustaining seven months in solitary confinement) where he remained (except for two months at Butyrki, another Moscow prison) until released on August 4, 1941. His interrogations had been in the hundreds— sometimes five times a week—and extended up to the time Russia was invaded by Germany. From these interrogations—always by the NKVD—General Anders concluded the Russians intended to wait until France, Great Britain, and Germany destroyed one another; then Russia would "occupy the whole of Europe, and that Russia will terminate the war where she began it." "Where will that be?" "In Spain!"[74] Implicit in the understanding gained by General Anders was that the desires and plans of Russia had been aimed at the occupation and control of the entire world, with Soviet Russia as the core. Any alliances would be ones of expediency with world conquest as the ultimate end.

When Germany attacked Russia, no information of any kind had been passed to the prisoners in Lubianka. The bombing of Moscow had been passed off as training exercises, or so the guards of the prison said. But the buildings had been sandbagged, the windows painted over, and the brief walk through the prison discontinued. Ten days after the German attack General Anders said the attitude toward him changed considerably; the Russians became friendly in the interrogations. He had been told that some sort of a mutual agreement for cooperation should be reached, that the past must be forgotten, and that the Russians and Poles must fight together against the Germans. By July 20, 1941, the interrogations were very friendly and the diet improved; in fact the General said he was taken to the barber who shaved off his beard and gave him cologne water. Near the end of July he had been told negotiations with the Polish government were making progress.

On August 4, 1941, the day of his departure from prison, he said he had been called out of his cell in the usual manner but the arm twisting behind his back had been stopped, and the NKVD commander of the prison, a colonel, accompanied the guards. He was limping and on crutches because he could not walk without support; the bullet was still lodged in his leg. He had been led "to fine quarters": a large room where he had been introduced to Mr. Beria, commander of the NKVD, and Mr. Merkulov, commander of the NKBD. (The NKVD was the parent unit that included all interior security agencies and took care of all affairs of the Ministry of the Interior; the NKBD, a subordinate unit, was responsible exclusively for the jails and prisons.) These two men, Beria and Merkulov, told General Anders he had been nominated as commander-in-chief of the Polish army to be formed in Russia. The oft-quoted reminder of cooperation and mutual assistance was presented in various ways and assurances; one being that all Polish prisoners would be released.

General Anders was given his freedom that very day. A few days thereafter he heard from General Bogusz-Szyszko who had been to Moscow as the chief of the Polish military mission from London. General Bogusz-Szyszko briefed him on the details of the German invasion, informed him about the agreements reached between the governments of Poland and Russia, and presented him with orders from his commander-in-chief, General Sikorski, Premier of the Polish Government in Exile in London.

As General Anders began re-organizing the Polish army, the shortage of officers became obvious. He had been told there would be approximately 1,000 officers and 20,000 soldiers, but he remembered the Pravda article on the first anniversary of the invasion of Poland by Russia in which the claim of taking 225,000 prisoners of war had been made by the Soviets. He knew there should be available about 15,000 Polish officers, but in the first six conferences with the Russian military authorities—always with the NKVD present—the Soviets made no mention of the officers, even though General Anders and General Bogusz-Szyszko brought up the officers' issue with no results. General Anders put Major Czapski to work on this missing officer problem. When the General visited Griazovietz, he found only a few more than 400 Polish officers who had survived Kozielsk, Ostashkov, and Starobielsk (via Pavlishchev Bor). Also, at Griazovietz he found the Polish officers who had been brought there from Lithuania. The startling fact that none of their friends had been heard from since the evacuation of the three camps in March and April, 1940, was upsetting. The internees were instructed by General Anders to start preparing lists of the names of the missing Polish officers they could remember. The officers at Griazovietz were recruited into the Polish army, and many of them were assigned to the General Staff.

At first the size of the Polish army was 1,700 officers and 20,000 soldiers, but when the headquarters moved to Tazhkent during February, 1942, from Buzuluk, the number of Polish soldiers soared to 73,000. The General even had soldiers arrive from Kolyma, which was described as a "horrible place." It had been said a person could survive only one winter there because the temperature would reach –70° Centigrade, or 100° below zero Fahrenheit. Of the 10,000 Poles sent to Kolyma, only 160 reported to General Anders for duty.

By the time of General Sikorski's visit with Premier Stalin, the missing officers' list totaled over 4,000. Major Czapski worked night and day interviewing internees who came from so many parts of Russia. The list as finally prepared went to General Anders and to General Sikorski for their meeting with Premier Stalin on December 3, 1941. General Anders had met General Sikorski in Teheran in November, 1941, and had accompanied him to Kuibyshev and on to Moscow to meet with Premier Stalin. It was at the close of this meeting that the list of 4,000 names of missing Polish prisoners of war had been handed to Premier Stalin by General Sikorski, who explained the list was constantly being revised, updated, and resubmitted. Also, Major Czapski was later given a note of introduction from General Sikorski to General Rajchman of the NKVD for the purpose of making inquiry about the missing Poles. This note was dated April 2, 1942. Major Czapski's activities will be reported later.

When the total number of Poles in the army in Russia exceeded 73,000 soldiers, with 40,000 women and children having arrived also, General Anders had been notified the Russians were reducing the rations for food to 26,000 people. He remonstrated with a telegram to Stalin which brought a response and a scheduled meeting with the Premier on March 18, 1942. General Anders took Colonel Okulinski, his chief of staff with him. At this meeting General Anders once more brought up the missing Polish officers. For the first time Stalin told them some of the Poles must have fled and become separated when the German army invaded the U.S.S.R. The first response on December 3, 1941, had been possible escape; now the story on March 18, 1942, had become one of being taken prisoner by the Germans. Why, then, had these prisoners been denied correspondence from the time of the closing of the three camps until the invasion by the Germans? Why had not a single prisoner escaped?

The result of this conference started the movement of the Polish army from Russia to the Middle East. While General Anders remained in Russia for a time, the evacuation of his army had begun. The Soviets had cut off the flow of new people to the Polish headquarters and camps. General Anders had thousands of people who had starved to death, no medicine had been provided for them, and the soldiers and been given no arms. General Anders reported the situation as "impossible." Ultimately, the message was received from the Russian government that in agreement with General Anders' request, permission to evacuate all the Poles to the Middle East had been approved. Even so, General Anders continued to request the return of the missing officers during the period.

General Anders and his headquarters completed the move to Iraq. On April 13, 1943, the announcement was made over the Berlin radio that the mass graves at Katyn had been discovered. When the German report was heard, every Pole in the Middle East was convinced the Russians had committed the massacre and for once the Germans had told the truth. Knowing how laboriously the Poles had searched for their missing prisoners of war, no one believed the Russian announcement when it came over the radio two days later. The Soviet report included lie after lie, and there had been no logic to the entire announcement. In response to the inevitable question concerning the establishment of guilt for the Katyn killings, General Anders responded:

> There is absolutely no question here. The 15,000 Polish officers from those three camps were unquestionably murdered by the Russians. We must remember the Russians were not retreating under the heavy German advance, they absolutely did not leave any prisoners fall into the hand of the Germans. They evacuated them through forced marches, if necessary, and they shot any prisoner who could not retreat with the Russians during that

143

advance. In many instances they murdered many prisoners in jails, in the prisons, when the Germans were advancing.[75]

Since only 4,143 bodies had been exhumed at Katyn, these undoubtedly were the missing Polish officers from Kozielsk. When asked what happened to the missing prisoners of war from Ostashkov and Starobliesk who had not been accounted for, General Anders replied: "There is no doubt, no question, that in Russia there are many more similar Katyns." He ended his testimony with this statement of concern:

I am deeply concerned that the murder of these 15,000 Polish soldiers is only a part of a deliberate and careful plan created over a period of many years toward the extermination of all people who may oppose bolshevism. I am deeply convinced that what has happened at Katyn and other Katyns is the aim of bolsheviks throughout the world.[76]

Chapter 11

SELECT COMMITTEE HEARINGS: FRANKFURT AND NAPLES

The overseas hearings moved from London to Frankfurt, Germany. The initial session convened on April 21, 1952,[1] in the main courtroom, Resident Officers Building, 45 Bockenheimer Anlager. After introductory remarks, the first witness, Josef Czapski,[2] a noted writer and painter, was called to testify. His book, *The Inhuman Land,* had been published in 1951.

Captain Czapski had been activated from his Polish army reserve status to active duty with the Eighth Regiment in Krakow on September 3, 1939. As the regiment was withdrawing from the Germans on September 27, he had been captured by the Russians and had been sent to the Polish POW camp at Starobielsk. Evacuation of this camp began on April 5, 1940, with groups of sixty to two-hundred-fifty men being moved to an unknown destination. On April 25 a select group of sixty-three had departed Starobielsk for Pavlishchev Bor; Josef Czapski had been in another group of sixteen that left Starobielsk the next day on its way to Pavlishchev Bor and later to Griazovietz. The total number of survivors of the Starobielsk camp had been the seventy-nine from these last two prisoner movements. Prior to the camp evacuation there had been 3,920 POWs at Starobielsk; including all ranks: generals; doctors, professors, intellectuals; many youths; many priests, including Reverend (Major) Anthony Alexandrowicz; the Superintendent of the Protestant Church in Poland; Rabbi (Major) Baruch Steinberg, the Rabbi-in-Chief of the Polish Army; Reverend (Major) Jan Potocki; and others.

In answering the questions as to why and who committed the murders, Captain Czapski's response included the opinion that the decision had been made in the Kremlin. He testified that after the cooperation between Hitler and Stalin began, the Kremlin decided to execute these Polish officers as a form of ". . . revenge. For these Poles constituted the elite of my country."[3] By permitting a few POWs to survive Russia could make these few remnants available if a later demand were made.

The witness stated the "Haven of Bliss" was a villa outside Moscow where twenty officers had been taken because the Soviets thought these individuals could be fashioned into Polish communists who would organize a Red-Polish army in Russia. Some of these officers were present when Berling, who would have become the leader, asked the question of Beria, the NKVD senior officer, about a need for officers in this new Polish army in Russia. Beria agreed with Berling that Polish officers of all political beliefs should be included. Berling commented that these officers would be available at the camps in Kozielsk and Starobielsk; therefore, officers would be immediately available for all units necessary to form a complete army. At this point Beria made his classic response, which has been oft quoted, "Oh, no, no, not those at Kozielsk and Starobielsk. With those we have made a grave mistake."[4] General Beria's assistant, General Merkulov, was also present and repeated the admission. Mr. Czapski indicated he had heard this same statement from three separate people at different places while on his search for the missing officers. Also, the committee included "in the record" the fact that witnesses under oath had already testified before the committee about hearing Beria's statement. For obvious reasons, the earlier witnesses and the committee members had been impressed with this reported incident.

Mr. Czapski became an officer of assistance as the first Polish division was being mobilized, and as such had interviewed all the soldiers and officers from the various POW camps. After the data had been accumulated, General Anders was briefed. Later, General Anders placed Captain Czapski in charge of the entire search for the missing Polish personnel. When the list was completed, it had been given to General Sikorski, who finally presented it to Premier Stalin at their meeting on December 3, 1941.

Captain Czapski, personally, had searched for the missing officers on Russian soil. First, he had gone to Czkalow because the chief of the Soviet camps, General Nasetkin, operated from there. His letter of introduction from General Anders had stated Premier Stalin had ordered the release of all Polish prisoners. Their first meeting was cordial; however, General Nasetkin asked for a few days' time. Obviously, he had received instructions from Moscow or Kuibyshev, the alternative capital (because the German attack was moving toward Moscow), for at their meeting the next day General Nasetkin advised Captain Czapski that he did not have permission to talk. At the same time General Anders was notified by the NKVD that "Czapski has no right to roam around the country."[5] General Anders immediately dispatched Captain Czapski to the headquarters of the NKVD at Kuibyshev, and later to Moscow, where he hoped the Captain could meet with Beria or Merkulov. Captain Czapski saw neither NKVD officer, but he did have the opportunity to talk to General Rajchman on February 2, 1942, to whom he gave a multipage listing of the Polish officers who had disappeared from the three POW camps. He also cited Premier

Stalin's promises, the fact that the missing captives were not being returned and the opinion that he believed the missing internees were not still alive. General Rajchman read the memorandum and assured Captain Czapski he would be given a reply. Finally, several days later, General Rajchman called Captain Czapski at midnight, indicated he had no knowledge of the matter, and suggested Captain Czapski see Deputy Minister of Foreign Affairs Vyshinsky in Kuibyshev. Captain Czapski reminded General Rajchman that Ambassador Kot had already communicated directly, in person, with Mr. Vyshinsky on eight separate occasions, and the Deputy Minister had said he had no knowledge of the missing officers.

Captain Czapski had returned to Iraq with the Polish army and was serving as Chief of the Propaganda Agency when the German announcement of Katyn had been broadcast. He stated that there had not been one person there who doubted that Russians had committed the crimes. The eyewitnesses to life as experienced in the Russian POW camps knew that the Soviets would not leave any prisoners to fall into the hands of the Germans. The witness concluded his testimony with the opinion that the Soviets murdered the Polish prisoners of war; then, he added that in a country such as the U.S.S.R. where centralized policies, orders, and directives are normal and expected, the decision for the crime and its ". . . full responsibility rests with Beria and Stalin."[6]

Josef Czapski had been a valuable witness. His military search has been oft-quoted as a valiant effort. His authorship on the subject of POW life has become a classic example of personal commitment, competence, and professional talent dedicated to a virtuous purpose.

In a brief, succinct, but effective way, the testimony of Werner Stephan,[7] the second witness, was interesting. Mr. Stephan served as Ministerial Councilor in the Ministry of Propaganda directly for the Chief of the Minister of Propaganda, Dr. Goebbels. Mr. Stephan was a journalist who had been visited on April 1 or 2, 1943, by a close friend, Hans Meyer, also a journalist, who had been conscripted into service and was at that time with the German army near Smolensk. Meyer told Stephan of the persistent rumors from the Russian population that mass graves of Polish officers were nearby, that exhumations had started about two weeks earlier, and that bodies of Poles had been found; but since Meyer felt the military might not handle the announcement properly because it was a political matter, he had gone to Berlin. Mr. Stephan arranged for Hans Meyer to see Dr. Goebbels immediately. The two talked alone, but Meyer debriefed Mr. Stephan after the conference. Dr. Goebbels had been extremely surprised that the good fortune of this news should come directly to him. He quickly delivered the information to the Fuehrer, Adolf Hitler, and the outcome of their meeting was that Goebbels received authority to pursue the situation, and that thereafter the armed forces were instructed to transfer their reports to him: a noteworthy victory for Goebbels within the highest level of the Third

Reich. Within two weeks, on April 13, 1943, Dr. Goebbels made the first public announcement of the Katyn atrocities from Berlin radio.

The last and third witness for April 21, 1952, was Colonel Albert Bedenk[8] who was the regimental commander of the Signal Regiment No. 537 which provided communication between the various armies of the German Central Army Group (Field Marshall von Bock). Colonel Bedenk arrived in Smolensk on July 28, 1941, before his unit; but when it arrived the regimental staff established its headquarters in a house right on the banks of the Dnieper River, some 1,000 meters from the road, which was in the Katyn Forest; and four kilometers west of the headquarters of the Central Army group. The witness described the forest as a thick, dense, mixed woods that included pine and evergreen trees with some young trees in those parts where the grave-sites were later found. He stated the soil was light in color.

Colonel Bedenk stated his staff was a small one; only eight or nine enlisted men. The group had heard that the house earlier had belonged to the GPU (NKVD) and was used as a recreation home for the commissars in Smolensk. Colonel Bedenk heard no stories of Polish officers being executed there, nor was he aware of the gravesites. The stories heard of earlier shootings in the woods had been assumed to be tales concerned with the front-line fighting nearby. The house was two stories in height with continuous balconies encircling the building on both floors. The first level consisted of two large rooms, approximately 20 by 40 feet each, and four or five smaller rooms. The upper floor had one large room and four or five smaller rooms. The principal outbuilding had a kitchen and six or eight smaller rooms.

Colonel Ahrens joined the regiment on October 20, 1941, and worked with Colonel Bedenk to learn the job; then he took command when Colonel Bedenk departed on November 20, 1941. Colonel Bedenk stated he neither saw any Polish prisoners of war nor did he receive any orders to execute any Polish prisoners of war. As the officer in charge in the fall of 1941 he stated there was no shooting of weapons in the forest, or he would have heard of it. He indicated, in response to a question, the Soviet report on the massacre at Katyn and the indictment at Nuremberg charged that the murders had been committed by the German Construction Regiment 537 under the command of a Colonel Ahrens. The witness testified, "This accusation is wrong in every detail."[9]

In responding to the Russian allegation that there had been three camps within close proximity to Katyn where the Polish prisoners of war were confined and which were left behind when the Russians withdrew, the Colonel's answer was, "I never saw any such installation which might have been camps."[10] Colonel Bedenk visited near Katyn one more time, in August, 1943, to check out with General Oberhaeuser because he was being transferred. The exhumations had already taken place, as had the reburial of the bodies.

The Select Committee reconvened on April 22, 1952, and heard the testimony of the fourth witness, Eugen Oberhaeuser,[11] who held the rank of Lieutenant General in the German armed forces and served as Chief of Communications of the Central Army Group under Field Marshall von Bock. His headquarters had been about three kilometers from Katyn and about ten kilometers from Smolensk; and he was there from July, 1941, through October, 1943, when they displaced. General Oberhaeuser confirmed the earlier testimony of Colonel Bedenk, his subordinate in the communications organization. The two would walk back and forth on the narrow dirt road which led off to the south from the Smolensk-Vitebsk Highway, an asphalt-covered road between Smolensk and Katyn. General Oberhaeuser made staff visits to Colonel Bedenk's headquarters several times a week and the two would discuss communications matters as they exercised and breathed the fresh air by hiking back and forth on the unsurfaced road. They detected no odor, and there was no indication that within 600 meters of the Dnieper Castle a gravesite was located on a spot in a sort of clearing where some of the birch trees were only three feet in height, and the ground covered with heather.

General Oberhaeuser had been a witness at Nuremberg (June 26, 1946), and had prepared a sketch and statement at that tribunal which had been provided to the Select Committee. On the question of over 4,000 Polish prisoners of war being executed by Colonel Bedenk's unit, the answer indicated it would have been impossible for this to occur. There had been no order, no exceptionally large truck movement of troops, and no shooting. When Colonel Ahrens replaced Colonel Bedenk in November, 1941, General Oberhaeuser was present at the change-of-command ceremony. Colonel Ahrens had been an instructor at the training regiment of the German Army Communication School at Halle, Saxony, during the timeframe the Russian Report indicated (July-October, 1941) he had been at Katyn in command and responsible for the murders of Polish POWs.

General Oberhaeuser did visit the Katyn Forest when the bodies were being exhumed and examined. He testified he had been there for "two or three visits" during his performance of staff visits to the Signal Regiment 537. He had witnessed an autopsy being performed by Professor Buhtz, and he recalled that the Polish

> . . . dead bodies were very well clad, in good uniform, all of them still had either their greatcoats or capes on, and very good boots, so that it gave me impression that the killings must have been done in a hurry, in view of the fact that wallets and all sorts of valuables were found on the bodies. It is quite unusual, according to my experience, that the Russians, after executing people, would bury them with all their clothes on. That astonished me.[12]

In summary, the Select Committee quoted three conclusions from the Russian investigation. For each one General Oberhaeuser gave clear reasons why the Soviet report was faulty from his "on-the-ground," eyewitness, in-command responsibility.

The fifth witness to testify was Lieutenant Reinhardt von Eichborn[13] who had been a case worker for communication affairs in the German Central Army group. Earlier, until the winter of 1940, he had been a member of the Signal Regiment No. 537. He testified that while on communication duty he would visit his old outfit when it was located in Katyn Forest in the summer and fall of 1941 just to see his old companions. At that time nothing about the area gave any indication it had been a mass grave site. His testimony coincided with General Oberhaeuser's, whom he had followed to the witness chair.

Regarding the so-called "commissar order" (the directive from Adolf Hitler to execute Soviet commissars who were taken prisoner by the Germans), Lieutenant von Eichborn testified he had been asked by Field Marshal von Bock to effect a communication link to Field Marshal von Kluge. He stated that as a communication officer it was his duty to see that the call could not be moni-tored; which meant he must man the transmitter switchboard himself and have another communication officer man the receiver switchboard at the other end of the line. For additional communication security the conversation was carried via high-frequency generator through an inverter (scrambling) device. Field Mar-shals von Bock and von Kluge agreed that they and the other two field marshals on the Russian front, von Runstedt and von List, should discuss with Hitler the possibility of having this order rescinded because it was unanimously decided such an order "was absolutely incompatible with the honor of a Prussian officer."[14]

Lieutenant von Eichborn summarized his testimony by emphasizing that it would have been impossible to execute and inter 4,000 people (the Rus-sians said 11,000) in the fall of 1941 without residents in the locale knowing about it.

The sixth witness was Friederich Ahrens,[15] who as a lieutenant colonel had been sent from a position as commander of a training regiment in a signal training school in Halle, Saxony, to the Smolensk area during the first few days of November, 1941. His assignment had been the command of Signal Regiment No. 537 at Katyn Forest. He remained there from the time he replaced Colonel Bedenk through August, 1943, when the Germans withdrew; in fact, he had been there all through the exhumations of the bodies of POWs in the late winter of 1942–43, through the spring of 1943, and until exhumations ceased on June 2, 1943. During the time the 537th was located at Katyn, like Colonel Bedenk and General Oberhaeuser before him, Lieutenant Colonel Ahrens had not antici-pated the presence of the mass graves. In the Russian investigation, however, Lieutenant Colonel Ahrens, as the officer in charge, had been accused of perpetrating the atrocities at Katyn by ordering the Polish prisoners of war murdered during the months of July, August, September, and October, 1941. He first heard about these allegations against him in February, 1946. Lieutenant Colonel Ahrens (whose name was misspelled "Arnes" in the Russian report) went to see Dr. Stahmer, the senior defense attorney for the Germans at the Nuremberg trial. Dr. Stahmer provided him with a copy of the Russian investigation, and Lieutenant Colonel Ahrens made himself available to the disposal of the court and did testify before the tribunal. He was not named a party to the trial, which he considered unusual; in fact, he reported the entire charge was dropped after the defense by the Germans.

Lieutenant Colonel Ahrens told the committee the first human bones had been found at Katyn by some of the Hiwis (Russians who were employed by the Germans or prisoners working for the Germans) at the very end of January or early in February, 1943. About four weeks later, after the snow began to thaw, these human bones were shown to Lieutenant Colonel Ahrens. He thought the bones had belonged to soldiers who had fallen in action, and he had notified the officer in charge of war graves so the matter could be investigated. Since such findings were considered to be a normal progression of events, this instance was not considered unusual. The Hiwis had found the human bones by a little hole while it was yet winter. Later, when the snow began to thaw, it was seen that a wolf, or some other wild animal, had been digging and had unearthed the human bones; also, with the snow melting it could be observed there were graves in that area. Although the witness testified he saw one birch cross sticking in the ground, he had not considered its presence unusual, for he had seen single crosses or a helmet marking grave sites elsewhere on battlefields.

The committee asked Lieutenant Colonel Ahrens why the Russian report called the 537th organization a "construction battalion" posing under the pretext of being a "signal battalion." The witness repeated the statements of others who had indicated the regimental flag posted near the road was square in shape with the numerical designator 537 included. Since battalion flags were triangular, how could the Russians mistake the square flag of 537 as the flag of an engineering battalion; in fact, Lieutenant Colonel Ahrens asked, "For whom did we have to use it as a disguise?"

Rudolph von Gersdorff,[16] the seventh witness, testified he was a Major General in the German army, and that even before the attack on Russia he had been on the general staff of the Central Army Group serving as chief intelligence officer on the Russian front from April, 1941, to September, 1943. He testified he had not seen a live Polish officer or soldier while there; however, he had seen the deceased Polish prisoners of war at Katyn, and they had been the first Poles, dead or alive, he had seen during the entire Russian campaign.

General von Gersdorff stated it would have been impossible for any German unit to have perpetrated the Katyn massacre without his knowing about it. Even the so-called "Einsatzgruppen" or "Einsatzkommandos"—who were under the direct order of the higher SS and police chiefs, who, in turn, were under the direct command of Heinrich Himmler—could not have committed the massacre for any one of three reasons: First, the commander (Field Marshal von Kluge, in this case) could demand the withdrawal of the specific Einsatzgruppen because it was hampering the strategic and tactical employment of the combat troops. Second, the chief of the police units (an officer named Nebe) and the witness were not only close friends but also co-members of the resistance movement (meaning both were against Adolf Hitler and national socialism); and this officer would never have carried out such an order without informing the General, who would never have approved it. Third, it would have been impossible to have carried out such order in secrecy without the General's knowledge because the location where the murders took place was too near the Smolensk-Vitebsk highway not to be observed. In other words, this atrocity could not have occurred without the knowledge of General von Gersdorff, the chief of intelligence.

This witness also noted that located near Gniezdovo were the prehistoric Russian cairns; old, ancient tombs inside of caves which were all badly overgrown with shrubs. When the graves of the Polish officers were discovered, the atrocity was not called the murders of Gniezdovo, even though the grave sites were actually closer to the village of Gniezdovo than they were to the village of Katyn on the far (or west) side of the Katyn Forest in order to distinguish the locale of the POW graves from those found in the old, prehistoric tombs of Gniezdovo.

The witness then testified that the very first information about Katyn had come from Field Police Secretary Voss who had been in charge of the small police unit responsible for internal security, and who at all times had been in close communication with the population in the vicinity of the staff headquarters. The General recalled that one day in February, 1943, Secretary Voss, whose duties corresponded to those in the rank of lieutenant, reported to him that some Polish auxiliary volunteers working for the infantry divisions had been making their way to the front lines, had taken temporary billeting in and near Gniezdovo, and had been asking whether Polish prisoners had been seen in that vicinity. Some of the local inhabitants had indicated to them that in the spring of 1940, trains filled with Polish prisoners had arrived at the Gniezdovo station. After these prisoners had detrained, they had been taken away in large black prison vans to the forest west of the station; and there they simply disappeared. Moreover, during these transport maneuvers the Dnieper Castle and the forest had been cordoned off by guards. After this information had been passed on to the operations officer and the chief of staff, General von Gersdorff had been instructed to investigate the matter further. Follow-through included continued conversations with the Russian workers that resulted in more productive interrogations and a clarification of the situation; also, instructions had come from higher echelons for the General to increase the investigative effort.

Although General von Gersdorff remained in charge of the military responsibility at Katyn Forest, Professor Buhtz of Breslau University had been put in charge of exhumations with express instructions to investigate any infringements of the Hague Convention. When the exhumations began in March, 1943, the military field police had been solely responsible for security duty, but later a company of Polish volunteers took up guard duty near the graves. The Polish Red Cross had been requested to send delegations to supervise and arrange for identification of victims, safekeeping of personal possessions, etc.; also, the International Red Cross had been advised of the situation. Exhumations continued until June, 1943; then were stopped. Due to the increase in summer temperatures, the military physicians had become concerned about the strong odor and stench as well as the health of the men engaged in the work.

While the graves were being opened, numerous visiting delegations had been received. The Ministry of Propaganda had sent many representatives of their own in addition to the delegations of journalists and experts of judicial medicine. General von Gersdorff had welcomed and spoke to many visitors, including members of the International Medical Commission with whom he had dined. Also, he had conversed with American, British, and Polish prisoners of war; the Archdeacon of Krakow, Dr. Yuzinski; and a great number of German delegations from various troop units and the homeland. He described the first grave as

> . . . approximately ten meters long and twenty meters wide and very deep. In this grave the dead bodies were stacked twelve layers on top of each other. Then later, a second grave was opened which was not as large as the first one, but in this grave all the dead bodies were fettered. They had their hands tied up. It may be assumed that in that case these Polish prisoners had perhaps tried to resist at the last moment.[17]

The witness testified that the hands of the victims had been tied behind their backs; that "sacks or tunics" had been pulled over their heads; and that, as shown to him by Dr. Buhtz, some had sawdust in their mouths.[18] He explained about the bullet holes through the skull; how one bullet hole marked the entry at the base of the skull, and how another hole marked the exit of the bullet in the forehead between the hairline and the eyebrow. Also, he stated that most of the bodies he saw had an "amulet," a "scapular," a "crucifix," or "little crosses" around their necks and under their underwear.

Then the witness spent some time describing the documents found on the cadavers; such as diaries, notebooks, letters and postcards from relatives and friends, photographs, large amounts of paper bank notes (out of circulation and without value), etc. He cited some entries in the diaries—like "destination unknown?" "Were they returning to their homeland?"—and reported that the dates on the various documents included March and April, 1940; then ceased. Also, he explained that the documents had been treated chemically because of being soaked in body fluids, and stated that many of the documents had been displayed on the porch of the building where the military field police had been billeted. He emphasized that first the bodies had been identified and numbered; then entries had been made concerning the contents of what had been found on each body, and this documentation had been packed into chests and sent away.

At the dinner which the Central Army Group had for the members of the International Medical Commission, General von Gersdorff had been seated between Dr. Naville, the Swiss pathologist, and Dr. Markov of Bulgaria. Both men were members of the commission and, in the words of Dr. Naville, had commented they were "absolutely convinced that only the Russians could have committed this crime."[19] The General reminded the Select Committee that Dr. Markov later recanted his testimony after his country had been overrun and occupied by the Russians, and he personally had been accused of crimes against the state. These accusations had been dropped after Dr. Markov had appeared at Nuremberg as a witness for the Russians, and had charged in his testimony that the Germans had forcibly included him in the commission. General von Gersdorff then responded to this charge by commenting that from the time the members of the International Medical Commission had reached Smolensk, they had been given the liberty to move about and investigate what they liked, to talk to whomever they wanted, and to engage in activities of their own choosing; in fact, he said he had issued orders that the free movement of these gentlemen should be safeguarded.

In response to one last question from the committee concerning the Russian report, General von Gersdorff concluded:

> It appears to me quite impossible that, as from the date of the German occupation of that territory, or of that area, a crime of such magnitude could have been committed in the immediate vicinity of the main supply road of the army group, and, likewise in the vicinity of the army group proper. This highway carried an extremely heavy supply traffic day and night. And even in the case of SS troops or some other unit carrying out such an action, it would at all events have to come to our knowledge.
>
> Apart from the previously stated facts, the documents recovered from the bodies, the expert advice given by the physicians is so convincing that there should not be any doubt as to who committed the crime.[20]

The eighth witness was one of the members of the small security unit of Field Police Secretary Voss. Albert Pfeiffer[21] had been a Russian interpreter

154

who had been present at the Katyn Forest exhumations "from the very first day," which had been estimated to be about "the middle of March, 1943," when "the first spade entered the ground," "to the end of exhumations," which occurred approximately in the beginning of June, 1943."[22] He testified that the first grave had been found in a forest clearing under a mound of dirt piled up approximately to a height of three feet that had become overgrown with heather, bushes, scrub-growth and small fir trees about three and one-half feet tall; all of which had to be removed before digging commenced. The first bodies had been found after digging had reached a depth of two and one-half meters (about eight feet or one foot less than three yards) from the top of the mound.

The job of the witness had been not only to clear the pockets of the clothes on the bodies, to remove the items found therein, and to store these items in a large numbered envelope for record purposes; but also to identify the deceased from the documents found. The best source of identification had been the pay books which each victim carried, and literally thousands of paybooks had been found. The witness told of the various delegations that came, some of whom identified personnel in photographs. He also told of the reburial site where "it was decided for reasons of piety, to make several graves"[23] instead of one huge grave; therefore, seven large graves had been prepared. Ground elevations and square plats with a cross marking on the earth itself identified the locations; as did the wooden crosses which had been placed at each of the seven gravesites. After the Germans had supervised the exhumation of the bodies, and the Germans and Poles had processed the identification and documentation records, then the Polish Red Cross supervised the reburial of the bodies. In addition, two individual graves each with a wooden cross had been prepared for the two Polish Generals who had been exhumed. The reburial site had been in the direction of the Katyn-Smolensk highway some one hundred meters from the original place where the graves had been found. The witness told of the chests of documents as well as the hearsay evidence about the boxes being taken to Krakow so the personal memorabilia could be distributed to the next-of-kin, or relatives, of the murdered men. He confirmed that the documents had been in good condition; also, that no document, diary, letter, or newspaper had included a date after April, 1940.

In response to the statement in the Russian report that the Germans had murdered 500 Russians after using them to dig the graves in which the Poles had been buried, the witness said that no Russian prisoners had been shot, that the total number of workers had been thirty peasants, and that the Russian report was "nonsense."

In a brief but complementary presentation the ninth witness, Paul Vogelpoth,[24] an editor of a paper in Mittag, Duesseldorf, identified himself as a member of German Propaganda Unit W Stationed on the Russian front at Smolensk, starting in February, 1942, and extending through the Katyn period. He stated he had first heard about the killings in March, 1943. He had been assigned the special duty of security arrangements for visitors in the area of the graves, including groups of 150 to 200 people selected from the large number of soldiers and civilians who would come to the forest to see the graves. Although most delegations had been managed by Lieutenants Slovenczyk and Voss who served as their guides, Lieutenant Vogelpoth had handled the other visitors who came to the grave site, including the delegations of journalists and authors. A part of the job of all three guides had been to answer questions and provide explanations. Paul Vogelpoth reported that Berlin had asked for an estimate of how many Polish prisoners of war were buried at Katyn Forest. Since his Propaganda Unit W had heard from the Poles that almost 13,000 Polish officers were missing, and since Unit W did not know the victims at Katyn had been from Kozielsk only, the unit incorrectly assumed all victims had been massacred at Katyn and guessed a total of 11,000 victims. This number was forwarded to Berlin, who used the number of 10,000 officers in the estimate circulated on the initial broadcast about Katyn on April 13, 1943. The witness testified that Propaganda Unit W did not know at that time there had been two other camps (Ostashkov and Starobliesk) whose prisoners of war were involved too; but later they realized their error when they learned the prisoners from the other two camps had not been murdered at Katyn. Lieutenant Vogelpoth commented that the fact remained the Polish POWs at Ostashkov and Starobliesk, both military and civilian, had not been accounted for to date; also, that it was believed there had been many more Polish officers murdered at Katyn than the 4,143 actually exhumed and examined for identification because Grave Number 8, the one opened and closed immediately about June 1 and 2, 1943, might have included many more bodies than estimated. The closure had been ordered by the health and sanitation authorities who feared an epidemic and did not want to take that risk.[25] The witness emphasized that interrogations of the local population brought a steady response of "10,000 Poles" as the estimate of how many POWs had detrained at Gniezdovo and embarked aboard the lorries for the journey to Katyn beginning in April, 1940.

Dr. Paul R. Sweet,[26] the head of the American team in England working on the war documents project, was the tenth witness. Dr. Sweet testified that the German documents captured by the American military forces under the command of the Supreme Commander, Allied Expeditionary Forces, General Dwight D. Eisenhower, had been turned over to the British and American governments for joint custody, and that a project had been initiated to publish a series of documents that would report the overall record of German foreign policy.

Dr. Sweet introduced approximately twenty documents primarily concerned with the exchange of messages and negotiations between all the involved governments. Specifically introduced were documents that concerned the German involvement with the International Red Cross and other relevant matters. In a message on April 13, 1943, Dr. Goebbels telephoned from the Ministry of Propaganda to ask the Foreign Ministry to invite the International Red Cross to send a commission to witness the exhumations of the bodies of Polish officers found in the mass graves in the Smolensk region. Delegations of Polish scientists, physicians, artists, and industrialists as well as the Polish Red Cross had already been invited. Dr. Goebbels told the Foreign Ministry, "The Fuehrer has now given the order that the affair should be given the widest possible use and publicity, with every means available."

Dr. Sweet presented message transmissions from the German Red Cross to the International Red Cross and the responses; plus similar communications from the Polish Government in Exile. He reported that trails of the summaries had been recorded and that one of the first reports of April 11, 1943, had indicated 160 bodies had been exhumed and identified, including the bodies of two Polish Generals (Smorawinski and Bohaterwicz). It had been estimated that in the largest grave 2,000 to 3,000 bodies would be found, for it was likely 250 cadavers would be found in a single row stacked in twelve layers one on top of the other ($12 \times 20 = 240$, or approximately 250).

The witness presented a letter from the Ministry of Propaganda to the Foreign Ministry, dated April 15, 1943, as a classic example of how important data could be reported in a succinct two-page summary, along with enclosures of photographs and interrogation reports. (See Appendix 4.) These interrogation reports proved how important the results of knowledge can be when gathered from people near the scene. Local inhabitants confirmed that Katyn Forest (the Kosigorie [sometimes Kosi-gory] portion) had been used as an execution location for the secret police as early as 1918. They told about how in 1931 the Kosigorie portion of the forest had been fenced in, after which the natives could no longer walk around and gather mushrooms; and they remembered the dacha being built in 1934. The interrogation reports included one touching story about a man who in 1921 had been feeding his horses when an open truck loaded with ten to fifteen men guarded by the secret police passed by enroute to Kosigorie. Two men aboard the truck called out, "Goodby, Uncle!" The man recognized them as his nephews. Later he had been informed by their parents the two were shot in Kosigorie because they were "anticommunistically inclined."[27]

The witness told some of the complications and intrigue involved in the developments rotating around the invitations to attend the International Red Cross meeting in Geneva. The invitation recipients had become convinced the Russians were using stalling tactics. The International Red Cross had responded to the German Red Cross and the Polish Government in Exile by stating that in accordance with the memorandum of September 12, 1939, the IRC could not participate in an identification process unless all interested parties requested it to do so. The key to this mandate had been that in suspected violations of international law the International Red Cross would never initiate an inquiry unless it had been requested to do so by all parties in the conflict. Dr. Sweet testified that the Soviet government not only did not participate but used the Polish Government in Exile's request-response to the International Red Cross as a breech of confidence of the "Allies"; then forthwith broke off diplomatic relations with them. From all the strategies available, Stalin had made the choice to follow this course of action.

Dr. Sweet also included with his testimony a copy of the Protocol of the International Medical Commission. (See Appendix 5.)

In a brief testimony, the eleventh witness, Hans Bless,[28] had been to the Katyn exhumations. He had been on the front lines and had been sent to Katyn about March 20, 1943, to participate in viewing the bodies of the POWs. While there, he had talked to an aged Russian civilian who repeated the stories of the Polish officers being brought to Katyn by railroad and lorry in March and April, 1940. The witness stated he personally saw the victims with their hands tied behind their backs and further testified a German who spoke Polish had read to them from a diary lying on the body of a Polish officer. The diary entries had been very thorough; reporting the officer's capture, his imprisonment, the camp closing, and how the inmates had been taken away. The last entry was made on April 20, 1940; ironically Adolf Hitler's birthday. Mr. Bless reported he had this jocular thought at the time of the reading; "Well, as a reward from the Russians to Adolf Hitler for having given them a portion of Poland, the Russians killed those officers."[29]

One of the signers of the Protocol of the International Medical Commission was the twelfth witness. Dr. Helge Tramsen's[30] testimony had been valued by the Select Committee, for this witness was a practicing physician in Copenhagen, a lecturer at the university and the high school of physical training, a surgeon and commander in the Danish Navy and for four years had worked at the University Institute of Medico-Legal Medicine where he conducted daily post-mortems on victims of murder and sudden death by unnatural causes.

Dr. Tramsen had become involved with the Katyn massacre on April 22, 1943, when the Danish Foreign Office had invited him to be a member of a committee, consisting of scientists and medico-legal specialists who were to go to Katyn and investigate the tombs and conduct post-mortems on the cadavers there. He had been told by the Copenhagen foreign affairs secretary that the invitation had been extended directly from the Reichsgesundheitsfuehrer, Dr. Conti, in Berlin. On April 27, 1943, by special plane, Dr. Tramsen had been flown to Berlin. There he had been introduced by Dr. Zietz from the Reichsgesundheitsamt to the other members of the medical-scientific committee: eleven other recognized pathologists with international reputations. The group had selected Dr. Orsos as chairman, not only because of his eminence as a specialist but also because he spoke Russian fluently, having been a Russian prisoner of war for four years during World War I. The next morning, April 28, 1943, the group had taken off from Templehof in a German military airplane, had landed midway at Warsaw, and finally landed at Smolensk about six in the evening; a sixteen-hundred-mile flight. In Berlin the group had met Professor Mueller-Hesse, the chief from the University Institute of Forensic Medicine in Berlin and his assistant, Dr. Huber. They had been met by Dr. Buhtz at Smolensk. Dr. Buhtz, as director of the expedition and all examinations while the commission was at Smolensk and Katyn had been considered by all to be their medical leader.

By 10:00 AM the next morning, the entire group had arrived at Katyn Forest. Dr. Tramsen testified he observed first the sparseness of fir tree in the woods; then noticed the terrible smell of decay. The next panorama to confront him had been the lane where dead bodies already "extracted from the tombs: had been laid out in a long line of rows. These exhumed Poles (twenty rows of fifteen bodies in each row) were still fully clothed in typical dress uniforms, including boots in rather good condition. Seven "tombs" of various depths situated on a sloping hill could be seen in the immediate area, and each one could be entered for examination by the members of the commission. The witness stated that members of the commission were using similar descriptive terms or terms having similar meanings; such as referring to the number of rows of bodies from top to bottom as "levels," or "layers," or "tiers," or "sheets." The commission's final estimate was that no less than 2,500 Polish officers had been buried in the largest or "L-shaped" grave, and that the numbers buried in the small graves would vary according to the size of each.

With Dr. Buhtz's guidance, the commission selected a dead body, to be extracted from its place in the grave and placed on one the numerous wooden autopsy tables. The commission gathered around as Dr. Buhtz went through the process of identifying the body by clearing out the uniform jacket pockets (often with scissors) which contained the personal papers and letters of the deceased.

By 9:15 AM on April 30, 1943, the commission members had arrived at Katyn to continue investigating the graves and observing and conducting post-mortem autopsies. Since all the members of the commission were not specialists in forensic medicine, the group decided that only the nine with forensic medical specialist training would conduct post-mortems. The Germans had provided typists, interpreters, secretaries; also, surgical instruments, rubber gloves, rubber aprons, etc. By 10:00 AM Dr. Tramsen testified had had entered one of the graves to choose a body to be placed on a table for the identification examination. The body was dressed in a Polish uniform and was wearing a cap affixed with a badge that had the Polish eagle on it. Also, the witness had found on the body of the deceased his military pass with his address which provided positive identification. Other effects found with the body included personal papers;

newspapers; and a pocketbook containing professional cards indicating the soldier had been a chemist, an envelope containing Russian and Polish stamps indicating he could have been a stamp collector, and Polish bank notes (currency) and coins. Dr. Tramsen stated he had taken possession of these personal effects and had turned them over to the Select Committee to photograph and include "in the record." Important, too, had been documents found on other bodies being examined by other pathologists of the commission and turned over to Dr. Tramsen. Two of these documents had dates on them: one, a Polish poem signed in Kozielsk had been dated April 26, 1940; the other, a roster of officers and marked Kozielsk had been dated April 12, 1940. This roster listed the names of thirty officers along with their birthdays and military ranks.

Dr. Tramsen testified that as he prepared to do the post-mortem he noted the means of restraint and the kinds of clothing on the cadaver he had selected. The body had been dead for

> . . . quite a long while, a long time, with underclothes compact with the skin. But the uniform was the proper size and all buttoned up, very warmly dressed, with two kinds of underwear and a thick wooly scarf. The boots were in good condition. The hands were tied behind the back with a thick white rope which had cut through the skin, nearly to the bone, which probably occurred after death. Of 800 bodies exhumed, only a few were not tied with the hands behind them.[31]

The witness stated he had seen several victims who had been bound with wire and one with a strip of leather, probably a belt. Most of the overcoats had been military—a few civilian—styles and made of very thick material. All of the bodies had been wearing winter clothes; and some wore fur skins between garments.

Concerning the condition of the body he had chosen to post-mortem, Dr. Tramsen reported,

> The state of the body itself was in an extraordinary kind of decay. I would call it more or less mummified, and I might say that this has been caused by the immense pressure of the weight of hundreds of dead bodies and the tons of heavy sand over them.[32]

In regard to the skull of the victim, Dr. Tramsen showed a photograph to the Select Committee that illustrated his medical findings which he stated in a layman's terms; however, upon request he would also verbalize in his pathologist's medical language. He said his finding

> . . . shows the skull of a Polish officer. The soft tissue from the neck has been removed, and it is clearly to be seen in the picture that a pistol-shot

wound in the occipital bone has entered the skull in this way. You can see that because the bones of the skull consist of an outer and an inner layer, between which you see, in the bone, small parts, and what is called cells. And a shot that enters the bones like that will make an absolutely round hole on the outside and a greater hole on the inside of the bone, and we have seen that in practically all of the skulls that were examined by cutting the bone through.[33]

Regarding the execution weapon being held at point-black range, he explained,

In the soft tissue, in this area we always found a lot of marking of black powder, which has more or less been pushed into the skin because the shot had been fired with the muzzle straight touching the skin and pointed forward, upwards, with the exit of the gunshot wound near the right or left temple (level) at the fore (front) of the head (indicating).[34]

And, about the internal impact of the bullet, he stated,

The direction of the bullet in that skull was such as it couldn't possibly have avoided a lesion, a serious lesion, of the bottom of the brain and the so called medulla oblongata, the nerve center of respiration, with an absolutely deadly effect.[35]

A body of a dead woman in a single, old Russian grave had been found further into the woods and away from the Polish POW graves. She had been dead much longer than the Polish officers. Her head had been covered with a "sort of sacking," her hands had been tied behind her back, and the string which bound her head extended down to the bound hands. Dr. Tramsen had been present when this body had been exhumed. The significance of finding this body, in addition to its bound hands and hood, related to its cause of death: the bullet that had entered at the rear of the skull and exited at the front of the head had been "exactly similar" to those that caused the deaths of the Polish officers.

Concerning the caliber of the bullet used in each execution-style killing, Dr. Tramsen reported that measurements of the bullet entry had been made by the commission members and had been as "we put it in the protocol, below eight millimeters"[36]; meaning the estimated caliber of 7.65 millimeters which had surfaced throughout the entire investigation had been entirely credible. The Germans also told the commission that the ammunition, which could be traced from the numerous casings found in the graves, had been of German manufacture. They further stated that much of this type of ammunition for pistols and other weapons had been delivered to Russia before the war.

The bayonet wounds examined by the commission had been typically recognizable wounds, often in the back and "of a special square kind." Obviously it could have been difficult to judge whether the wound marks were triangular or square in shape; however, Dr. Tramsen testified he had identified one wound that had been so distinct, he had been positive about its square (+) shape.

In order to establish the time of death, some of the skulls of the Katyn victims had been taken to Smolensk after the post-mortems had been conducted. Professor Orsos, of Budapest, a specialist in conducting skull post-mortems to determine a time of death, had developed a new technique for examining the inside of a skull interred for at least two years. The method had been reported in forensic medical journals but some of the committee members had not yet practiced it.

> If the skull is left in the ground for a certain time, at least for two years, the pulp of the brain will sort of lay down in a compact mass at the lowest part of the skull, and if you cut the skull through, with the lowest part still lying low, then you will cut through this pulp of the brain lying at the bottom of the skull and notice certain layers of grayish and yellowish stripes formed by the various chemicals isolated in the brain, the liquids and phosphor acids and salts of various kinds, lying down in a special layer that you can notice. But, as Professor Orsos stated, this will not take place unless the skull has been lying in the same position for at least two years, and we did notice that symptom in several of the skulls that were cut through.[37]

Dr. Tramsen advised the committee that other terms such as "calcium type of formation," "claylike state," or "heavily compressed clay" could have been applied to this condition; then he stated members of the commission had witnessed such masses.

Absolutely no insects had been found on the cadavers. Dr. Tramsen indicated that the commission had been looking for any evidence of insects, eggs, mites, or ants; but nothing had been found and the members had concluded that the bodies had been buried during an insect-free time of the year, such as the cold weather of wintertime. Too, this conclusion had been compatible with the obvious lack of body decay; especially in the Smolensk area where Russian winters are very cold and summers very hot.

Dr. Tramsen repeated the quote of the German forestar, von Herff, regarding his estimate that the small fir trees had been transplanted about three years earlier. He indicated this fact could have been articulated microscopically by cuts showing the growth of the rings of the trees which had a point of arrest.

In summary, Dr. Tramsen emphasized these points:
1. A total of seven large graves filled with Polish officers had been wit-

nessed while the commission had been at Katyn; not counting the older Russian graves.

2. Regarding the crucial issue of date of death, the last date on a Russian newspaper had been April 20, 1940, and the last date entered in a diary had been April 21, 1940.

3. Professor Orsos talked to the civilians since he spoke Russian. He had asked the questions of the peasants and received their answers concerning the trains coming into Gniezdovo in the spring of 1940 and the detraining of Polish prisoners of war. These men had been promptly transported to the Katyn woods from which shooting had been heard in the early morning hours, and where Russian guards had patrolled the area so no civilians could come near the woods.

The testimony of Dr. Tramsen of Denmark was followed and complemented by the testimony of Dr. Wilhelm Zietz,[38] the thirteenth witness, who was the Deputy Chief of the Reich Public Health Service and Reich Physicians Chamber with the Foreign Office, and whose immediate superior was Dr. Conti. When Dr. Zietz heard Dr. Goebbels' first announcement of the discovery of a massacre beyond description at Katyn, he learned also that his old friend, Dr. Buhtz, had been placed in charge of exhumations. He telephoned Dr. Buhtz, in Smolensk, and learned first hand of the extreme atrocities that had been discovered in connection with the gruesome execution of Polish officers. Dr. Zietz had asked if it would be desirable to dispatch a commission of international scientists to the scene of the crimes to corroborate the findings, and Dr. Buhtz supported the offer. Dr. Buhtz concluded their conversation with the opinion that the Russians had committed the murders.

Although Dr. Zietz was not a medical doctor, he proceeded to prepare a plan approved in its entirety by Dr. Conti; likewise, by the Foreign Office prior to being approved by Foreign Minister Ribbentrop. To avoid a possible stigma of political significance as the Reich health leader he was invited to host the delegation, and the Foreign Office extended invitations to participate to all friendly nations, neutral nations, and allies of Germany.

Since Dr. Zietz did not want to duplicate Dr. Tramsen's medical testimony, he concentrated his testimony on the goals and responsibilities of being the host.

The witness testified that thirteen countries had been represented and that the flight of commission members to Smolensk took place on April 28, 1943. Twelve of the members had assumed full authority to act; the thirteenth member, a psychologist, had come as an observer from the French Vichy government. Dr. Zietz served as the personal host who greeted the visitors as they arrived at Berlin's Adlon Hotel. After all were present, the arrivals had dined and visited together. Also, a number of Germany's physicians had made themselves available for visits with the commission members; such as Dr. Mueller-Hesse, Berlin's most prominent doctor of forensic medicine who subsequently went to Katyn with a team of German physicians that concurred with the commission's conclusions.

After arriving at Smolensk, the visitors had met Dr. Holm, the General Surgeon of the Central Army group, with whom they dined that evening. He promised them every freedom during their inspection, plus the full support and cooperation of everyone at Katyn. The primary objective of Doctors Holm and Buhtz had been for each member of the commission to get an independent impression of this Katyn atrocity, and Dr. Zietz testified this intention remained unaltered throughout the stay of the International Medical Commission. He participated with the team as its host during the entire trip; e. g. he visited the display of diaries, pocketbooks, tobacco pouches, etc. contained in glass showcases, and noted every document had been made available for examination by the commission members. Also, he observed the visitors had made extensive trips to the graves; in fact, to the entire woods and its surrounding areas. Facilitating details had been meticulously organized; e. g. the wooden tables upon which the autopsies had been conducted were always ready, and typewriters on small tables were conveniently situated for preparation of the autopsy reports. Moreover, if some members of the commission wanted to work in pairs, they did; if one wanted to work alone, he did. There to assist the members of the commission were people from the Institute of Forensic Medicine, medics, non-coms, and Polish and Russian laborers to carry the cadavers.

In his testimony, Dr. Zietz brought up the preparation of the protocol. He emphasized this issue had not been brought up by "the German side"; it had been a concern of the commission who had defined Dr. Buhtz's role as a person who served as charge d'affaires of negotiations; not as a person responsible for input in the commission's protocol content. The spokesman for the committee, its chairman Professor Orsos, had been primarily responsible for this feat in negotiation. The members of the group agreed with no discrepancies of opinion upon the contents of the protocol; the discussion was concerned more with the problem of form and the extent of the statement to be made. The twelve acting participants voluntarily discussed the statement and voluntarily signed the protocol. Dr. Zietz pointed out that no member debated before signing the document, or refused to sign it, or said his government had not authorized him to sign it, etc.; in fact, each member had signed with alacrity. The French representative, a psychologist, who announced from the very beginning that he had been sent as an observer only and not as a qualified pathologist, did not sign nor had it been expected that he should sign.

The Protocol of the International Medical Commission had been delivered to Dr. Conti, the day the group returned to Berlin. Dr. Zietz testified Dr. Conti had asked him to deliver a copy to the Foreign Office, which he had done.

By the following morning photostatic copies had been made, including signatures, and Dr. Zietz delivered a copy to each member of the commission. The group went to the Institute of Forensic Medicine in Berlin, bought textbooks, and visited other people and places; then each departed individually for his own country.

Dr. Zietz told the Select Committee that when the Foreign Office had started what was called the White Book of the Katyn incident, he had cooperated and assisted by providing photographs and documents, including the medical report of Dr. Buhtz. After the book had been completed, he had sent a copy to each member of the International Medical Commission and had received friendly letters of gratitude from each in return.

Concerning non-participants the witness stated Portugal had been invited but had not replied; Spain had been invited but had not wished to participate; Sweden had been invited but its participant had been involved in an automobile accident just before he was scheduled to depart from Stockholm and had been in a plaster cast for an entire year.

Dr. Zietz reminded the Select Committee that Dr. Markov, the Bulgarian, and Dr. Hajek, the Czechoslovakian, both members of the commission, had later recanted their opinions and signatures and claimed the Germans had forced them to sign the protocol. This same question had been put to Dr. Tramsen earlier, who had responded by saying those members had signed the document and at that time had said they agreed with its content. Dr. Zietz responded in much the same vernacular; then further commented on the impeccable character of both Dr. Markov and Dr. Hajek and added that both resided in countries occupied by the U.S.S.R. as a "protectorate." As eyewitnesses both "had occasion to see at Katyn how such things were done."[39]

The fourteenth witness, Fritz von Herff,[40] was a skilled forester serving with the German armed forces. He had been providing wood for troops billeted around Smolensk; hence his testimony confirmed the fact that the small fir tree saplings, planted over the Katyn gravesite probably would be five years old and would have been transplanted in 1940, for he had observed them under a microscope in 1943. He stated a fir tree added a ring each year; however, when a tree had been transplanted, as had probably occurred at Katyn Forest, the tree's growth would have been stunted while adjusting to the new soil. The witness said obviously the growth of the small fir trees examined at Katyn had been stunted.

The Select Committee reconvened at 10:00 AM on April 24, 1952. The fifteenth witness, Wladyslaw Kawecki,[41] a second lieutenant in the Polish army, and a journalist before the war, had been the first to testify. On April 9, 1943, he had been summoned by the Press Chief of the Governor General in Krakow who told him of the mass graves being found at Katyn. As yet, no public announcement had been made. Mr. Kawecki said he left the next day,

April 10, 1943, on a plane that went from Krakow to Warsaw, picked up additional Polish passengers there, then went to Smolensk where they spent the night. By 9:30 AM, April 11, 1943, this Polish group had arrived at Katyn where they had been introduced to a group of high ranking German officers by their guide, Lieutenant Slovenczyk. The first grave they visited was the largest grave; "a horrible sight." Also, they had been shown exhumed bodies, including the mortal remains of General Smornawinski and General Bohaterewicz, both of whom could be recognized by their uniforms and the medals they were wearing. General Bohaterewicz was wearing a fur coat suggesting he had been executed in the winter or early spring months.

The witness testified the visiting group had been given complete freedom and permission to select bodies to be exhumed, to search for records, and to try to determine how the victims had died—which obviously had been a bullet shot into the back of the head that came out the front of the head. By mingling with the Russian workers, the visitors tried to determine when these Polish officers had been executed; and they were told it had been March to May, 1940. One of the Russians Mr. Kawecki spoke with was Kisselev, whom he addressed in his own language—Russian. The old peasant spoke willingly and stated no Germans had been nearby during the time-frame mentioned. Kisselev recounted the story told to him by his friends in Gniezdovo of unknown soldiers, not Russians, who had been transferred by train to Gniezdovo and by truck to Katyn; then never seen to return. Another native told the witness of seeing the NKVD vans, the "black ravens," bringing the soldiers into Katyn Forest.

Mr. Kowecki, who returned the next day with his data to Poland, recalled it had been an unnerving experience. He had compiled a list of those identified; approximately fifty positive identifications of the first seventy bodies exhumed. His newspaper published the list which brought an immediate response from the readers who suspected that their family members might also be buried at Katyn since the Germans said 10,000 bodies might be there.

Dr. Adam Szebesta of the Polish Red Cross had been another visitor who wanted a list of the deceased because the names were being telephoned back in such a roundabout connection: via Minsk to Wilno, to Koenigsberg, to Danzig, and finally to Krakow. Mr. Kawecki stated he had made a second trip to Katyn in mid-May, 1943, as a substitute for Dr. Moliszewski who had broken a leg prior to departure. This second assignment had been to compile a complete list of POWs; hence he remained at Katyn until the end of May, 1943, in his attempt to prepare such a list. While there he witnessed documents, newspapers, diaries, letters, etc., and he had become convinced the Russians had been responsible for the murders. He had worked closely with Dr. Szebesta, head of the Polish Red Cross, and both agreed the Russians had committed the crimes; in fact, the witness stated that in 1942 both he and Dr. Szebesta had been arrested by the Gestapo and jailed for some months in Krakow. Mr. Kawecki then testified he had been told Dr. Szebesta, through a press release dated March 28, 1952, from East Germany, had been quoted as saying he had changed his opinion. According to the testimony of Mr. Kawecki, this change of opinion had been "unfortunate" because he, too, had been approached in Rome in May, 1947, by an officer of the Warsaw Government in Poland who offered a bribe if he would sign a statement denouncing his position of 1943. He not only refused the money (a pile of American $20 bills) but also refused to sign the statement which had been prepared for him. He left Rome in 1948 and since then had been living in Wuerzburg, Germany.

The sixteenth witness to be heard had been Erwin Allgaver.[42] He had served in the Fifth Company of the Eighth Railroad Engineer Regiment who used the road about August 1 or 2, 1941, that passed Katyn to Smolensk. His job had been to find a billet in which their unit could be quartered. When nothing could be found in or near Smolensk, they retraced their steps back toward Katyn and observed a fence and a narrow road, which led them to investigate the area. They found the Dnieper Castle and remained there with their unit about three weeks. In his opinion, they had been the first German troops to occupy the building. They saw no Polish POWs in the area, but they did hear stories of "people being shot there." They knew nothing of the graves of Katyn. If the Germans had shot anyone, the people who lived in the forest area would have known it. Most of the unit was ill with dysentery; also, there had been an "incredible number of insects" and "an awful lot of flies." As a result, the company moved out quickly.

Two witnesses testified concerning the fourteen boxes of Polish POW's personal possessions that had been moved from the mass gravesite to Krakow. One, the seventeenth, was Karl Herrmann,[43] a member of the security forces in 1943–1945 in Krakow. The witness testified the boxes had actually left Dresden; then he had been ordered to retrieve them. Finally, the fourteen boxes had made the trip on the last train from Krakow to Dresden, had been unloaded safely and stored on the station platform, and later had been moved by truck to Radebeul, a suburb of Dresden; which had been as far as they went. The date of arrival had been sometime in February, 1945. Each box had been marked for the Reich Security Office in Berlin at the time it had been moved to Radebeul.

The eighteenth witness, Dr. Werner Beck,[44] then picked up the story of the fourteen boxes. Dr. Beck had served with the German Ministry of the Interior, and at the time of the hearings was serving in Krakow, Poland, as Director of the State Institute for Forensic Medicine. Dr. Beck's chief at Breslau years earlier had been Dr. Buhtz. Dr. Beck had cooperated with the Polish Red Cross by providing people from the institute to go to Katyn to assist with exhumations. He testified the personal possessions of the Polish POWs had totaled fourteen locked boxes (some estimates had indicated sixteen) for which he had the keys. He said that even though the Germans had ordered the documents destroyed, the order had not been obeyed.[45] The chemical tests had been rendered in an attempt to read the documents and to make photostatic copies; but it had not been possible to distribute the documents to the next-of-kin because of the stench—the odor had been unbearable.

Permission had been granted to move the fourteen boxes to Breslau, and there they had been stored in a special room at the University of Breslau (Anatomical Institute). In January, 1945, the boxes had been moved to Dresden; then finally to a suburb of Dresden—Radebeul, where they had been stored in a railway forwarding depot.

Dr. Beck testified he had been trying to get the boxes to the International Red Cross in Prague. Because he had found no vehicles available, he had traveled to Prague alone. On his return he had made another attempt to retrieve the boxes. He said he got as far as Pilsen early in May, 1945. There the United States armed forces had given him a traveling pass to Dresden; however, the Russians occupied Dresden, so he returned to the United States zone of Bavaria in June, 1945. In the meantime, he had given the order to the railroad agent to burn the boxes if the Russians came for them. He had hoped the Americans would occupy Dresden. He had been aware that his every move and destination had been known to the Russian secret police who had been right behind him. Later, an informant had told him the boxes had been burned.

Dr. Beck further testified that his family had been interrogated and that his mother had been incarcerated in jail for six months. The railway agent had been deported by the "Russian police in those gray uniforms, with green bands around the caps; Russian secret police,"[46] and never heard from again.

Finally, in his testimony Dr. Beck indicated his laboratory studies had proved the rope or cord used to tie the victims at Katyn had been of Russian hemp and manufacture.

On Friday, April 25, 1952, the Select Committee met for its last day in Frankfurt, Germany. The nineteenth witness had been Christer Jaederlunt,[47] a Swedish journalist for the newspaper STOCKHOLM TIDNINGEN, who had been sent to Berlin in 1928 and had been still there representing his newspaper in April, 1943. One of his articles, dated April 17, 1943, had been a follow-up on the Katyn affair. From the viewpoint of the London-Polish government the article had been asking the International Red Cross to investigate the deaths of the Polish officers. Too, the German government had submitted an investigation request to the International Red Cross; however, the investigation never occurred because the Russians had refused to participate.

Mr. Jaederlunt testified he had returned to Berlin from a trip to France where, with other journalists he had visited the so-called Atlantic defense wall. He had received a telephone call from the German Ministry of Propaganda asking if he could be prepared to fly to Smolensk, Russia, with a similar group of journalists the next day. The evening before the visit to Katyn this group of five or six international journalists had been told by the guide officer about the mass graves.

The descriptions of this witness had been identical to testimonies of other witnesses; the number of bodies exhumed, the slight extent of their decay, the type and preservation of their clothing, the description of the seven pits, the selection process of a body for post-mortem autopsy, the death wound in the back of the skull, the hands tied behind their backs with rope or wire, the head-coverings on some, the sawdust in some victims' mouths, the identification process, the confirmation that no documents had been dated after April, 1940, etc.

One significant aspect of the visit by Mr. Jaederlunt had been the fact that he had been included on the very first visit by journalists, which could have been as early as April 10, 1943; although the witness could not recall the exact date. He testified that very few exhumations had been completed, and that the visit had been prior to Dr. Goebbels' Berlin radio announcement of April 13, 1943. Some newspapers, including the STOCKHOLM TIDNINGEN, had withheld the article because of the uncertainty about what the Germans would do with the story.

Mr. Jaederlunt also reported that the Russian peasants talked not only about the executions in Katyn Forest but also told him that the Poles working for the German army had asked about other Poles and been told of the execution of Polish officers, that the shovel had been borrowed, that the gravesites had been found, that the bodies had already been exposed, that the birch crosses marked the graves, and that the rumors about the Katyn atrocity had been circulated. He commented that these rumors or stories reached the Germans, the interviews commenced and the investigations had been successful.

Once at Katyn, Mr. Jaederlunt had stayed for several days because there were no planes returning to Berlin. He said he had been given great freedom to roam around the forest, talk to the peasants, watch exhumations, and inspect the identification process being conducted on the cadavers. As his exchanges with the Russian inhabitants became more friendly and cordial, he had been told more and more stories of what had been witnessed three years earlier; such as stories about the trains arriving at Gniezdovo, the "black ravens" carrying the Polish POWs to Katyn and the men never being seen again. He observed that many of the Russians did not like the Nazis, but neither did they like the Bolsheviks. It had been evident to him in his conversations with the local population that they felt strongly about receiving warnings from the NKVD which forbade them the privilege of going near the forest; in fact many predicted that not only would the deceased Polish officers be found but also the Germans would "find a number of bodies executed before the war and in former times."[48]

Mr. Jaederlunt also testified that shortly after exhumations began the Germans had reported seeing for extended periods Russian observation aircraft circling over Katyn. Moreover, he noted that while the correspondents had been enroute to Katyn from Smolensk, they had become suspicious about the activities of Dr. Goebbels and his Ministry of Propaganda. The newsman thought they had been sent to learn about conditions in Russia; but if any bodies were witnessed, they thought those findings could be reported near the end of any article. The back-home newspapers and Swedish press, however, informed them to "Leave atrocity stories to Goebbels."

> But when I stood in front of the mass graves and when I realized what an atrocious crime had been perpetrated here, all my suspicions vanished and my own newspaper, at first, was not prepared to publish this report, but I insisted upon the report being published because I said: 'The world must know about this matter.'[49]

Mr. Rudi Kramer,[50] the twentieth witness, had been a lieutenant in Propaganda Unit W in Smolensk, who when asked if he had been there when the graves were discovered, answered that he had been there "from the beginning to the end."[51] Early in March, 1943, while working with the local population to engender pro-German feeling at Gniezdovo and Krasny Bor, he had been talking to a local peasant, who lived right on the railroad line near the forest. This old person had told him about the mass graves in the forest, of the crosses erected there, and how local people would take flowers on holidays to put on the ground at the gravesite; also, he confirmed the graves had come into existence three years earlier. Mr. Kramer had reported this information to the army group and had been told to continue his investigation; hence, he had gathered additional data about the railroad station, the forest, the timeframe, the small wooden crosses, the Dnieper Castle, etc.; all of which had been forwarded to his unit, and then to the army group that had given the order to commence digging.

This witness introduced the committee to the systematic method of determining the depth of the grave and the techniques of side-to-side digging. He provided vivid descriptions of the bodies; stating each POW had been clad in a uniform with a leather belt, and had been wearing leather boots. He said, too, that the hands of some victims had been tied behind their backs. Mr. Kramer spoke of Dr. Buhtz and said he had known him earlier in Breslau. He told how he learned so much from Dr. Buhtz, who had provided explanations and opportunities for him to see and learn what had been going on. Also, he corroborated the testimonies of others regarding visitors: "commissions"; medical experts; foreign journalists, writers, authors, artists; and western allied officers who were themselves prisoners of war in Germany. He remembered, too, visits by Polish clergymen, relatives, and next-of-kin of the murder victims; and he confirmed that the dates of entry in diaries, letters, and documents had ended between April 16 and 19, 1940. Forestry experts had told him the small trees had been placed over the gravesite three years earlier, and had been moved there from somewhere else.

As the weather warmed up, Mr. Kramer recalled the environment in which everyone worked had become more obnoxious, especially the smell; hence due to acceleration of temperatures exhumations ceased. The plan had been to start exhumations again in September; however, the Germans had started to withdraw by that time. Since Mr. Kramer's unit had been transferred from Smolensk to Italy, he would not have been there in the fall. In his opinion, Mr. Kramer testified that had the Germans kept digging, more bodies undoubtedly would have been found. He estimated that probably only one-third of the bodies buried in Katyn had been exhumed.

Mr. Matvey Skarginsky,[52] the twenty-first witness was a Russian who had left the Soviet Union after the Revolution. He had moved around but was living in Yugoslavia up to May, 1941, when the Germans occupied that country and he had been sent to Berlin by the Labor Office. While there he had been conscripted into the German army and assigned as an interpreter to the staff headquarters of the Ninth Army in Smolensk. He had interviewed and interrogated three railroad officials who had been in Smolensk under the Russians, and who had stayed on to work for the Germans; in fact, several other Russian officials had remained at the Gniezdovo station. The witness said the whole railroad story had been unfolded to him; how the trains had arrived without orders, how NKVD guards sat on the train where brakemen usually sat, how the timeframe could be identified as early in the year of 1940, how the Polish POWs had been moved to Gniezdovo, etc. The interrogations of the railroad officials were crucial to the German investigation because these men had seen the railroad prison cars being unloaded, and the prisoners being taken by truck or marched to Katyn Forest. Mr. Skarginsky also identified Boris Basilovsky as the "second in charge," or deputy mayor, in Smolensk, who shortly before the Germans had to evacuate the city of Smolensk, "crossed over to the Soviets."[53]

The former president, and currently a trustee of the Gustav Genschow Company, Mr. Karl Genschow,[54] was the twenty-second witness. This German company had manufactured the ammunition with which the Polish prisoners of war were murdered at Katyn Forest. The witness said the company maintained a principal office in Berlin, although the manufacturing plant was at Durlach near Karlsruhe. The factory had been in operation since early 1887, and the ammunition works had started in 1906. The witness affirmed that the company did manufacture pistol ammunition in the 7.65 caliber, and elaborated that the caliber was a very common type for pistol ammunition. Although the trademark had changed several times over the years Mr. Genschow said the shells of this caliber had carried the word "Geco" on the bottom of the shell, and under "Geco" the "7.65." He made two points: one, that this caliber could be used in various

171

kinds and makes of pistols because it was a standard type of cartridge; and two, that it was used internationally by various nations as well as police and armed forces. He testified the company had sold this ammunition to the Soviet Union until 1928; but after that year even though the quantities sold to them had become small, the company had continued to sell to the Soviet Union. Other eastern European countries—in particular the three Baltic States: Estonia, Latvia, and Lithuania—purchased considerably larger quantities than the shipments exported to the U.S.S.R. The witness testified that each of the Baltic States generally purchased 50,000 rounds per year; whereas the Soviets received only 2,000 to 3,000 rounds per year. The German High Command asked for specific quantities exported to the eastern European countries, the Baltic States, and the U.S.S.R.; a request which would require the Genschow Company to provide accurate statistics on all exports—including quantities shipped, in what years, and to which foreign countries.

Dr. Ferene Orsos,[55] the twenty-third witness, had been a member of the International Medical Commission that visited the Katyn gravesite near the end of April, 1943; in fact, he had served as spokesman for the commission. At that time he was a professor of judicial medicine; also, the director of the Department of Judicial Medicine at Budapest University, and of the Institute for Judicial Medicine serving all high courts in and near Budapest. He had been selected as a member of the commission by the Hungarian Foreign Office. Since Hungary was occupied by the Soviet Union, Dr. Orsos had been living in Mainz, Germany.

As a witness Dr. Orsos discussed the backgrounds of Dr. Conti, Dr. Buhtz, and Dr. Zietz relating to Katyn. He also, discussed Katyn Forest in terms of the protocol, assured the Select Committee that everything of a scientific nature had been inclined therein, and assured his presence as a witness had been simply to confirm the points of the protocol. He modestly stated that he had been the chairman, if the others said he was; but actually he had chaired the professional discussions only as a spokesman and as the oldest member.

The last, and twenty-fourth, witness to testify was another International Medical Commission member, Dr. Francis Naville[56] of Geneva, Switzerland, who had been asked to join the commission by the German Consulate in Geneva. Dr. Naville repeated that the Polish Red Cross and the German Red Cross had asked for an International Commission to be formed. When the Russian government disapproved the idea of an investigation, a private commission had been formed; however, he had met Dr. Conti, Dr. Buhtz, and Dr. Zietz only as a member of the commission. He identified Dr. Conti as the chief of the Reich Health Ministry, Dr. Buhtz as the general administrator in charge of all forensic affairs at Katyn, and Dr. Zietz as a philologist (an expert in the science of language), not as a physician, in charge of the commission's administrative affairs.

Dr. Naville testified the commission members had spent two days in the woods at Katyn where they saw 800 to 1,000 exhumed bodies and conducted about ten autopsies. He stated each member had selected a corpse from the untouched bodies in the pit—that is, the grave; and confirmed the Germans had not interfered but had cooperated in every way. He repeated the conversations with the Russian peasants, and stated the death shots in the back of the skull from a very near distance had caused the powder burns. His observations had been that the victims probably were in a standing position when killed, and that the executioners were experienced in the use of pistols within six inches (ten centimeters) of the skull. He testified that he had a positive identification of a piece of clothing that had a square hole in it caused by a four-edged bayonet. Too, he had witnessed victims with their hands tied behind their backs, and some with a cloth pulled over their heads and tied around their necks with a rope. He confirmed the cadavers had been dressed in winter-weight clothing: Polish uniforms; in fact, he had brought some buttons along to be used as exhibits. Again the report of the forester about the age of the trees was repeated; the small trees had been about five years old and had been transplanted some three years earlier. Also, Dr. Naville provided pictures and objects from the graves for the record; then stated no valuables—such as rings, watches, fountain pens—had been found on the bodies of the victims. He testified the latest date on any document which he witnessed had been April 22, 1940.

Dr. Naville discussed Dr. Orsos' theory of calcification in the inside of the back part of the skull, and affirmed that calcification was present in any corpse lying in the ground more than two years; then, he confirmed this condition had been witnessed in the bodies of the Katyn victims. Also, he discussed the two commission members, Dr. Markov of Bulgaria and Dr. Hajek of Czechoslovakia, who had signed the protocol but recanted later when their countries had been occupied by the Russians. Finally, Dr. Naville stated there had been no pressure exerted on the commission members by the Germans; which, he said, gave him cause to be "very much surprised, because it is a very well-known fact among the public since World War I, I have hated the Germans so much."[57]

The Select Committee left Frankfurt and met next in Naples, Italy, on Sunday, April 27, 1952, in order to provide an opportunity for the members to hear the testimony of Dr. Vincenzo Mario Palmieri,[58] the Italian representative to the International Medical Commission. Dr. Palmieri was a specialist in forensic medicine and criminology. His invitation to be a commission member had been extended from the Italian Ministry of Foreign Affairs on April 23, 1943. When he arrived in Berlin, he had met the entire commission at the Adlon Hotel.

Dr. Palmieri testified that at Katyn, there had been no pressures from the Germans and the graves had been open. He stated the primary question confronting the commission had been this one: When did these victims die? Was it April, 1940? or September, 1941? He likewise, referred to the studies of Professor Orsos regarding the calcification that takes place in a body interred for two years. Also, he commented about the trees that had been transplanted three years earlier; definitely a contributing factor in determining an answer to the major question. He told the committee he was aware of the non-medical findings—actually non-technical arguments—such as documents in the uniform pockets, personal letters, newspapers, diaries, etc.; none of which had dates later than April, 1940. He testified that his conclusion was the victims had been killed not later than April or May, 1940. Dr. Palmieri confirmed he had voluntarily signed the protocol. When asked about Dr. Markov of Bulgaria, and Dr. Hajek of Czechoslovakia, who signed the protocol but later said they had been forced or coerced to sign, Dr. Palmieri stated all the committee members had signed voluntarily; and if anyone had not wanted to sign the protocol, he could have refused.

Dr. Palmieri reported further that since signing the protocol, he had made many examinations of other cadavers; and that he had found in recent autopsies, as he had at Katyn, the pseudo-growth calcium deposits within the skull of a body buried two or more years. He, too, noted the cooperation of the Germans at Katyn, and how each member of the commission had been allowed to go voluntarily into the pit to select the body upon which to perform the autopsy:

> We went down in the graves and pointed out which one (body) we wanted to pull out since the heads were out—the grave was only three meters deep. It looked like a wine cellar with the necks of the bottles showing.[59]

With the completion of the testimony of Dr. Palmieri, the overseas hearings of the Select Committee had been completed. With the literal gold mine of witnesses and valuable testimony provided, the trips of the committee to London, Frankfurt, and Naples had been successful beyond expectation, which made it difficult to understand why the House Resolution to fund the overseas hearings had passed in Congress by only a nine-vote margin. If these same United States Representatives had the opportunity to reassess the immeasurable value of there hearings and could vote a second time, the funding bill should pass unanimously.

Chapter 12

SELECT COMMITTEE HEARINGS CONCLUDE: WASHINGTON

At the hearings in London (commencing April 16, 1952) the committee had agreed to accept materials that had been presented by many Polish witnesses, which at that time had been included as Exhibits 32 and 33. These reports had turned out to be a record of facts and documents compiled by the Polish Government in Exile in London. Because of their significant volume and attention to detail the committee had published them under separate cover; however, they would be included as a part of the Select Committee's testimony[1] under the title, *Polish White Paper on Katyn.*

The Select Committee reconvened in Washington, D.C., on Tuesday, June 3, 1952.[2] The chairman noted for the record that this was the sixth in a series of separate hearings, five of which already had been conducted. The overseas hearings from London (thirty-two witnesses) and Frankfurt (twenty-eight witnesses) had been completed. One trip had been made to Naples to accept the testimony of Dr. Palmieri, a member of the International Medical Commission who had been unable to go to Frankfurt. The chairman further indicated that although the responsibility of guilt for the Katyn massacre practically had been concluded, these Washington sessions would review what had happened to certain reports which had been submitted to various government departments.

The timing of the committee's Washington hearings was also significant because 1952 was a general election year in the United States. Primary elections were being held in the winter and spring, and political party nominations were being decided in the summer. Dwight D. Eisenhower had been chosen as the presidential nominee for the Republicans; Adlai Stevenson for the Democrats. Even though committee members were busy attending meetings and giving political speeches, all members were present when the Select Committee reconvened in Washington.

As the chairman had pointed out when the meeting opened, the pri-

175

mary direction of these hearings was to review testimony concerning the whereabouts of formal reports referred to in preceding testimonies. When checking for the whereabouts of the original Van Vliet report, which should have gone from the Assistant Chief of Staff, G-2, of the Army to the State Department, it had been found this report had never left the originating office and was now missing. The report had been written in May, 1945; the month the war ended in Europe. Two months later, when the G-2 office forwarded the Gilder report (a report from a British officer who was with Van Vliet and other Allied prisoners of war taken to Katyn) to the State Department, the covering letter made a comparison and a reference to the Van Vliet report thinking the latter was already at the State Department when it had not left the office in which it had been written and was now unaccounted for.

Although the June, 1952, meetings of the Select Committee were to be primarily concerned with administrative matters of handling classified materials—their interpretation, value, etc.—one witness had made a contribution to the placement of responsibility for the Katyn massacre. A Russian, Boris Olshansky,[3] was an associate professor of mathematics at Voronezh State University, in Voronezh, U.S.S.R. In September, 1941, after Germany attacked Russia, he had been called to active duty in the Russian army as a major in the Engineering Corps. He had been part of the Stalingrad operations (1942–1943), later had been involved in the Bielo-Russian operations (1943–1944), and had continued with the Fifth Army under Marshal Zhukov (1944–1945) until the war ended. After the termination of hostilities he remained in East Berlin as an inspector of the German peoples' education under Soviet military administration (1946–1947).

Mr. Olshansky's father had been a doctor and a good friend of Professor Burdenko; a professional relationship that began in 1919 (though 1923) when both were in Voronezh. Their personal friendship had continued after Professor Burdenko departed for Moscow. Even after Mr. Olshansky's father died in 1929, the witness had continued the association with Dr. Burdenko with visits each time he was in Moscow; in fact, the association had been so friendly that Professor Burdenko had assisted the witness in completing his education as well as financially.

Professor Burdenko, from 1936 on, had been the physician in the Kremlin, a position that included such duties as being the personal physician of Premier Josef Stalin: and resulted in his joining the Communist party in 1939. He was considered to be an outstanding scientist and held membership in the Union Academy of Sciences. In 1944, after the witness had been wounded and was recovering in the hospital in Gomel, Dr. Burdenko, as chief surgeon of the Red Army with the highest rank in the Medical Corps of lieutenant general, had visited him during a hospital inspection visit.

Mr. Olshansky testified he had heard of Katyn from the Soviet press and had been suspicious the media version was more Soviet propaganda; an opinion held by many fellow Red Army officers. When he had entered Poland as a part of Marshal Rokossovsky's army, he heard from many Polish people that the Russians had been responsible for the atrocity. In April, 1946, with the war concluded, the witness testified he had been traveling to Moscow on assignment, so he made it a point to visit Dr. Burdenko, who was ill. Dr. Burdenko told him he had served as president of the Academy of Medical Sciences, was at that time a member of the Supreme Council of the U.S.S.R., and had been chief member of the Russian medical team and one of the signers of the medical report concerning Katyn.

Mr. Olshansky's visit had lasted approximately forty minutes. When he brought up the subject of Katyn, Professor Burdenko had said the Russians had to "straighten out" the protocol given out by the Germans; then elaborated by stating that Katyns were existing and more would be existing—that any person who would be digging out in the country of Russia could find them. The witness then quoted Professor Burdenko as saying: "I was appointed by Stalin personally to go to the Katyn place. All the corpses were four years old. For me as a medical man, this problem is quite clear. Our NKVD friends made a mistake."[4] Mr. Olshansky stated he had not asked why Dr. Burdenko would sign the medical report because for every Soviet citizen the reason was obvious: one would loss one's head if one would not sign. Professor Burdenko was sixty-seven years of age at the time of this visit and the witness learned that seven months later Dr. Burdenko died, in November, 1946.

Mr. Olshansky returned to East Berlin and was at Karlshorst in 1948 when he escaped with his family. At Regensburg he reported to the American military government who provided protection and allowed him and his family to immigrate to the United States on January 2, 1952.

In June the Select Committee decided to file an interim report with Congress prior to adjournment in July, 1952, for the purpose of establishing guilt of the nation responsible for Katyn. In the past, responsibility for perpetrating an atrocity of the magnitude of Katyn that violated human rights would have been placed with one nation; but the committee pointed out that for the first time in world history, Katyn had been an international crime in which two nations disputed the guilt: the reason why the Congress of the United States, through the House of Representatives, had authorized this special committee to attempt officially to determine the responsibility of guilt. By a unanimous vote of members, the Select Committee concluded in the interim report the testimony revealed that the Soviet government had been responsible for murdering Polish officers, soldiers, and intellectual leaders at Katyn. (See Appendix 7.)

In addition to establishing the Russians as the responsible party for the Katyn crime, and also by unanimous approval of committee members, the interim report made four requests to the Congress of the United States:

1. That the President of the United States forward the testimony, evidence, and findings of this committee to the United States delegates at the United Nations.
2. That the President of the United States issue instructions to the United States delegates to present the Katyn case to the General Assembly of the United Nations.
3. That the appropriate steps be taken by the General Assembly to seek action before the International World Court against the Union of Soviet Socialist Republics for committing a crime at Katyn which was in violation of the general principles of law recognized by civilized nations.
4. That the President of the United States instruct the United States delegation to seek the establishment of an international commission which would investigate other mass murders and crimes against humanity.[5]

Following the autumn elections of November, 1952, the Select Committee reconvened to conduct hearings. The first meeting was held on Armistice Day, November 11, 1952; normally a holiday, but the committee met in the spirit of completing its work. At this time their first witness had been the Honorable Robert H. Jackson,[6] Associate Justice, United States Supreme Court, who had been the representative and chief counsel for the United States at the Nuremberg Tribunal. In his opening statement, Justice Jackson pointed out that the guilt for the Katyn Forest massacre had not been adjudged by the Nuremberg Tribunal; a position consistent with that of the United States prosecutor.

As reported earlier, the four Allies involved in the international trial of Hermann Goering, et al, had divided the areas of responsibility so that each country could concentrate on the preparation and presentation of one issue pertinent to the case; thereby avoiding duplication and expediting a trial of unprecedented complexity. The area assigned to the United States had been the overall conspiracy to incite a war of aggression; Great Britain's, the violation of specific treaties and crimes on the high seas; and France and Russia's, the violation of the laws of war in relation to crimes against humanity. France's responsibility for prosecution had been related to Western Europe; Russia's to Eastern Europe—an area largely under Soviet occupation with no other country having access. This Soviet area included Poland and Katyn, although no other prosecutor knew the massacre would be introduced until the Soviet prosecutor brought it up when the indictment had been delineated at the London conference. The initial charge of the Soviet prosecutor stated: "In September, 1941, 925 Polish officers who were prisoners of war were killed in Katyn Forest near Smolensk."[7] Any British and American protests had been overcome by this rationalization: if the Russians could prove their lack of guilt for the Katyn atrocity, they should be entitled to do so, since it had been included in their area of responsibility.

In Berlin, Justice Jackson (who had not been at the London meeting) protested strongly when at the very last minute the Soviets amended the Katyn charge to include 11,000 victims instead of the original 925. The Soviets claimed to have evidence that highlighted the Nazi intent to exterminate the inhabitants of Poland; a country in which no other country had been allowed access to investigate. The Russians had been warned that no help would be provided for them through the Tribunal (such as providing countercharges and developing a good defense) if the Germans denied the charge. Justice Jackson succinctly summarized the Nuremberg Tribunal results on the Katyn murders in this manner:

> The Russian prosecutor appeared to have abandoned the charge. The tribunal did not convict the German defendants of the Katyn massacre. Neither did it expressly exonerate them, as the judgment made no reference to the Katyn incident. The Soviet judge dissented in some matters, but did not mention Katyn.[8]

The Select Committee brought up the question that had proper testimony been presented at the Nuremberg Tribunal, could the four-power nature of the trial have placed the guilt for the Katyn murders on the Soviets? and the answer had been that the Russians could not be convicted because they had not been indicted. The authority of prosecution had been to prepare and prosecute charges of atrocities and war crimes "against such of the leaders of the European Axis Powers and their principal agents and accessories as the United States may agree with any of the United Nations to bring to trial before an international military tribunal."[9]

Justice Jackson also made clear that as United States prosecutor he had no knowledge of the important reports of Colonel Van Vliet, Lieutenant Colonel Stewart, and Colonel Szymanski, which had indicated Russian guilt in the Katyn killings. If this information had been known before the indictments had been drawn (October, 1945), the United States position would have been strengthened by keeping the charge from being made against the Germans.

Moreover, the American prosecutor had not known that Poland's General Anders had been invited by Mr. Stahmer, the counsel for Hermann Goering, to appear in the German defense. General Anders had declined, which was understandable since he would have been defending the Germans whose harm to the Polish people had been beyond measure; however, General Anders had offered to testify if invited to do so by the Nuremberg Tribunal. At that time Justice Jackson had not been privy to this information since it went to the tribunal and not to the prosecutor; he had learned about the situation three years later when he read General Anders' book published in 1949.

On the other hand, Justice Jackson did know of the protocol prepared by the special medical commission sent by Germany to Katyn and that it had been signed by twelve internationally-known pathologists; too, he had heard of the Russian team of experts who had accused the Germans of the crime. The American prosecutor also had heard of Dr. Naville (one of the signers of the protocol, who had been located in Switzerland) who saw no reason to come to the aid of "Goering and his crowd." Likewise, this had been the attitude of General Anders. On the point of judgment of the Presiding Judge Lawrence that each side could use three witnesses only, it had been defended as a sound decision; especially since the Russians had alleged they had 120 witnesses on Katyn alone. As structured, the Nuremberg Tribunal took nine months to complete.

Mr. Jackson ended his testimony by complimenting the Select Committee on the vast store of evidence it had amassed that had not been available at Nuremberg, and alerting the committee to the fact that "the Polish Government then in power in Warsaw (communists) kept a delegation at Nuremberg which cooperated closely with the Soviets in all matters."[10]

The hearings continued on Wednesday, November 12, 1952, with the testimony of the second witness, Admiral William H. Standley,[11] U.S. Navy, (Retired), who had served as United States Ambassador to Moscow, beginning in April 14, 1942. But even before his appointment as ambassador, Admiral Standley had been to Moscow with the Beaverbrook-Harriman mission (Lend-Lease to Russia) in September, 1941, when the Polish situation had been discussed. The discussion concerned some 10,000 Polish officers the Russians had seized when they invaded eastern Poland, and the effort being made to locate these missing Poles. After his appointment as ambassador in the latter part of 1941, Admiral Standley had involved himself with the agencies and individuals who would be concerned with the missing Polish officers. Upon his arrival in Moscow, he had received instructions from the State Department to avoid the questions upon which he had been briefed in Washington. He protested immediately because he had not yet made his report to Mr. Kalinin, the President of the Soviet Union, and placed him a position in which he could not bring up the Polish question on his first visit with Mr. Molotov. At this initial meeting with the Soviet foreign minister, the new American ambassador had expressed his knowledge and interest in the Polish situation. Included in their discussion had been the suggestion to have an American officer as a liaison between the Russians and the Poles; however, Mr. Molotov indicated such a plan would not be necessary because he deemed the availability of the naval and military attaches to the Poles as sufficient for this purpose.

Admiral Standley testified he had been made aware of the military significance of the Germans pressing toward Moscow when the Russians had moved their government headquarters to Kuibyshev. This move meant Admiral Standley would be dealing with Deputy Foreign Minister Vyshinsky and his assistant, Mr. Lozovski, in Kuibyshev. Although Mr. Molotov had been there for a time, he returned to the capital; and Mr. Stalin never left Moscow. Since

Mr. Vyshinsky "never made a decision on anything," Admiral Standley had to travel between the two capitals frequently. The witness stated he had worked very well with Polish Ambassador Kot and later with his successor, Ambassador Romer. The Polish ambassadors had been cooperative and had enlisted the assistance of both the American and British ambassadors in their effort to improve Soviet-Polish relations through an attempt to find the missing Polish officers.

Admiral Standley had witnessed the unfortunate plight of the first 28,000 Polish soldiers—together with families, women, and children—after their arrival in Teheran. These Poles had been among the first evacuees from the U.S.S.R. The American ambassador had inspected the Polish camps; thereby he had been provided an opportunity to become sensitive to the terrible predicament of the Polish people; their poor health, malnutrition, and squalid environment. He testified that he was able to imagine the harsh conditions under which the Poles had existed while deported to Russia, which were worse, more severe and hostile.

In the summer of 1942 Admiral Standley had asked Mr. Molotov to continue to evacuate the Poles to the Middle East to relieve the U.S.S.R. of the burden of caring for them, but Mr. Molotov resisted restarting the evacuation by saying:

> If we had evacuated the Polish women and children in the beginning, it would have been alright. But to evacuate them now would give the Germans the idea that we could not take care of them. It would create a disturbance, and we just feel that we are not in a position now to evacuate these women and children and soldiers.[12]

Admiral Standley testified he had kept the State Department aware of this growing problem which had worsened steadily. In the fall of 1942, the Germans and Italians had moved almost to Alexandria, Egypt; a move that threatened the entire Middle East. The Russian government at that time had agreed to allow three Polish divisions and their families to depart Russia; however, the release of the 10,000 missing Polish officers had not been included.

Mr. Wendell L. Willkie, who had been the defeated Republican candidate for president in the 1940 election against Franklin D. Roosevelt, had asked for and received permission from President Roosevelt to be his special representative to Moscow in September, 1942. He had been advised by the President to look into the Polish situation, including the status of the missing officers. Mr. Willkie's trip had been a failure in the opinion of Admiral Standley because so many clandestine events had occurred. Mr. Molotov had indicated the arrangements to see Premier Stalin, which had been the ultimate goal of Mr. Willkie, would be made "through the American Embassy;" but the arrangements had been made by private invitation to Mr. Willkie only, thereby bypassing the Embassy and excluding the American Ambassador. Even though Mr. Willkie had debriefed Admiral Standley the next day, he stated that some information had been "so secret that he couldn't even tell it to the American Ambassador."[13] No information had been gleaned from Mr. Willkie's visit concerning the improvements in the Soviet-Polish situation or the status of the missing officers; in fact, his visit only opened the door for Soviet officials to presume an attitude that discredited the senior American representative. Admiral Standley stated he then asked to return home to consult with the President, gained approval for the organizational changes he wanted to implement, and returned to the Soviet Union.

Admiral Standley also testified about the exchange of correspondence between President Roosevelt and Premier Stalin; especially the Premier's message of April 24, 1943, which announced the Soviet Union's break in relations with the Polish Government in Exile in London and the President's reply which expressed hope that the U.S.S.R. could term the problem as a "suspension of conversations" with the Government of Poland in London rather than a "complete severance of diplomatic relations." The latter context prevailed. The Select Committee then pursued the idea that the Soviet Union had been looking for an excuse to sever relations with Poland and the request for the International Red Cross to investigate the Katyn massacre, and the letter-exchange had provided them that opportunity. The point the committee was trying to establish was whether this was the time the Soviets seized the opportunity to absolve their responsibility for the missing Polish officers; and obviously, it had been that "time."

As a member of the diplomatic function, Admiral Standley always had tried to effect an aura of conciliation, negotiation, give and take, etc.; in fact, the ambassador's message to President Roosevelt and Secretary Hull, dated April 28, 1943, indicated the foreign correspondents at first used the expression "suspension of relations," but later the censors had approved terms such as "a break" or "a rupture" of relations. His message went on to say the communist Polish Patriots' Union had been vocal in its criticism of the Sikorski government in London; especially in the desire of that government to organize in the Soviet Union some Polish military units that would fight beside the Red Army against Hitler. Obviously, this development ended any hope of reconciliation between the U.S.S.R. and the Polish Government in Exile in London. The same day (April 28, 1943) Admiral Standley had sent a second message (a telegram) to the Secretary of State outlining the intention of the "Free Polish Government" to operate from the Soviet Union, and to alone represent the real "Polish people in Poland" now currently occupied by Germany.

The American Ambassador then reviewed for the committee the announcement by Dr. Goebbels of the discovery of the Katyn grave site on April 13, 1943, and how his broadcast had been followed by Moscow radio broadcasts that indignantly denied the Nazi charge. The sentence, "At last, these new German lies reveal the fate of the Polish officers whom the Germans used for construction work in the Smolensk area," resulted in Tass publishing an entire article about Katyn the next day which reported the Russian version of the Red Army's withdrawal under the German attack of 1941, the capture of the Poles by the Third Reich's army, the construction work around Smolensk, etc. The cold, hard facts of the truth, however, so incensed the Poles that the Ambassador stated "the Poles were wild." He pointed out that if the Soviets had known these prisoners had been captured in 1941, why had they permitted the Polish leaders to search for them hopelessly for almost two years (July, 1941 to April, 1943). Ambassador Romer had advised caution, for everyone knew the Soviets had never used the answer "captured by the Germans" in response to requests by the American, British, and Polish inquiries. No information on location or disposition had ever leaked out. Admiral Standley, who had been nominated in the fall of 1941 to be the American Ambassador to Moscow and submitted his credentials in April, 1942, departed for America in October, 1943.

The Honorable Sumner Welles,[14] former Under Secretary of State (May 26, 1937, to July, 1943) was the third witness. Earlier he had been Ambassador to Cuba and Assistant Secretary of State. Mr. Welles confirmed the testimony of Admiral Standley regarding the events during his tenure as Ambassador to Moscow and his succinct analysis of those events; then emphasized that the primary purpose of our traditional policy and governmental objective had been to conclude the war successfully. Mr. Welles stated the goal of the United States had been for Poland to be a free, independent, and self-governing nation; also, for Poland to exist in peace without the fear of friction developing between it and the Soviet Union. This, too, had been the position of General Sikorski, the Head of the Polish Government in Exile, who Mr. Welles considered to have been a great patriot and for whom Americans had a high admiration. Mr. Welles noted that as the months passed, General Sikorski had become concerned about the Soviet failure to carry out the commitments made with regard to the repatriation of Polish forces to the Middle East.

Neither Mr. Welles nor Admiral Standley, who had preceded him as a witness, had been privy to such information as the message addressed by President Roosevelt to Marshal Stalin regarding the initial impact of the Katyn Forest massacre on the Polish Government in Exile and its response in requesting an International Red Cross investigation. Although Mr. Welles agreed that Poland's "common-sense" approach had been correct insofar as the objective had been concerned, he believed more forethought should have been given to the procedure pursued. Had the Poles asked for Mr. Roosevelt and Mr. Churchill's support prior to requesting intervention from the International Red Cross, the decision by the Russians to sever diplomatic relations with the Polish Government in Exile would have been made more difficult; then the Poles could have gone direct to the Russians after having gained the support of the Americans and the British. Mr. Welles concluded that in any event the outcome probably would have been the same; that is, if the Russians had been looking for a reason to sever relations with Poland, this had been their best opportunity for the Soviets to seize it. At the time, there had been no League of Nations (Russia had been expelled for invading Finland) or United Nations, but there had been the International Red Cross. The diplomatic opinion of both Admiral Standley and Mr. Welles had been that the action of the Poles in requesting an impartial investigation did not justify the severance by the U.S.S.R. of diplomatic relations with Poland's Government in Exile. Both witnesses agreed the step taken by the Soviets had been merely a pretext for the policy which had been determined some previous time.

Since Mr. Welles had ventured the opinion that General Sikorski had been assassinated, the Select Committee pursued the thinking in this direction with vigor. General Sikorski's plane had crashed just as it was taking off from Gibraltar in a return trip to London from North Africa. Two or three similar incidents had occurred previously; such as the one the year earlier on his trip to the United States when his plane had taken off from Montreal, rose to an altitude of one hundred feet, and then crashed. It had been generally conceded that the commitments made to General Sikorski by Premier Stalin and Commissar Molotov could be avoided more easily with the death of the Polish Prime Minister.

As early as January 16, 1943, when the Russian government declared all Poles to be Russian citizens, the understanding between the two countries began to deteriorate. The suspicion existed that Russia at that time needed to reinforce and give voice to its desires for territorial expansion; an indication the probable intent had been to break off diplomatic relations with Poland, one of its Allies. The letter dated June 24, 1942, which the witness had written as Under Secretary of State to General Watson, Secretary to President Roosevelt, had included a significant reference to the Polish situation; for forwarded with it had been the letter from the American Ambassador to London, A. J. Drexel Biddle, dated June 2, 1942, requesting State Department and Presidential support for General Sikorski's attempt to locate his missing officers. Ambassador Biddle, in London, had made an herculean attempt to follow up with what he termed the "last chance to save those who may still be alive."[15] Immediately after the Katyn Forest murders had been announced by the Germans, Ambassador Biddle, on May 20, 1943, had forwarded to the State Department another important diplomatic document which correctly referenced all materials previously forwarded; and included a seven-part document that provided background and made forecasts in accord with the Czapski Report—a report that had reviewed the value of a strong Polish army. The first purpose of Ambassador Biddle's communication had been to aid the U.S.S.R. in defending itself against Germany; the second, to inform the United States about military operations in the Near East. The Ambassador had believed that forming a Polish army would be not only a humanitarian move toward Poland but also a realistic military effort to win the war.

Mr. Welles also noted in his testimony that the former Ambassador from Poland to Moscow had appeared before the Select Committee and pointed out that over a period of two years some fifty separate and distinct requests regarding the whereabouts of the missing Polish officers had been made to the Soviet government. The United States government had been active in its support. Secretary of State Cordell Hull, Under Secretary of State Sumner Welles, and the American ambassadors had been in communication with the various Soviet ambassadors in regard to many subjects, including Soviet-Polish relations and the fate of the missing Polish officers. A strong feeling existed in the State Department that President Roosevelt would review these relevant points when talking to Mr. Molotov or Mr. Litvinof; unfortunately, however, the President rarely kept memoranda of his conversations with foreign diplomats or visiting foreign statesmen. The position on removal of the Polish army from Soviet soil to the Middle East had been one issue in which the United States diplomatic support had aided the Poles. Likewise, on the issue of the missing officers the American diplomats had contributed support in 1943, 1942, and as early as 1941.

The summary of Mr. Welles' testimony initiated a hypothetical discussion of the United Nations by the Select Committee and how this body had been organized immediately after the termination of hostilities in World War II. If the Van Vliet Report had not been lost and if its impact on the countries of the world had been immediate would the Soviet Union have been admitted to the United Nations? Or, would the United States have joined the United Nations? Or, more likely, would the organization itself never have come into existence?—all thought-provoking theories. The committee did conclude there could be no compassionate difference between an Adolf Hitler and a Josef Stalin, each had been a classic example of a totalitarian dictator.

The fourth witness was the United States Ambassador who had replaced Admiral Standley in October, 1943: the Honorable William Averell Harriman.[16] In that same month Mr. Harriman and Secretary of State Cordell Hull had attended the Moscow Conference; hence, the members of the Select Committee quickly directed the testimony of the witness to the subject of Yalta and the formulation of the Polish Provisional Government that had been in control from 1945 through 1947 when the "free and unfettered" elections supposedly had taken place. Then the committee asked about the sixteen underground leaders of the Polish Government in Exile who had been lured out of hiding about April, 1945, on the premise they were being taken to Moscow for a conference in which they would be included as participants; rather they had been imprisoned.

Mr. Harriman had been a participant of the Beaverbrook (Great Britain) -Harriman (United States) Commission to Moscow (Lend- Lease to Russia) in September, 1941. He had spent much time in London, and knew General Sikorski well. At President Roosevelt's suggestion he had sent a telegram to Premier Stalin seeking cooperation for the establishment of a Polish army in Russia.

When the Soviets invited the foreign press in Moscow to go to Katyn (January, 1944), Mr. Harriman had suggested it would be cogent if a member of the Embassy went along, although this had not been a custom of the Soviet government. He asked his daughter to go as his emissary, along with Mr. John Melby, a member of the American Embassy staff. Each one filed an independent report regarding what had been seen and heard, and expressed her/his opinion. These reports had been filed with the State Department, and messages had been sent to the President and Secretary of State.

As Ambassador to Moscow, Mr. Harriman had discussed with the Soviets the renewal of recognition of the Polish Government in Exile in London. Conferences, including Yalta, had been held in an attempt to get the Russians to agree to a Free Poland, and to accept the American principles that had been set forth for the protection of Polish interests. When Yalta occurred, the Russian army had been in occupation of Poland and had established the Lublin government there, with Mr. Beirut as its leader. This Lublin government had been organized in Russia, used the Red army as its controlling mechanization, and had no connection whatsoever with the Polish government in Exile in London or the underground which that government had operated so effectively in Poland itself during the war.

Only three governments had been represented at Yalta: Great Britain, the United States of America, and the Union of Soviet Socialist Republic. The Lublin government had assumed control of Poland after it had been released from German control by the Red army. The discussions at Yalta had envisioned a broadening of the base of that Lublin government that would include not only democratic leaders from within the borders of Poland but also outside Poland; meaning, of course, the London government. Mr. Harriman indicated that

> agreements were reached with Stalin, in which he undertook to cooperate with the American and British Governments in the establishment of a broadly based democratic government, with the participation of the other leaders both inside and outside Poland and the holding, as promptly as possible, of free and unfettered elections.
>
> That agreement was reached, and the fact that Stalin broke that agreement is the reason why Poland is now under Soviet domination.[17]

Before Yalta there had been discussions over a long period of time that attempted to get the Soviet government to recognize the Polish Government in Exile in London as the official government of Poland. Secretary of State Cordell Hull, in October, 1943, at the Moscow Conference, had attempted to get the Soviets to recognize the Polish Government in Exile in London, but his efforts had been unsuccessful. Apparently, all negotiations had failed because the Soviet government had placed into operation its plan to establish the Lublin government. The governments of Great Britain and the United States initially had not recognized the Lublin government; in fact, they continued to recognize the Polish Government in Exile in London until July 5, 1945.

President Roosevelt and Prime Minister Churchill had tried to work out arrangements with Premier Stalin to insure Poland's freedom, and both thought this had been accomplished with the latter's pledge of free and unfettered elections. President Roosevelt wanted the occupation of Poland by the Red army to cease. If the Soviets would not recognize the Polish Government in London, the President wanted some other method to be developed whereby the Poles would be free and the Polish nation would not be enslaved; but the Russians forbade the Polish Government in Exile in London to return to its homeland after the war to participate in "free and unfettered" elections. The people of Poland had refused to recognize the Lublin government. The plan had been to develop a provisional government in cooperation with Great Britain and the United States so a free election in Poland could be conducted, and the people again would have their freedom.

Mr. Harriman, when asked about Poland's leadership possibilities, referred to one of Admiral Standley's dispatches as Ambassador to Moscow after the Katyn announcement in which he had said that no Polish individuals had been left by Russia of sufficient stature to be a leader. His concern had related to the killing of future leaders at such places as Katyn. The witness testified the members of the Lublin government had been Poles brought to Moscow after 1943 who had been working among the communists in Poland trying to develop a communistic movement within the country. The committee's conclusion had to be that there had never been a "free election" in Poland, as prescribed at Yalta. Never!

Mr. Harriman had agreed with the assessment of James F. Byrnes that President Roosevelt, Prime Minister Churchill, and Premier Stalin had spent considerable time discussing Poland at Yalta:

> Not only Poland's boundaries, but Poland itself was one of the most serious issues of the entire conference. More time was spent on this subject than any other. Because of the intensity of argument, Mr. Roosevelt would assume the role more of an arbiter than of an advocate, although he, as well as Prime Minister Churchill, urged the establishment of a new Polish Gov-

ernment in Warsaw. The Soviet Union, on the other hand, wanted to continue the Lublin government. Stalin was willing to add a few persons, but he wanted to make certain that those added did not affect the Soviet Union's control of the government.[18]

The only governments represented at Yalta had been Great Britain, the United States, and the Union of Soviet Socialist Republics. Poland's Prime Minister Mikolajczyk, who had replaced General Sikorski after the latter had been killed, had visited Moscow in August, 1944, and again in October, 1944, and had been involved in talks in London with the Allies, but had not participated in Yalta.

Since the Yalta conference had not consummated with a satisfactory solution, it had been determined there that Ambassador Kerr (Great Britain), Ambassador Harriman (United States), and Minister of Foreign Affairs Molotov (U.S.S.R.) would meet in Moscow in June, 1945. At Yalta the hope had been that an interim government would have sufficient non-communist members to insure there actually would be free elections in Poland, but the agreement had been unsuccessful. The only guarantee given Great Britain and the United States had been the pledge of Stalin that "free and unfettered" elections would be held in Poland. At both Yalta and the June conference the participants had agreed that representatives from Great Britain, the United States, and the Soviet Union would conduct the elections; however, the Russians always refused to let that happen. The result had been that the present government had not been representing the Polish people but had been a puppet government of the Soviet Union; a situation that had existed since the occupation of Poland by the Red Army in World War II.

The witness made reference to the sixteen Polish underground leaders who had been induced to come out of hiding to go to Moscow in order to assist in the conferences on representative government and elections in Poland but who instead had been imprisoned. Mr. Harriman stated that Secretary of State Edward R. Stettinius vigorously had protested this chicanery with Foreign Minister Molotov at the San Francisco United Nations Conference, May 7, 1945; but to no avail.

Mr. Harriman, who had retained the post of Ambassador to the U.S.S.R. until late in 1945, testified he had been a representative at all three tri-power conferences: Teheran, Yalta, and Potsdam; and his conclusion had been any agreement made with Russia would have no value unless it had been based on a position of such strength that the Soviets could be forced to carry out its terms. He noted that in April, 1945, President Truman had put intrepid pressure on Mr. Molotov when the latter visited him in Washington to have the Soviet Union fulfill its obligations toward Poland; again to no avail.

The testimonies of witnesses five and six—Kathleen Harriman Mortimer[19] and John F. Melby[20]—followed. The Soviet authorities had invited approximately twenty members of the foreign press to visit Katyn. As the daughter of the American Ambassador to Moscow, Mrs. Mortimer had been asked to go to Katyn instead of a medical authority because it would be hard for the Russians to refuse the Ambassador's request if she were selected. The overnight train ride of approximately 200 kilometers to Smolensk had been made on January 21-23, 1944. The foreign correspondents had been primarily British and American. Mrs. Mortimer had been accompanied by Mr. Melby, the third Secretary of the Embassy. After the trip had been completed, a separate report had been submitted by each representative to the Ambassador who forwarded them to the Secretary of State with a covering letter dated February 23, 1944. Mrs. Mortimer's entire report indicated the planned Russian trip had lacked credibility by using terms such as "staged," "rigged," "phoney," "testimony was petty," "a sham," etc. Nonetheless, she placed the blame for the Katyn atrocity on the Germans. Mr. Melby also referred to the "staged" visit, and indicated the Russian case had been "incomplete" and "badly put together"; however, he also put the blame on the Germans. After Mrs. Mortimer read the committee's interim report, she concluded her judgment had been incorrect and that it had been the Russians that killed the Poles. She complimented the committee on its effort to present "every side of the picture," and said she had not been able to have any input other than the Russian version. The visiting correspondents had been told the murders occurred in August and September, 1941; however, they had challenged the presence of the winter uniforms on the cadavers in their discussions on the train back to Moscow. Even though the Soviet members of the Foreign Office had been trying to gain assurance from the representatives that the Russian version had been accepted, the correspondents had expressed their uncertainty about what they had seen.

The committee assailed the performance of Ambassador Harriman's daughter, Kathleen Harriman Mortimer, and John Melby because their reports had not accurately presented the correct information available to them, and their conclusions had not followed the evidence presented. A postscript to their reports would be to compare them to the thinking of the average American in this timeframe: every American wanted very much to believe in the Russians, their belated Ally. The hope for some thread of morality, honesty, and trust to be found running through the cloth of the wartime version of Soviet communism had not waned. There had to be one bad "blunder" for the bubble to burst—forever!

The Select Committee continued the Washington hearings on Thursday, November 13, 1952, with the testimony of the seventh witness, Stanislaw Mikolajczyk,[21] President of the International Peasants Union. Mr. Mikolajczyk had been born in Germany; later he moved to Poland where, in 1918, he had participated in the uprising against the Germans for a free and independent Poland. In

1920 he fought against the bolsheviks; in 1939 he fought against the Germans. He had been interned in a prisoner of war camp in Hungary from which he had escaped and made his way to France. While there he had been entrusted by General Sikorski to prepare the plan for the formulation of a parliament in exile. The Polish Parliament in Exile in France had been formed in 1939 with Mr. Paderewski as Chairman, and Mr. Mikolajczyk as Vice Chairman. Its first seat had been in Paris later in Angers, France; then in 1940 it had been moved to London. In 1941 the witness had been appointed Vice Premier and Minister of the Interior, and had held these positions until the death of General Sikorski in the plane crash at Gibraltar in July, 1943; then Mr. Mikolajczyk became Prime Minister.

The reports from Poland in 1939 and 1940 had been that the Polish officers taken by the Russians as POWs would be released and sent back under German occupation. When all letters and news stopped, the agreements, the personal conversations, the diplomatic requests, the notes, etc., all followed with no success. Finally, the German announcement of April 13, 1943, reported the discovery of the mass grave sites at Katyn. With all the background material available, including the data from the Polish underground, immediately it had been clear that the Russians had perpetrated the killings.

The witness, now testifying in his role as Prime Minister, related how the underground, some 300,000 strong, had been caught between the Nazi occupation and the advancing Russians. In June, 1944, he stated he had met with President Roosevelt and had laid before him all the problems facing Poland, including the restoration of the boundaries of Poland to their pre-war locations. President Roosevelt had responded that he thought he could help save or retain Lwow, Tarnopol, the potash mines in Kaluez, and the oil in Drohobycz and Kalisz; but he had been doubtful that Stalin would give up Wilno.

In public the Soviets had demanded two conditions for the restoration of Polish-Soviet relations: first, changes had to be made in the Polish Government in London; and second, the so-called Curzon Line had to be recognized. The first demand had included, unofficially, a denouncement by the Poles of their initial request for an International Red Cross investigation, and a public proclamation that the Polish government had been wrong in asking for the investigation in the first place.

The witness testified that the situation had been worsening inside the Polish underground, for orders had been given to fight the Germans and then try to contact the advancing Russian armies since the Soviets had been favorable and had supported the underground army in the eastern portion of Poland. The Poles, however, had not understood what the officers of the Red army meant who told them, "Wait two or three days and you will see what will happen."[22] In actuality it had meant that after the underground had spent itself in blood and sweat against the Germans, and had its ranks thinned by casualties, those Poles who survived had been arrested by the same Red army they had supported and sent to Siberia.

In October, 1944, Mr. Mikolajczyk testified he had attended a meeting in Moscow to discuss, among other things, the eastern boundary of Poland. Also in attendance had been Premier Stalin, Mr. Molotov, Prime Minister Churchill, Mr. Eden, Ambassador Averell Harriman, Professor Gravski, and Ambassador Romer. When as Polish Prime Minister the witness had been arguing with Premier Stalin about the boundary, Mr. Molotov arose and said: "But, gentlemen, what are we speaking about? This problem has already been settled in Teheran."[23]

The Big Three conference had been held in Teheran in December, 1943. If the eastern boundaries of Poland had been established, the event had occurred nine or ten months earlier. The Poles had not been represented at Teheran, nor had they been informed of any settlements that occurred there. Prime Minister Mikolajczyk had pressed for a settlement of the boundary issue at the October, 1944, meeting because it appeared this would be the last opportunity for recognition of the Polish Government in Exile in London by the Soviets; therefore, he had not brought up the Katyn issue without Russia's support on the boundary issue. At the meeting the British had acknowledged the boundary situation, however, Mr. Harriman had indicated there had been a misunderstanding about the settlement he would have to consult with the President. A series of letters had resulted in Mr. Harriman's return to the United States for a visit with the President. On his way back to Moscow he stopped in London and had told the Prime Minister that the President had asked him to approach Premier Stalin once more about the southeastern portion of Poland only. When Prime Minister Mikolajczyk had explained this proposal to his government in London, the majority of the members had thought the entire border could be regained; however, it had been his opinion the time had come to accept the consequences and try to recover that portion of the border which might be returned by the Soviets. The witness said he had been supporting the American position, but because he had been in the minority and could not convince the majority he had resigned as Prime Minister to become a private citizen and chairman of the Polish Peasants Union.

Mr. Mikolajczyk's further testimony confirmed that the Soviet government had established the Lublin group as an administrative body on July 25, 1944, because this body had signed the agreement concerning the Curzon Line that had conceded all territory east of that line to the U.S.S.R. In addition, he stated it had been agreed the Poles in the whole Polish territory would receive just treatment under the leadership of the military commander of the Red army. The next step had been the announcement by the Lublin administrative body that, in effect, it had become the government of authority in Poland. The Soviets quickly extended diplomatic recognition to this body on January 7, 1945. Since this recognition had preceded Yalta, reference to Poland at that meeting had been made in terms of the "reconstruction of this government." In March, 1945, the sixteen leaders of the Polish underground had promised to come out in the open for a conference with General Iwanow in Warsaw. They had been told they would be flown to a political conference in Moscow, after which they could fly to London if they desired. Instead, their plane had landed one hundred miles from Moscow, and they had been taken by train to the Moscow prison. In April, 1945, Mr. Stalin and Mr. Bierut of the Lublin government had reached an agreement concerning a military and political alliance between Poland and U.S.S.R. Then, in May, 1945, Mr. Molotov publicly announced the capture of the sixteen Polish leaders at the San Francisco (United Nations) meeting.

George Howard Earle,[24] the eighth witness to testify, had served during World War II as Minister to Bulgaria, Minister to Austria, and President Roosevelt's Special Emissary for Balkan Affairs in Turkey. Before the war Mr. Earle had been the Governor of Pennsylvania. Although his testimony covered a wide range of ideas, his remarks regarding Katyn had been of primary concern to the Select Committee. Mr. Earle had been a close personal friend and confidant of President Roosevelt. As the Special Emissary of the President to Turkey he had been capable of gathering much intelligence data.

Mr. Earle had operated from Istanbul, Turkey, an anti-Russian country since the Turks had known the Soviets wanted their warm water seaports since the days of the Czars. One of Mr. Earle's agents had brought him photographs of the Katyn massacre. Another agent in Bulgaria had brought him three letters; two from separate members of the Bulgarian Red Cross, and the other from a Romanian Red Cross member: and Mr. Earle had known two of the three writers. Each of these three men stated by affidavits that they had gone to Katyn and inspected the gravesites, and that all evidence, including body decomposition, had clearly indicated the Russians committed the massacre of Polish officers. He testified he had entrusted copies of the larger photographs of Katyn to a close professional friend, Captain Trammel, to deliver; however, he had kept all affidavits and the small photographs to deliver personally to President Roosevelt (who had used a magnifying glass to inspect them) during a consultation with him in May, 1944. Even though Mr. Earle had acquired the data in February, 1944, he had waited to deliver the information and documents when he would be able to discuss Katyn with the President. The two men had disagreed about the evidence: Mr. Earle had been convinced the Russians had been guilty of the Katyn murders, but he could not convince the President of their guilt. The Commander-in-Chief had believed Katyn had been a "German propaganda" trick and a "German plot." Mr. Earle used the expression "hopeless" in describing his inability to convince the President that the Russians had been guilty. [Note: Before the President died in April, 1945, and after he had experienced promise after promise being broken by Premier Stalin, he had been heard to remark in deriding terms that he had been taken in by Stalin and the Soviets because he thought they had been honest when they were not.]

Mr. Earle's observation had been that Josef Stalin's decision to sever diplomatic relations with Poland's Government in Exile had resulted because the Soviets actually had committed the crime at Katyn and could have been exposed if there had been an international investigation; hence, there had been no other practical solution—in other words, it had been Russia's only defense.

The ninth witness had been Arthur Bliss Lane,[25] who had been a career diplomat in the State Department for thirty-one years. He had been the American Minister to Yugoslavia; but in 1941 when the Germans came he had left there after four years in office. Next he had been appointed Minister of Costa Rica and later Ambassador to Columbia; then followed his appointment as Ambassador to the Polish Government in Exile in London. He had been confirmed by the Senate and had waited from September, 1944, to July, 1945 to fulfill his mission to London; instead he had been sent to Warsaw. The only data he had been able to find on Katyn had been the Kathleen Harriman Mortimer report in the State Department files. That was all! He testified he had talked to Ambassador Ciechanowski on the subject; also, to a Mr. Durbrow who had been in charge of the Polish desk at the time.

Mr. Lane stated that his first information concerning Katyn had come after his arrival in Poland via the underground who indicated the Russians had been guilty. He testified he had developed such an anticommunist philosophy as a result of his tour in Poland that he knew he would have to resign when he opposed the loan of $90,000,000 to the Polish Government in Warsaw; and he left Poland on February 24, 1947. In 1949, back in the United States, he had been asked by Mr. Julius Epstein to help organize and serve as chairman with a private committee to investigate the Katyn massacre; long before Congress had become involved. This bipartisan effort had included not only Democrats and Republicans but also Catholics, Protestants, and Jews. Although funding had been difficult, progress had been achieved. The most favorable result had been to stimulate an interest in the Congress regarding the importance of bringing out the truth. Mr. Lane ended his testimony by complimenting the committee on its procedures, results, and accomplishments in educating the American public on the dangers of communism.

Julius C. Holmes,[26] the tenth witness, had been a member of the Foreign Service as American Minister in London. In World War II he had served as executive officer with the combined Chiefs of Staff in Washington. He had been overseas for most of the war and as a brigadier general had been ordered back to Washington in January, 1945, to serve as Assistant Secretary of State. An effort had been made to determine what had happened to the missing original of the Van Vliet report of May 22, 1945, for the report had never been received by the State Department. This testimony had been supported by the eleventh witness,

Frederick B. Lyon,[27] the Consul General of the United States Embassy in Paris, who had been Acting Director of the Office of Controls in the State Department in May, 1945.

The thirteenth, and last, witness to testify had been Julius Epstein,[28] the Executive Secretary of the private American Committee for the Investigation of the Katyn Massacre, Inc., who spoke of its background and how it had gained support from Congressmen Sheehan, Flood, Madden, and Dondero.

Almost anticlimactically, the hearings of the Select Committee ended on November 14, 1952. The hours of planning, preparation, conferences, executive sessions, formal hearings of testimony, and the publication of proceedings had been completed. The unanimous vote concerning Russian guilt had never been changed or challenged. The Select Committee filed its report with the Speaker of the House and held a final press conference in December, 1952. All branches of the government and the American population at large had appreciated the committee's contribution to the "voice" of justice, for the finest capability of the American congressional investigative system would be represented forever through its findings.

PART III

IN REVIEW

Chapter 13

IN REVIEW

From one end of the spectrum to the other Americans wanted to believe in the credibility of all their Allies. "Mr. and Mrs. Average American" and the wartime president, Franklin D. Roosevelt, had the feeling the intentions of the Allies represented "good" (i.e. freedom, liberty, trust, et cetera), including the goals of the Atlantic Charter that stated no territorial gains would await the military victors. The 1930's had developed an international atmosphere in which Americans had endeavored to assess the forces of "bad." Adolf Hitler and Josef Stalin had been watched closely; but, in comparing the knowledge and data available, neither system—Nazism or Communism—seemed better than the other, although Hitler appeared to be the more maniacal of the two men. This appearance could have been because of the obvious and stated expansionist concepts of the Third Reich; for even though the Russian expansionist ideas were known, they had not been as obviously publicized. When the Russo-German Pact had been agreed to in the summer of 1939, it appeared both governments had been equally sadistic; a paradox which the peace-loving nations had to confront when Germany attacked western Poland and a short time later Russia attacked eastern Poland. Also, in November, 1939, Russia appeared more greedy than Germany, when it attacked Finland and was expelled from the League of Nations within a month. Then, when Hitler attacked Russia in 1941, after having brought France to its knees and Great Britain to the threshold of defeat, the attitude of the free world worked against Hitler and in favor of Stalin whose country had been attacked.

The Americans had been so convinced the war-time atmosphere of the Allies (including Russia) had been "good" and the Axis "bad" that the American news media used the handling of the Katyn incident as a classic example. The average American wanted to believe the Germans had been guilty of perpetrating the Katyn killings; not the Russians. The news broadcast by Elmer Davis, a distinguished radio commentator, whose remarks on May 3, 1943, for the Office of War Information, have often been quoted as an example. As he addressed himself to the Katyn massacre, Mr. Davis reported:

197

But while the German armies are finding it pretty tough going, the German propaganda won a striking success last week when it succeeded in bringing about a break in diplomatic relations between Russia and the Polish Government in Exile. The way the Germans did this is a good example of the doctrine Hitler preached in *Mein Kampf,* that it is easier to make people swallow a big lie than a little one. When the Germans had beaten Poland in September, 1939, the Russians moved in and occupied eastern Poland, taking thousands of Polish troops prisoners. In June, 1941, when the Germans attacked Russia, they overran all of this territory and have held it since. Now, almost two years later, they suddenly claim to have discovered near Smolensk the corpses of thousands of Polish officers, who, according to the Germans, were murdered by the Russians three years ago. In several respects, this story looks very fishy. At first, the Germans were quite uncertain about the number of killed. At one time the Japanese and the Vichy French came up with a story of Romanians murdered in Odessa, not Poles in Smolensk. First, they said 10,000, then 2,000, and then 5,000, before finally deciding on 12,000. Rome and Berlin disagreed as to how they had been killed. The remains must have been better preserved than usual after three years. The Russians were said to have tried hard to conceal the graves, yet they buried every man in uniform with his identification tag. Suggestions of an investigation by the International Red Cross mean nothing, for the Germans control the area. It would be easy for them to show the investigators corpses in uniform with identification tags. There is no way the investigators could determine whether these men were killed by Russians or by Germans, as they probably were.

Two additional paragraphs elaborated on the topic, but his point had been made. Mr. Davis, in his presentation before the Select Committee in 1952, stated that after nine-and-one-half years and working with the new evidence now available, he was convinced the Russians were guilty of the crime.

The spirit of the time had reached all the way to the oval office of the White House. President Roosevelt had been at the peak of his political career in gaining unprecedented third and fourth terms in the elections of 1940 and 1944. All Americans had been convinced things were "going" right. The nation had survived the worst business depression on record which had begun with the "Crash of 1929" and became the international "Depression of the 1930s." The nation had not embraced any intrusions of totalitarian systems in the depression days although their revolutionary voices (American Nazi Party and Communist Internationale) had been heard. The parapets of the Atlantic and Pacific Oceans which seemed to protect the American arsenals of democracy had been altered by the Japanese sneak attack on Pearl Harbor; likewise, by Hitler's declaration of war against the United States immediately thereafter. Understandably, President Roosevelt supported the Allied cause and unity with every energy left to him. Like the nation he had been elected to lead, he wanted to believe that the loyal and generous material support which America had been providing the U.S.S.R. would generate a moderate communist approach in return. Before he died in Warm Springs, Georgia, on April 12, 1945, he reached his oft-quoted conclusion regarding the Premier of the Soviet Union: "We can't do business with Stalin. He has broken every one of the promises he made at Yalta."

Many people and governments look at warfare as something to be avoided completely; or if it comes, to win the war as quickly as possible and return to a peacetime atmosphere. To a totalitarian thinker wartime is only a normal period of operation because additional expansionist goals can be achieved in the chaos of war, for confusion covers up the intent to attain those goals.

The main thrust of this review had been the issue of the Polish prisoners of war being murdered on Soviet soil. Although the blame points to the Russians, the German government's capability for mass homicide has been well documented. Concentration camps had been started in Germany as early as 1933 when the dictatorship of Adolf Hitler commenced; and once the war began, their operation had been expanded and the camps had served as a cloak to conceal Hitler's other nefarious deeds. These German concentration camps have been analyzed in many studies[1] and often have been called either *death camps* or *forced labor camps*, depending upon their intended use;[2] moreover, the studies have recorded that the Nazis killed approximately eleven million people, approximately six million being Jews. For example, the Germans decimated over three million of the Polish Jewish population of approximately 3,300,000 during World War II. Jews from Russia, Hungary, Romania, Austria, Netherlands, France, Czechoslovakia, Greece, Belgium, Yugoslavia, Bulgaria, and Italy had been victimized in the Holocaust.[3] Four of the so-called "main German concentration camps"—Auschwitz, Treblinka, Belzec, and Chelmno—had been located in Poland; three—Dachau, Buchenwald, and Bergen-Belsen—in Germany. Actually, hundreds of concentration camps or forced labor camps had been located in Germany; proof of which has been found in the records made available to numerous analysts and writers after Germany lost the war.

In comparison, after the Soviet "Iron Curtain"[4] descended, penetration to review and analyze U.S.S.R. records has been impossible; therefore, outsiders have had rare glimpses of the internal management of Russian concentration camps, forced labor camps, or general operation of the Soviet system. This secretive, furtive, clandestine approach to Russia's internal control has been true since the days of the Russian Revolution. Even though Russian literature pinpoints the existence of this undercover system of government, compared to the availability of records of a defeated government accurate statistics and data about Russia have been difficult to find and assess.

Since the elevation of Pope John Paul II to the Papacy in the Vatican, many think of his home country of Poland as primarily a Catholic country;

however, all religions are represented in that country, just as the clergymen and laymen of all religions had been represented among the victims at Katyn. The outcome has been that all faiths have found a mortal enemy in the atheistic policies of the U.S.S.R. "Death to the enemies," a slogan of the NKVD, had been practiced at Katyn with the murders of enemies of the state long before World War II; then practiced again with the assassinations of Polish officers as herein reviewed.

In considering the efficiency of the Nazi system there can be no doubt the Germans could develop and execute (literally) a mass extermination effort, but the data herein reviewed establishes they did not commit the killings at Katyn. Because the German High Command knew they were innocent of this atrocity their primary concern was to expose the truth. To prove the Russians guilty brought the companion need for the Germans to prove themselves innocent; an herculean effort. Invitations to foreign journalists, to prisoners of war of many nations, to many Polish agencies (i.e. Red Cross), and to individuals (physicians, clergy, etc.), were intelligent public relations activities; especially the decision to invite the International Red Cross to make its investigation at Katyn. Also, should that possibility of proof fail because the Russians would not cooperate with the Germans and Poles, the move to organize an International Medical Commission had been a wise decision.

Although Dr. Buhtz and his colleagues had done an outstanding job in providing conclusive evidence through the application of the principles of forensic medicine, the testimonies of the well-respected members of the International Medical Commission overwhelmingly confirmed Russia's guilt for the Katyn Massacre. Many analysts have offered reasons why the dastardly killings of the Polish prisoners of war had been committed by the Russian secret police, for their deaths had occurred on Soviet soil at a time when the Russians had been in complete control of the Polish prisoners of war and of their own countryside which was at peace. Absolutely critical to their conclusion would be "when" the murders in Katyn Forest had been perpetrated. The German doctors of forensic medicine and the International Medical Commission who conducted the investigations and autopsies while the German army occupied Smolensk (and Katyn) confirmed the time as three years before the investigation; or about April and May, 1940. Although the International Medical Commission confirmed the "when" the forensic-medical findings[5] became the strong factor in determining that April and May, 1940, had to be "when" the killings had been committed.

The physical evidence found on the bodies became another powerful factor in determining the "when;" for the dates on the numerous letters, postcards, diaries, newspaper clippings and other documents had been no later than May, 1940. Also, under a microscope the rings of growth of the small fir trees transplanted over the grave site showed the trees had to be about five years old;

an indication the trees had been transplanted three years earlier, and their stunted growth had been due to adjustment to the soil.

Yet another important finding at Katyn had been the discovery of graves containing bodies of people who had been executed long before World War II started in 1939. These Russian bodies had been hooded and their hands bound behind the back in almost the exact manner as the bodies of so many Poles killed in 1940. Another factor that confirmed the statements of the peasants who lived in the immediate Katyn vicinity that these earlier victims had been "enemies of the state." Obviously, the later executions of the Polish officers simply had been a continuation of the same brutality.

Such accurate detailed evidence could lead only to these conclusions: The Russians did execute the Polish prisoners of war at Katyn. The killings took place during April and May, 1940. The decision to eliminate these POWs had been made by the highest ranking officials in the Kremlin. The operation itself had been conducted by the Russian secret police—the NKVD.

The only possible way the Russians could prove their innocence would be to prove the guilt of the Germans. The Soviets' first announcement of April 15, 1943, as reported in Chapter 3, had been a defensive measure issued two days after the initial German announcement. Later, after taking Smolensk, the Soviets announced the formation of an investigative body whose report on January 24, 1944, has been introduced in Chapter 4; and the document has been recorded in its entirety in Appendix 6.

The initial Russian response to the German announcement stated the Germans had been guilty of the Katyn Killings. The Soviets claimed that these cadavers had been "former Polish prisoners of war who in 1941 were engaged in construction work in areas west of the Smolensk region and who fell into the hands of the Germans." This was the first statement of the Russians that indicated Poles had been in the area. In response to the questions from Ambassadors Kot and Romer, Generals Anders and Sikorski, and other allied representatives, the senior Kremlin members and their ambassadors during 1941, 1942, and 1943 would not provide information as to the whereabouts of the Polish officers, their activities or whether they were alive. Why were the Poles not permitted to write to their families and friends after April, 1940, if they were "west of Smolensk" and "engaged in construction work?" Before that time they had been permitted to write and to receive communications. Too, why, if they had done no work before April, 1940, were they then required to be "engaged in construction work?"

The Russian announcement on April 15, 1943, mentioned the "archeological excavations of the historic 'Gniezdovo burial place.'" This reference could have been a suggestion by the Russians that the Germans had located the historic gravesite and were somehow trying to tie it into the deaths of the Polish officers since the mere mention of the "historic Gniezdovo burial place" suggested subterfuge. Actually, the Germans knew the background of the historic burial sites, including Gniezdovo; in fact, the reason why the Germans called the site of the killings of the Polish officers the Katyn Forest massacre instead of the Gniezdovo massacre was to alleviate any confusion about "historic burial" backgrounds. Although the railroad station of Katyn was far beyond (west of) the forest, and the town of Katyn was even farther (south of the Dnieper River), the name "Katyn" became indelibly inked in infamy when it was linked with the name of the forest where the gravesites had been located.

The Russian "Report of Special Commission for Ascertaining and Investigating the Circumstances of the Shooting of Polish Officers by the German-Fascist Invaders in the Katyn Forest" had been formally published and dated January 24, 1944. This report had indicated the Russian investigation found "11,000" bodies; almost three times the number exhumed (4,143) by the Germans. According to the report only nine items of evidence and documentation had been removed from six of the "11,000" numbered bodies. The fact remains that the Germans had exhumed 4,143 bodies most of whom had been identified by means of literally thousands of newspaper articles, letters, diaries, paybooks, and other documentation found on their bodies. The Russians had almost 7,000 more cadavers than the Germans, which should have provided them with a bonanza of dated evidence to cinch their establishment of "when" as "September-December, 1941." Statistically speaking, if the Russian body-count almost tripled the German, then the amount of physical evidence could conceivably be tripled, also.

The testimony of witnesses as reported in the first version of the Russian document indicated the killings had occurred in August and September, 1941; the January 24, 1944, final report stated the dates as "September-December, 1941." When the Allied newsmen had been taken on a tour of Katyn by the Russians in January, 1944, the press questioned why the bodies had been wearing winter clothing if the deaths occurred in August and September, 1941. This questioning had been particularly sententious during the return trip by train when the Soviet guides asked the newsmen if they had been convinced the Germans had been guilty of committing the Katyn massacre. Apparently, the newsmen had found a flaw in the unpublished report which prompted the Russians to change the dates in the official version; hence publishing the press releases had to be delayed to coincide with date of publication of the official report. As a matter of fact to this day the estimated "when" of the killings in the formal Russian report remains between September-December, 1941, the stipulations in the depositions of the witnesses remains August and September, 1941.

The foreign (Allied) correspondents also reported the "show" had been "staged" with a tight routine in contrast to the professional, free-access atmosphere in which the German investigation had been conducted. The attitude that permeated throughout the group while the Russians had been present appeared to create an atmosphere of uncertainty. Yet another contrast of the two investigations related to selection of participants: the International Medical Commission that confirmed the German findings had members from twelve separate countries with no Germans being formally on the commission; the Russian commission had been composed exclusively of Russians.

The Russian report stated all three POW camps—Kozielsk, Ostashkov, and Starobliesk—had been closed down completely and all Polish officers had been incarcerated at three locations—Camps 1, 2, and 3—spread out over an area from fifteen to twenty-eight miles (twenty-five to forty-five kilometers) west of Smolensk; yet no records have been provided to establish this allegation. No camp population reports have been available, although attention to detail on camp rosters always has been a known military necessity. No specific camp locations have been established, and no interrogation of peasants ever confirmed the presence of these three alleged POW camps. If the primary camps had been closed and all the prisoners incarcerated in three (Numbers 1, 2 and 3) camps along the way, why were all the prisoners detrained at Gniezdovo? Logically, from a logistical and security point of view, the prisoners could have been detrained all along the route. Too, with 11,000 Poles working on construction in about a thirteen-mile area (twenty-eight miles less fifteen miles), personnel congestion along the work area would surely have been in evidence. Moreover, with approximately 11,000 prisoners in such a seemingly temporary billeting arrangement near the "construction work," the possibility of escape by the Poles would have been greatly enhanced.

The flaws of the Russian investigation have been numerous and obvious and have been reviewed in detail in Chapter 4 and included in Appendix 6. These "in review" comments have been merely summarizations.

In comparing the German information with the data in the Russian investigation, an analysis of events provides a probable explanation of what occurred.

In cooperation with the Polish Red Cross, the Germans exhumed 4,143 cadavers of Polish POWs graves one through seven between March and June, 1943, and made a positive identification of about 68 percent of those bodies. Also, the Germans recovered and retained thousands of documents and items that had been removed from these bodies before their reburial in six new graves. The German investigators included their own pathologists and the invited members of the International Medical Commission who confirmed the "when" of death as being during April and May, 1940. To substantiate the evidence the Germans invited journalists of many nations, Allied prisoners of war, Polish representatives, and others to be present at the exhumation. In contrast the Special Commission established by and composed of Soviets arrived on October 26, 1943, to make its investigation of the area. Then, in January, 1944, the

Russian government invited foreign correspondents to share in a briefing and "show" of their findings. In that same month the Russian report was published, which stated they had found 11,000 bodies—almost 7,000 more than had been found by the Germans. The Russians had not identified the bodies by name; only by numbers. According to the report, only nine pieces of physical documentation had been located on six numbered bodies. In contrast, the German investigators recorded the identification of each Polish officer exhumed by name and rank and whatever other information could be gleaned from the physical documents found on the body.

The German investigation had been specific on details, such as the bound hands and hooded heads, and referred to documents as belonging to an individual person; i.e. Solski's Diary. Other details reported had been cause of death; specific reference to time of death; reasons for the pathologists' estimate of time of death, including medical evidence; physical evidence of dated documents, and even an estimate by foresters of tree growth. The Russian report included in its medical comments the fact that 925 bodies had been exhumed and examined, and referred to both 7.65 millimeter and 9.0 millimeter bullet holes in the skull; however, most of the medical comments were little more than cursory observations.

Observations concerning stab wounds from bayonets, the "various stages of body decay," reasons for broken bones and limbs, etc. were included in the German report. The Russian report omitted such small but important details. Also, the German report commented about the absence of insects, the cold weather, the bodies lying undisturbed for three years, the winter clothing on bodies from Graves Numbers One through Seven, and the summer clothing on bodies in Grave Number Eight—the final grave discovered in which exhumations had just begun but had been cancelled and the grave resealed due to moderating weather. Similar meticulous details were not recorded in the Russian report.

The Germans concluded the killings occurred in April and May, 1940, thereby making the Russians responsible. The Russian report claimed the Germans killed 11,000 Poles during September to December, 1941, after the Third Reich army had captured Smolensk. Obviously, just reviewing the variations in the two reports regarding the Katyn killings reveals an overwhelming pattern of circumstantial evidence against the Russians.

From the assembled evidence presented, this "in-the-record" data of the Katyn massacre justifiably concludes that official murder is an instrument of Soviet policy. Past records confirm this allegation, and later events could be cited to reaffirm it.

In March, 1985, a United States army officer, Major Arthur D. Nicholson, Jr., was shot twice and killed by the Russians while on a legal mission in East Germany. Sergeant Jessie G. Shatz was involved in the same incident when he was prevented from giving first aid to Major Nicholson; in fact, the Russian medical personnel present were prevented from administering first aid for thirty minutes. The spokesman for the United States State Department described the event as "murder." Editorials across the country called the incident another example of "official murder" being used as an instrument of Soviet policy.

In East Germany in 1984, a member of a French observation team was killed under similar circumstances. Also, in 1984, a Polish priest[6] was murdered by members of the Polish secret police who had been trained and were controlled by the Soviet secret police. In 1981 an attempt had been made to assassinate Pope John Paul II in Rome and Italian authorities linked the Bulgarian secret police with this tragic event; a group also trained and controlled by the Russian secret police. To the most naive spectator such intimidations and intolerances sound a literal death knell that reminds the world Russia wants to be the country "in charge." The shooting down in September, 1983, by a Soviet military aircraft using air-to-air missiles, of an unarmed Korean aircraft in which 269 passengers were killed emphasizes the "in charge" point.

As far back as the Russian Revolution examples of similar atrocities can be noted; such as the 1940 assassination in Mexico of Leon Trotsky, arch rival of Josef Stalin, by the long arm of the Soviet secret police. Also, many historians think the death of Trotsky's daughter in Berlin was a planned murder by the same Soviet secret police who "staged her suicide." The same suspicions can be associated to the death of Ivan Kriwozercew, the old Russian peasant who had been an eyewitness to the exhumations of the investigating teams at Katyn since his home was so close to the forest. He had escaped to London, assumed a new name (Michael Loboda), and found a new job; then later, under mysterious circumstances, was found hanged in an ancient workshop. More examples of Russia's intrusion into European and other countries include Poland (1980), Afghanistan (1979), Czechoslovakia (1968), Hungary (1956), etc. Such examples as Africa (Angola, Ethiopia, etc.) and Latin America (Cuba, Nicaragua, etc.) indicate the same official use of "murder" as an instrument of Soviet policy. That Russia was responsible for the "murders" of approximately 15,000 Polish POWs should not be a truth to question. Although the names of the leaders could change (Lenin, Stalin, etc. through Brezhnev, Andropov, Cherenko, and Gorbachev), the policy or strategy appear to remain the same: world-wide domination via the official use of "murder" as one of the enforcing instruments. (All this in spite of Mikhail Gorbachev's stated new policy of "openness," [glasnost].)

To this day the Russian decision at the highest level to kill methodically the Polish officers at Katyn, and elsewhere, has left a pall over all of Poland. Hatred that has seethed just below the surface for centuries between the two peoples erupts from time to time. While successful by Soviet communist standards in following policies of extermination of enemies, the Katyn "blunder" has created a cloud of doubt, suspicion, lack of trust, and bitterness that will in the long run prove costly as knowledgeable world opinion continues to polarize against the threat of Soviet communism as perpetrated in the Katyn killings.

On Tuesday, January 13, 1987, Poland's communist leader, General Wojciech Jaruzelski, met with Pope John Paul II at the Vatican. They spoke privately in their native Polish for seventy minutes, as reported by Vatican officials. The Pope asked that greater voice be given to "ordinary Poles in running their country." The talks were "serious, frank and in depth." The Vatican source also noted "the differences remain."[7]

Prior to his visit, the communist leader had released hundreds of "political prisoners" to improve government relations inside and outside the country (including relations with the Holy Father). Many of the "political prisoners" were involved with the Solidarity trade union movement which had provided a great motivation to the Polish people who were hoping for enhanced freedom and human rights. But as the Solidarity trade union movement succeeded, it gained the attention and disfavor of the Kremlin which perceived the threat and so the communist Polish government declared martial law in December, 1981. Solidarity was outlawed. This was the traditional Soviet response of the prevailing hard line communist theoreticians and practitioners against the Solidarity trade union movement which began in Gdansk (formerly Danzig) many months earlier and had captured the hearts and minds of the Polish workers. Solidarity had spread throughout the societal and class structure of the non-government elements of the country. It was only a question of time until the Kremlin would act/react to "break the back" of any movement which did not adhere to the party line completely.

The Solidarity trade union movement or simply Solidarity[8] brought with it a strong clandestine publishing movement.[9] One of the results has been the response by Polish communists who do not bother to deny the Soviet responsibility for the atrocity of Katyn. In addition, Polish homes which were not allowed, earlier, to honor the dead of Katyn[10] have more recently been permitted to do so, provided it is not too provocative to the Soviet Union. The Kremlin perhaps adjudges this more seemingly tolerant attitude of allowing the deceased to be so honored and respected as the preferred decision than to "slam the door" on the suggested atmosphere of "openness" and thereby focus even more attention on the issues of the Katyn Forest Massacre.

The possible temporary indulgence by the hard line communist policy is contrary to the official ". . . Control of Press" policy in which the communist controlled Warsaw government continues to follow the recommended "Great Soviet Encyclopedia" which attempts to shift the blame of Katyn from the Russians to the Germans by conveniently shifting the dates of death of the Polish prisoners of war from 1940 to 1941 when the Germans occupied the Smolensk area. This is done by quoting the Russian Special Commission Report of January 24, 1944, as the specific reference.[11]

In the summer and fall of 1987 it was reported,[12] in a story emanating in Giby, in the northeast corner of Poland, that a farmer named Stefan Myszczynski had located, on June 29, 1987, in a large (600 square mile) forest, what ultimately became an unmarked, sizable gravesite by initially finding three human skeletons. News of his discovery tore open old scars of over forty years for near the end of World War II in 1945 hundreds of Polish citizens were arrested and collected by Soviet soldiers, taken to the forest and never heard from again. It had been presumed by the local Poles that these victims were considered enemies of the state and as such were executed in the forest. Although no evidence of mass executions had been unearthed, it was known that after the Germans withdrew from the region in 1944, the occupying Russians were constantly searching for remnants of the Polish Home Army. These loyal Poles had fought valiantly against the Germans, but were viewed as a threat to communism by the occupying Red army. Those arrested were never seen alive again. Indeed, there was no trace until mid-1987.

The local inhabitants could arrive at two possible conclusions. One was the mass deportation into Soviet Russia, as happened to so many Poles, or secondly, that there had been mass executions in the forest into which the prisoners had disappeared. As no information had reached the families of the victims for such an extended period of time the obvious presumption of death by execution prevailed.

With the discovery of the gravesite the word of mouth and official reports circulated to a widely disturbed citizenry. Many visitors made their way to the forest to pray for the victims, burn votive candles, and erect primitive wooden crosses.

When it was announced the Polish War Crimes Commission would conduct a formal investigation, the Polish people assumed the matter would be officially and objectively reported. But the truth appears to have been suppressed once more. The Polish Government-in-Warsaw, under the yoke of the Kremlin, reported after a single week-long investigation that the skeletons were those of Nazi soldiers, based on items of equipment and other objects obtained during the "exhumation and identification of the grave's contents," as the official report stated. Actually three large gravesites were found and investigated, the exact number included in stories which had circulated for years. The formal investigation was concluded.

Published reports resulting from interviews with the Polish villagers indicate that not a single local resident believes the conclusions of the War Crimes Commission. Neither do they believe the investigation was adequately conducted nor was the truth exposed. What the results do indicate is the continuing problems of the Polish Government-in-Warsaw in its formal political relationship with the U.S.S.R. The Soviet official policy of "glasnost" or "openness" might be the stated, current Kremlin public relations goal, but the actual implementation of the doctrine deviates from the theory and deprives the Polish citizenry of the truth.

Because there was no war declared between Russia and Poland in 1939, the Katyn incident might be rationalized on the basis the Polish officers were not POWs but political prisoners who had to be eliminated; and, they were! Even after almost fifty years the Russian leadership will not admit guilt because by Soviet standards the elimination of political opponents is the established policy of state; "right" if it serves the state; "wrong" if it does not. Since the Polish prisoners of war were both military and political victims they had only two choices: embrace communism and convince their captors, or as an enemy of the state pay the penalty of death.

Could the modest hope for justice eventually prevail? Could a logical precis include the fact that historians and legal scholars have yet to be heard? The circumstantial evidence against the Soviets regarding Katyn is so overwhelming that it has given support, meaning, and encouragement to the Polish people who are resisting, as exemplified by the lofty and worthwhile goals of the Solidarity trade union movement. Why has no international body such as the United Nations attempted to establish responsibility for the Katyn Forest Massacre? Has the de-Stalinization of the U.S.S.R. reached the level where guilt could be affixed to an errant decision? If not, then it could well mean the status quo or the policy of the "enemies of the state must be eliminated" remains the same. And the "quo vadis" or the future policy also remains the policy of the past—unchanged.

So far, in the free world of reality, no court or objective investigative body has absolved the Russians of guilt for the Katyn massacre; in fact, the Select Committee states positively the Russians were guilty of the "murders" of the Polish POWs. When the Russians brought the charges against the Germans for Katyn at the Nuremberg Tribunal, the international court did not find the Germans guilty; thus establishing the guilt for the Katyn atrocity on the Russians where it will remain from generation to generation.

The hearings of the Select Committee have been a tribute to the American system of democratic government; and those witnesses who testified before the committee, and experienced the strain and concern of getting things "in the record," have an appreciation of the value of testimony under oath. *In The Record* is a synthesis of the testimonies heard by this committee that travelled not only within the United States but also to London, Frankfurt, and Naples for never-before-attempted overseas hearings by members of Congress. The goal had been to place accurately and absolutely "in the record" the testimony of those witnesses so all the world will be aware of the atrocities which can be promulgated. There are people everywhere, and especially in Poland, who feel justice, mercy, and honor will not be served until the guilt has been established for the atrocity at Katyn. The fact remains, however, that the Select Committee shed light on the guilt or innocence of the countries involved in the massacre so the world's people could judge those who were responsible for the Katyn Massacre and at least hope that justice would prevail in the future.

The interim report of the Select Committee to Conduct an Investigation and Study of the Facts, Evidence and Circumstances of the Katyn Forest Massacre of the United States House of Representatives was filed on July 2, 1952; however, the committee continued to conduct hearings and take testimony under oath during the balance of the year and submitted its report to the Speaker of the House on December 22, 1952. The unanimous conclusion in the interim report (and never changed) of the Select Committee follows:

> This committee unanimously agrees that evidence dealing with the first phase of its investigation proves conclusively and irrevocably the Soviet NKVD (Peoples' Commissariat of Internal Affairs) committed the massacre of Polish Army officers in the Katyn Forest near Smolensk, Russia, not later than the spring of 1940.
>
> This committee further concludes that the Soviets had plotted this criminal extermination of Poland's intellectual leadership as early as the fall of 1939—shortly after Russia's treacherous invasion of the Polish nation's borders. There can be doubt this massacre was a calculated plot to eliminate all Polish leaders who subsequently would have opposed the Soviet's plans for communizing Poland.

NOTES: CHAPTER 1

1. Collier's World Atlas and Gazetteer, (P. F. Collier and Son Corporation, New York, 1946).
2. Thorndike-Barnhart Dictionary, (Scott, Foresman and Company, 1952, also published in 1942 and 1935).
3. Henry Wilson Littlefield's *History of Europe, 1500–1848,* (Barnes and Noble, Inc., 1939).
4. This research on Poland's past utilizes older references. For a series of more current discussions of Poland's immediate past see William P. Lineberry's *Poland,* (The W. H. Wilson Company, New York, 1984).
5. Adolf Hitler's *Mein Kampf, (My Battle),* was originally written while in prison in the early 1920's. (Abridged and translated by E. T. S. Dugdale, Boston and New York, Houghton-Mifflin Company, 1933. Also translated by Ralph Manheim, Houghton-Mifflin Company, Boston, 1943).
6. The First Reich, most research concludes, lasted about 1,000 years; from the coronation of Charlemagne in 800 A.D. to 1806. The term Second Reich extended from the victory over the French in the Franco-Prussian War of 1870, in 1871, to the abdication of Kaiser Wilhelm at the end of World War I in 1918. The Third Reich covered the tenure of Adolf Hitler, from 1933 to 1945, and was concluded with the termination of hostilities of World War II.
7. By design or not, an oddity or coincidence appears when Adolf Hitler refers to "natural law." For such an approach is reminiscent of the methodology used by Adam Smith in *The Nature and Causes of the Wealth of Nations* in 1776. Smith's monumental presentation laid down the foundation for modern economic thought in the free world. Although Smith started in the natural-law direction, his philosophy was modified by succeeding authors who, when taken in unison, provided the background for establishment of current economic systems outside the totalitarian world. The oddity is that the roots of the free enterprise system are the natural laws of competition, whereas Hitler's totalitarian dictatorship uses the term "natural law" as factor in economic control.
8. Another "tempest in a teapot" concerning the rise of Hitler's Nazi Party and the decline of the Weimar Republic started with the 1981 publication of the book, *The Collapse of the Weimar Republic,* (Princeton Press), by David Abraham, a Marxist, whose research and writing on the subject was his doctoral dissertation. In his view, the Weimar Republic failed as a democracy because the businessmen opposed it and instead supported Hitler financially in return for his promises of monopoly. This radical and flawed approach has been taken to task by a number of competent au-

thors, including Henry Ashley Turner, Jr., whose 1985 presentation, *German Big Business and the Rise of Hitler,* (Oxford University Press), states "only through gross distortion can big business be accorded a crucial, or even major role in the downfall of the republic." In a nutshell, then, big business had no reason to support the Nazis because the Weimar Republic had highly successful firms which as cartels were already protected by the German government.

9. The beginning of World War II with Hitler's invasion of Poland was covered in major newspapers as page-one material; i.e. three-line headlines in the *New York Times* of September 1, 1939. See *"Page One—Major Events, 1920–1975"* as reported in the *New York Times,* (Acno Press, New York, 1975).

10. B. H. Liddell Hart's *History of the Second World War,* (a Paragon book by G. H. Putnam's Sons, 1979), pp. 27–31. Hart critiques the Polish army's initial positions by noting the fact that had they been behind a river barrier they would have been better located defensively against an armored attack. Nonetheless, he notes the overwhelming reasons for deploying the Polish army as it was and fighting as it did.

11. The 8:00 A.M. broadcast of Russian Foreign Minister Molotov on September 17, 1939, summarized the contents of the "note" and added the reasons why the Soviet Union was invading Poland. Mr. Molotov's message stated in part, "events arising out of the Polish-German War have revealed the internal dissolution and obvious impotence of the Polish state. Polish ruling circles have suffered bankruptcy . . . Warsaw as the capital of the Polish state no longer exists. No one knows the whereabouts of the Polish government . . . The Polish state and its government has virtually ceased to exist . . ."

12. A reference from an article about the fighting around Grodno in the northeast of Poland. Other hotly contested fighting occurred at Lwow, Baranowicze, Dubno, and Tarnopol. The Russian writer quoted was Corps Commissar S. Kojevnikow; his article was entitled: "An Historic March."

13. This Soviet version of psychological warfare against the Polish soldiers had no impact on the individual Pole and his fighting capability. If anything, it sharpened his will to resist. In addition, no Polish records show any indication of "negotiators" coming from the Polish side being shot by the Poles. Quite the reverse, the records do show the senior Polish officer, General Wilczynski, Commanding Officer of the 3d Corps Area and officers with him, near Grodno (village of Sopockine), going forward to discuss a local armistice being shot and killed by the Russians.

   Another psychological ploy was to invite the Poles to surrender with the promise they would be allowed to "go south" into Romania where they would be reorganized to fight against the Germans. No data of this happening exists. Some Polish soldiers could have fled this route on their own; i.e. they had not yet been captured by the Germans or the Russians and evaded capture enroute to the border of Romania where they joined other Poles to fight against the Germans.

14. Some of the Polish enlisted men tried to protect and hide their officers while in the Russian POW camps for enlisted men. In some instances this practice was successful and lasted from the time of capture until their release in September, 1941, when they formed a Polish army on Russian soil. Earlier, some were sent from Russian to German POW camps.

15. Population estimates of prisoners of war at each camp, according to Polish records were as follows: Kozielsk with 4,500 officers, reserve officers, and cadet officers; Ostashkov with 6,500 officers, policemen, military policemen, and frontier guards; Starobielsk with 3,900 officers, reserve officers, and cadet officers.

16. Josef Czapski, *The Inhuman Land,* (London: Chatto and Windus, 1951). Major Czapski wrote as an eyewitness since he was a Polish prisoner of war at Starobielsk. As one of the seventy nine survivors who were not killed, he was sent to Pavlishchev Bor and finally to Griazovietz. The Polish officers there lived to join the Polish army formed in Russia in accord with the Russian-Polish pact of 1941. Major Czapski was a productive witness before the Select Committee when hearings were held in Frankfurt, Germany.

17. Of the 14,920 Polish prisoners of war reviewed here, only 448 were "selected" and transferred to Pavlishchev Bor. Later even fewer made it to Griazovietz. (At Kozielsk, for instance, 400 were initially chosen, but this number was later reduced to 245 who actually went to Pavlishchev Bor. Further screening significantly reduced the number of survivors.) The remnants of these 448 were later released in September, 1941, to become a part of a Polish military unit formed on Russian soil. These few Poles were the only eyewitnesses to the "closing" of the three Russian prisoners of war camps.

18. Some authors indicated that 2,000,000 German troops were involved in the initial assault upon the U.S S.R.; others pushed the number up to 3,000,000, a fifty per cent increase. Different authors applied different references and developed different answers.

19. Nikolai Tolstoy, *Stalin's Secret War,* New York: Holt, Rinehart and Winston, 1982, pp. 245–248. Tolstoy quotes Kravchenko, Ekart, et al who were particularly effective in reporting terminal acts of inhumanity on prisoners of the Soviet Union.

20. Victor Kravchenko, *I Chose Freedom,* London & New York: C. Scribner's Sons, 1946, pp. 356, 405.

21. Antoni Ekart, *Vanished Without Trace; The Story of Seven Years in Soviet Russia,* London: Max Parrish & Co., Ltd. 1954, pp 91–95.

22. Nikolai Tolstoy, op. cit. p. 241.

23. Ibid. p. 204.

24. Ibid. p. 232.

25. Most reports details the efficiency of the NKVD and the killing of thousands of "political prisoners." Wholesale slaughters were reported in Minsk, Smolensk, Kiev, Kharkov, Dnepropetrovsk, and Zapovozhve. In Kabardinor, in the Balkan Republic, hundreds of prisoners were machine gunned "to the last man and woman" by order of the local commissar. On June 28, 1941, the advancing Germans found five hundred dead and mutilated bodies, including many children, at Dubno. Another five hundred prisoners were slaughtered in the courtyard of the building at Provienka. At Tartu one hundred ninety two prisoners had been shot to death and their bodies placed in a well. Massacres were also recorded at Uman, Rovno, and Tallinn. At Tcherwene, in White Ruthenia, thousands upon thousands of prisoners were reported killed; including Poles, Ruthenians, Ukrainians, Russians, and Lithuanians. Many records referred to the closing of prisons within the Soviet Union

when confronted with the emergency of the German invasion of June, 1941. Too few escaped the slaughter. A German officer stated that "five or six thousand prisoners of the Soviet prisons" were seen on the road from Minsk to Smolensk.

26. Nikita Khrushchev. *Khrushchev Remembers,* Little, Brown and Company, 1970, pp. 101, 104. In addition to this reference, the *LIFE* Magazine series of reviews that started on November 27, 1970, emphasized in Part III, "The Menace of Beria," other strong remarks by Khrushchev; such as "Beria is a butcher and an assassin." (See also Nikita Khrushchev, *Khrushchev Remembers—The Last Testament,* Volume II, Little, Brown and Company, 1974.)

27. Lavrenti (sometimes Lavrenty) P. Beria was a Georgian, as was Premier Josef Stalin. Beria was named head of the Party Organization in Transcaucasia in 1931. Transferred in the mid-1930's to the position of secret police chief in Moscow, Beria took full command of all police organizations in December, 1938. He held this position for fifteen years and was referred to as the Commissar of Internal Affairs. In the aftermath of Stalin's death in March, 1953, he was removed from power in June, 1953, and executed for crimes against the state in December, 1953. Beria instituted an increased level of deprivation in the concentration camps, heightened the level of terror imposed by the secret police, and increased mass deportations. He was without a doubt a most feared and powerful party official during the last years of Josef Stalin. When named to the Politburo in 1946, he was the first secret police chief ever admitted as a full member to the Politburo, the Soviet ruling body. (See also Thaddeus Wittlin, *Commissar: The Life and Death of Lavrenty Pavlovich Beria,* the MacMillan Company, New York; Collier—MacMillan Limited, 1972).

28. In some research, the fact is omitted that the entire tragic massacre could have happened as "a misunderstanding" or failure to achieve a "meeting of the minds." This body of research maintains the event was well planned and executed from start to finish. However, so "no stone be unturned" and all possibilities covered to accomplish thoroughness in research, this study includes the possibility that an error of great magnitude could have occurred, even though the error-concept is offered only as a hypothetical possibility. Beria's reference to the "great error" or "great blunder" in the presence of some Polish prisoners of war confirms the concept that the massacre was planned, logistically and administratively supported, and literally executed on order of Moscow's highest authority.

29. *The Winston Dictionary,* published by the John C. Winston Company, 1943. Almost any dictionary uses similar definitive interpretations. *The Thorndike-Barnhart Dictionary,* 1952, (also 1942 and 1935), states: "settle the accounts of (a business); clear up the affairs of (a bankrupt)," then adds: "get rid of: the French Revolution liquidated the nobility." *The Webster's Collegiate Dictionary,* G. & C. Merriam Co. Springfield, Massachusetts, U.S.A., 1946, adds: "Figuratively, to clear up and dispose of as if by such process, as to liquidate 'illiteracy'."

30. The standard military operations procedures known to every commander and staff officer at every level. After the military order is given, the senior officer asks, "Are there any questions?" If there are none, or after further clarification is provided, every person moves to assure successful completion of the order. Even if not invited to ask questions, the rule applies. Why would Beria, an NKVD general, not have

asked questions and followed the military custom? Was it because of his arrogance or vanity, as Khrushchev suggests?

31. The Dzerzhinsky case can be used as an example, or precedent, of what would happen two decades later at Katyn Forest. Felix (sometimes Felicks) Dzerzhinsky was the founder and first chief of the Cheka, Lenin's secret police. A personally unselfish bleak ascetic with a friendly smile, he was utterly ruthless and merciless to political opponents. Dzerzhinsky was called the "knight of the proletariat."

At a meeting Lenin once scribbled a note to Dzerzhinsky asking how many political and other prisoners the Cheka had in jail. "About 1,500," the secret police chief wrote on the bottom of the note, which was returned. Lenin read it, muttered something, jotting an " + " or " × " beside the figure (Lenin's technique of indicating he had seen the message) and had it returned once more to Dzerzhinsky. This mark signified that Lenin had noted the figure, but Dzerzinsky mistook the meaning of the " + ." Silently, he left the room and had all 1,500 shot.

NOTES: CHAPTER 2

1. The United States of America became an Ally in the aftermath of the naval attack on Pearl Harbor, Hawaii, by the Japanese on December 7, 1941; for America and Great Britain declared war on Japan the next day, December 8, 1941. Hitler declared war on the United States three days thereafter (December 11, 1941), as did Italy, Germany, Japan, Hungary, Romania, and Bulgaria, the Axis Nations thereby became pitted against the Allied Nations: Great Britain, France, Russia, Poland, and the United States.

Worldwide confrontation had become a reality, and the United States proposed that all nations hostile to the Axis Nations pledge their cooperation to wage war and agree not to make a separate peace or armistice. A declaration to this effect was signed in Washington, D.C. (January 1, 1942) by the representatives of twenty-six governments: The United States of America, United Kingdom of Great Britain and Northern Ireland, Union of Soviet Socialist Republics, China, Australia, Belgium, Canada, Costa Rica, Cuba, Czechoslovakia, Dominican Republic, El Salvador, Greece, Guatemala, Haiti, Honduras, India, Luxembourg, the Netherlands, New Zealand, Nicaragua, Norway, Panama, Poland, South Africa and Yugoslavia. These nations were joined later in 1942 by Mexico, the Philippine Commonwealth, and Ethiopia. Joiners in 1943 were Iraq, Brazil, Bolivia, and the Free French. Thirty-three governments of the New and Old World were united and known as the "Allies."

2. A number of sources pinpoint verbal exchanges between Ambassador Kot and Deputy Commissioner for Foreign Affairs Vyshinsky (October 7, 13, 14, and November 1, 2, 1941; and July 8, 1942), plus written exchanges as well. Some sources indicated eight meetings were held, which is probably an accurate number.

3. The modern symbol of the cross, the traditional grave marker for military men and women for centuries, has a strong meaning for Christian minds. One of these crosses was still upright; the larger of the two had fallen over.

4. The logic of why the German High Command picked the number of "10,000 Polish officers" is unique. The Polish government in London was searching for almost 15,000 missing prisoners of war. The approach of the Germans was that 10,000 Polish officers were missing, plus the "intelligentsia," including educators, clergy, cadets, border and frontier guards, etc., and the Germans thought they had found the 10,000 officers. Actually, about 3,000 officers were already being exhumed.

5. The initials GPU (or OGPU) were the previous initials of the Soviet secret police which had already changed its name. The new initials NKVD (Narodny Kommissariat Vnutrennikh Del) were now in vogue. Later, this police group would become MVD; still later, KGB; and so it goes. The secret police can trace its roots back to the original Cheka, from Russian Revolution time frames. (The Cheka used the title "executioner" as a position description, and many members were formally photographed holding a handgun as a mark of authority or status symbol. One of the Cheka motivators was "Commission: Death to the Enemies."

   The secret police, NKVD, as a special detachment of governmental security within the U.S.S.R., dealt with the political prisoners (Politicheski Zakliuschene).

6. Most researchers agree on the tell-tale mark of Russian bayonets as the four sided plus sign (+). Some eye witnesses used the expression "fluted, four sided," which had the same meaning. Some few used the expression "fluted" with "three sided" or "triangular shaped." What these accounts express is that bayonets have "more than two sides" without specifically using the term "fluted," meaning "four sided."

7. The fact that the victims were buried in their uniforms was not always the rule for captives who were assassinated. In many "death camps" the nude bodies of victims were disposed of in whatever way was convenient.

   One respectful commentary on uniformed deceased military personnel is the recollection of the story of Rev. William E. Corby, a Holy Cross priest, later President of the University of Notre Dame, who served as a Union Chaplain at Gettysburg in the American Civil War. Before the Army of the Potomac collided with the Army of Northern Virginia in the wheat field in the early phases of the fighting at Gettysburg, July 1–3, 1863, Father Corby, C.S.C. gave a blessing (July 2, 1863) to the Union soldiers (of all denominations). He reminded them that no Christian burial would be provided for those who fled the battlefield; then he reported later that he included the absolution and prayers for the dead because he knew many of the soldiers being given the blessing were wearing "their burial shrouds."

8. Later testimony noted that when the weather moderated and exhumations loosened the soil, an eyewitness commented that the ground became like "light yellow-colored sand."

9. The final report of the German Field Police dated June 10, 1943, submitted by Lieutenant Ludwig Voss, the secretary:

> The work of exhuming, examining and identifying the bodies of Polish officers came to an end on June 7, 1943. In the first place it must be stressed that the Kosogory Forest was used as a place of execution of those sentenced to death by the NKVD or the Committee of 'The Three,' as early as 1925. Preliminary excavations undertaken in various parts of the wooded area invariably led to the discovery of mass-graves ('fraternal graves') in which the bodies of Russians of both sexes were found. Some of

these bodies were carefully examined and it was proved that, without exception, death was caused by a shot in the back of the neck. From the documents found, it appeared that they were prisoners from the NKVD jail in Smolensk, the majority being political prisoners.

The seven mass-graves of murdered Polish officers which have been cleared cover a relatively small area.

Of 4,143 exhumed bodies, 2,815 have been definitely identified. Identification was based on identity cards, birth certificates, and award certificates found in their pockets together with their personal correspondence.

In many cases identity cards, documents and considerable sums of zloty banknotes were sewn into the legs of their boots. Their clothes left no doubt as to their being Polish officers, for instance, the long cavalry boots of a shape normally worn by Polish officers.

A large number of hitherto unidentified bodies will undoubtedly be identified by the Polish Red Cross.

The number of officers of various ranks is given below:

Generals	2
Colonels	12
Lt.-Colonels	50
Majors	165
Captains	440
Lieutenants	542
2nd Lieutenants	930
Paymasters	2
Warrant Officers	8
Other NCOs	2
Identified as officers	101
Identified as "in uniform"	1,440
Medical Officers	146
Veterinaries	10
Chaplains	1
Civilians	221
Names only identified	21
Unidentified	50
	4,143

Bodies identified as 'being in uniform' must also be regarded as officers, for corresponding epaulettes were found in their pockets.

After the identification (during which each body was given a serial number) and after the forensic medical examination, the bodies were buried in the newly-dug graves with the assistance of members of the Polish Red Cross. The new graves are numbered from 1 to 6 and the numbers can be found on the reverse side of the crosses. The single graves of the generals were marked in a similar way.

A name roll of all identified persons was made in order to facilitate meeting further inquiries from the families.

From the translation of diaries, of memoirs and notes found with the bodies, it was proved that the officers had been taken prisoner by the Soviet Army in 1939, were sent to various camps: Kozielsk, Starobielsk, Ostashkov, Putiviel, Bolotov, Pavlishchev Bor, Shepyetovka, Gorodok. The majority of those killed in Katyn Forest had been in the Kozielsk camp (250 Kilometers south-east of Smolensk on the railway-line

Smolensk-Tambov). A few are known to have been brought from Starobielsk to Katyn through Kozielsk.

From the end of March, until the first day of May, 1940, the prisoners from Kozielsk arrived by rail. The exact dates cannot be established. A few short intervals apart, a batch left almost every day; the number of prisoners varied between 100 and 300 persons.

All trains were sent to Gniezdovo near Smolensk. Thence, in the early morning, the prisoners proceeded in special lorries (trucks) to the Katyn Forest, situated three kilometers west of Gniezdovo. There the officers were immediately shot, thrown into the waiting graves and buried, as may be seen from the evidence of witness Kisselev, who had seen the ditches being prepared.

That the shooting took place immediately after arrival of a batch of prisoners is proved by witnesses who heard shots after every arrival. There was no accommodation in the forest apart from the rest house, which had a limited capacity. The notes of Major Solski merit attention: the translation of his diary is preserved with other documentary evidence of the crime. Major Solski made a few entries in his diary during the last hour of his life.

A certain number of spent cartridge-cases with the stamp "Geco 7.65D" were found beyond the area of the graves; some single spent cases were found among the bodies in the graves. With a few exceptions, all the bodies show pistol-shots in the head; generally the place of entry of the bullet is below the protrusion on the back of the skull and the exit is in the forehead above the eye. (Cf. detailed photographs and the report of the medical expert, Professor Dr. Buhtz, as well as the evidence of a Polish doctor, Wodzinski.) In many instances the bullets had not left the skull. The calibre of the bullets found, 7.65 mm, would account for the damage to the skulls. The ammunition used was manufactured by the German firm of 'Genschow'. According to information given by the German High Command on May 31, 1943 (Ch. H. Rust und Befehlshaber des Ersatzheeres), ammunition for pistols of that calibre and actual pistols were supplied to Soviet Russia and Poland. It remains to be established whether the ammunition and pistols came from Russian dumps or from Polish equipment captured by the Russians when they overran the eastern part of Poland.

From the position of the bodies it may be assumed that the majority were murdered outside the graves. The bodies were in a complete tangle, except in graves Nos. 1, 2 and 4, where some of them lay side by side or on the top of each other. On some bodies spent cartridge cases were found between the collar of the victim's greatcoat and his neck, and there were holes in the collars of all the greatcoats. Every one of the collars was turned up. In other instances the bullets were found between the forehead and the inside of the cap. The number of persons shot in the graves totalled between 500 and 600.

Very many of the dead men had their hands tied behind their back. In the case of a small number of bodies there was evidence that the head had been covered by the service dress or greatcoat and that a cord of the type used for hanging curtains had been tied around the neck.

A few wedding rings and gold coins, etc., were the only valuables found in the victims' pockets. From the notes and diaries of the murdered persons it was evident that all valuables had been taken away from them in the camps. If anybody still possessed something of that kind, he had to hand it over immediately before the execution. They were left with zloty banknotes and these were found in great quantities.

In spite of repeated announcements and searches, no eyewitnesses of the murders could be traced. The only known name is that of the administrator of the Rest House who lived there. The evidence of witnesses confirm that access to the forest was forbidden.

Not all the bodies of the murdered officers had been exhumed when the work was interrupted, since a new grave of unknown capacity has recently been found. The possibility that further graves may come to light is not ruled out.

The papers and personal effects were kept separately marked with the serial numbers of the victims and were always mentioned in routine reports.

Voss,
Secretary of the Field Police

10. The report made by Dr. Gerhard Buhtz, Professor of Forensic Medicine and Criminology at Breslau University, as senior medical officer in charge of the German forensic medicine investigation:

On March 1, 1943, I received for examination a report from the Secret Field Police dated February 28, 1943, concerning the discovery in Katyn Forest of mass-graves of Polish officers shot in 1940 by NKVD personnel. Together with the representatives of the Secret Field Police I carried out a number of experimental exhumations and myself soon became convinced that the evidence collected during the interrogation of the inhabitants of a nearby village was confirmed by the facts. The frozen ground did not allow the exhumation and examination of the bodies to be started.

On the instructions of the German High Command the exhumation began on March 29, 1943.

Up to June 1, 1943, seven mass-graves containing the bodies of officers of the Polish Army were found in the area of Katyn Forest. These graves were situated near each other in a clearing in the wood and had young pine trees planted on the top of them.

The seven graves occupied a total area of at least 478 square metres.

The depth of the various graves was between 1.85 and 3.30 metres. The central sector of the longer arm of the L-shaped graves was the deepest place. The differences in the depth could be explained by the varying levels of the bottom of the graves. Thus the depth of grave No. 6 at its north-eastern end was 2.10, at the south-western end only 1.74 metres.

As a rule the graves were filled with bodies up to within 1.5 metres of the surface.

Grave No. 8 was discovered in the south-western part of the marshy lowlands on June 1, 1943, about 100 metres from the area occupied by graves Nos. 1 to 7.

In the woods north-east of the area of graves Nos. 1–7 on the other side of a forest track leading to the Rest House, and to the south-east of grave No. 8, several experimental excavations were carried out. They led to the discovery of the graves of many Russian civilians; this definitely confirmed previous information received to the effect that the Katyn Forest had been used for many years as a place of execution of the victims of the NKVD and of its predecessors, the Cheka and GPU.

On June 3, 1943, the exhumation work had to be temporarily stopped by the sanitary police on account of the heat and the flies.

Doctor Wodzinski, from Cracow, a representative of the Polish Red Cross, was recently made responsible for the work of protecting the bodies, which service had previously been carried out by specially trained German personnel assisted by workmen recruited from among local inhabitants.

All bodies exhumed from the seven graves were duly buried in new graves situated to the north-west of the original grave area. Thirteen bodies of Polish Army personnel from the grave No. 8 were re-buried in the same grave after examination and the securing of proof of identity.

All the bodies from graves 1–7 wore winter clothing, for most part military great-coats, leather or fur jerkins, pullovers and sweaters. Only two of the bodies exhumed from grave No. 8 on June 1, 1943, were in overcoats but not wearing warm under-clothes, the remainder were in summer clothes (officers in service dress).

We may deduce from this that the executions were carried out at different times of the year; this is corroborated by the various Russian and Polish newspapers, whole or fragmentary, found amongst the victims' personal papers. Whilst the newspapers found in graves Nos. 1–7 were dated March or the first half of April, 1940, those found in grave No. 8 bore dates ranging from the latter part of April to the beginning of May, 1940. For example, there were fragments of the Polish newspaper Glos Radziecki (edited in Kiev), dated April 26 and 28, 1940, with an editorial headed 'Catchwords for the First of May', as well as Russian newspapers dated May 1 and 6, 1940.

The uniforms in which the exhumed bodies were clothed were unquestionably those of the Polish Army, for with them were found the following articles: Polish eagles on the buttons, badges of rank, awards and medals, regimental badges, Polish type boots, field flasks, aluminum cups, and markings on the linen. It must be pointed out that amongst the victims there were many officers of Marshal J. Pilsudski's First Cavalry Regiment. This is proved by shoulderstraps found in grave No. 8 with the letters 'J. P.' It was a crack Polish Cavalry regiment.

The highest awards for gallantry were found on many victims' uniform; for instance, the Silver Cross, 'Virtuti Militari' (corresponding to the German Knight's Cross), the Polish Cross of Merit, the Cross for Valor, etc.

For the most part the uniforms were well cut and a good fit; the boots too were well-fitting. Often personal monograms were found on the underclothing. In all instances the uniforms and the underclothes were well-buttoned. Braces and belts were in good order. Apart from a few instances of damage by bayonets, the clothing had not been interfered with and there were no traces of violence.

All these facts lead to the conclusion that the victims were buried in the uniforms worn in captivity prior to their deaths, and that the bodies lay untouched until the opening of the graves. A theory, widely disseminated by the enemy, that the bodies were later dressed in Polish officers' uniforms is therefore without foundation. It is disproved by the medical examination of the bodies; moreover, forensic medicine has taught us that it would be out of the question to remove the clothes of thousands of dead bodies and then for the sake of camouflage, to cloth them in well-fitting lines and uniforms.

No watches or rings were found on the bodies; detailed entries in the diaries of certain victims indicate, however, that they had their watches with them up to the last. On one of the bodies a well concealed emerald ring of great value was found; several other bodies had valuables concealed on them, particularly silver cigarette cases. The gold from teeth had not been removed. Crosses, gold chains, etc., were found under the shirts.

Apart from small change (Polish paper money, nickel and copper coins), larger sums of money in zloty bank notes were found on the victims. In many instances wooden, hand made cigarette cases were found together with partly filled tobacco pouches, cigarette holders engraved with monograms, inscriptions and the dates 1939 or 1940. Often the work 'Kozielsk' was engraved on articles; this is the name of the camp, situated 250 kilometres south-west of Smolensk and 120 kilometres north of Orel, where the majority of the murdered officers were held. There was also personal correspondence from relatives and friends addressed to Kozielsk. Documents found on the victims (identity cards—but not military passports—diaries, letters, postcards, calendars, photographs, drawings, etc.) gave the name, age, profession, origin and family relations of the victims. Pathetic entries in the diaries testify to the treatment of the victims by the NKVD. Letters and postcards from relatives in Upper Silesia, in the "General Government" and in the Russian occupied zone, written, to judge the post office stamps, between Autumn, 1939 and March or April, 1940, clearly point to the time of the crime (spring, 1940).

Dr. Buhtz summarized his report by enumerating each fact briefly so that an accurate forensic medical conclusion would be recorded:

(1) As a result of the investigation in Katyn Forest 4,143 bodies of the members of the Polish Army were exhumed from the mass-graves. Out of this number 2,815 (67.9 per cent) were identified. On June 3, 1943, the exhumations had to be stopped for sanitary reasons (heat, flies). A lot more victims await exhumation, identification and forensic medical examination.

(2) Besides two major generals, the following victims were identified on the spot: 2,250 officers of various ranks, 156 medical and veterinary officers, 406 officers of unknown rank, warrant officers and cadet officers and one chaplain. Identification of remaining bodies continues, based on correspondence and other personal effects found upon them.

(3) On all the bodies were found small objects of a personal nature, including souvenirs, letters, documents, diaries. They wore well fitting Polish uniforms on which the rank badges, awards and medals could be recognized. In addition, many articles of military equipment were found on the bodies. The bodies from graves Nos. 1–7 were in winter uniform, those from grave No. 8 in summer clothing.

(4) Upon examination of the bodies, there was no suggestion that disease might have been the cause of death. With a few exceptions the usual bullet shot in the nape of the neck from a 7.65mm pistol was found. Corroboration is provided by corresponding spent cartridge cases and bullets (some lodged in bodies) and by one live cartridge found at the place of execution. In many instances the shots in the nape of the neck had passed through the raised collar of the greatcoat. Up to date physical, chemical and optical methods of investigation showed that the shots were fired at extremely close range.

(5) The execution most probably took place outside the graves.

(6) A uniform method of binding the hands across the back had been used on a considerable number of the victims. Others (particularly those from grave No. 5) had greatcoats thrown over their heads and in some cases sawdust was found between the coat and the face of the victim. Forensic medical examination brought to light distinct signs of torture.

(7) Numerous stab marks were found, undoubtedly inflicted prior to execution with a dagger like weapon corresponding to the fluted Russian bayonet. No doubt these stabs were a means of urging the victims on their way to the place of execution.

(8) Broken jaws, obviously suffered by the victims when they were still alive, prove that they were battered or beaten with rifle butts prior to the murder.

(9) The uniform shot in the nape of the neck and uniform method of tying the victim's hands and binding his head show that this was the work of skilled men.

(10) The bodies were in various stages of decay. In a few cases mummification of

the uncovered parts had taken place (bodies from the upper layers), but generally the formation of adipocere had started with the fat penetrating into the clothing.

(11) Initially, the decomposition of the bodies was not affected by the ground, but after some time it was partly influenced by the acids in the soil (formation of adipocere and preservation of inner organs). On the other hand the products of the decomposition caused characteristic (chemical and structural) changes in the soil. These phenomena show that the bodies lay undisturbed for years in their original place.

(12) The material discovered in the graves (amongst others, documents found there) and the evidence of witnesses (Russian inhabitants of the neighboring villages) prove that the bodies had lain in the graves for three years. The changes that had taken place, as ascertained during the post mortem, and the other findings at the inquest, bear this out.

(13) The execution and the burial of the victims were carried out in a cool season, when there were no insects. The documents, correspondence, diaries and newspapers found on the bodies prove that the officers were murdered in March, April and May, 1940.

NOTES: CHAPTER 3

1. Louis FitzGibbon, in a masterful style, used the title, *Katyn; Crime Without Parallel,* New York, Charles Scribner's Sons, 1971.
2. Thadeusz Romer, former Polish Ambassador to Moscow in testimony before the U.S. House of Representatives Select Committee to Conduct an *Investigation of the Facts, Evidence and Circumstances of the Katyn Forest Massacre,* Part 2, Washington D.C. (February 4, 5, 6 and 7, 1952) p. 126.
3. Facts brought out at the hearings before the Select Committee to Conduct an Investigation of the Facts, Evidence, and Circumstances of the Katyn Forest Massacre, Part 5, Frankfurt, Germany. Testimony of Dr. Tramsen, Danish member, International Medical Commission, p. 1465.
4. Protocol of the International Medical Commission, April 30, 1943. See Appendix 5.
5. Nikoli Tolstoy, *Stalin's Secret War,* Holt, Rinehart & Winston, 1982. Tolstoy's review of prison/jail closings is precise, especially with the German attack in progress.
6. In layperson's language, what does using comparables mean, when the estimate of murdered prisoners of war states, "approximately 15,000?" In America, if a person attended a football game at the University of Notre Dame Stadium which has a seating capacity of approximately 60,000, then one-fourth of the entire seating area would equal "approximately 15,000." Or, if one attended an athletic contest at the Hoosier Dome in Indianapolis, Indiana, again one-fourth of the seating capacity of 60,000 would equal "approximately 15,000."

NOTES: CHAPTER 4

1. Report of the Special Commission for Ascertaining and Investigating the Circumstances of the Shooting of Polish Officer Prisoners Of War by the German Fascist Invaders in the Katyn Forest.

2. Ibid. Introduction, page 1
3. Foreign correspondents invited to the Katyn Forest in January, 1944, during the time the Russians were conducting their investigation included the daughter of American Ambassador Averell Harriman. She (and others) asked the Soviet authorities why the deceased Polish officers were wearing winter clothing if they were killed by the Germans in August and September, 1941, and were told that the weather was unpredictable in that part of Russia. This explanation might be the reason why the Russians added "autumn, 1941" to the Soviet version of the massacre as the time frame for the deaths. The fact that the news stories of the foreign correspondents were held up by the Russian censors for three days so the stories could coincide with the publication of the Russian report suggests again the possibility of a need to adjust the time estimate for the deaths of Polish POW's.

NOTES: CHAPTER 5

1. Louis Fischer, *The Road to Yalta,* Soviet Foreign Relations, 1941–1945, Harper and Row, New York, Evanston, San Francisco, London, 1972. Page 75 commences his description of "Murder in the Forest," the logic of relating its importance, and why it should have been included in diplomatic relations and negotiations.
2. In July and August, 1945, the Potsdam Conference was held. This was after the death of President Roosevelt (April 12, 1945). His successor, President Harry Truman, represented the United States and was chosen Chairman. The post-conference announcements stated that there were to be "territorial adjustments in Poland and East Prussia;" also that "freedom of the press" and "unfettered elections in Poland" would be assured.
3. *Colliers World Atlas and Gazetteer,* P. F. Collier and Son Corporation, New York, 1946.
4. See cartographer's sketch map of pre-war and post-war boundaries of Poland (1939 and 1946).
5. The statements in reports and on maps indicating "The United States Government has not recognized the incorporation of Estonia, Latvia and Lithuania into the Soviet Union," do not ease the fact that the countries named have been taken over by Russia.
6. Also, a map-study will indicate that part of eastern Czechoslovakia (Carpatho-Ukraine) disappeared to become part of the U.S.S.R. which provided the latter with a frontier adjacent to Hungary (a necessary adjunct for the invasion of Hungary by the Soviets in 1956). This fact is mentioned here because this part of Czechoslovakia also bordered on Romania.
7. Paul Johnson, *Modern Times: The World from the Twenties to the Eighties,* Harper and Row, 1983.
8. The U.S.S.R. appropriated other gains, too. In earlier accords before Yalta, both the United States and Britain were in complete agreement that none of the Allies should seek territorial gains at the end of the war. This policy can be cited in the Atlantic Charter (August, 1941), the United Nations Declaration (January, 1942), and the Anglo-Russian Treaty of Alliance (May, 1942). At Yalta, however, Premier Stalin

gave a promise to enter the war against Japan, but his price was a high one because it included recognized territorial claims of Soviet control of Outer Mongolia, southern Sakhalin and nearby islands, concessions in Manchuria and China, and the outright annexation of the Kurile Islands. When President Roosevelt and Prime Minister Churchill yielded to Premier Stalin on these points, it assured the Soviets of naval and military power in the northern Pacific.

9. *Hearings of the Select Committee to Conduct an Investigation of the Facts, Evidence, and Circumstances of the Katyn Forest Massacre.* Part 7, Washington D.C., November 12, 1952. p. 2074.

10. Harsh critics of Prime Minister Churchill and President Roosevelt offered the opinion that the governments of Great Britain and the United States might not yet have received the first Van Vliet Report (May 22, 1945) or the Gilder Report (July, 1945), but that other information such as the Colonel Henry I. Szymanski reports of November 23, 1942, and May, 1943, were available.

In 1972 with the declassification of Foreign Office documents after the required thirty-year period, it was learned that the British Ambassador to Poland, Owen O'Malley, wrote to Foreign Minister Anthony Eden in 1943; "Most of us are convinced that a large number of Polish officers were indeed murdered by the Russian authorities." The harsh circumstances of the Katyn killings were quoted in this letter along with the official British diplomatic position of saying nothing about the atrocity to the Russians for fear of disrupting Allied unity. In the message Ambassador O'Malley concluded; "We have, in fact, perforce used the good name of England to cover up the massacre." (*TIME* Magazine, July, 1972, p. 31.)

11. Bill D. Ross, *IWO JIMA: Legacy of Valor,* Vanguard Press, New York, 1985, p. 322.

NOTES: CHAPTER 6

1. Some references use the spelling *Nurnberg.* In the Select Committee testimony at Frankfurt, Germany, separate and different spellings appear, sometimes on the same page.

2. Francis Biddle, *In Brief Authority,* Doubleday and Company, Inc. Garden City, New York, 1962.

3. Justice Robert Jackson had authored a worthwhile article in the "Atlantic Monthly" which detailed the far-reaching impact of conducting international trials, and expressed his professional views about the need for such a restitution of justice. President Truman appointed him immediately after the agreement had been reached by the conference in San Francisco.

4. Robert Falco signed the London Agreement and Charter for France, General Nikitchenko for the U.S.S.R., Justice Robert Jackson for the United States, and Lord Chancellor Jowitt for Great Britain.

5. *Record of hearings before the Select Committee to Conduct an Investigation of the Facts, Evidence and Circumstances of the Katyn Forest Massacre* conducted in Frankfurt, Germany, on April 24, 1952, p. 1539.

6. Ibid. p. 1541.

7. Ibid. p. 1542.
8. Ibid, pp. 1534–1548 and 1549–1556.
9. Ibid. p. 1550.
10. Ibid. p. 1554.
11. Ibid. p. 1554.

NOTES: CHAPTER 7

1. The Democrats were: Ray J. Madden, Indiana, Chairman; Daniel J. Flood, Pennsylvania; Foster Furcolo, Massachusetts; and Thaddeus M. Machrowicz, Michigan. The Republicans were: George A. Dondero, Michigan; Alvin E. O'Konski, Wisconsin; and Timothy P. Sheehan, Illinois.
2. *Interim Report of the U.S. Congressional Select Committee, July 2, 1952. Select Committee to Conduct an Investigation and Study of the Facts, Evidence and Circumstances of the Katyn Forest Massacre.*
3. *Final Report of the U.S. Congressional Select Committee, December 22, 1952 (Press Conference). Select Committee to Conduct an Investigation and Study of the Facts, Evidence and Circumstances of the Katyn Forest Massacre.*
4. Op. cit.
5. This "violation of human lives" in Poland has continued to be a strong criticism of the U.S.S.R. to this day. On Saturday, June 22, 1985, Polish Foreign Minister Stefan Olszowski had a private forty-minute audience with Pope John Paul II at the Vatican. When the Foreign Minister reported new churches were being built, etc., the Pope rebuked him and responded with the premise that church-state relations "are not the main concern. The real problem is between the society and the state." The Pope was expressing his displeasure with the (Moscow-controlled) Polish government's judicial conviction of three Solidarity leaders. (Vatican News Release of Sunday, June 23, 1985.)

NOTES: CHAPTER 8

1. Lieutenant Colonel Stewart's testimony was summarized as introductory material by American eyewitnesses. Other testimonies confirmed its details. *Hearings before the Select Committee to Conduct an Investigation of the Facts, Evidence and Circumstances of the Katyn Forest Massacre,* Part 1, Washington, D.C. October 11, 1951. p. 7.
2. Ibid. p. 10.
3. Ibid. p. 11.
4. Ibid. p. 12.
5. Ibid. p. 13.
6. Ibid. p. 13.
7. Ibid. p. 28.

8. *Hearings Before the Select Committee to Conduct an Investigation of the Facts, Evidence and Circumstances of the Katyn Forest Massacre*, Part 2, Washington, D.C. February 4, 5, 6 and 7, 1952. pp. 32–73.
9. Ibid. p. 40.
10. Ibid. p. 45.
11. Ibid. p. 53.
12. Ibid. p. 55. Colonel Van Vliet's Second Report is included as Appendix 1 (as is the initiating letter of April 26, 1950).
13. Ibid. p. 103.
14. Ibid. p. 125.
15. Ibid. p. 125.
16. Ibid. p. 181.
17. Ibid. p. 182.
18. Ibid. p. 184.
19. Ibid. p. 201.
20. Ibid. p. 201.
21. Ibid. p. 209.
22. Ibid. p. 209.

NOTES: CHAPTER 9

1. *Hearings before the Select Committee to Conduct an Investigation of the Facts, Evidence and Circumstances of the Katyn Forest Massacre*, Part 3, Chicago, Illinois, March 13 and 14, 1952.
2. Ibid. pp. 310–334.
3. Ibid. pp. 335–340.
4. Ibid. pp. 502– (The original roster numbered some 317 pages. It was reduced later to two small pages per page of testimony.) Mr. Moszynski introduced the list by stating his purpose: "In this manner, I hope to repay Providence for sparing my life and at the same time give the service to all those fellow prisoners of war who through the tragic dictates of fate had paid with their lives."
5. Ibid. pp. 340–358.
6. Ibid. p. 342.
7. Ibid. pp. 358–368.
8. Ibid. pp. 368–374.
9. Ibid. pp. 375–384.
10. Ibid. p. 377.
11. Ibid. p. 379.
12. Ibid. pp. 384–415.
13. Ibid. p. 385.
14. Ibid. p. 412.
15. Ibid. pp. 414–415.
16. Ibid. p. 416–501.
17. Ibid. p. 472.

NOTES: CHAPTER 10

1. *Hearings before the Select Committee to Conduct an Investigation into the Facts, Evidence and Circumstances of the Katyn Forest Massacre.* Part 4: London, England; April 16, 17, 18 and 19, 1952.
2. Ibid. pp. 503, 504.
3. Ibid. p. 504.
4. Ibid. p. 506–517.
5. Ibid. p. 508.
6. Ibid. p. 509.
7. Ibid. p. 515.
8. Ibid. pp. 517–523.
9. Ibid. p. 520.
10. Ibid. p. 523.
11. Ibid. pp. 524–551, 552–556, 571–603.
12. Ibid. p. 525.
13. Ibid. p. 550.
14. Ibid. p. 553.
15. Ibid. p. 555.
16. Ibid. pp. 551–552, 556–571.
17. Ibid. pp. 603–611. (later identified as Professor Stanislaw Swianiewicz)
18. Ibid. p. 610.
19. Ibid. pp. 611–613, 618.
20. Ibid. p. 612.
21. Ibid. pp. 614–618.
22. Ibid. p. 618.
23. Ibid. pp. 618–628.
24. Ibid. pp. 624–628.
25. Ibid. p. 627.
26. Ibid. p. 628.
27. Ibid. pp. 628–632.
28. Ibid. p. 631.
29. Ibid. pp. 632–636.
30. Ibid. pp. 636–638.
31. Ibid. pp. 638–647.
32. Ibid. p. 647.
33. Ibid. pp. 648–653.
34. Ibid. p. 651.
35. Ibid. p. 652.
36. Ibid. p. 653.
37. Ibid. pp. 656–665.
38. Ibid. p. 661.
39. Ibid. p. 663.
40. Ibid. p. 665.
41. Ibid. pp. 665–679.

42. Ibid. p. 670.
43. Ibid. p. 679.
44. Ibid. pp. 680–707.
45. Ibid. p. 691.
46. Ibid. p. 689.
47. Ibid. pp. 708–738.
48. Ibid. p. 711.
49. Ibid. p. 735.
50. Ibid. pp. 738–756.
51. Ibid. p. 739.
52. Ibid. p. 740.
53. Ibid. p. 746.
54. Ibid. p. 747.
55. Ibid. pp. 760–769.
56. Ibid. p. 768.
57. Ibid. pp. 771–774.
58. Ibid. p. 773.
59. Ibid. p. 774.
60. Ibid. pp. 775–778.
61. Ibid. p. 777.
62. Ibid. p. 777.
63. Ibid. pp. 779–785.
64. Ibid. pp. 785–790.
65. Ibid. pp. 790–798.
66. Ibid. pp. 867–881.
67. Ibid. p. 881.
68. Ibid. pp. 881–929.
69. Ibid. p. 904.
70. Ibid. p. 913.
71. Ibid. pp. 926, 927.
72. Ibid. pp. 931–968.
73. Ibid. p. 934.
74. Ibid. p. 935.
75. Ibid. p. 967.
76. Ibid. p. 967.

NOTES: CHAPTER 11

1. *Hearings before the Select Committee to Conduct an Investigation of the Facts, Evidence and Circumstances of the Katyn Forest Massacre,* Part 5, Frankfurt, Germany, April 21, 22, 23, 24 and 25. 1952.
2. Ibid. pp. 1230–1244.
3. Ibid. p. 1233.
4. Ibid. p. 1234.

5. Ibid. p. 1236.
6. Ibid. p. 1244.
7. Ibid. pp. 1246–1249.
8. Ibid. pp. 1249–1262.
9. Ibid. p. 1257.
10. Ibid. p. 1259.
11. Ibid. pp. 1263–1281.
12. Ibid. p. 1277.
13. Ibid. pp. 1281–1287.
14. Ibid. p. 1284.
15. Ibid. pp. 1287–1302.
16. Ibid. pp. 1303–1318.
17. Ibid. p. 1310.
18. Ibid. p. 1311.
19. Ibid. p. 1313.
20. Ibid. p. 1318.
21. Ibid. pp. 1318–1329.
22. Ibid. pp. 1320, 1321, 1322.
23. Ibid. p. 1324.
24. Ibid. pp. 1329–1335.
25. Ibid. p. 1334.
26. Ibid. pp. 1337–1416.
27. Ibid. pp. 1363, 1364.
28. Ibid. pp. 1416–1419.
29. Ibid. p. 1419.
30. Ibid. pp. 1420–1470 and pp. 1475–1485.
31. Ibid. p. 1455.
32. Ibid. p. 1455.
33. Ibid. p. 1464.
34. Ibid. p. 1464.
35. Ibid. p. 1465.
36. Ibid. p. 1467.
37. Ibid. p. 1468, 1469.
38. Ibid. pp. 1485–1491.
39. Ibid. p. 1491.
40. Ibid. pp. 1491–1495.
41. Ibid. pp. 1497–1505.
42. Ibid. pp. 1505–1509.
43. Ibid. pp. 1509–1511.
44. Ibid. pp. 1511–1519.
45. Ibid. p. 1515.
46. Ibid. p. 1517.
47. Ibid. pp. 1557–1567.
48. Ibid. p. 1567.
49. Ibid. p. 1567.
50. Ibid. pp. 1568–1573.

51. Ibid. p. 1569.
52. Ibid. pp. 1574–1577.
53. Ibid. p. 1576.
54. Ibid. pp. 1577–1580.
55. Ibid. pp. 1597–1602.
56. Ibid. pp. 1602–1615.
57. Ibid. p. 1613.
58. Ibid. pp. 1617–1621.
59. Ibid. p. 1621.

NOTES: CHAPTER 12

1. *Hearings Before the Select Committee to Conduct An Investigation of the Facts, Evidence and Circumstances of the Katyn Forest Massacre.* Part 6, pp. 1623–1823.
2. *Hearings Before the Select Committee to Conduct An Investigation of the Facts, Evidence and Circumstances of the Katyn Forest Massacre.* Part 7, June 3, 4, and November 11, 12, 13, 14, 1952.
3. Ibid. pp. 1939–1942.
4. Ibid. p. 1941.
5. Ibid. p. 1944.
6. Ibid. pp. 1945–1978.
7. Ibid. p. 1946.
8. Ibid. p. 1951.
9. Ibid. p. 1953.
10. Ibid. p. 1958.
11. Ibid. pp. 2042–2056, 2060–2074.
12. Ibid. p. 2044.
13. Ibid. p. 2050.
14. Ibid. pp. 2075–2103.
15. Ibid. p. 2086.
16. Ibid. pp. 2103–2131.
17. Ibid. p. 2107.
18. Ibid. p. 2115.
19. Ibid. pp. 2132–2149.
20. Ibid. pp. 2149–2153.
21. Ibid. pp. 2155–2173.
22. Ibid. p. 2162.
23. Ibid. p. 2163.
24. Ibid. pp. 2196–2215.
25. Ibid. pp. 2216–2226.
26. Ibid. pp. 2226–2241.
27. Ibid. pp. 2241–2246.
28. Ibid. pp. 2266.

NOTES: CHAPTER 13

1. David S. Wyman, *The Abandonment of the Jews: America and the Holocaust, 1941–1945,* New York: Pantheon Books, 1984.
2. Lucy S. Dawidowicz, *The War Against the Jews, 1933–1945,* New York: Holt, Rinehart, and Winston, 1975.
3. Martin Gilbert, *Atlas of the Holocaust,* New York: MacMillan Publishing Company, Inc., 1982.
4. Winston Churchill, wartime Prime Minister of Great Britain, delivered a postwar speech in Fulton, Missouri, (1946), in which he used the term "iron curtain" to describe effectively the clandestine activities of the satellite governments of the U.S.S.R. and the government of Russia itself. The term has continued to be used extensively for four decades as a short, succinct description for communist countries.
5. "Forensic medicine" is a valuable scientific tool practiced by the legal-medical field currently and in the timeframe of this study. In June, 1985, a team of international medical personnel, specializing in forensic medicine, investigated what was thought to be the remains of Josef Mengele, the "Angel of Death," who as a German physician conducted gristly human experiments at the Auschwitz death camp during World War II. Mengele was apparently the victim of a drowning in Brazil, South America, in February, 1979. When his body was exhumed in 1985, there were only a few bones remaining; however, the doctors of forensic medicine concluded from the remains—along with certain comparisons of physical evidence, photos, and medical records—that the deceased was in all probability Josef Mengele.
6. Father Jerzy Popieluszko was abducted, beaten, and tortured to death (October, 1984). The entire Polish nation was shocked and enraged at the inhuman treatment of the defenseless priest after his bound, gagged and battered body had been removed from a reservoir. He was one of the priests of Solidarity, and is spoken of as a Polish martyr. Visitors to Poland, including diplomatic dignitaries, pay him honor by visiting his grave.
7. *Wall Street Journal,* Wednesday, January 14, 1987, p. 1. Also *Muncie Star,* Wednesday, January 14, 1987, p. 24.
8. The Independent Self Governing Trade Union Solidarity (its formal name is rendered in Polish abbreviations as NSZZ SOLIDARNOSC).
9. Leonard R. Sussman, Article: Press Freedom, Secrecy and Censors, in *Freedom At Issue,* January-February, 1987, p. 9.
10. *TIME* Magazine, July 17, 1972, p. 31.
11. Jane Leftwich Curry, translated and edited by, *The Black Book of Polish Censorship,* Random House, New York, 1984, pp. 340–42. These Polish censorship documents were smuggled out of the country by Tomasz Strzyzewski, an official of the Krakow censors office.
12. Los Angeles Times, Sunday edition of September 28, 1987, by Times Staff Writer, Charles T. Powers was one. Others included the Indianapolis Star of July 21, 1987, with a story by Benjamin R. Cole.

Appendix 1

Colonel Van Vliet's Second Statement Regarding Katyn (including letter
requesting the report)

Quarters 165
Ft. Lewis, Washington
11 May, 1950

Subject: THE KATYN CASE

To: F. L. PARKS,
        Major General, USA
        Chief of Information

1. Pursuant to your letter of 26 Apr 1950 (incl #1) I am personally
typing this report of my recollections concerning the KATYN Case. I am retain-
ing one carbon copy for my personal file.

2. Since five years have elapsed since I made the first report to Maj.
Gen. Bissell, this report will have to omit some details such as names which I
have forgotten. In order to assist in locating my original report here are the
circumstances under which it was made.

On 22 May 1945 Gen. Bissell discussed the case with me alone in his
private office in the Pentagon for about 20 minutes. He decided that it was
important and directed his civilian female assistant (secretary ? stenographer ?) to go with me to closed room across the hall and take dictation. I
dictated my report, she typed it up and we added the photographs as inclo-
sures. The General read the finished report, directed that it be marked "Top
Secret" and filed. He then dictated the letter directing me to silence, and
had me sign a copy of it in his presence. He explained the importance of my
remaining silent, gave me my copy of the letter and thanked me.

3. Narrative: I was a prisoner of war at Oflag IX/AZ in Rotenburg,
Germany in April, 1943. It was primarily a British Officers prison camp headed
by Brigadier Nicholson (who had been the defender of CALAIS). I was the

senior of the 125 (approx.) American officers in the camp. At this time the German press began a big splurge on the KATYN case. So also did the German radio.

(Note: mention of this radio violates the certificate I had to sign upon being processed as a returned POW.)

Hauptman HEYL, the German camp commander, told Brig. Nicholson and me that he had orders to send two American officers and one British officer to the RR station at KASSELL, Germany where they would be met by British Maj. Gen. FORTUNE (from another nearby POW camp. He had commanded the British 1st Division in France).

Hauptman Heyl stated that I would be one of the two U.S. officers; that I would select the other one; that together with other Allied prisoners we would be a "Board of Inquiry" to investigate the Katyn Massacre. I flatly refused to have any part of it. Brig. Nicholson backed me up on this and together we wrote a letter to the Swiss Protecting Power which stated that no officers from the camp would make any visit to Katyn or make any investigation, or express any opinion. That if we were forced to go it would be only as individual prisoners under guard and against our protest. That we could not be considered as representatives of the prison camp, our army, or our nation, and that we protested violently this apparent attempt to use us for German Propaganda Purposes.

Our protest did no good. Using armed guards, the Germans took me and Capt. Donald Stewart, FA (regular army) to the Kassel RR station where they expected to meet Maj. Gen. Fortune. He did not arrive, to the surprise of the German guards. We were then taken to Berlin and jailed in an Arbeits Kommando (sp?)—a building overlooking the Spree River, housing PWs of several nationalities who were performing labor in Berlin.

In this Jail we met several U.S. soldiers who had been brought from a nearby PW camp for the same reason that we had. One of these[1] was a CPL TAUSSIG who had been in the same regiment with me for the invasion of Algiers by the 168th Inf. There were also several British soldiers and a British civilian (internee) as well as[2] LT COL STEVENSON (British, South African, Sig corps) and a British captain, medical corps, whose name I cannot now remember. In my opinion these men were actually what they appeared to be and did not include any "plants." We prisoners of war were very careful in our efforts to make certain identification.

---

[1] I knew Taussig personally.

[2] Lt. Col. Stevenson was from the same camp as Capt. Stewart and myself. He had come to Berlin with us. We knew him.

Soon we were taken, one by one, to the jail office where we were interviewed by several German staff officers and some civilian officials who appeared to be from both the foreign office and the propaganda ministry. The procedure appeared about the same for all of us: "Since you have volunteered to investigate this terrible Katyn atrocity, we are taking you to the scene. You will of course sign a parole not to escape."

"The hell we did volunteer. We don't want to go. Send us back to our camps." Great surprise and much chatter among the Germans. Then the same thing over again.

Finally they announced that since we wouldn't give our paroles they would have to place guards on the airplane with us. This meant that some prisoners would not make the trip, to make room for the guards. The American soldiers were left back.

Lt. Col. Stevenson was the senior in the group. We cautioned the entire group to do no talking, to give no indications of opinion, and not to cooperate in any way with the Germans. All agreed. It was evident to all of us that we were involved in an international mess with terrific political implications.

An English-speaking German captain was placed in charge of the group together with an English-speaking Sonderfuhrer (sp?) who gave the name of Von Johnson, spoke idiomatic American, and said he had attended school at Rice in the USA.

We were flown from Templehof to Smolensk about the 6th of May, 1943. At that time Smolensk was about 60 miles from the front and appeared to contain only garrison troops. We were billeted in some of the remaining intact buildings, of which there were only a few. Some sort of a German service unit maintained an officers mess where we all ate. While in Smolensk we were taken on a sight-seeing tour by the local service unit commander and a major who appeared to be an agricultural expert and enthusiast who was trying to rehabilitate the land with the remnants of the Russian peasant population. His efforts included a model village. In my opinion this "hospitality" was spontaneous and was prompted partly by his own enthusiasm for his work and partly because he hadn't had many visitors. It didn't appear to be organized on orders from Berlin.

A German Lt. (spoke no English) appeared from the group that was in charge of operations at the scene of the Mass Graves in KATYN Forest. He acted as our guide. We were driven to the site where there was a gate, guarded by young soldiers in Polish uniforms. A sickly-sweet odor of decaying bodies was everywhere. At the graves it was nearly overpowering. There were several graves. Professor Herr Doktor BUTZ (BOOTZ?), a German expert in forensic medicine was present together with other technicians. Several Polish Red Cross workers were present. Civilian labor was being used to remove bodies from the graves. Each body was searched very carefully, examined, identified, and reburied in a nearby mass grave which was to become a national shrine with suitable monuments. The articles removed from each body were placed in a large manilla envelope for safekeeping. The search of the bodies was very thorough, including removal of shoes or boots where it was possible. (Sometimes the whole leg from the knee down came off with the boot). The examiners wore rubber aprons and rubber gloves. A typist was present recording the findings on each body.

We followed our guide right into each of the graves—stepping on bodies that were piled like cord wood, face down usually to a depth of about 5 to 7 bodies covered with about 5 feet of earth. About 300 bodies were laid out beside one of the graves. These all had their hands tied behind them with cord. The rest appeared not to have been tied. All bodies had a bullet hole in the back of head near the neck with the exit wound of the bullet being in the forehead or front upper part of the skull.

The graves on the down-hill part of the slope were more moist than the others. One end of one grave had standing water in it. German photographers were present and took both still and motion pictures of our party while we inspected the graves. Copies of the still pictures were later given to us. We never saw or heard anything of the movies.

After we inspected the graves we were shown several other test holes which had been dug in the vicinity, together with very old human bones, i.e., no meat left on them, which were said to have been dug up there. I am inclined to believe the story, although there was no proof. The Germans made much of the fact that this wooded knoll was a long-standing burial site used by the Russian secret police. I forget whether they called them the OGPU, NKVD, or MVD. There was a rustic lodge on the low bluff overlooking the small landing on the river (Dneiper River, I believe). This lodge was allegedly the scene of frequent tortures, drinking parties, and various other orgies held by the Russian police as matters of amusement and recreation as well as routine business. The Germans produced an old peasant, Russian, who claimed that this forest of Katyn had an evil reputation—it was forbidden ground—that he had seen big closed vans go from the railroad siding (some miles distant) into the forest and that there were stories of shots being heard very often in the woods. This was supposed to confirm that the Russians had brought the victims to the mass graves by rail and truck some time before the Germans occupied the area.

The British medical captain in the group understood German very well and a little Russian which he had learned while taking care of Russian prisoners.

About a mile down the road the Germans had taken over a house as a field museum and office. The porch and front rooms were filled with glass showcases containing items removed from bodies in the graves. There were sample uniform insignia ranging from General to Lieutenant, there were several

Geneva arm bands, many letters, photographs, diaries, news clippings, personal souvenirs, etc. These items were just the better samples. In the back rooms of the house there were the individual envelopes containing the items removed from the corpses. This building was also permeated with the smell of the graves, coming from the showcases and the envelopes.

At this point the Germans produced two small drinks for everyone and then we returned to our billets in Smolensk.

We were flown back to the same Jail in Berlin and stayed there about 10 days. During this time the Germans were apparently trying to decide what to do with us. (The British soldiers and the civilian internee were returned to their respective camps before the end of this ten day period—or so we were told—leaving us four officers to wonder what it was all about. An English speaking German soldier or Sonderfuhrer Von Johnson would take us for walk through the Tiergarten every day, along with guards. It was during this walk period that we had a chance to talk without fear of microphones. Our discussion while in the Jail always avoided any mention of what we thought about who had committed the murders at Katyn.

During these walks, Lt. Col. Stevenson did a lot of talking with the Germans. Told them that he had once published a book and that as soon as he returned home he was going to get permission from his superiors to write a book about this experience. We couldn't get him to shut up about any subject at any time except the big question of "Whodunnit?" He was a windbag. He claimed to be a member of a group of amateur investigators of the supernatural. He even carried a feather in his wallet which he said was from the headdress of the American Indian Chief (spirit) whom he had contacted through a medium in S. Africa.

We gathered from the Germans that the front office didn't know what to do with us. There was some hopeful implication that we might be released, possibly through Spain.

One afternoon Lt. Col. Stevenson was bundled off by the Germans on about ten minutes notice. He seemed very surprised and quite uneasy as he left the Jail. We never saw or heard of him again. That night Capt. Stewart and I were returned to our original prison camp, where we were met by Hauptman Heyl. We asked him what kind of a story he had told us about going to meet Maj. Gen. Fortune. He replied that Fortune had been seriously ill with bronchitis.

(I later met Maj. Gen. Fortune and he had not been sick at all.)

[Insert] Prior to leaving Berlin we were told that Germany had not and would not make any propaganda use of our visit to the graves or the pictures taken of the visit. I have never heard of their doing so. Throughout the rest of our time in prison camps Capt. Stewart and I refused to discuss our experiences concerning Katyn and never stated what opinion we had formed.

I reached the American lines in the sector of the 104th Inf. Div. near Duben, Germany at the MULDE River line on 5 May 1945, still carrying the photographs given me at KATYN.

I showed the photographs to G-2 of the 104th Div. (I had previously showed these to only one other person apart form the German prison camp security personnel who conducted periodic searches, but always allowed me to keep the photographs because they had been stamped "Gepruft". This other person was Col. Thomas D. Drake, Senior officer of Oflag 64 who was repatriated for stomach ulcers. Before he left the prison camp to be repatriated Capt. Stewart and I talked with him, showed him the pictures and asked that he report the matter to the War Dept. He laughed at me and said that I had been taken in completely by the German Propaganda Experts. I don't know if he ever mentioned the matter when he reached the States).

G-2 of the 104th Div. recognized that my report was one of interest to both the State and War Depts. and provided transportation to Hq. VII Corps in Leipzig. General J. Lawton Collins then commanded the VII Corps.

Gen. Collins (who has known me since I was a child) discussed the matter with me and set the necessary wheels in motion to get me back to the Pentagon with all haste.

In Paris I stayed with Gen. Barker and at his suggestion discussed the matter with a full colonel (whose name I have forgotten) connected with War Crimes Investigations. He decided it was a matter for the War Dept. and the State Dept. and took no action.

COL. DRAKE, GEN. COLLINS, GEN. BISSELL, AND GEN. BISSELLS' STENOGRAPHER ARE THE ONLY PERSONS I HAVE EVER TOLD OF MY CONCLUSIONS CONCERNING WHO MURDERED THE POLISH OFFICERS AT KATYN. (Except, of course, the other members of the party who visited the site with me.)

4. CONCLUSIONS: I believe that the Russians did it. The rest of the group that visited the site stated to me that they believed that the Russians did it. (Capt., now Major, Donald Steward, FA, can be asked to verify this. I don't know his present address. He is regular army).

5. Discussion: At the beginning of the newspaper publicity concerning KATYN I believed the whole thing to be one huge, well managed, desperate lie by the Germans to split the Western Allies from Russia.

I hated the Germans. I didn't want to believe them. At that time, like many others, I more or less believed that Russia could get along with us.

When I became involved in the visit to KATYN I realized that the Germans would do their best to convince me that Russia was guilty. I made up my mind not to be convinced by what must be a propaganda effort.

The apparent weak spot in the German story was the fact that Germany had occupied the ground around Smolensk for a long time before announcing the discovery of the graves. (The exact dates are a matter of record. I don't have the facilities to look them up for entry in this report).

I wanted to believe that whole thing was a frame-up. Could these be bodies from an extermination camp, dressed as Polish officers and "planted"?

Could the letters, diaries, identification tags, news clippings—all be forgeries?

What about the state of decomposition of the bodies? Did it appear to agree with the German story of when they must have been buried? After all, I'm no expert on body-decomposition. What about the temperature, moisture, soil bacteria? What about the German statements that Polish families had been trying to locate their relatives, known to have been imprisoned when Russia occupied part of Poland? Was it true that these Polish relatives ceased to get answers from their imprisoned relatives-that a cloak of mystery descended all at once? Where is PROOF of who killed these men? Who saw it done?

And so on and so on—I tried every way I knew how to avoid believing that Russia had done it. I tried every way to convince myself that the Germans had done it. I wanted to believe that the Germans had done it.

Since the graves were already opened when we were there, it was not possible to see for ourselves what sort of ground had existed on top of the graves, in order to see how long the graves had existed. And if we had been present, how could we know that the Germans hadn't cleverly transplanted older bushes to give the appearance of age to the graves?

So you see that we pursued every line of attack to weaken the German story and avoid the conclusion that the Russians had done the killing. It was only with great reluctance that I decided finally that it must be true; that for once the Germans weren't lying, that the facts were as claimed by the Germans. I have thought about this a lot in the past seven years, and freely admit that there never was presented to me any single piece of evidence that could be taken as an absolute proof. But the sum of circumstantial evidence, impressions formed at the time of looking at the graves, what I saw in the peoples faces—all forces the conclusion that Russia did it.

The uniforms on the bodies were obviously of the best material and tailor made. The footwear appeared to be of the best and included many pairs that were obviously made to order. The uniforms and footwear all were obviously well-fitted. This convinced me that the bodies were truly those of Polish officers. The degree of wear on the clothing and particularly the wear on the shoes led me to believe that these officers had been dead a long time, otherwise the shoes and clothing would show much more wear. This was a point that was not called to our attention by the Germans. It is one of the strongest arguments by which to fix the date of the killing.

6. Last summer I received some letters from MR. MONTGOMERY M. GREEN. I wrote the Dept. of the Army for instructions on how to reply to

Mr. Green. In order to clear my files and possibly to be of assistance to Captain Semple, I am enclosing some papers marked: "MONTGOMERY GREEN and related papers."

(signed) John H. Van Vliet, Jr.
JOHN H. VAN VLIET, JR.
Lt. Col, 23rd Infantry

Incl. #1: Ltr, Request for Intel. Rpt.
       Gen Parks to Lt. Col. V. V.
Incl. #2: "MONTGOMERY GREEN and related papers"
Incl. #3: Cert. true cpy, Directive from Gen. Bissell to Lt. Col. V. V.

April 26, 1950

Subject: Request for Intelligence Report

To: Lt. Col. John H. Van Vliet, Executive Officer, 23rd Infantry Regiment, 2nd Infantry Division, Fort Lewis, Washington

    1. Reference is made to telephonic conversation of 24 April 1950 with Captain Malcolm M. Semple, Public Information Division, and Mr. Thomas E. Connor, Consultant to the Chief of Information.

    2. A thorough search has been made in the files of G-2, and the report which you made to General Bissell on 22 May 1945 has not yet been found. A search is being continued with the various intelligence agencies; however, until such time as the report is located, it is requested that another report be rendered on your experience with the Katyn case.

    3. The memorandum addressed to you on 22 May 1945 by the then Assistant Chief of Staff, G-2, General Bissell, directing you to silence regarding the Katyn case, is rescinded for the purpose of rendering the above-requested report. However, it must be pointed out that the exception to silence is valid only for this particular report, and, until further notice, the order directing you to silence will again become effective.

    4. Request the report be classified "Secret" and returned to me personally.

F. L. Parks,
Major General, USA,
Chief of Information

In the lower left-hand corner is "Incl. #1."
On the reverse side of this exhibit in the upper left-hand corner is:

AMBAG—0201 Van Vliet, John H. (O), 1st Ind., JJM/f

Subject: Request Made of Lt. Col. Van Vliet for Summary of Certain War Observations.

Hq., 2d Infantry Division, Fort Lewis, Washington, 20 September 1949

Appendix 2

(Translated From Russian)
Peoples Commissariat For Foreign Affairs
V. Molotov's Note of April 25, 1943

Moscow, April 25th, 1943

Mr. Ambassador,

On instruction of the Government of the Union of Soviet Socialist Republics, I have the honour to inform the Polish Government of the following:

The Soviet Government finds the behaviour of the Polish Government during the last period of time absolutely abnormal, infringing all the rules and norms of mutual relations as between two Allied States.

The Polish Government has been eager to pick up, and the Polish official press is in every way inflaming, the calumnious campaign launched by German fascists regarding the Polish officers killed by the German armies in the district of Smolensk which they were occupying. Not only has the Polish Government failed to counteract the base fascist calumnies about the USSR, but it has not even found it necessary to address a question to the Soviet Government or ask for explanations in the matter.

The Hitlerite authorities, having accomplished a monstrous crime on Polish officers, are now enacting the comedy of an investigation, in which they are using Polish fascist elements whom they have carefully selected in occupied Poland, a country thoroughly dominated by Hitler and where no honest Pole can openly express his opinion.

The Polish Government on a par with the Hitlerite Government, has called on the International Red Cross to carry out an "investigation" staged by Hitler against the background of his terroristic regime with its gallows and mass destructions of peaceful populations. Obviously such an "investigation", carried on behind the back of the Soviet Government, cannot inspire confidence in anyone possessing even a modicum of honesty.

The fact that a hostile campaign against the Soviet Union has started simultaneously in the German and the Polish press and is conducted on an

242

identical platform, can leave no doubt of a plot between the common enemy of the Allies: Hitler, and the Polish Government.

At a time when the nations of the Soviet Union, shedding their blood in the desperate fight against Hitlerite Germany, unite for the defeat of the common enemy of the Russian and Polish peoples and of all freedom-loving democratic countries, the Polish Government bowing to Hitler's tyranny aims a treacherous blow at the Soviet Union.

It has been brought to the notice of the Soviet Government that the Polish Government have taken advantage of Hitlerite falsifications to start hostile campaign against the Soviet Union, so as to extort concessions at the expense of the Soviet Ukraine, Soviet Byelorussia and Soviet Lithuania.

The above circumstances force the Soviet Government to state that the present Polish Government, having descended to the level of plotting with the Hitlerite authorities, has in fact as an Ally violated its relationship with the USSR, and has adopted an attitude which is hostile towards the Soviet Union.

In consequence, the Soviet Government have decided to break off relations with the Polish Government.

Please accept, Mr. Ambassador, the expression of my highest respect.

Signed: V. Molotov

Mr. T. Romer
Ambassador Extraordinary and Plenipotentiary of the Republic of Poland
Moscow

Appendix 3

(Translated From Polish)
Polish Ambassador T. Romer's Note of April 26, 1943

April 26th, 1943

To Mr. V. Molotov
People's Commissar for Foreign Affairs
Moscow

Sir,

Today at 0.15 a.m. you were good enough to invite me with the purpose of reading to me a note signed by you, dated the 25th inst., informing me of the decision of the Soviet Government to break off diplomatic relations with the Polish Government. On hearing the text of the note I declared that nothing was left to me but to express my great regret at this decision for which the Soviet Government will have to take full responsibility. At the same time, I emphatically protested against the suggestions and conclusions contained in the note read to me. It inadmissibly accuses the Polish Government of conduct and intentions which are contrary to fact, thus rendering the note itself unacceptable.

I also pointed out that, contrary to statements in the Note, the Polish Government has, for the past two years, made numerous unsuccessful efforts to obtain an explanation from the Soviet Government concerning the fate of the lost Polish officers and lately has again repeated this request in a note of the 20th inst. addressed to Ambassador Bogomolow.

In spite of my firm refusal to accept your note, I find that it has been delivered to my hotel in a sealed envelope of the People's Commissariat for Foreign Affairs. I therefore have the honour to return it in accordance with my position as set out above.

I have the honour to be, etc.

Signed: Tadeusz Romer

Appendix 4

(Translated From German)
Minister of Propaganda Goebbel's Letter to Foreign Ministry of April 15, 1943, Concerning Discovery of Mass Graves (with enclosures)

Berlin 15 April 1943
Kurfurstenstr. 137

German Foreign Office
Kult Pol L VI 6716
Annexes
Concerning: Discovery of mass graves of murdered Polish Officers

To the German Embassy—Bern

In the annex will be found photographs which were sent of murdered Polish officers discovered in the forest at Katyn and copies of the examinations of local Russians.

The photographs show:
1. A view of the site of discovery
2. Position of corpses in the mass graves
3. Single corpses, the hands tied behind backs
4. One corpse with the tunic and hands tied together above the head

All photographs concern the bodies of murdered Polish officers. From the statements of the Russians it can be deducted:

1. The site was from 1918–1929 an execution ground belonging to GPU
2. In March and April 1940 thousands of Polish officers, a few Polish civilians, suspected members of the intelligentsia as well as several Polish clergy, were brought daily in columns to the place of execution. The Poles allegedly came from the prison camp in Kosielsk, were brought by train to Gniesdowe and were there loaded onto lorries.

The following comment can be made on the circumstances leading up to the discovery: In the summer of 1942 Polish members of the Wehrmachtsgefolges heard that Poles had been deported to the place in question. On their own initiative they dug, found several corpses, marked the place with a wooden cross but made no report in spite of their discovery. In February 1943 the Secret Security Forces [end of sheet 5827/E424381] heard rumours about an alleged mass grave, inspected the indicated spot in March, and began major excavation at the beginning of April as soon as the weather allowed.

Until April 6th digging experiments were made in seven different places, and all these led to the discovery of corpses.

Until now only a few of the Polish and Russian graves have been opened. The largest Polish grave had been opened to a length of twenty-eight meters and breadth of sixteen meters by April 11th. 250 corpses lie in twelve layers one on top of the other. In this one grave 2,000–3,000 Polish officers ought to be lying. Close by is a wider grave in which apparently Polish staff officers were buried. The corpses lie face downwards and all show shots in the neck, according to present examinations.

One section of the officers who were found in another grave again a few meters away, had their hands tied behind their backs; a few had uniform tunics or sacks tied over their heads.

With a few exceptions the officers had no valuables on them, but in nearly every case identity cards and papers were found.

By April 11th, 160corpses had been taken out of the graves and identified. Among these were two Polish generals, Brigadier-General Smorawinsky, Mecyslaw of Lublin Pl, Litwenski 3 and General Bronislaw Bogaterewitsch. Until now all ranks of officers from lieutenant to general have been identified. A strikingly large section of the officers are wearing the traditional braid of the Pilsudski Regiments. Of the corpses in the Polish mass graves it is estimated that 90% are officers. [end of sheet E424382] The total number of buried Polish corpses in the said woodland is estimated (on the grounds of statements made by civilian persons about the constant unloading in March and April 1940) at about 10,000.

The corpses were examined by forensic pathologists of Army Group Mitte and the report will be made as soon as possible. It will give information about possible mutilations and the exact nature of the shooting. Mutilations on the 160 corpses could not be determined. The position of the corpses indicates that the officers were forced to climb into the grave and to lie down in it. Only the corpses in the upper layer were found lying obliquely one on top of the other, from which fact it can be assumed that they were thrown into the grave after being shot.

Only a small section of the Russian graves have been opened so far, but here also I could see that sacks had been tied over the heads of some corpses; a few had their mouths stuffed with sawdust.

The exhumations are being continued but probably only until the beginning of May, as then the graves have to be closed because of fear of epidemic at the entry of warmer weather.

It is suggested that you should make as much public use of this as possible.

By order

Six

O. U. the 27 February 1943

On verbal invitation, appeared the Russian,
Kieselow, Parfeon,
72 years old,
Farmer
Resident in Kosegorie
and declared, on interrogation, the following,

"Since 1907 I have lived in Kosegorie. Approximately ten years ago, the castle and the woodland was first used as a sanitorium for senior NKVD officials. The whole wooded area was surrounded by barbed wire to the height of about two metres. Moreover everything was guarded by armed sentries. No civilians were allowed entry. I did not know any of the officials, only the house servant, who was also watchman. His name was Roman Sergejewitsch allegedly from Vjasmir.

"In the spring of 1940, daily, for four to five weeks, three to four lorries loaded with people were brought to the woodland and there presumably shot, by the NKVD. The lorries were closed, so that no one could see what they contained. One day, as I was standing on Gniesdowa station, I saw men dismounting from the train and getting into the familiar lorries, which drove away in the direction of the wood. What happened to the men, I could not say, as no one dared to go near. The sounds of shots and men screaming could be heard in my house. It is to be assumed that the men were shot. In the vicinity no bones were made of the fact that Poles had been shot by the NKVD. The people in the village said that about 10,000 Poles were shot. After the area had been occupied by German troops, I went into the wood to convince myself. I was of the opinion that I might find some corpses but in vain, because I found only a few thrown up mounds. I was convinced that the dead could only be lying under the mounds.

In the summer of 1942, certain Poles were with a German unit at Gniesdowa. One day ten of them came to me and asked me to show them where their countrymen, who had been shot by the NKVD, were buried. I led them to the wooded site and showed them the new mound. The Poles then asked me to lend them a hoe and a spade, which I did. After about an hour, they came to me very indignant and abusive of the NKVD. They explained that in one of the mounds they had found corpses. They marked the spot with two crosses made of birchwood which are there to this day.

"I am unable to make any further statement."
Translated into Russian and read aloud.

Sealed xyz

signed xyz

Sergt of Hilfspolizei
Interpreter xyz
NCO

O. U. the 6 April 1943

Before the local headquarters appeared the Russian
Schigulow, Michail
Born 10 Jan 1915 in Novo Bateki
Resident there in House No. 16
Married, one child, no party.
Since 1942, with the Russian OK
and stated:

"Already as a child I heard that people from Smolensk prison were taken to the wood near Kosigorie and were there shot. I often saw open powered trucks on the highway on which prisoners under guard were transported, coming from Smolensk and travelling in the direction of Kosigorie.

"One day in 1927 I, together with some other village boys, was looking after horses. We saw a powered truck coming form the direction of Smolensk and stopping on the highway near the Kosigorie wood. Eleven people dismounted and were led off into the woodland. A short time after this we heard shots; again after some time the guards came back and the truck returned in the direction of Smolensk. Out of curiosity we boys ran into the wood in order to examine more closely the spot where people had been shot. I myself lost courage before reaching the spot and remained behind. Afterwards the others told me that they had found the grave. On the edge of it they had seen very fresh bloodstains. And moreover, the corpses had only been covered with a little earth so that they saw hands and feet sticking out.

"I should like to comment that at this time the woodland near Kosegorie was not shut off. The boys with whom I was at Kosegorie at that time were all conscripted into the Red Army."

Translated into Russian and read before me.

Signature	Signed
N.C.O. and Auxiliary	Eichholz
Policeman	N.C.O. and Interpreter

O. U. 6 April 1943

On invitation the Russian Sladkow, Alexei, appeared, born 17.3.1785 in Chorowschawa, County Demodow, resident in Krassny-Bor, House No. 75 and deposed.

"I lived in the years 1939–41 in Novo Bateki and travelled by train to Smolensk every day where I worked. In this way I had the opportunity to witness the transfer of the Poles to Kosie Gorie with my own eyes. One day in March 1940 four or five passenger coaches (Luxus wagons) stood on a railway siding of the Gnesdowa station, in the vicinity of the loading platform. The passengers were not allowed to leave the carriages and two armed sentries stood in front of them. I myself passed the carriage and saw officers and civilians sitting at table on which were bottles of wine and various types of food, such as sausage and ham. The passengers were mostly civilians with a few women among them. They were all well-fed and decently dressed and from this already recognizable as foreigners. Women from Bateki had to carry water to the carriages but were not allowed to enter them. I was also witness when in the evening a section of the passengers were loaded onto two trucks. They all had heavy suitcases with them and a few also carried cushions under their arms. The unloading was continued for four to five days until the carriages were empty. The carriages disappeared during the night and after eight days they were again on the same spot, fully occupied. This performance was repeated unceasingly in March and April 1940. At that time the local population described these people as 'Polish hostages'.

"I am unable to make any further statement."

Translated into Russian and read aloud (to me)

	Signature.
	Witnessed
Interpreter	Boscke
Special officer	NCO and Auxiliary
Signature	Policeman

O. U. the 27 Feb 1943

On invitation appeared the Russian,
  Gwiwasorzow Iwan,
  Born on 20.6.1916 in Nowo Bateki
  Resident there House No. 119
  Turner
  Bachelor
  Non party
  employed since July 1942 with Russian OD
and made the following statement:

"In the year 1940 I was working in the village Gniesdowa on the collective farm. As my job was quite near the railway I noticed in March and April 1940 three to four trains consisting of three to four carriages which I recognized from the barred windows as obvious prison carriages, coming daily from Smolensk. These prison carriages stopped at Gniesdowa station. My sister Daria then told me that she herself had seen Polish soldiers, civilians and a few clergy leaving the carriages and being loaded into closed trucks. Generally one heard that the lorries had been driven to Kosigorie by the NKVD and that there the people had been shot. I myself saw nothing of this and my sister did not go into further details.

"I am unable to give further information."

Translated into Russian and read before me.

	Signature
Sealed	Interpreter
Signature	Eichholz
NCO and Auxiliary Policeman	NCO

Note. The sister of Griwasorzow, Iwan, at the approach of German troops to drive cattle from the collective farm was kidnapped by the Bolshevists and her present whereabouts are unknown.

Signed
NCO and Auxiliary Policeman

O. U. the 5 April 1943

The Russian citizen
  Kriwoserzew, Ivan,
  born 20.7.1915 in Novo Bateki
  Bachelor

Ironworker
resident in Novo Bateki House no. 119
County Smolensk
Non party
since July 1942 and OD man
appeared at the office and made this statement:

"From my parents, who are well known in the village, I heard that the woodland of Kosi-Gory (Goats' Hill) has been used as a place of executions since 1918 first by the Tscheka, then the GPU, OGPU and later by the NKVD.

"Until 1931 we, the villagers, were allowed to walk in the woodland and to gather mushrooms and berries. As a boy I picked mushrooms in Kosi-Gory. On this occasion I was repeatedly shown the new graves by the older people.

"In 1931 the woodland of Kosi-Gory was fenced in and entry prohibited by notice-boards signed by the OGPU. I heard that in 1934 a large house was built inside the wooded area which was meant as a sanatorium for the NKVD.

"Executions were carried out in Kosigorie from 1918 to 1929 and from 1940 onwards. In the intervening period no transport lorries were seen to drive into the area.

"From 1940 the woodland was additionally guarded by sentries and dogs. In March and April 1940 many prison transport waggons arrived in Gniesdowa; the prisoners were cooped up into prison lorries commonly known as 'black raven' and the lorries then travelled along the road from Gniesdowa station in the direction of Katyn. I never heard any shots from the Kosi Gory wood."

Translated into Russian and read before me.

	Signature
Sealed	Interpreter
Hohne	Eichholz
Corporal of Aux. Police	NCO

O. U. 28 February 1943

On invitation appeared the Russian
Andrejew, Ivan
born on 22.1.1917 in Novo Bateki
Resident there House No. 2.
Locksmith
married

Non party
and made as witness the following statement:

"Approximately from the middle of March until the middle of April 1940, three to four trains arrived daily in Gniesdowa. Two to three carriages of each were decidedly arrest carriages. These stopped at the station. Passengers who were mostly Polish soldiers whom I recognised from their caps, as well as civilians, were taken from the carriages and loaded into closed lorries. The lorries were driven along the station road towards the railway and then turned left in the direction of Katyn. I noticed several times that they turned off the highway two and a half kilometres from here and were driven in the direction of Kosigory. I never saw it myself but heard several times, that these people were shot in Kosigory by the NKVD.

"I am unable to make any further statement."
Translated into Russian and read before me.

Sealed
  NCO and Aux. Policeman   Interpreter
                 NCO

              O. U. the 5 April 1943

On invitation appeared the Russian
 Godonow Kusma
 born on 25.10.1877 in Novo Bateki
 Married Five children
 Farmer
 Resident since birth in Novo Bateki House without number
 Non Party
and made the following declaration:

"Since 1918 I have been employed as an ostler on the collective farm at Novo Bateki. It was known to all the people in the neighbourhood that Kosigorie was being used as a place of execution by the Tscheka. I still remember that in 1921 between the end of May and the beginning of June, the two sons of Ivan Kurtschanowa from the village of Satylki, County Kaspliansk, were shot in Kosigori. As I left my house on that day at about three o'clock, to feed the horses, I was met on the highway by an open truck loaded with ten to fifteen men all guarded by the Tscheka. As it passed two of the men called to me 'Goodbye Uncle!' I immediately recognized the two sons of Ivan Kortschanowa. When I met their parents about two weeks later, my suspicions were confirmed because they had been informed that their two sons had been shot in Kosigorie.

"Approximately in the middle of July, Feodar Isatschenkow was also arrested in the village of Sarubinki, County Kasplianski, and sentenced to death by the 'Troika', in Smolensk. His parents told me that their son Feodor was also shot at Kosigorie.

"The reasons for the shootings are unknown to me. Judging by the statements of the parents and acquaintances, the victims were anticommunistically inclined.

"When executions were not taking place, the Kosigorie woodland was open to all until 1931. Children who gathered mushrooms there always told of new gravemounds.

"I am unable to give further information."

Translated into Russian and read before me.

(Signed) Klodynof
Interpreter
NCO

Sealed
Sgt. of Aux. Police

O. U. 4 March 1943

To: Secret Field Police Group 570 via Aok 4.

Subject: Discovery of a Massgrave of Poles shot in 1940 by the NKVD, in the wooded area by the road Smolensk Motor road (approach from Vitezsk) North East of Katyn.

At the beginning of February it was reported by a contact, that in the vicinity of Katyn several thousand Poles are buried, having been shot by members of the NKVD in April and May 1940.

Investigations revealed the truth of the statement. In the woodland north of Katyn there were several thrown-up mounds under which lie the buried corpses. Because of ground frost only a part two metres square could be uncovered of one of the mounds. At a depth of two metres numerous corpses were found lying close together, decomposition having set in for the greater part. Judging by the position of the bodies it must be assumed that they are lying in several layers, one above the other. A button bearing the Polish Eagle was removed from the clothes of one of the corpses. How far the corpse shows mutilation, can only be determined by excavations carried out on a larger scale.

In order to discover details, several inhabitants of the neighbouring locality were interrogated. A 72 year old Russian states that a sanitorium for senior NKVD officials has been situated in the woodland for about ten years. Entrance to the area, fenced in and guarded by sentries, was prohibited to unauthorised persons. Daily for several weeks in the spring of 1940 the Russians saw three to four closed lorries on which the people who were later shot were transported from Gniesdowa station to the woodland in question. At times he heard men's screams and shooting coming from the wood in question, in his house which was a considerable distance away.

According to the reports of others, about 10,000 people seem to have been involved.

Another inhabitant who was at the time employed on the unloading station states, that in the months of March and April 1940, daily nine to twelve prison waggons arrived at the Gniesdowa station. Passengers are reported to have been Polish soldiers, civilians, and a few clergy. He also noticed that they were taken away in closed lorries in the direction of Katyn.

A third inhabitant of the locality made a similar statement.

Eyewitnesses of the shooting itself have so far not been discovered.

The original of the previous report has been laid before the Ic/AO of Army Group Mitte, with a reference to the possibility of its use for propaganda purposes, for his decision.

From there a copy was sent to the Supreme Army Command (OKH) for a decision on its use: a second copy was passed for information to the senior forensic pathologist Professor Dr. Buhtz at the Medical Army Group.

After the arrival of further instructions the exhumations will be carried out with the participation of Professor Dr. Buhtz and Propaganda Section W.

> Voss,
> Secretary
> Field Police

Appendix 5

(Translated From German)
Protocol of the International Medical Commission of April 30, 1943

Smolensk, 30 April 1943

PROTOCOL,

drawn up on the occasion of the examination of the mass graves of Polish officers in the Katyn wood near Smolensk, which was carried out by a commission composed of leading exponents of Medical Jurisprudence and Criminology at European universities and of other renowned medical professors.

In the period from 28 to 30 April 1943, a commission composed of leading exponents of Medical Jurisprudence and Criminology from European universities and of other renowned medical professors subjected the mass graves of Polish officers in the Katyn wood near Smolensk to a thorough scientific examination.

The Commission consisted of the following men:
1. Belgium: Dr. Speleers, Professor in Ordinary of Ophthalmology at the University of Ghent
2. Bulgaria: Dr. Markov, lecturer in Medical Jurisprudence and Criminology at the University of Sofia
3. Denmark: Dr. Tramsen, Prosecutor at the Institute of Medical Jurisprudence in Copenhagen
4. Finland: Dr. Saxen, Professor in Ordinary of Pathological Anatomy at the University of Helsinki
5. Italy: Dr. Palmieri, Professor in Ordinary of Medical Jurisprudence and Criminology at the University of Naples
6. Croatia (a province of Yugoslavia):
   Dr. Miloslavich, Professor in Ordinary of Medical Jurisprudence and Criminology at the University of Agram
7. Netherlands: Dr. de Burlet, Professor in Ordinary of Anatomy at the University of Groningen

8. Protectorate of Bohemia and Moravia:
   Dr. Hajek, Professor in Ordinary of Medical Jurisprudence and Criminology at Prague
9. Roumania: Dr. Birkle, Medico-legal Adviser to the Roumanian Ministry of Justice and First Assistant at the Institute of Medical Jurisprudence and Criminology in Bucharest
10. Switzerland: Dr. Naville, Professor in Ordinary of Medical Jurisprudence at the University of Geneva
11. Slovakia: Dr. Subik, Professor in Ordinary of Pathological Anatomy at the University of Bratislava, Head of the Public Health Department of Slovakia
12. Hungary: Dr. Orsos, Professor in Ordinary of Medical Jurisprudence and Criminology at the University of Budapest

During the work and consultations of the Delegation there were further present the following:

1. Dr. Buhtz, Professor in Ordinary of Medical Jurisprudence and Criminology at the University of Breslau, delegated by the Supreme Command of the German Army to direct the exhumations at Katyn.
2. Dr. Costedoat, Medical Inspector, delegated by the head of the French Government to attend the work of the Commission.

The discovery of mass graves of Polish officers in the Katyn wood near Smolensk, recently come to the notice of the German authorities, has caused Dr. Conti, Reich Health Leader, to invite the above-named experts from different European countries to inspect the place of discovery in Katyn, in order to assist in the clarification of this unique case.

The Commission personally examined some Russian witnesses, inhabitants of the Katyn district, who stated, i.e., that in the months of March and April 1940 large rail transports of Polish officers were detrained almost daily at the station at Gniesdowa near Katyn, transported to the Katyn wood in prisoners' trucks, and were later never seen again; the Commission further took note of the findings and discoveries made so far and inspected the evidence which had been found. According to these, by 30 April 1943 982 corpses were disinterred. Of these, about 70 percent were immediately identified, while the papers of the others can be used for identification purposes only after careful preliminary treatment. The corpses disinterred before the arrival of the Commission were all inspected and to a great extent also dissected by Professor Buhtz and his collaborators. Up to the present, seven mass graves have been opened, the biggest of which contains as far as can be judged 2,500 officers' corpses.

Nine corpses were dissected by the members of the Commission personally, and numerous specially selected cases were subjected to an autopsy.

MEDICO-LEGAL RESULTS OF THE INSPECTIONS AND EXAMINATIONS CARRIED OUT

In all the corpses so far disinterred, the cause of death has been without exception established as due to shots in the head. It is a question throughout of shots in the nape of the neck and indeed predominantly of single shots in the nape of the neck, in a few cases of two shots in the nape of the neck, and in one single case of three shots in the nape of the neck. The entry-hole of the bullet is without exception situated low at the nape of the neck and goes into the bone-structure of the occipital bone near the foramen magnum, while the place of exit of the bullet lies, as a rule, in the region of the frontal hair-line and only in very rare cases, lower down. Without exception the shots are from pistols of a calibre of less than eight millimeters.

From the blasting of the skull and the findings of powdermarks at the occipital bone near the place of entry of the bullet and also from the similarity in the position of the entry shot, it can be concluded that the shot was fired at point-blank or at very close range especially as the direction of the bullet track is, with very few deviations always the same. The remarkable similarity of the injuries and the position of the entry-shot within a very restricted area in the occipital region, indicate a practised hand. In numerous corpses the tying of the hands in identical fashion and in a few cases also four-edged bayonet wounds in clothing and skin could be established. The method of tying corresponds with that discovered on the corpses of Russian civilians who were also disinterred in the Katyn wood and had been buried much earlier.

$$* \quad * \quad * \quad * \quad * \quad * \quad *$$

There are different stages and types of decomposition, conditioned by the arrangement of the corpses inside the pit and with relation to each other. There is mummification at the surface and the edges of the mass of corpses and, in the middle of this mass, liquid decomposition. The coagulation and congealing together of neighbouring corpses by congealed liquid from the corpses, particularly the malformations corresponding to and conditioned by reciprocal pressure, indicate beyond doubt contemporaneous burial.

$$* \quad * \quad * \quad * \quad * \quad * \quad *$$

SUMMARIZED CONCLUSIONS

In the Katyn wood, mass graves of Polish officers were examined by the Commission, seven of which have so far been opened. From these, 982 corpses have so far been recovered, examined, partly dissected, and 70 percent identified.

The corpses show exclusively that death was due to shots in the nape of the neck. From the statements of witnesses, letters, diaries, newspapers, etc.

257

found on the corpses, it is concluded that the shootings took place in the months of March and April 1940. The findings at the mass graves and in individual corpses of the Polish officers, as described in the Protocol, are in complete accordance with this.

(sgd.)	Dr. Speleers	Dr. Hajek
	Dr. Saxen	Dr. Subik
	Dr. de Burlet	Dr. Tramsen
	Dr. Naville	Dr. Miloslavich
	Dr. Markov	Dr. Birkle
	Dr. Palmieri	Dr. Orsos

Appendix 6

(Translated from Russian)
Report of Special Commission For Ascertaining and Investigating the
Circumstances of the Shooting of Polish Officer Prisoners by the
German-Fascist Invaders in the Katyn Forest

The Special Commission for Ascertaining and Investigating the Circumstances of the Shooting of Polish Officer Prisoners by the German-Fascist Invaders in the Katyn Forest (near Smolensk) was set up on the decision of the Extraordinary State Committee for Ascertaining and Investigating Crimes Committed by the German-Fascist Invaders and Their Associates.

The Commission consists of Academician N. N. Burdenko, member of the Extraordinary State Committee (chairman of the Commission); Academician Alexei Tolstoy, member of the Extraordinary State Committee; Metropolitan Nikolai, member of the Extraordinary State Committee; Lt. Gen. A. A. Gundorov, president of the All-Slav Committee; S. A. Kolesnikov, chairman of the executive committee of the Union of the Red Cross and Red Crescent Societies; Academician V. P. Potemkin, People's Commissar of Education of the Russian SFSR; Col. Gen. P. E. Melnikov, chairman of the Smolensk Regional Executive Committee.

To accomplish the task assigned to it the Commission invited the following medico-legal experts to take part in its work: V. I. Prozorovsky, chief medico-legal expert of the People's Commissariat of Health Protection of the U.S.S.R., director of scientific research in the Institute of Forensic Medicine; Doctor of Medicine V. M. Smolyaninov, head of the faculty of forensic medicine of the Second Moscow Medical Institute; P. S. Semenoysky and Docent M. D. Shvaikova, senior staff scientists of the State Scientific Research Institute of Forensic Medicine under the People's Commissariat of Health of the U.S.S.R.; and Prof. D. N. Voropayev, chief pathologist of the front, major of Medical Service.

The special Commission had at its disposal extensive material presented by the member of the Extraordinary State Committee Academician N. N. Burdenko, his collaborators, and the medico-legal experts who arrived in Smolensk on September 26, 1943, immediately upon its liberation, and carried out preliminary study and investigation of the circumstances of all the crimes perpetrated by the Germans.

The special Commission verified and ascertained on the spot that 15 kilometers from Smolensk, along the Vitebsk highway, in the section of the Katyn Forest named Kozy Gory, 200 meters to the southwest of the highway in the direction of the Dnieper, there are graves in which Polish war prisoners shot by the German occupationists were buried.

On the order of the special Commission, and in the presence of all its members and of the medico-legal experts, the graves were excavated. A large number of bodies clad in Polish military uniform were found in the graves. The total number of bodies, as calculated by the medico-legal experts, is 11,000. The medico-legal experts made detailed examinations of the exhumed bodies and of documents and material evidence discovered on the bodies and in the graves.

Simultaneously with the excavation of the graves an examination of the bodies, the special Commission examined numerous witnesses among local residents, whose testimony establishes with precision the time and circumstances of the crimes committed by the German occupationists.

The testimony of witnesses reveals the following:

The Katyn Forest

The Katyn Forest had for a long time been the favorite resort of Smolensk people, where they used to rest on holidays. The population of the neighborhood grazed cattle and gathered fuel in the Katyn Forest. Access to the Katyn Forest was not banned or restricted in any way. This situation prevailed in the Katyn Forest up to the outbreak of war. Even in the summer of 1941 there was a Young Pioneers' Camp of the Industrial Insurance Board in this forest, which was not disbanded until July 1941.

An entirely different regime was instituted in the Katyn Forest after the capture of Smolensk by the Germans. The forest was heavily patrolled. Notices appeared in many places warning that persons entering without special passes would be shot on the spot.

The part of the Katyn Forest named Kozy Gory was guarded particularly strictly, as was the area on the bank of the Dnieper, where 700 meters from the graves of the Polish war prisoners there was a country house—the rest home of the Smolensk Administration of the People's Commissariat of Internal Affairs. When the Germans arrived this country house was taken over by a German institution named Headquarters of the Five Hundred and Thirty-seventh Engineering Battalion.

Polish War Prisoners in the Smolensk Area

The Special Commission established that, before the capture of Smolensk by the Germans, Polish war prisoners officers and men, worked in the western district of the region, building and repairing roads. These war prisoners were quartered in three special camps named: Camp No. 1 O. N., Camp No. 2 O. N., and Camp No. 3 O. N. These camps were located 25 to 45 kilometers west of Smolensk.

The testimony of witnesses and documentary evidence establish that after the outbreak of hostilities, in view of the situation that arose, the camps could not be evacuated in time and all the Polish war prisoners, as well as some members of the guard and staffs of the camps, fell prisoner to the Germans.

The former Chief of Camp No. 1 O. N., Major of State Security V. M. Vetoshnikov, interrogated by the Special Commission, testified: "I was waiting for the order on the removal of the camp, but communication with Smolensk was cut. Then I myself with several staff members went to Smolensk to clarify the situation. In Smolensk I found a tense situation. I applied to the chief of traffic of the Smolensk section of the Western Railway, Ivanov, asking him to provide the camp with railway cars for the evacuation of the Polish war prisoners. But Ivanov answered that I could not count on receiving cars. I also tried to get in touch with Moscow to obtain permission to set out on foot, but I failed.

"By this time Smolensk was already cut off from the camp by the Germans, and I do not know what happened to the Polish war prisoners and guards who remained in the camp."

Engineer S. V. Ivanov, who in July 1941 was acting Chief of Traffic of the Smolensk section of the Western Railway, testified before the Special Commission: "The Administration of Polish War Prisoners' Camps applied to my office for cars for evacuation of the Poles, but we had none to spare. Besides, we could not send cars to the Gussino line, where the majority of the Polish war prisoners were, since that line was already under fire. Therefore, we could not comply with the request of the camps' administration. Thus the Polish war prisoners remained in Smolensk region."

The presence of the Polish war prisoners in the camps in Smolensk region is confirmed by the testimony of numerous witnesses who saw these Poles near Smolensk in the early months of the occupation up to September 1941 inclusive.

Witness Maria Alexandrovna Sashneva, elementary schoolteacher in the village of Zenkovo, told the Special Commission that in August 1941 she gave shelter in her house in Zenkovo to a Polish war prisoner who had escaped from camp.

"The Pole wore Polish military uniform, which I recognized at once, as during 1940 and 1941 I used to see groups of Polish war prisoners working on the road under guard. . . . I took an interest in the Pole because it turned out that, before being called up, he had been an elementary schoolteacher in Poland. Since I had graduated from a pedagogical institute and was preparing to be a teacher, I started to talk with him. He told me that he had completed normal school in Poland and then studied at some military school and was a junior lieutenant of the reserve. At the outbreak of war between Poland and Germany he was called up and served in Brest-Litovsk, where he was taken prisoner by Red Army units. . . . He spent over a year in the camp near Smolensk.

"When the Germans arrived they seized the Polish camp and instituted a strict regime in it. The Germans did not regard the Poles as human beings. They oppressed and outraged them in every way. On some occasions Poles were shot without any reason at all. He decided to escape. Speaking of himself, he said that his wife, too, was a teacher and that he had two brothers and two sisters. . . ."

On leaving next day the Pole gave his surname, which Sashneva put down in a book. In this book, Practical Studies in Natural History, by Yagodovsky, which Sashneva handed to the Special Commission, there is a note on the last page: "Juzeph and Sofia Loek. House 25, Ogorodnaya St., town, Zamostye." In the lists published by the Germans, under No. 3796, Lt. Juzeph Loek is put down as having been shot at Kozy Gory in the Katyn Forest in the spring of 1940.

Thus, from the German report, it would appear that Juzeph Loek had been shot 1 year before the witness Sashneva saw him.

The witness, N. V. Danilenkov, a farmer of the Krasnaya Zarya collective farm of the Katyn Rural Soviet stated: In August and September 1941 when the Germans arrived, I used to meet Poles working on the roads in groups of 15 to 20."

Similar statements were made by the following witnesses: Soldatenkov, former headman of the Village of Borok; A. A. Kolachev, a Smolensk doctor; A. P. Ogloblin, a priest; T. I. Sergeyev, track foreman; P. A. Smiryagin, engineer; A. M. Moskovskaya, resident of Smolensk; A. M. Alexeyev, chairman of a collective farm in the village of Borok; I. V. Kutseyey, waterworks technician; V. P. Gorodetsky, a priest; A. T. Bazekina, a bookkeeper; E. N. Vetrova, a teacher; I. V. Savvateyev, station master at the Gnezdovo station, and others.

Round-Ups of Polish War Prisoners

The presence of Polish war prisoners in the autumn of 1941 in Smolensk districts is also confirmed by the fact that the Germans made numerous round-ups of those war prisoners who had escaped from the camps.

Witness I. M. Kartoshkin, a carpenter, testified: "In the autumn of 1941 the Germans not only scoured the forests for Polish war prisoners, but also used police to make night searches in the villages."

M. D. Zakharov, former headman of the village of Novye Bateki, testified that in the autumn of 1941 the Germans intensively combed the villages and forests in search of Polish war prisoners.

Witness N. V. Danilenkov, a farmer of the Krasnaya Zarya collective farm, testified: "Special round-ups were held in our place to catch Polish war prisoners who had escaped. Some searches took place in my house two or three times. After one search I asked the headman, Konstantin Sergeyev, whom they were looking for in our village. Sergeyev said that an order had been received from the German Kommandantur according to which searches were to be made in all houses without exception, since Polish war prisoners who had escaped from the camp were hiding in our village. After some time the searches were discontinued."

The witness collective farmer T. E. Fatkov testified: "Round-ups and searches for Polish war prisoners took place several times. That was in August and September 1941. After September 1941 the round-ups were discontinued and no one saw Polish war prisoners any more."

Shootings of Polish War Prisoners

The above-mentioned Headquarters of the Five Hundred and Thirty-seventh Engineering Battalion quartered in the country house at Kozy Gory did not engage in any engineering work. Its activities were a closely guarded secret. What this headquarters engaged in, in reality, was revealed by numerous witnesses, including A. M. Alexeyeva, O. A. Mikhailova, and Z. P. Konakhovskaya, residents of the village of Borok of the Katyn Rural Soviet.

On the order of the German Commandant of the settlement of Katyn, they were detailed by the headman of the village of Borok, V. I. Soldatenkov, to serve the personnel of headquarters at the above-mentioned country house.

On arrival in Kozy Gory they were told through an interpreter about a number of restrictions: they were absolutely forbidden to go far from the country house or to go to the forest, to enter rooms without being called and without being escorted by German soldiers, to remain on the grounds of the country house at night. They were allowed to come to work and leave after work only by a definite route and only when escorted by soldiers.

This warning was given to Alexeyeva, Mikhailova, and Konakhovskaya, through an interpreter, personally by the Chief of the German Institution, Oberstleutnant [Lt. Col.] Arnes, who for this purpose summoned them one at a time.

As to the personnel of the headquarters, A. M. Alexeyeva testified:

"As in the Kozy Gory country house there were always about 30 Germans. Their chief was Lieutenant Colonel Arnes, and his aide was First Lieutenant Rekst. Here were also a Second Lieutenant Hott; Sergeant Major Lumert; noncommissioned officer in charge of supplies Rose; his assistant

Isikes; Sergeant Major Grenewski, who was in charge of the power station; the photographer, a corporal whose name I do not remember; the interpreter, a Volga German whose name seems to have been Johann, but I called him Ivan; the cook, a German named Gustav; and a number of others whose names and surnames I do not know."

Soon after beginning their work Alexeyeva, Mikhailova, and Konakhovskaya began to notice that "something shady" was going on at the country house.

A. M. Alexeyeva testified:

"The interpreter Johann warned us several times on behalf of Arnes that we were to hold our tongues and not chatter about what we saw and heard at the country house.

"Besides, I guessed from a number of signs that the Germans were engaged in some shady doings at this country house. . . .

"At the close of August and during most of September 1941 several trucks used to come practically every day to the Kozy Gory country house.

"At first I paid no attention to that, but later I noticed that each time these trucks arrived at the grounds of the country house they stopped for half an hour, and sometimes for a whole hour, somewhere on the country road connecting the country house with the highway.

"I drew this conclusion because some time after these trucks reached the grounds of the country house the noise they made would cease. Simultaneously with the noise stopping, single shots would be heard. The shots followed one another at short but approximately even intervals. Then the shooting would die down and the trucks would drive up right to the country house.

"German soldiers and noncommissioned officers came out of the trucks. Talking noisily they went to wash in the bathhouse, after which they engaged in drunken orgies. On those days a fire was always kept burning in the bathhouse stove.

"On days when the trucks arrived more soldiers from some German military units used to arrive at the country house. Special beds were put up for them in the soldiers' casino set up in one of the halls of the country house. On those days many meals were cooked in the kitchen and a double ration of drinks was served with the meals.

"Shortly before the trucks reached the country house armed soldiers went to the forest, evidently to the spot where the trucks stopped, because in half an hour or an hour they returned in these trucks, together with the soldiers who lived permanently in the country house.

"Probably I would not have watched or noticed how the noise of the trucks coming to the country house used to die down and then rise again were it not for the fact that whenever the trucks arrived we (Konakhovskaya, Mikhailova, and myself) were driven to the kitchen if we happened to be in the courtyard near the house; and they would not let us out of the kitchen if we happened to be in it.

"There was also the fact that on several occasions I noticed stains of fresh blood on the clothes of two lance corporals. All this made me pay close attention to what was going on at the country house. Then I noticed strange intervals in the movement of the trucks and their pauses in the forest. I also noticed that bloodstains appeared on the clothes of the same two men—the lance corporals. One of them was tall and red-headed, the other of medium height and fair.

"From all this I inferred that the Germans brought people in the truck to the country house and shot them. I even guessed approximately where this took place, as when coming to and leaving the country house, I noticed freshly thrown-up earth in several places near the road. The area of this freshly thrown-up earth increased in length every day. In the course of time the earth in these spots began to look normal."

In answer to a question put by the Special Commission—what kind of people were shot in the forest near the country house—Alexeyeva replied that they were Polish war prisoners, and in confirmation of her words, stated:

"There were days when no trucks arrived at the country house, but even so soldiers left the house for the forest from which came frequent single shots. On returning the soldiers always took a bath and then drank.

"Another thing happened. Once I stayed at the country house somewhat later than usual. Mikhailova and Konakhovskaya had already left. Before I finished the work which had kept me there, a soldier suddenly entered and told me I could go. He referred to Rose's order. He also accompanied me to the highway.

"On the highway 150 or 200 meters from where the road branches off to the country house I saw a group of about 30 Polish war prisoners marching along the highway under heavy German escort.

"I knew them to be Poles because even before the war, and for some time after the Germans came, I used to meet Polish war prisoners on the highway wearing the same uniform with their characteristic four-cornered hats.

"I halted near the roadside to see where they were being led, and I saw that they turned toward our country house at Kozy Gory.

"Since by that time I had begun to watch closely everything going on at the country house, I became interested in this situation. I went back some distance along the highway, hid in bushes near the roadside, and waited. In some 20 or 30 minutes I heard the familiar, characteristic single shots.

"Then everything became clear to me and I hurried home.

"I also concluded that evidently the Germans were shooting Poles not only in the daytime when we worked at the country house, but also at night in our absence. I understood this also from recalling the occasions when all the officers and men who lived in the country house, with the exception of the sentries, woke up late, about noon.

"On several occasions we guessed about the arrival of the Poles in Kozy Gory from the tense atmosphere that descended on the country house. . . .

"All the officers left the country house and only a few sentries remained in it, while the sergeant major kept checking up on the sentries over the telephone. . . ."

O. A. Mikhailova testified: "In September 1941 shooting was heard very often in the Kozy Gory Forest. At first I took no notice of the trucks which arrived at our country house, which were closed at the sides and on top and painted green. They used to drive up to our country house always accompanied by noncommissioned officers. Then I noticed that these trucks never entered our garage, and also that they were never unloaded. They used to come very often, especially in September 1941.

"Among the noncommissioned officers who always sat with the drivers I began to notice one tall one with a pale face and red hair. When these trucks drove up to the country house, all the noncommissioned officers, as if at a command, went to the bathhouse and bathed for a long time, after which they drank heavily in the country house.

"Once this tall red-headed German got down from the truck, went to the kitchen and asked for water. When he was drinking the water out of a glass I noticed blood on the cuff of the right sleeve of his uniform."

O. A. Mikhailova and Z. P. Konakhovskaya witnessed the shooting of two Polish war prisoners who had evidently escaped from the Germans and had been caught.

Mikhailova testified:

"Once Konakhovskaya and I were at our usual work in the kitchen when we heard a noise near the country house. On coming out we saw two Polish war prisoners surrounded by German soldiers who were explaining something to Non-commissioned Officer Rose. Then Lieutenant Colonel Arnes came over to them and told Rose something. We hid some distance away, as we were afraid Rose would beat us up for being inquisitive. We were discovered, however, and at a signal from Rose the mechanic Grenewski drove us into the kitchen and the Poles away from the country house. A few minutes later we heard shots. The German soldiers and Non-commissioned Officer Rose, who soon returned, were engaged in animated conversation. Wanting to find out what the Germans had done to the detained Poles, Konakhovskaya and I came out again. Arnes' aide, who came out simultaneously with us from the main entrance of the country house, asked Rose something in German, to which the latter answered, also in German, "Everything is in order." We understood these words because the Germans often used them in their conversation. From all that took place I concluded that these two Poles had been shot."

Similar testimony was given by Z. P. Konakhovskaya.

Frightened by the happenings at the country house, Alexeyeva, Mikhailova, and Konakhovskaya decided to quit work there on some convenient pretext. Taking advantage of the reduction of their wages from 9 to 3 marks a month at the beginning of January 1942, on Mikhailova's suggestion they did not report for work. In the evening of the same day a car came to fetch them, they were brought to the country house and locked up in a cell by way of punishment—Mikhailova for 8 days and Alexeyeva and Konakhovskaya for 3 days each.

After they had served their terms all of them were discharged.

While working at the country house Alexeyeva, Mikhailova, and Konakhovskaya had been afraid to speak to each other about what they had observed of the happenings there. Only after they were arrested, sitting in the cell at night, did they share their knowledge.

At the interrogation on December 24, 1943, Mikhailova testified:

"Here for the first time we talked frankly about the happenings at the country house. I told all I knew. It turned out that Konakhovskaya and Alexeyeva also knew all these facts but, like myself, had been afraid to discuss them. I learned from them that it was Polish war prisoners the Germans were shooting at Kozy Gory, since Alexeyeva said that once in the autumn of 1941, when she was going home after work, she saw the Germans driving a large group of Polish war prisoners into Kozy Gory Forest and then she heard shooting."

Similar testimony was given by Alexeyeva and Konakhovskaya.

(On comparing notes Alexeyeva, Mikhailova, and Konakhovskaya arrived at the firm conviction that in August and September 1941 the Germans had engaged in mass shootings of Polish war prisoners at the country house in Kozy Gory.)

The testimony of Alexeyeva is confirmed by the testimony of her father, Mikhail Alexeyev, whom she told as far back as in the autumn of 1941, during her work at the country house, about her observations of the Germans' activities at the country house. "For a long time she would not tell me anything," Mikhail Alexeyev testified. "Only on coming home she complained that she was afraid to work at the country house and did not know how to get away. When I asked her why she was afraid she said that very often shooting was heard in the forest. Once she told me in secret that in Kozy Gory Forest the Germans were shooting Poles. I listened to my daughter and warned her very strictly that she should not tell anyone else about it, as otherwise the Germans would learn and then our whole family would suffer."

That Polish war prisoners used to be brought to Kozy Gory in small groups of 20 to 30 men escorted by five to seven German soldiers, was also testified to by other witnesses interrogated by the Special Commission: P. G. Kisselev, peasant of Kozy Gory hamlet; M. G. Krivozertsev, carpenter of Krasny Bor station in the Katyn Forest; S. S. Ivanov, former station master at Gnezdovo in the Katyn Forest area; I. V. Savvateyev, station master on duty at the same station; M. A. Alexeyev, chairman of a collective farm in the village of Borok; A. P. Ogloblin, priest of Kuprino Church, and others.

These witnesses also heard shots in the forest at Kozy Gory.

Of especially great importance in ascertaining what took place at Kozy Gory country house in the autumn of 1941 is the testimony of Professor of Astronomy B. V. Bazilevsky, director of the Smolensk Observatory.

In the early days of the occupation of Smolensk by the Germans, Professor Bazilevsky was forcibly appointed assistant burgomaster, while to the post of burgomaster they appointed the lawyer, B. G. Menshagin, who subsequently left together with them, a traitor who enjoyed the special confidence of the German command and in particular of the Smolensk Commandant von Schwetz.

Early in September 1941 Bazilevsky addressed to Menshagin a request to solicit the Commandant von Schwetz of the liberation of the teacher Zhiglinsky from war prisoners' camp No. 126. In compliance with this request Menshagin approached von Schwetz and then informed Bazilevsky that his request could not be granted since, according to von Schwetz, "instructions had been received from Berlin prescribing that the strictest regime be maintained undeviatingly with regard to war prisoners without any easing up on this matter.

"I voluntarily retorted," witness Bazilevsky testified, 'Can anything be stricter than the regime existing in the camp?' Menshagin looked at me in a strange way and bending to my ear, answered in a low voice: 'Yes, there can be. The Russians can at least be left to die off, but as to the Polish war prisoners, the orders say that they are to be simply exterminated.'

" 'How is that? How should it be understood?' I exclaimed.

" 'This should be understood literally. There is such a directive from Berlin,' answered Menshagin, and asked me 'for the sake of all that is holy' not to tell anyone about this. . . .

"About a fortnight after this conversation with Menshagin, when I was again received by him, I could not keep from asking: 'What news about the Poles?' Menshagin paused for a moment, but then answered: 'Everything is over with them. Von Schwetz told me that they had been shot somewhere near Smolensk.'

"Seeing my bewilderment Menshagin warned me again about the necessity of keeping this affair in the strictest secrecy and then started 'explaining' to me the Germans' policy in this matter. He told me that the shooting of Poles was one link in the general chain of anti-Polish policy pursued by Germany, which became especially marked in connection with the conclusion of the Russo-Polish Treaty."

Bazilevsky also told the Special Commission about his conversation with Hirschfeld, the Sonderfuehrer of the Seventh Department of the German Commandant's Office, a Baltic German who spoke good Russian:

"With cynical frankness Hirschfeld told me that the harmfulness and inferiority of the Poles had been proved by history and therefore reduction of Poland's population would fertilize the soil and make possible an extension of Germany's living space. In this connection Hirschfeld boasted that absolutely no intellectuals had been left in Poland, as they had all been hanged, shot, or confined in camps."

Bazilevsky's testimony is confirmed by the witness I. E. Yefimov, professor of physics, who has been interrogated by the Special Commission and whom Bazilevsky at that time, in the autumn of 1941, told about his conversation with Menshagin.

Documentary corroboration of Bazilevsky's and Yefimov's testimony is supplied by notes made by Menshagin in his own hand in his notebook.

This notebook, containing 17 incomplete pages, was found in the files of the Smolensk Municipal Board after the liberation of Smolensk by the Red Army.

Menshagin's ownership of the notebook and his handwriting have been confirmed both by Bazilevsky, who knew Menshagin's hand well, and by expert graphologists.

Judging by the dates in the notebook, its contents relate to the period from early August 1941 to November of the same year.

Among the various notes on economic matters (on firewood, electric power, trade, etc.) there are a number of notes made by Menshagin evidently as a reminder of instructions issued by the German commandant's office in Smolensk.'

These notes reveal with sufficient clarity the range of problems with which the Municipal Board dealt as the organ fulfilling all the instructions of the German command.

The first three pages of the notebook lay down in detail the procedure in organizing the Jewish "ghetto" and the system of reprisals to be applied against the Jews.

Page 10, dated August 15, 1941, contains the following note:

"All fugitive Polish war prisoners are to be detained and delivered to the commandant's office."

Page 15 (undated) contains the entry: "Are there any rumors among the population concerning the shooting of Polish war prisoners n Kozy Gory (for Umnov)?"

It transpires from the initial entry, firstly, that on August 15, 1941,

Polish war prisoners were still in the Smolensk area and, secondly, that they were being arrested by the German authorities.

The second entry indicates that the German command, worried by the possibility of rumors circulating among the civilian population about the crime it had committed, issued special instructions for the purpose of checking this surmise.

Umnov, mentioned in this entry, was the chief of the Russian police in Smolensk during the early months of its occupation.

Beginning of German Provocation

In the winter of 1942–43 the general military situation changed sharply to the disadvantage of the Germans. The military power of the Soviet Union was continually growing stronger. The unity between the U.S.S.R. and her allies was growing in strength. The Germans resolved to launch a provocation, using for this purpose the atrocities they had committed in the Katyn Forest, and ascribing them to the organs of the Soviet authorities. In this way they intended to set the Russians and Poles at loggerheads and to cover up the traces of their own crimes.

A priest, A. P. Ogloblin, of the village of Kuprino in the Smolensk district, testified:

"After the events at Stalingrad, when the Germans began to feel uncertain, they launched this business. The people started to say that 'the Germans are trying to mend their affairs.'

"Having embarked on the preparation of the Katyn provocation, the Germans first set about looking for 'witnesses' who would, under the influence of persuasion, bribes, or threats, give the testimony which the Germans needed.

"The attention of the Germans was attracted to the peasant Parfen Favrilovich Kisselev, born in 1870, who lived in the hamlet nearest to the country house in Kozy Gory."

Kisselev was summoned to the Gestapo at the close of 1942. Under the threat of reprisals, they demanded of him fictitious testimony alleging that he knows that in the spring of 1940 the Bolsheviks shot Polish war prisoners at the country house of the administration of the People's Commissariat of Internal Affairs in Kozy Gory.

Kisselev testified before the commission:

"In the autumn of 1942 two policemen came to my house and ordered me to report to the Gestapo at Gnezdovo station. On that same day I went to the Gestapo, which had its premises in a two-story house next to the railway station. In a room I entered there were a German officer and interpreter. The German officer started asking me through the interpreter how long I had lived in that district, what my occupation and my material circumstances were.

"I told him that I had lived in the hamlet in the area of Kozy Gory since 1907 and worked on my farm. As to my material circumstances, I said that I had experienced some difficulties since I was old and my sons were in the war.

"After a brief conversation on this subject, the officer stated that, according to information at the disposal of the Gestapo, in 1940, in the area of Kozy Gory in the Katyn Forest, staff members of the People's Commissariat of Internal Affairs shot Polish officers, and he asked me what testimony I could give on this score. I answered that I had never heard of the People's Commissariat of Internal Affairs shooting people at Kozy Gory, and that anyhow it was impossible, I explained to the officer, since Kozy Gory is an absolutely open and much frequented place, and if shootings had gone on there the entire population of the neighboring villages would have known.

"The officer told me I must nevertheless give such evidence, because he alleged the shootings did take place. I was promised a big reward for this testimony.

"I told the officer again that I did not know anything about shootings, and that nothing of the sort could have taken place in our locality before the war. In spite of this, the officer persistently insisted on my giving false evidence.

"After the first conversation about which I have already spoken, I was summoned again to the Gestapo only in February 1943. By that time I knew that other residents of neighboring villages had also been summoned to the Gestapo and that the same testimony they demanded of me had also been demanded of them.

"At the Gestapo the same officer and interpreter who had interrogated me the first time again demanded of me evidence that I had witnessed the shooting of Polish officers, allegedly carried out by the People's Commissariat of Internal Affairs in 1940. I again told the Gestapo officer that this was a lie, as before the war I had not heard anything about any shootings, and that I would not give false evidence. the interpreter, however, would not listen to me, but took a handwritten document from the desk and read it to me. It said that I, Kisselev, resident of a hamlet in the Kozy Gory area, personally witnessed the shooting of Polish officers by staff members of the People's Commissariat of Internal Affairs in 1940.

"Having read this document, the interpreter told me to sign it. I refused to do so. The interpreter began to force me to do it by abuse and threats. Finally he shouted: 'Either you sign it at once or we shall destroy you. Make your choice.'

"Frightened by these threats, I signed the document and thought that would be the end of the matter."

Later, after the Germans had arranged visits to the Katyn graves by various "delegations," Kisselev was forced to speak before a "Polish delegation" which arrived there.

Kisselev forgot the contents of the protocol he had signed at the Gestapo, got mixed up, and finally refused to speak.

The Gestapo then arrested Kisselev, and by ruthless beatings, in the course of 6 weeks again obtained his consent to make "public speeches."

In this connection Kisselev stated:

"In reality things went quite a different way.

"In the spring of 1943 the Germans announced that in the Kozy Gory area in Katyn Forest they had discovered the graves of Polish officers allegedly shot in 1940 by organs of the People's Commissariat of Internal Affairs.

"Soon after that the Gestapo interpreter came to my house and took me to the forest in the Kozy Gory area.

"When we had left the house and were alone together, the interpreter warned me that I must tell the people present in the forest everything exactly as it was written down in the document I had signed at the Gestapo.

"When I came in to the forest in saw open graves and a group of strangers. The interpreter told me that these were 'Polish delegates' who had arrived to inspect the graves.

"When we approached the graves the 'delegates' started asking me various questions in Russian in connection with the shooting of the Poles, but as more than a month had passed since I had been summoned to the Gestapo I forgot everything that was in the document I had signed, got mixed up, and finally said I did not know anything about the shooting of the Polish officers.

"The German officer got very angry. The interpreter roughly dragged me away from the 'delegation' and chased me off.

"The next morning a car with a Gestapo officer drove up to my house. He found me in the yard, told me that I was under arrest, put me into the car and took me to Smolensk Prison. . . .

"After my arrest I was interrogated many times, but they beat me more than they questioned me. The first time they summoned me they beat and abused me mercilessly, stating that I had let them down, and then sent me back to the cell.

"The next time I was summoned they told me I had to state publicly that I had witnessed the shooting of Polish officers by the Bolsheviks, and that until the Gestapo was convinced that I would do this in good faith I would not be released from prison. I told the officer that I would rather sit in prison than tell people lies to their faces. After that I was badly beaten up.

"There were several such interrogations accompanied by beatings, and as a result I lost all my strength, my hearing became poor and I could not move my right arm.

"About 1 month after my arrest a German officer summoned me and said: 'You see the consequences of your obstinacy, Kisselev. We have decided to execute you. In the morning we shall take you to Katyn Forest and hang you.' I asked the officer not to do this, and tried to convince him that I was not fit for the part of 'eyewitness' of the shooting as I did not know how to tell lies and therefore I would mix everything up again. The officer continued to insist. Several minutes later soldiers came into the room and started beating me with rubber clubs.

"Being unable to stand the beatings and torture, I agreed to appear publicly with a fallacious tale about the shooting of the Poles by the Bolsheviks. After that I was released from prison on condition that at the first demand of the Germans I would speak before 'delegations' in Katyn Forest.

"On every occasion, before leading me to the open graves in the forest, the interpreter used to come to my house, call me out into the yard, take me aside to make sure that no one would hear, and for half an hour make me memorize by heart everything I would have to say about the alleged shooting of Polish officers by the People's Commissariat of Internal Affairs in 1940.

"I recall that the interpreter told me something like this: 'I live in a cottage in Kozy Gory area not far from the country house of the People's Commissariat of Internal Affairs. In the spring of 1940, I saw Poles taken to the forest on various nights and shot there.' And then it was imperative that I must state literally that 'this was the doing of the People's Commissariat of Internal Affairs."

"After I had memorized what the interpreter told me, he would take me to the open graves in the forest and compel me to repeat all this in the presence of 'delegations' which came there. My statements were strictly supervised and directed by the Gestapo interpreter.

"Once when I spoke before some 'delegation' I was asked the question: 'Did you personally see these Poles before they were shot by the Bolsheviks?' I was not prepared for such a question and answered the way it was in fact, i.e., that I saw Polish war prisoners before the war, as they worked on the roads. Then the interpreter roughly dragged me aside and drove me home.

"Please believe me when I say that all the time I felt pangs of conscience, as I knew that in reality the Polish officers had been shot by the Germans in 1941. I had no other choice, as I was constantly threatened with the repetition of my arrest and torture."

P. G. Kisselev's testimony regarding his summons to the Gestapo, subsequent arrest, and beatings are confirmed by his wife Aksinya Kisseleva, born in 1870, his son Vasili Kisselev, born in 1911, and his daughter-in-law Maria Kisseleva, born in 1918, who live with him, as well as by track foreman Timofey Sergeyev, born in 1901, who rents a room in Kisselev's hamlet.

The injuries caused to Kisselev at the Gestapo (injury of shoulder, considerable impairment of hearing) are confirmed by a report of medical examination.

In their search for "witnesses" the Germans subsequently became interested in railway workers at the Gnezdovo station, 2-1/2 kilometers from Kozy Gory. In the spring of 1940 the Polish prisoners of war arrived at this station, and the Germans evidently wanted to obtain corroborating testimony from the railwaymen. For this purpose, in the spring of 1943, the Germans summoned to the Gestapo the ex-station master of Gnezdovo station, S. V. Ivanov, the station master on duty, I. V. Savvateyev, and others.

S. V. Ivanov, born in 1882, gave the following account of the circumstances in which he was summoned to the Gestapo:

"It was in March 1943. I was interrogated by a German officer in the presence of an interpreter. Having asked me through the interpreter who I was and what post I held at Gnezdovo station before the occupation of the district by the Germans, the officer inquired whether I knew that in the spring of 1940 large parties of captured Polish officers had arrived at Gnezdovo station in several trains.

"I said that I knew about this.

"The officer then asked me whether I knew that in the same spring, 1940, soon after the arrival of the Polish officers, the Bolsheviks had shot them all in the Katyn Forest.

"I answered that I did not know anything about that, and that it could not be so, as in the course of 1940–41, up to the occupation of Smolensk by the Germans, I had met captured Polish officers who arrived in spring, 1940, at Gnezdovo station, and who were engaged in road-construction work.

"Then the officer told me that if a German officer asserted that the Poles had been shot by the Bolsheviks it meant that this was the case. 'Therefore,' the officer continued, 'you need not fear anything, and you can sign with a clear conscience a protocol saying that the Polish officers who were prisoners of war were shot by the Bolsheviks and that you witnessed it.'

"I replied that I was already an old man, that I was 61 years old, and did not want to commit a sin in my old age. I could only testify that the Polish prisoners of war really arrived at Gnezdovo Station in the spring of 1940.

"The German officer began to persuade me to give the required testimony, promising that if I agreed he would promote me from the position of watchman on a railway crossing to that of station master of Gnezdovo Station, which I had held under the Soviet Government, and also to provide for my material needs.

"The interpreter emphasized that my testimony as a former railway employee at Gnezdovo Station, the nearest station to Katyn Forest, was extremely important for the German command, and that I would not regret it if I gave such testimony.

"I understood that I had landed in an extremely difficult situation, and that a sad fate awaited me. However, I again refused to give false testimony to the German officer.

"After that the German officer started shouting at me, threatening me with beating and shooting, and said I did not understand what was good for me. However, I stood my ground.

"The interpreter then drew up a short protocol in German on one page, and gave me a free translation of its contents.

"This protocol recorded, as the interpreter told me, only the fact of the arrival of the Polish war prisoners at Gnezdovo Station. When I asked that my testimony be recorded not only in German but also in Russian, the officer finally was beside himself with fury, beat me up with a rubber club, and drove me off the premises. . . ."

I. V. Savvateyev, born in 1880, stated:

"In the Gestapo I testified that in spring 1940, Polish war prisoners arrived at the station of Gnezdovo in several trains and proceeded further by car, and I did not know where they went. I also added that I repeatedly met these Poles later on the Moscow-Minsk highway, where they were working on repairs in small groups.

"The officer told me I was mixing things up, that I could not have met the Poles on the highway, as they had been shot by the Bolsheviks, and demanded that I testify to this. I refused.

"After threatening and cajoling me for a long time, the officer consulted with the interpreter in German about something, and the interpreter wrote a short protocol and gave it to me to sign. He explained that it was a record of my testimony. I asked the interpreter to let me read the protocol myself, but he interrupted me with abuse, ordering me to sign it immediately and get out. I hesitated a minute. The interpreter seized a rubber club hanging on the wall and made a move to strike me. After that I signed the protocol shoved at me. The interpreter told me to get out and go home, and not to talk to anyone or I would be shot. . . ."

The search for "witnesses" was not limited to the above-mentioned persons. The Germans strove persistently to locate former employees of the People's Commissariat of Internal Affairs and extort from them false testimony.

Having changed to arrest E. L. Ignatyuk, formerly a laborer n the garage of the Smolensk Regional Administration of the People's Commissariat of Internal Affairs, the Germans stubbornly, by threats and beatings, tried to extort from him testimony that he had been a chauffeur and not merely a laborer in the garage and had himself driven Polish war prisoners to the site of the shooting.

E. L. Ignatyuk, born in 1903, testified in this connection:

"When I was interrogated for the first time by Chief of Police Alferchik, he accused me of agitating against the German authorities, and asked what work I had done for the People's Commissariat of Internal Affairs. I replied that I had worked in the garage of the Smolensk Regional Administration of the

People's Commissariat of Internal Affairs as a laborer. At this interrogation, Alferchik tried to get me to testify that I had worked as a chauffeur and not as a laborer.

"Greatly irritated by his failure to obtain the required testimony from me, Alferchik and his aide, whom he called George, bound up my head and mouth with some cloth, removed my trousers, laid me on a table and began to beat me with rubber clubs.

"After that I was summoned again for interrogation, and Alferchik demanded that I give him false testimony to the effect that the Polish officers had been shot in Katyn Forest by organs of the People's Commissariat of Internal Affairs in 1940, of which I allegedly was aware, as a chauffeur who had taken part in driving the Polish officers to Katyn Forest, and who had been present at their shooting. Alferchik promised to release me from prison if I would agree to give such testimony, and get me a job with the police, where I would be given good living conditions—otherwise they would shoot me. . . .

"The last time I was interrogated in the police station by examiner Alexandrov, who demanded from me the same false testimony as Alferchik about the shooting of the Polish officers, but at this examination, too, I refused to give false evidence.

"After this interrogation I was again beaten up and sent to the Gestapo. . . .

"In the Gestapo, just as at the police station, they demanded from me false evidence about the shooting of the Polish officers in Katyn Forest in 1940 by Soviet authorities, of which I as a chauffeur was allegedly aware."

A book published by the German Ministry of Foreign Affairs, and containing material about the "Katyn Affair," fabricated by the Germans, refers to other "witnesses" besides the above-mentioned P. G. Kisselev: Godesov (alias Godunov), born in 1877; Grigori Silverstov, born in 1891; Ivan Andreyev, born in 1917; Mikhail Zhigulev, born in 1915; Ivan Krivozertsev, born in 1915; and Matvey Zakharov, born in 1893.

A check-up revealed that the first two of the above persons (Godesov and Silverstov) died in 1943 before the liberation of the Smolensk region by the Red Army; the next three (Andreyev, Zhigulev, and Krivozertsev) left with the Germans, or perhaps were forcibly abducted by them while the last—Matvey Zakharov—formerly a coupler at Smolensk Station, who worked under the Germans as headman in the village Novo Bateki, was located and examined by the special commission.

Zakharov related how the Germans obtained from him the false testimony they needed about the "Katyn Affair."

"Early in March 1943 an employee of the Gnezdovo Gestapo, whose name I do not know, came to my house and told me that an officer wanted to see me.

"When I arrived at the Gestapo a German officer told me through an interpreter: 'We know you worked as a coupler at Smolensk Central station and you must testify that in 1940 cars with Polish war prisoners passed through Smolensk on the way to Gnezdovo, after which the Poles were shot in the forest at Kozy Gory.' In reply, I stated that in 1940 cars with Poles did pass Smolensk westward, but I did not know what their destination was.

"The officer told me that if I did not want to testify of my own accord he would force me to do so. After saying this he took a rubber club and began to beat me up. Then I was laid on a bench, and the officer, together with the interpreter, beat me. I do not remember how many strokes I had, because I soon fainted.

"When I came to, the officer demanded that I sign a protocol of the examination. I had lost courage as a result of the beating and threats of shooting, so I gave false evidence and signed the protocol. After I had signed the protocol I was released by the Gestapo. . . .

"Several days after I had been summoned by the Gestapo, approximately in mid-March 1943, the interpreter came to my house and said I must go to a German general and confirm my testimony in his presence.

"When I came to the general he asked me whether I confirmed my testimony. I said I did confirm it, as on the way I had been warned by the interpreter that if I refused to confirm the testimony I would have a much worse experience than I had on my first visit to the Gestapo.

"Fearing a repetition of the torture, I replied that I confirmed my testimony. Then the interpreter ordered me to raise my right hand, and told me I had taken an oath and could go home."

It has been established that in other cases also the Germans used persuasion, threats, and torture in trying to obtain the testimony they needed, for example, from N. S. Kaverzney, former deputy chief of the Smolensk Prison, and V. G. Kovalev, former staff member of the same prison, and others.

Since the search for the required number of witnesses failed to yield any success, the Germans posted the following handbill in the city of Smolensk and neighboring villages, an original of which is in the files of the Special Commission:

"Notice to the population.

"Who can give information concerning the mass murder of prisoners, Polish officers and priests, by the Bolsheviks in the forest of Kozy Gory near the Gnezdovo-Katyn highway in 1940?

"Who saw the columns of trucks on their way from Gnezdovo to Kozy Gory, or

"Who saw or heard the shootings? Who knows residents who can tell about this?

"Rewards will be given for any information.

"Information to be sent to Smolensk, German Police Station, No. 6, Muzeinaya Street, and in Gnezdovo to the German Police Station, house No. 105 near the railway station.

> "Foss
> "Lieutenant of Field Police,
> "May 3, 1943."

A similar notice was printed in the newspaper Novy Put, published by the Germans in Smolensk—No. 35 (157) for May 6, 1943.

The fact that the Germans promised rewards for the evidence they needed on the "Katyn Affair" was confirmed by witnesses called by the Special Commission: O. E. Sokolova, E. A. Puschchina, I. I. Bychkov, G. T. Bondarev, E. P. Ustinov, and many other residents of Smolensk.

Preparing Katyn Graves

Along with the search for "witnesses" the Germans proceeded with the preparation of the graves in Katyn Forest; they removed from the clothing of the Polish prisoners whom they had killed all documents dated later than April 1940—that is, the time when, according to the German provocational version, the Poles were shot by the Bolsheviks—and removed all material evidence which could disprove this provocational version.

In its investigation the Special Commission revealed that for this purpose the Germans used up to 500 Russian war prisoners specially selected from war prisoners' camp No. 126.

The Special Commission has at its disposal numerous statements of witnesses on this matter.

The evidence of the medical personnel of the above-mentioned camp merits special attention.

"Just about the beginning of March 1943, several groups of the physically stronger war prisoners, totaling about 500, were sent from the Smolensk camp No. 126 ostensibly for trench work. None of these prisoners ever returned to the camp."

Dr. V. A. Khmyrov, who worked in the same camp under the Germans, testified:

"I know that somewhere about the second half of February or the beginning of March 1943, about 500 Red Army men prisoners were sent from our camp to a destination unknown to me. The prisoners were apparently to be used for trench digging, for the most physically fit men were selected. . . ."

Identical evidence was given by medical nurse O. G. Lenkovskaya, medical nurse A. I. Timofeyeva, and witnesses P. M. Orlova, E. G. Dobroserdova, and B. S. Kochetkov.

The testimony of A. M. Moskovskaya made it clear where the 500 war prisoners from camp 126 were actually sent.

On October 5, 1943, the citizen Moskovskaya, Alexandra Mikhailovna, who lived on the outskirts of Smolensk and had worked during the occupation in the kitchen of a German military unit, filed an application to the Extraordinary Commission for the Investigation of Atrocities Perpetrated by the German Invaders, requesting them to summon her to give important evidence.

After she was summoned she told the Special Commission that before leaving for work in March 1943, when she went to fetch firewood from her shed in the yard on the banks of the Dnieper, she discovered there an unknown person who proved to be a Russian war prisoner.

A. M. Moskovskaya, who was born in 1922, testified:

"From conversation with him I learned the following:

"His name was Nikolai Yegorov, a native of Leningrad. Since the end of 1941 he had been in the German camp No. 126 for war prisoners in the town of Smolensk. At the beginning of March 1943 he was sent with a column of several hundred war prisoners from the camp to Katyn Forest. There they, including Yegorov, were compelled to dig up graves containing bodies in the uniforms of Polish officers, drag these bodies out of the graves and take out of their pockets documents, letters, photographs, and all other articles.

"The Germans gave the strictest orders that nothing be left in the pockets on the bodies. Two war prisoners were shot because after they had searched some of the bodies, a German officer discovered some papers on these bodies.

"Articles, documents, and letters extracted from the clothing on the bodies were examined by the German officers, who then compelled the prisoners to put part of the papers back into the pockets on the bodies, while the rest were flung on a heap of articles and documents they had extracted, and later burned.

"Besides this, the Germans made the prisoners put into the pockets of the Polish officers some papers which they took from cases or suitcases (I don't remember exactly) which they had brought along.

"All the war prisoners lived in Katyn Forest in dreadful conditions under the open sky, and were extremely strongly guarded. . . .

"At the beginning of April 1943 all the work planned by the Germans was apparently completed, as for 3 days not one of the war prisoners had to do any work. . . .

"Suddenly at night all of them without exception were awakened and led somewhere. The guard was strengthened. Yegorov sensed something was wrong and began to watch very closely everything that was happening. They marched for 3 or 4 hours in an unknown direction. They stopped in the forest at a pit in a clearing. He saw how a group of war prisoners were separated from the rest and driven toward the pit and then shot.

"The war prisoners grew agitated, restless, and noisy. Not far from Yegorov several war prisoners attacked the guards. Other guards ran toward the place. Yegorov took advantage of the confusion and ran away into the dark forest, hearing shouts and firing.

"After hearing this terrible story, which is engraved on my memory for the rest of my life, I became very sorry for Yegorov, and told him to come to my room, get warm and hide at my place until he had regained his strength. but Yegorov refused. . . . He said no matter what happened he was going away that very night, and intended to try to get through the front line to the Red Army. But Yegorov did not leave that evening. In the morning, when I went to make sure whether Yegorov had gone, he was still in the shed. It appeared that during the night he had attempted to set out, but had only taken about 50 steps when he felt so weary that he was forced to return. This exhaustion was caused by the long imprisonment at the camp and the starvation of the last few days. We decided he should remain at my place several days longer to regain his strength. After feeding Yegorov I went to work.

"When I returned home in the evening my neighbors Maria Ivanovna Baranova and Yekaterina Viktorovna Kabanovskaya told me that in the afternoon, during a search by the German police, the Red Army war prisoner had been found, and taken away."

As a result of the discovery of the war prisoner Yegorov in the shed, Moskovskaya was called to the Gestapo, where she was accused of hiding a war prisoner.

At the Gestapo interrogation Moskovskaya stoutly denied that she had any connection with this war prisoner, maintaining she knew nothing about his presence in her shed. Since they got no admission from Moskovskaya, and also because the war prisoner Yegorov evidently had not incriminated Moskovskaya, she was let out of the Gestapo.

The same Yegorov told Moskovskaya that besides excavating bodies in Katyn Forest, the war prisoners were used for bringing bodies to the Katyn Forest from other places. The bodies thus brought were thrown into pits along with the bodies that had been dug up earlier.

The fact that a great number of bodies of people shot by the Germans in other places were brought to the Katyn graves is confirmed also by the testimony of Engineer Mechanic P. F. Sukhachev, born in 1912, an engineer mechanic of the Rosglavkhleb combine, who worked under the Germans as a mechanic in the Smolensk city mill. On October 8, 1943, he filed a request that he be called to testify.

Called before the Special Commission, he stated:

"Somehow during the second half of March 1943 I spoke at the mill to a German chauffeur who spoke a little Russian. Learning that he was carrying flour to Savenki village for the troops, and was returning on the next day to

Smolensk, I asked him to take me along so that I could buy some fat in the village. My idea was that making the trip in a German truck would do away with the risk of being held up at the control stations. The German agreed to take me, at a price. On the same day, at 10 p.m. we drove on to the Smolensk-Vitebsk highway, just myself and the German driver in the truck. The night was light, and only a low mist over the road reduced the visibility. Approximately 22 or 23 kilometers from Smolensk, at a demolished bridge on the highway, there is a rather deep descent at the bypass. We began to go down from the highway, when suddenly a truck appeared out of the fog coming toward us. Either because our brakes were out of order, or because the driver was inexperienced, we were unable to bring our truck to a halt, and since the passage was quite narrow we collided with the truck coming toward us. The impact was not very violent, as the driver of the other truck swerved to the side, as a result of which the trucks bumped and slid alongside each other. The right wheel of the other truck, however, landed in the ditch, and the truck fell over on the slope. Our truck remained upright. The driver and I immediately jumped out of the cabin and ran up the truck which had fallen down. I was struck by a heavy stench of dead bodies, evidently coming from the truck. On coming nearer, I saw that the truck was carrying a load covered with a tarpaulin and tied up with ropes. The ropes had snapped with the impact, and part of the load had fallen on the slope. It was a horrible load—human bodies dressed in military uniforms.

"As far as I can remember there were some six or seven men near the truck: One German driver, two Germans armed with tommy guns—the rest were Russian war prisoners, as they spoke Russian and were dressed accordingly.

"The Germans began to abuse my driver and then made some attempts to right the truck. In about 2 minutes' time two more trucks drove up to the place of the accident and stopped. A group of Germans and Russian war prisoners, about 10 men in all, came up to us from these trucks. . . . By joint efforts we began to raise the truck. Taking advantage of an opportune moment I asked one of the Russian war prisoners in a low voice: 'What is it?' He answered very quietly: 'For many nights now we have been carrying bodies to Katyn Forest.'

"Before the overturned truck had been raised a German noncommissioned officer came up to me and my driver and ordered us to proceed immediately. As no serious damage had been done to our truck the driver steered it a little to one side and got onto the highway, and we went on. When we were passing the two covered trucks which had come up later, I again smelled the horrible stench of dead bodies."

Sukhachev's testimony is confirmed by that of Vladimir Afanasievich Yegorov, who served as policeman in the police station during the occupation.

Yegorov testified that when, owing to the nature of his duties, he was guarding a bridge at a crossing of the Moscow-Minsk and Smolensk-Vitebsk highways at the end of March and early in April 1943, he saw going toward Smolensk on several nights big trucks covered with tarpaulins and spreading a heavy stench of dead bodies. Several men, some of whom were armed and were undoubtedly Germans, sat in the driver's cabin of each truck, and behind.

Yegorov reported his observations to Kuzma Demyanovich Golovnev, chief of the police station in the village of Arkhipovka, who advised him to "hold his tongue" and added: "This does not concern us. We have no business to be mixing in German affairs."

That the Germans were carrying bodies on trucks to the Katyn Forest is also testified by Frol Maximovich Yakovlev-Sokolov (born in 1896), a former agent for restaurant supplies in the Smolensk restaurant trust and, under the Germans, chief of police of Katyn precinct. He stated that once, early in April 1943 he himself saw four tarpaulin-covered trucks passing along the highway to Katyn Forest. Several men armed with tommy guns and rifles rode in them. An acrid stench of dead bodies came from these trucks.

From the above testimony it can be concluded with all clarity that the Germans shot Poles in other places, too. In bringing their bodies to the Katyn Forest they pursued a triple object: first, to destroy the traces of their crimes; second, to ascribe their own crimes to the Soviet Government; third, to increase the number of "victims of Bolshevism" in the Katyn Forest graves.

"Excursions" to the Katyn Graves

In April 1943, having finished all the preparatory work at the graves in Katyn Forest, the German occupationists began a wide campaign in the press and over the radio in an attempt to ascribe to the Soviet Power atrocities they themselves had committed against Polish war prisoners. As one method of provocational agitation, the Germans arranged visits to the Katyn graves by residents of Smolensk and its suburbs, as well as "delegations" from countries occupied by the German invaders or their vassals. The Special Commission questioned a number of delegates who took part in the "excursions" to the Katyn graves.

K. P. Zubkov, a doctor specializing in pathological anatomy, who worked as medico-legal expert in Smolensk, testified before the Special Commission: "The clothing on the bodies, particularly the overcoats, boots and belts, were in a good state of preservation. The metal parts of the clothing—belt buckles, button hooks, and spikes on shoe soles, etc.—were not heavily rusted, and in some cases the metal still retained its polish. Sections of the skin on the bodies, which could be seen—faces, necks, arms—were chiefly a dirty green color and in some cases dirty brown, but there was no complete disintegration of the tissues, no putrefaction. In some cases bared tendons of whitish color and parts of muscles could be seen.

"While I was at the excavations people were at work sorting and extracting bodies at the bottom of a big pit. For this purpose they used spades and other tools, and also took hold of bodies with their hands and dragged them from place to place by the arms, the legs or the clothing. I did not see a single case of bodies falling apart or any member being torn off.

"Considering all the above, I arrived at the conclusion that the bodies had remained in the earth not 3 years, as the Germans affirmed, but much less. Knowing that in mass graves, and especially without coffins, putrefaction of bodies progresses more quickly than in single graves. I concluded that the mass shooting of the Poles had taken place about a year and a half ago, and could have occurred in the autumn of 1941 or the spring of 1942. As a result of my visit to the excavation site I became firmly convinced that a monstrous crime had been committed by the Germans."

Testimony to the effect that the clothing of the bodies, its metal parts, shoes, and even the bodies themselves were well preserved was given by numerous witnesses who took part in "excursions" to the Katyn graves and who were questioned by the Special Commission. The witnesses include I. Z. Kutzev, the manager of the Smolensk water supply system; E. N. Vetrova, a Katyn schoolteacher; N. G. Shchedrova, a telephone operator of the Smolensk communications bureau; M. A. Alexeyev, a resident of the village of Borok; N. G. Krivozertsev, a resident of the village of Novo Bateki; I. V. Savvateyev, the station master on duty at Gnezdovo station; E. A. Pushchina, a citizen of Smolensk; T. A. Sidoruk, a doctor at the Second Smolensk hospital; P. M. Kessarev, a doctor at the same hospital; and others.

Germans Attempt to Cover Up Traces of Their Crimes

The "excursions" organized by the Germans failed to achieve their aims. All who visited the graves saw for themselves that they were confronted with the crudest and most obvious German-Fascist frame-up. The German authorities accordingly took steps to make the doubters keep quiet. The Special Commission heard the testimony of a great number of witnesses who related how the German authorities persecuted those who doubted or disbelieved the provocation. These doubters were discharged from work, arrested, threatened with shooting.

The Commission established that in two cases people were shot for failure to "hold their tongues." Such reprisals were taken against the former German policeman Zagainev, and against Yegorov, who worked on the excavation of graves in Katyn Forest. Testimony about the persecution of people who expressed doubt after visiting the graves in Katyn Forest was given by M. S.

Zubareva, a woman cleaner employed by drug store No. 1 in Smolensk; V. F. Kozlova, assistant sanitation doctor of the Stalin District Health Department in Smolensk, and others.

F. M. Yakovlev-Sokolov, former chief of police of the Katyn precinct, testified:

A situation arose which caused serious alarm in the German commandant's office, and police organs around about were given urgent instructions to nip in the bud all harmful talk at any price, and arrest all persons who expressed disbelief in the 'Katyn affair.' I, myself, as chief of the area police, was given instructions to this effect at the end of May 1943 by the German commandant of the village of Katyn, Oberleutnant Braung, and at the beginning of June by the chief of Smolensk district police, Kametsky.

"I called an instructional conference of the police in my area, at which I ordered the police to detain and bring to the police station anyone who expressed disbelief or doubted the truth of German reports about the shooting of Polish war prisoners by the Bolsheviks. In fulfilling these instructions of the German authorities I clearly acted against my conscience, as I, myself, was certain that the 'Katyn affair' was a German provocation. I became finally convinced of that when I, myself, made an 'excursion' to the Katyn Forest."

Seeing that the "excursions" of the local population to the Katyn graves did not achieve their purpose, in the summer of 1943 the German occupation authorities ordered the graves to be filled in. Before their retreat from Smolensk they began hastily to cover up the traces of their crimes. The country house occupied by the "Headquarters of the Five Hundred and Thirty-seventh Engineer Battalion" was burned to the ground.

The Germans searched for the three girls—Alexeyeva, Mikhailova, and Konakhovskaya—in the village of Borok in order to take them away and perhaps to kill them. They also searched for their main "witness," P. G. Kisselev, who, together with his family, had succeeded in hiding. The Germans burned down his house.

They endeavored to seize other "witnesses" too—the former station master of Gnezdovo, S. V. Ivanov, and the former acting station master of the same station, I. V. Savvateyev, as well as the former coupler at the Smolensk station, M. D. Zakharov.

During the very last days before their retreat from Smolensk, the German-Fascist occupationists looked for Profs. Brazilevsky and Yefimov. Both succeeded in evading deportation or death only because they had escaped in good time. Nevertheless, the German-Fascist invaders did not succeed in covering up the traces of or concealing their crime.

Examination by medico-legal experts of the exhumed bodies proved irrefutably that the Polish war prisoners were shot by the Germans themselves. The report of the medico-legal experts' investigation follows:

Report of the Medico-Legal Experts' Investigation

In accordance with the instructions of the special commission for ascertaining and investigating the circumstances of the shooting of Polish officer prisoners by the German-Fascist invaders in Katyn Forest (near Smolensk), a commission of medico-legal experts was set up, consisting of V. I. Prozorovsky, chief medico-legal expert of the People's Commissariat of Health Protection of the U.S.S.R. and director of the State Scientific Research Institute of Forensic Medicine; Doctor of Medicine V. M. Smolyaninov, professor of forensic medicine at the Second Moscow State Medical Institute; Doctor of Medicine D. N. Vyropayev, professor of pathological anatomy; Dr. P. S. Semenovsky, senior staff scientist of the thanatology department of the State Research Institute of Forensic Medicine under the People's Commissariat of Health Protection of the U.S.S.R.; Assistant Prof. M. D. Shvaikova, senior staff scientist of the chemico-legal department of the State Scientific Research Institute of Forensic Medicine under the People's Commissariat of Health Protection of the U.S.S.R.; with the participation of Major of Medical Service Nikolsky, chief medico-legal expert of the western front; Captain of Medical Service Bussoyedov, medico-legal expert of the . . . Army; Major of Medical Service Subbotin, chief of the pathological anatomy laboratory No. 92; Major of Medical Service Ogloblin; Senior Lieutenant of Medical Service Sadykov, medical specialist; Senior Lieutenant of Medical Service Pushkareva.

During the period between January 16 and January 23, 1944, these medico-legal experts conducted exhumation and medico-legal examination of the bodies of Polish war prisoners buried in graves on the territory of Kozy Gory in Katyn Forest, 15 kilometers from Smolensk. The bodies of Polish war prisoners were buried in a common grave about 60 by 60 by 3 meters in dimension, and also in another grave about 7 by 6 by 3–1/2 meters. Nine hundred and twenty-five bodies were exhumed from the graves and examined. The exhumation and medico-legal examination of the bodies were effected in order to establish: (a) Identity of the dead; (b) causes of death; (c) time of burial.

Circumstances of the case: See materials of the Special Commission. Objective evidence: See the reports of the medico-legal examination of the bodies.

Conclusion

On the basis of the results of the medico-legal examination of the bodies, the commission of medico-legal experts arrived at the following conclusion:

Upon the opening of the graves and exhumations of bodies from them, it was established that:

(a) Among the mass of bodies of Polish war prisoners there were bodies in civilian clothes, the number of which, in relation to the total number of bodies examined, is insignificant (in all, 2 out of 925 exhumed bodies); shoes of army type were on these bodies.

(b) The clothing on the bodies of the war prisoners showed that they were officers, and included some privates of the Polish Army.

(c) Slits in the pockets, pockets turned inside out, and tears in them discovered during examination of the clothing show that as a rule all the clothes on each body (overcoats, trousers, etc.) bear traces of searches effected on the dead bodies.

(d) In some cases whole pockets were found during examination of the clothing and scraps of newspapers, prayer books, pocketbooks, postage stamps, postcards and letters, receipts, notes and other documents, as well as articles of value (a gold nugget, dollars). pipes, pocketknives, cigarette papers, handkerchiefs, and other articles were found in these pockets, as well as in the cut and torn pockets, under the linings, in the belts of the coats, and in footwear and socks.

(e) Some of the documents were found (without special examination) to contain data referring to the period between November 12, 1940, and June 20, 1941.

(f) The fabric of the clothes, especially of overcoats, uniforms, trousers, and tunics, is in a good state of preservation and can be torn with the hands only with great difficulty.

(g) A very small proportion of the bodies (20 out of 925) had the hands tied behind the back with woven cords.

The condition of the clothes on the bodies—namely, the fact that uniform jackets, shirts, belts, trousers, and underwear are buttoned up, boots or shoes are on the feet, scarves and ties tied around the necks, suspenders attached, shirts tucked in—testifies that no external examination of the bodies and extremeties of the bodies had been effected previously. The intact state of the skin on the heads, and the absence on them, as on the skin of the chests and abdomens (save in 3 cases out of 925) of any incisions, cuts, or other signs, show convincingly that, judging by the bodies exhumed by the experts' commission, there had been no medico-legal examination of the bodies.

External and internal examination of 925 bodies proves the existence of bullet wounds on the head and neck, combined in 4 cases with injury of the bones of the cranium caused by a blunt, hard, heavy object. Also, injuries of the abdomen caused simultaneously with the wound in the head were discovered in a small number of cases.

Entry orifices of the bullet wounds, as a rule singular, more rarely double, are situated in the occipital part of the head near the occipital protuberance, at the big occipital orifice or at its edge. In a few cases entry orifices of bullets have been found on the back surface of the neck, corresponding to the first, second, or third vertebra of the neck.

The points of exit of the bullets have been found more frequently in the frontal area, more rarely in the parietal and temporal areas as well as in the face and neck. In 27 cases the bullet wounds proved to be blind (without exit orifices), and at the end of the bullet channels under the soft membrane of the cranium, in its bones, in the membranes, and in the brain matter, were found deformed, barely deformed, or altogether undeformed cased bullets of the type used with automatic pistols, mostly of 7.65 millimeter caliber.

The dimensions of the entry orifices in the occipital bone make it possible to draw the conclusion that firearms of two calibers were employed in the shooting: in the majority of cases, those of less than 8 millimeter, i.e., 7.65 millimeter and less; and in a lesser number of cases, those of more than 8 millimeter, i.e., 9 millimeter.

The nature of the fissures of the cranial bones, and the fact that in some cases traces of powder were found at the entry orifice, proves that the shots were fired pointblank or nearly pointblank.

Correlation of the points of entry and exit of the bullets shows that the shots were fired from behind with the head bent forward. The bullet channel pierced the vital parts of the brain, or near them, and death was caused by destruction of the brain tissues.

The injuries inflicted by a blunt, hard, heavy object found on the parietal bones of the cranium were concurrent with the bullet wounds of the head, and were not in themselves the cause of death.

The medico-legal examination of the bodies carried out between January 16 and January 23, 1944, testifies that there are absolutely no bodies in a condition of decay or disintegration, and that all the 925 bodies are in a state of preservation—in the initial phase of desiccation of the body—which most frequently and clearly was expressed in the region of the thorax and abdomen, sometimes also in the extremeties; and in the initial stage of formation of adipocere (in an advanced phase of formation of a dipocere in the bodies extracted from the bottom of the graves); in a combination of desiccation of the tissues of the body with the formation of adipocere.

Especially noteworthy is the fact that the muscles of the trunk and extremities absolutely preserved their macroscopic structure and almost normal color; the internal organs of the thorax and peritoneal cavity preserved their configuration. In many cases sections of heart muscle have a clearly discernible structure and specific coloration, while the brain presented its characteristic structural peculiarities with a distinctly discernible border between the gray and white matter.

Besides the macroscopic examination of the tissues and organs of the bodies, the medico-legal experts removed the necessary material for subsequent microscopic and chemical studies in laboratory conditions.

Properties of the soil in the place of discovery were of a certain significance in the preservation of the tissues and organs of the bodies.

After the opening of the graves and exhumation of the bodies and their exposure to the air, the corpses were subject to the action of warmth and moisture in the late summer season of 1943. This could have resulted in a marked progress of decay of the bodies. However, the degree of desiccation of the bodies and formation of a dipocere in them, especially the good state of preservation of the muscles and internal organs, as well as of the clothes, give grounds to affirm that the bodies had not remained in the earth for long.

Comparing the condition of bodies in the graves in the territory of Kozy Gory with the condition of the bodies in other burial places in Smolensk and its nearest environs—Gedeonovka, Magalenshchina, Readovka, Camp No. 126, Krasny Bor, etc. (see report of the commission of medico-legal experts dated October 22, 1943)—it should be recognized that the bodies of the Polish war prisoners were buried in the territory of Kozy Gory about 2 years ago. This finds its complete corroboration in the documents found in the clothes of the bodies, which preclude the possibility of earlier burial (see point d of paragraph 36 and list of documents).

The commission of medico-legal experts—on the basis of the data and results of the investigation—

Consider as proved the act of killing by shooting of the Polish Army officers and soldiers who were war prisoners;

Asserts that this shooting dates back to about 2 years ago, i.e., between September and December of 1941;

Regards the fact of the discovery by the commission of medico-legal experts, in the clothes on the bodies, of valuables and documents dated 1941, as proof that the German-Fascist authorities who undertook a search of the bodies in the spring-summer season of 1943 did not do it thoroughly, while the documents discovered testify that the shooting was done after June 1941;

States that in 1943 the Germans made an extremely small number of post-mortem examinations of the bodies of the shot Polish war prisoners;

Notes the complete identity of method of the shooting of the Polish war prisoners with that of the shooting of Soviet civilians and war prisoners widely practiced by the German-Fascist authorities in the temporarily occupied territory of the U.S.S.R., including the towns of Smolensk, Orel, Kharkov, Krasnodar and Voronezh.

(Signed)

Chief Medico-Legal Expert of the People's Commissariat of Health

Protection of the U.S.S.R. Director of the State Scientific Research Institute of Forensic Medicine under the People's Commissariat of Health Protection of the U.S.S.R., V. I. Prozorovsky; Professor of Forensic Medicine at the Second Moscow State Medical Institute, Doctor of Medicine V. M. Smolyaninov; Professor of Pathological Anatomy, Doctor of Medicine D. N. Vyropayev; Senior Staff Scientist of Thanatological Department of the State Scientific Research Institute of Forensic Medicine under the People's Commissariat of Health Protection of the U.S.S.R., Doctor P. S. Semenovsky; Senior Staff Scientist of the Forensic Chemistry Department of the State Scientific Research Institute of Forensic Medicine under the People's Commissariat of Health Protection of the U.S.S.R., Assistant Professor M. D. Shvaikova.

Smolensk, January 24, 1944.

Documents Found on the Bodies

Besides the data recorded in the protocol of the commission of medico-legal experts, the time of the shooting of the Polish officer prisoners by the Germans (autumn, 1941, and not spring, 1940, as the Germans assert) is also ascertained by documents found when the graves were opened, dated not only the latter half of 1940 but also the spring and summer (March-June) of 1941. Of the documents discovered by the medico-legal experts, the following deserve special attention:

1. On body No. 92:
   A letter from Warsaw addressed to the Central War Prisoners' Bureau of the Red Cross, Moscow, Kuibyshev Street, House No. 12. The letter is written in Russian. In this letter Sofia Zigon inquires the whereabouts of her husband Tomas Zigon. The letter is dated September 12, 1940. The envelope bears the imprint of a German rubber stamp "Warsaw Sept. 1940" and a rubber stamp Moscow, Central Post Office, ninth delivery, Sept. 28, 1940" and an inscription in red ink in the Russian language: "Ascertain camp and forward for delivery, November 14, 1940" (signature illegible).
2. On body No. 4:
   A post card registered under the number 0112 from Tarnopol stamped "Tarnopol November 12, 1940."
   The written text and address are discolored.
3. On body No. 101:
   A receipt No. 10293 dated December 19, 1939, issued by the Kozelsk camp testifying receipt of a gold watch from Eduard Adamovich Lewandowski. On the back of the receipt is a note dated March 14, 1941, on the sale of this watch to the Jewelry trading trust.

4. On body No. 46:

A receipt (number illegible) issued December 16, 1939, by the Staro-belsk camp testifying receipt of a gold watch from Vladimir Rudolfovich Araszkevicz. On the back of the receipt is a note dated March 25, 1941, stating that the watch was sold to the Jewelry trading trust.

5. On body No. 71:

A small paper icon with the image of Christ, found between pages 144 and 145 of a Catholic prayer book. The inscription, with legible signa-ture, on the back of the icon, reads: "Jadwiga" and bears the date "April 4, 1941."

6. On body No. 46:

A receipt dated April 6, 1941, issued by camp No. 1–ON, showing receipt of 225 rubles from Araszkevicz.

7. On the same body, No. 46:

A receipt dated May 5, 1941, issued by camp No. 1–ON, showing receipt of 102 rubles from Araszkevicz.

8. On body No. 101:

A receipt dated May 18, 1941, issued by camp No. 1–ON, showing receipt of 175 rubles from Lewandowski.

9. On body No. 53:

An unmailed postcard in the Polish language addressed Warsaw Baga-tena 15, apartment 47, to Irene Kuczinska, and dated June 20, 1941. The sender is Stanislaw Kuczinski.

General Conclusions

From all the material at the disposal of the special commission, namely, evidence given by over 100 witnesses questioned, data supplied by the medico-legal experts, documents, and material evidence found in the graves in the Katyn Forest, the following conclusions emerge with irrefutable clarity:

1. The Polish prisoners of war who were in the three camps west of Smolensk, and employed on road building up to the outbreak of war, remained there after the German invaders reached Smolensk, until September 1941, in-clusive;

2. In the Katyn Forest, in the autumn of 1941, the German occupation authorities carried out mass shootings of Polish prisoners of war from the above-named camps;

3. The mass shootings of Polish prisoners of war in the Katyn Forest were carried out by a German military organization hiding behind the conven-tional name of "Headquarters of the Five Hundred and Thirty-seventh Engineer Battalion," which was headed by Lieutenant Colonel Arnes and his assistants, First Lieutenant Rekst and Second Lieutenant Hott;

4. In connection with the deterioration of the general military and po-litical situation for Germany at the beginning of the year 1943, the German

occupation authorities, with provocational aims, took a number of steps in order to ascribe their own crimes to the organs of the Soviet power, calculating on setting Russians and Poles at loggerheads;

5. With this aim:

(a) The German-Fascist invaders, using persuasion, attempts at bribery, threats, and barbarous torture, tried to find "witnesses" among Soviet citizens, from whom they tried to extort false evidence, alleging that the Polish prisoners of war had been shot by the organs of Soviet power in the spring of 1940;

(b) The German occupation authorities in the spring of 1943 brought in from other places bodies of Polish war prisoners whom they had shot and put them into the opened graves in the Katyn Forest, calculating on covering up the traces of their own crimes, and on increasing the number of "victims of Bolshevik atrocities" in the Katyn Forest;

(c) Preparing for their provocation, the German occupation authorities started opening the graves in the Katyn Forest in order to take out documents and material evidence which exposed them, using for this work about 500 Russian prisoners of war who were shot by the Germans after the work was completed.

6. It has been established beyond doubt from the evidence of the medico-legal experts that:

(a) The time of the shooting was the autumn of 1941;

(b) In shooting the Polish war prisoners the German executioners applied the same method of pistol shots in the back of the head as they applied in the mass execution of Soviet citizens in other towns, e.g., Orel, Voronezh, Krasnodar, and Smolensk itself.

7. The conclusions drawn from the evidence given by witnesses, and from the findings of the medico-legal experts on the shooting of Polish war prisoners by the Germans in the autumn of 1941, are completely confirmed by the material evidence and documents excavated from the Katyn graves;

8. In shooting the Polish war prisoners in the Katyn Forest, the German-Fascist invaders consistently carried out their policy of physical extermination of the Slav peoples.

(Signed:)
Chairman of the Special Commission, Member of the Extraordinary State Committee Academician N. N. Burdenko.
Members:
Member of Extraordinary State Committee, Academician Alexei Tolstoi, Member of the Extraordinary State Committee, Metropolitan Nikolai.
Chairman of the All-Slav Committee, Lt. Gen. A. S. Gundorov.

Chairman of the Executive Committee of the Union of the Red Cross and Red Crescent Societies, S. A. Kolesnikov.

People's Commissar of Education of the Russian SFSR, Academician V. P. Potemkin.

Chief of the Central Medical Administration of the Red Army, Col. Gen. E. I. Smirnov.

Chairman of the Smolensk Regional Executive Committee, R. E. Melnikov.

Smolensk, January 24, 1944
Translated from the Russian

Appendix 7

Select Committee to Conduct an Investigation and Study of the Facts,
Evidence and Circumstances of the Katyn Forest Massacre

(Interim Report of July 2, 1952)
U.S. House of Representatives

Ray J. Madden, Indiana, Chairman

Daniel J. Flood, Pennsylvania
Foster Furcolo, Massachusetts
Thaddeus M. Machrowicz, Michigan
George A. Dondero, Michigan
Alvin E. O'Konski, Wisconsin
Timothy P. Sheehan, Illinois
John J. Mitchell, Chief Counsel
Roman C. Pucinski, Chief Investigator
Barbara R. Booke, Secretary

Contents

VIII. Testimony of International Medical Commission
IX. Russian report
X. Nuremberg
XI. Conclusions
XII. Recommendations

The Katyn Forest Massacre

July 2, 1952.—Committed to the Committee of the Whole House on the State of the Union and ordered to be printed

Mr. Madden, from the Select Committee to Conduct an Investigation and Study of the Facts, Evidence, and Circumstances of the Katyn Forest Massacre, submitted the following

Interim Report
[Pursuant to H. Res. 390 and H. Res. 539]
I. Introduction

A. Creation and Purpose of Select Committee to Investigate Katyn Forest Massacre

On September 18, 1951, the House of Representatives unanimously adopted House Resolution 390. This resolution provided for the establishment of a select committee of Congress and authorized it to conduct a full and complete investigation concerning an international crime committed against soldiers and citizens of Poland at the beginning of World War II. This committee was given the responsibility to record evidence, take testimony, and study all facts and extenuating circumstances pertaining directly or indirectly to the barbarous massacre of thousands of Polish Army officers and civilian leaders buried in mass graves in the Katyn Forest on the banks of the Dnieper in the vicinity of Smolensk, U.S.S.R.

B. Organization of the Committee

The Speaker of the House of Representatives appointed the following members to this committee: Ray J. Madden (Democrat) Indiana, chairman; Daniel J. Flood (Democrat) Pennsylvania; Foster Furcolo (Democrat) Massachusetts; Thaddeus M. Machrowicz (Democrat) Michigan; George A. Dondero (Republican) Michigan; Alvin E. O'Konski (Republican) Wisconsin; and Timothy P. Sheehan (Republican) Illinois. The committee selected John J. Mitchell for counsel, Roman C. Pucinski as investigator, and Barbara Booke as secretary.

C. Procedure

This committee was confronted with the difficult task of determining whether the Germans or the Soviets were responsible for this colossal crime. Both countries had accused each other.

The task assigned this committee is without precedent in the history of the United States House of Representatives. But likewise without precedent is the fact that never before in the history of the world have two nations accused each other of such an atrocious crime with the identity of the nation actually guilty never having been sufficiently established.

Until the creation of this committee, this crime was destined to remain an international mystery and the conscience of the world could never have rested.

Fully aware then that this was the first neutral committee ever officially authorized by any government to investigate the Katyn massacre, this committee divided its investigation into two phases:

(1) Assemble evidence which would determine the guilt of the country responsible for the mass murder of these Polish Army officers and intellectuals in the Katyn Forest.

(2) Establish why the Katyn massacre with all of its ramifications never was adequately revealed to the American people and to the rest of the world. The committee likewise included in this phase an effort to determine why this crime was not adjudicated at the Nuremberg trials—where it should have been settled in the first instance if the Germans were guilty.

It was unanimously agreed by the committee that phase I of the investigation would be undertaken first and this interim report will include an analysis only of this phase. Testimony heard thus far has of necessity touched on phase II but additional study will be required before any conclusions can be reached.

This committee, for instance, heard testimony which clearly indicates certain reports and records relating to this massacre which were compiled by American observers had either disappeared or had been misplaced. What effect, if any, these reports might have had on this country's postwar foreign policy if the missing reports had been known and properly evaluated by all top level United States agencies will be the subject of subsequent hearings. The committee's conclusions on phase II will be incorporated in its final report.

D. Hearings

The committee's first public hearing was held in Washington on October 11, 1951. It heard the testimony of Lt. Col. Donald B. Stewart, a United States Army officer, who as a German prisoner-of-war, was taken by the Germans to view the mass graves at Katyn in May, 1943. (See Part 1 of the committee's published hearings.)

295

The next set of hearings was held in Washington on February 4, 5, 6, and 7, 1952. Seven witnesses appeared and rendered an account of their knowledge relating to the Katyn massacre. (See Part 2 of the published hearings.)

In Chicago on March 13, 14, 1952, eight other witnesses were heard by this committee. (See part 3 of the published hearings.)

In London on April 16, 17, 18 and 19, 1952, 29 witnesses were heard. (See Part 4 of the published hearings.)

In Frankfurt, Germany, on April 21, 22, 23, 24, 25, and 26, 1952, 27 witnesses were heard. (See Part 5 of the published hearings.)

In Berlin, Germany, on April 25, a subcommittee heard testimony from members of the German Commission on Human Rights and received approximately 100 depositions which had been taken by that organization.

In Naples, Italy, on April 27, testimony of Dr. Palmieri was heard.

In Washington on June 3 and 4, 1952, testimony was heard from five witnesses.

In the course of the hearings held by this committee to date, testimony has been taken from a total of 81 witnesses; 183 exhibits have been studied and made part of the record, and more than 100 depositions were taken from witnesses who could not appear at the hearings. In addition, the committee staff has questioned more than 200 other individuals who offered to appear as witnesses but whose information was mostly of a corroborating nature.

E.   Letters of Invitation

The committee unanimously agreed that in order to make this a full, fair, and impartial investigation, it would be willing to hear any individual, organization, or government having possession of factual evidence or information pertaining to the Katyn massacre.

Letters of invitation were forwarded to the Government of the USSR, the Polish Government in Warsaw, the Polish Government-in-Exile in London, and the German Federal Republic. The German Federal Republic and the Polish Government-in-Exile accepted the invitation.

The Soviet Government rejected the invitation of the committee with the statement that a Special Soviet Commission (composed of all Russian citizens) had thoroughly investigated the Katyn massacre in January 1944 and consequently there was no need for reopening the issue. However, the Soviet Government did attach to their reply the special commission's report and it later was made part of the permanent record of this committee. (See pp. 223 through 247, Part 3 of the published hearings.)

The Polish Government in Warsaw transmitted to the American Embassy a note likewise rejecting the committee's invitation, part of which is quoted as follows:

The attitude of the Polish Government re the activities of this committee was expressed in the declaration of the Polish Government published on March 1, 1952, and the Polish Government does not intend to return to this matter again.

The entire note may be found on page 504 of Part 4 of the public hearings of this committee.

The attitude of the Polish Government as quoted above was revealed by the vicious propaganda blast issued in the form of a press release and circulated to all newspaper correspondents by the Polish Embassy in Washington. The chairman of the committee published this press release in its entirety in the Congressional Record on March 11, 1952, and called upon the Secretary of State to take prompt action relative to the propaganda activities of the Polish Embassy here in Washington. The Secretary of State on March 20, 1952, delivered a stern reprimand to the Polish Embassy regarding such press releases and greatly restricted its activities in this field.

F. House Resolution 539

The first two series of hearings definitely established in the minds of this committee that it would be impossible to conduct a thorough investigation without obtaining the testimony of available witnesses in Europe. Consequently, the committee went before the House of Representatives on March 11, 1952, with House Resolution 539 which amended the original, House Resolution 390, and requested permission to take testimony from individuals and governments abroad. The House approved House Resolution 539 on March 11, 1952.

G. Findings

This committee unanimously agrees that evidence dealing with the first phase of its investigation proves conclusively and irrevocably the Soviet NKVD (Peoples' Commissariat of Internal Affairs) committed the massacre of Polish Army officers in the Katyn Forest near Smolensk, Russia, not later than the spring of 1940.

This committee further concludes that the Soviets had plotted this criminal extermination of Poland's intellectual leadership as early as the fall of 1939—shortly after Russia's treacherous invasion of the Polish nation's borders. There can be no doubt this massacre was a calculated plot to eliminate all Polish leaders who subsequently would have opposed the Soviets' plans for communizing Poland.

Appendix 8

General Wladyslav Anders' Statement Regarding Katyn of April 28, 1950

Although it is ten years now since the Katyn Crime was committed the Katyn Case as such can by no means be treated as closed. That is why I feel it my duty to raise it again and remind the Public Opinion of the Democratic Nations of its existence.

1. The Victims of the Crime, the Place and Date of Their Disappearance

The victims of this foul murder were my own Countrymen and my comrades-in-arms, most of them officers who—in the same way as I did—having fought in September 1939 against Hitler found themselves taken prisoners of war by the Red Army, the then German Ally, who joined Hitler in his assault by stabbing us in the back over the Eastern frontiers of Poland.

Two years later, after the outbreak of war between Germany and Russia and after the signing of an Agreement between the Polish Government in London and the Soviet Government, I was released from Soviet imprisonment and appointed Commander of a Polish Army to be formed in Russia from among the Polish prisoners-of-war, civilian prisoners and deportees. Soon after I had set about my task it became apparent that about 14,500 prisoners-of-war were missing, mostly officers who had been formerly inmates of three large P.O.W. camps in Kozielsk, Starobielsk and Ostashkov. It was further established that, ever since the disbandment of these three camps which had taken place in April and May 1940, except for some 400 men who had been transported to a camp in Griazowiec, all the others had vanished without a trace and without ever giving a sign of life. Not a clue about what had happened to them could be found in spite of a meticulous search which lasted nearly a year and in spite of several interventions at the highest level in Moscow including two personal interviews with Stalin himself at one of which General Sikorski was also present. All we ever got was a score of deceitful and vague answers. It was obvious that the Soviet Government was unwilling to explain what had happened with the thousands of missing prisoners-of-war taken by the Red Army in 1939.

2. The Katyn Graves and the International Consequences of Their Discovering

But when in April 1943 the Germans made their announcement about the discovery of the Katyn graves, the Soviet Government immediately came forth with a ready version about the alleged capturing by the Germans of several thousands of the missing Polish prisoners-of-war during the summer of 1941, and about the subsequent murdering of them by the Germans in August and September 1941. Furthermore, when the Polish Government headed by General Sikorski sent in a request to the International Red Cross asking for an investigation of the whole case, the Soviet Government not only refused its consent to any such investigation but moreover took this Polish initiative as an excuse for the severing of diplomatic relations with the Polish Government in London.

3. The Katyn Case Before the Nuremberg Tribunal

The Katyn Case came before the Nuremberg Tribunal as part of the general trial of the chief German war criminals by an International Tribunal. As prosecutor of this point of the indictment appeared the Soviet Union representative and therefore a representative of a Government which was a suspect No. 1 in the case of the Katyn Crime included in the indictment. Moreover, among the four members of the Jury there also sat a representative of this suspect Government. But there was no representative of Poland whose sons and soldiers were involved and who therefore was most entitled if not to accuse at least to plead and give evidence. True enough that delegates of the Warsaw Administration were sent to Nuremberg and did appear there although only in a secondary role but I do believe that there is no longer any doubt as to the real character of the Bierut Regime. But even to these agents of Soviet interests in Poland the right to speak in the Katyn case was denied.

Nevertheless and in spite of such a composition of the International Tribunal at Nuremberg, the Katyn Crime although included in the indictment was omitted from the judgment. There is no mention about this atrocity in the long list of inhuman crimes proved to have been committed by the Nazi Germans. The significance of this fact is enormous. It means that—since it was found impossible to prove that the Germans had perpetrated this crime—one of the greatest atrocities committed in this last war has been ignored and its culprit has escaped with impunity. The very principles of justice therefore call for the appointment of a new International Tribunal before which the Katyn case should be brought. Neither should it be thought that although this case no longer occupies the official bodies of International Justice or that at present nothing is heard about it at Lake Success, that it has been finally settled, that the crime will be forgotten and that the conspiracy of silence hovering over the mass graves of Katyn will last forever. On the contrary, to quote a sentence from an excellent article by Mr. G. F. Hudson in a recent issue of the quarterly 'International Affairs'—the unquiet dead of Katyn still walk the earth'.

4. The Uneven Struggle for Justice

We Poles will never forget Katyn. Having lost the right to raise our voice on the international forum after most of the countries had withdrawn their recognition of our Government, deprived of the possibility of appealing directly to Governments and to the institutions of International Justice, we have nevertheless prepared with perseverance our indictment. For years we collected every scrap of documentary evidence, we scrutinized every detail and we informed both the Governments of Democratic countries and the public opinion of the free countries about the result of our work.

Speaking of publications available to all, the most exhaustive material is to be found in the book 'The Katyn Crime in the Light of Documents' to which I have written a foreword and which was published in Polish in London in 1948, and in French in Paris in 1949. An English translation of this book is ready for publication and awaits a publisher. Further to this documentary work there is a whole chapter about Katyn in the book 'Stalin and the Poles' published last autumn by Hollis & Carter and containing a foreword written by the President of the Polish Republic. Important evidence is also contained in the memoirs of J. Czapski consisting of two books: 'Souvenirs de Starobielsk' and 'La Terre Inhumaine'. I have also related the story of the Katyn Crime in my memoirs which were published by Macmillan under the title 'An Army in Exile'. All these books are lying on this table ready for anyone who would care to look through them.

In our endeavors to make known the truth about Katyn we were by no means alone. Time and again we have found understanding among generous people not least of whom are here in Great Britain. They have never hesitated to stand up in defense of a righteous cause and have claimed justice for us in defiance of the materialistic considerations and the short-sighted attitude which seemed to dictate to many of the free Governments the policy of silence in the matter of Katyn in preference to the risk of irritating the Kremlin. I wish to express here my sincere thanks and appreciation to all those who preferred to put justice and truth before illusory political interests and especially may I be allowed to express my deep gratitude to those of our proved friends who are present here today.

5. The American Committee for the Investigation of the Katyn Massacre

Voices claiming justice in the Katyn case have been also raised many a time in other countries, especially in the United States of America. I wish to mention here particularly the speeches in Congress of the Hon. George A. Dondero on July the 7th, 1949 and of the Hon. Ray J. Madden on September the 29th, 1949, both of whom courageously and outspokenly demanded the conviction of these guilty of the Katyn crime.

Finally, towards the end of last year, an initiative in the U.S.A. which calls for our special gratitude has led to the formation of the "American Committee for the Investigation of the Katyn Massacre" under the chairmanship of Mr. A. Bliss-Lane, the former U.S.A. Ambassador in Poland. We greet the announcement of such an impartial investigation of the Katyn Case as an important and positive step towards the vindication of the principle of International Justice.

6. Polish Evidence is an Indispensable Element in Any Proceedings Relating to the Katyn Murder

I also hope that in any future proceedings relating to the Katyn Case the second essential misfeasance committed at Nuremberg will be avoided, namely that Polish evidence was not heard by the Court. By Polish I understand of course evidence given not by Soviet puppets but by free Poles entitled to demand the truth and to speak in the name of the victims and of the injury suffered in this case by the entire Polish Nation. Moreover hearing the Polish side in any Trial of the Katyn Case cannot be dispensed with not only because the very nature of legal procedure calls for it; it should be heard also because only when the material assembled by the Polish side can the evidence supplied by both the potential culprits be rightly estimated and the actual culprit determinated.

7. We Accuse the Government of the U.S.S.R.

I deem we are sufficiently prepared to appear before any Tribunal. Not only have we gathered all the available evidence but on the strength of the proof we possess we are positive *that the Soviet Government is guilty of having committed the Katyn Crime;* that the 14,500 Polish prisoners-of-war in Russian hands were murdered during April and the first half of May 1940, therefore at a time when Soviet Russia was still at peace and on friendly terms with Hitlerite Germany; that, therefore, the Kremlin is guilty of having calmly decided to murder in cold blood practically the whole of the Polish Officers Corps together with a few thousand other prisoners all of whom had fallen into the hands of the Red Army in September 1939, and whose only guilt was of having been the first to fight against totalitarian aggression.

I shall briefly sketch the following main points on which rests our firm conviction about the Soviet guilt and our indictment against the Soviet Government.

a/ It is an uncontested fact that all the murdered Polish prisoners were alive and in Soviet hands earlier in the spring of 1940. All statements brought forth by the Soviet Government that, while still alive, they had found themselves out of reach and no longer in the responsibility of the Soviet Authorities and that therefore they must have been murdered by someone else are false and obviously untrue and no proof can be given to support such statements.

301

b/ Throughout the ten months from August 1941 till July 1942 while vainly searching for the missing prisoners all over the Soviet Union, we had exchanged notes with the Soviet Government and had held innumerable conferences and interviews in this matter; but we never received any information about the falling of these men into the hands of the Germans in the neighborhood of Smolensk which was the story the Soviet Government put forth immediately after the revealed discovery of the Katyn graves.

c/ Soviet statements which claim that the Polish prisoners in question were alive till August-September 1941, at which time they were murdered by the Germans after having fallen into their hands when the Germans took over the Smolensk district, are absolutely with no foundation and no proof has ever been produced to support such a version. The truth is that ever since the spring of 1940, no sign of life has been given by any of the missing prisoners while every evidence retrieved from their bodies such as thousands of newspapers, letters and other documents proves irrefutably that the lives of the victims came to an end in spring 1940.

d/ The Soviet Government never gave its consent for the admittance of international impartial experts to the Katyn graves. It objected against it in April 1943 when the Polish Government requested the International Red Cross to investigate the case, neither did it invite a single international expert to investigate the graves when, six months later, the Katyn district was once again in Soviet hands. On the other hand the International Commission of Experts invited by the Germans to Katyn included, further to experts coming from countries occupied at the time by the Germans or allied to them also Dr. Fr. Naville, professor of Forensic Medicine in Geneva, and therefore from a country which was absolutely neutral. The report of this Commission dated 30th April, 1943, stated the Soviet guilt.

e/ The official Soviet Communique about the Katyn Massacre, published in January 1944 by a Commission composed entirely of Soviet citizens contains so many contradictions, obviously fictitious facts and false statements by feigned witnesses that it only strengthens the conviction about the guilt of the Soviet side.

f/ In spite of the privileged position the Soviet side had in Nuremberg no new arguments in favor of the Soviet version were produced at the trial. On the contrary, by failing to prove the guilt of the Germans the trial, although indirectly, also incriminated the Soviet Government.

8. The Group of Officers Who Escaped the Massacre

Before I end I should like to assure you that we welcome any inquiries and are willing to supply you with all explanations referring to our attitude in this matter and about the documentary material we possess. We also have among us a few of the former prisoners-of-war from the three camps which were liqui- dated in 1940. They belonged to that group of 400 sent first to the Pavlishtchev Bor and later to the Griazovetz camp and which was the only group to be spared from massacre. They can give you evidence particularly about the important circumstances of the evacuation of the camps and can testify about the ceasing of all correspondence with their lost comrades, a fact which they had learned from letters they received from their own families in the country.

9. My Appeal to the Public Opinion of the Free Nations

I thank you, Gentlemen, for having come here today and for your attention throughout my rather lengthy explanations. May I be allowed to appeal through you to the public opinion of the countries you represent as well as to that of other free and democratic countries and ask for their support of our endeavors tending to elucidate the Katyn Case and our plea for the appointment of a new International Tribunal which would be called upon to investigate this crime and to punish the culprits.

Because in my opinion, only if all the war-criminals of this last war will meet with adequate punishment will this be understood as a warning for the future and will give a guarantee that human principles will be maintained in case we find ourselves involved in a new armed conflict.

Appendix 9

Report to Polish Red Cross Directors in Warsaw from Casimer Skarzynski
(after Visiting Katyn Forest) of April 17, 1943
(Translated from Polish)

The next morning I submitted an oral report on my journey to the Central Board. The report was given in the minutes of the Presidium's meeting No. 332. From this report the following facts emerged:

1) At the locality of Katyn, near Smolensk, there are partially excavated mass graves of Polish officers;

2) Relying upon the examination of about 300 bodies so far exhumed, one may state that these officers were killed by bullets fired into the back of the head. The uniform nature of the wounds in all [the bodies] proves beyond doubt [that the executions were] mass executions.

3) The murder was not motivated by robbery, because the bodies are in uniforms, in boots, with distinctions, and a considerable number of Polish coins and banknotes were found on the bodies.

4) The murder took place in March–April 1940. This judgment is based upon the documents found on the bodies.

5) Up to now, only a small number of the murdered persons (150) have been identified.

6) If identification and registration of the murdered people is desired, the team sent to Smolensk should be increased by 5 or 6 persons.

7) The work of our Technical Commission can be developed and carried on only jointly with the work of the German military authorities competent in this area.

8) Our Commission received the kindest and fullest collaboration from the German military authorities in this area.

The first 6 of the above points do not require any discussion. With regard to point 7, the performance of an independent investigation by the Polish Red Cross alone at Katyn Forest was absolutely impossible. That the Polish Red Cross undertook the work of exhumation on such a scale outside the frontier of Poland, in a foreign country devastated by the war and occupied by our enemies, and moreover near the front (Smolensk is now only 30–40 km. from the front line), might [indicate that they] might have had in mind an investigation undertaken only with the assistance of the German army. It should be borne in mind that in the Katyn affair, as in all other affairs, the ends of German policy and those of the Polish Red Cross were totally different. The aim of the Polish Red Cross was to bury the bodies of the Polish officers in new graves as soon as the wearisome and complex work of exhumation and identification had been accomplished. The German authorities, however, were interested in propaganda. This discrepancy of aims has led to frictions which will be discussed *infra*. It was beyond any doubt that the German propaganda would give up the control of the work in order to ingratiate itself with Polish public opinion. Although this undertaking was in the interest of propaganda to some degree [propaganda] was nevertheless a secondary motive. The Polish Red Cross was to choose either to give up the work or to accept a modest executive function on the spot, under German control. For reasons mentioned above, the Polish Red Cross has decided to choose the latter alternative.

With regard to point 8, the Central Board having its Technical Commission near Smolensk in full dependence upon the German army, and having in mind the importance of the work of the Commission it [the Central Board] deemed it advisable to give . . .

[Translated by: Dr. Peter Siekanowscz, Foreign Law Section, Law Library. Library of Congress May 14, 1952.]

Appendix 10

Translated from Polish)
Polish Red Cross Technical (Field Team) Commission Report on Progress of
Work at Katyn

The following is the text of this report:

"On April 17, 1943, the Commission, provisionally composed of three persons, undertook the work, which was divided in the following way:

1) Mr. Rojkiewicz Ludwik—examination of documents at the Secretariat of Field Police;

2) Messrs. Kolodziejski Stefan and Wodzinowski Jerzy—searching for and securing of documents found on the bodies in Katyn Forest.

On this day, however, the work was interrupted because the delegation of Polish officers from German prison camps arrived. [They were:]

1) Lieutenant Colonel Mossor Stefan, Cavalry, Oflag II E/K No. 1449.

2) Captain Cynkowski Stanislaw, Oflag II E/K No. 1272.

3) Sub-Lieutenant Gostkowski Stanislaw, Oflag II D. No. 776/II/b.

4) Captain Kleban Eugenjusz, Oflag II D.

5) Sub-Lieutenant Rowinski Zbigniew, flier, Oflag II C. No. 1205/II/B.

6) Captain Adamski Konstanty, armored division, Oflag II C. No. 902/XI/A.

The members of the Polish Red Cross Commission had then to see the pits and documents jointly with the officers [who had arrived from German camps]. The behavior of the Polish officers toward the Germans was full of reserve and dignity. During a short talk apart, they acknowledged with apparent satisfaction that the Polish Red Cross had undertaken the technical functions of the exhumation, separating itself entirely from political [work].

On April 19, the members of the Commission were trying to get in touch with Lieutenant Slovenzik in order to settle the details of the operation. Since they had no means of transportation, these endeavors were unsuccessful. After waiting in vain until 14 o'clock on April 20, Mr. Ludwik Rojkiewicz went on foot to the Secretariat of the Field Police in order to get in touch with him. He turned back, however, having met a motorcar on the way, on which the members of the Polish Red Cross Commission, Messrs. Kassur Hugon, Jaworowski Gracjan, Godzik Adam, were riding. These members [of the Polish

Red Cross] left Warsaw on April 19 at 12:15 o'clock, together with representatives of the foreign press composed of a Swede, a Finn, a Spaniard, a Belgian, a second Flemish Belgian, an Italian, and a Czech, besides one Russian emigrant from Berlin and Professor Leon Kozlowski, former Prime Minister of the Polish Republic who lived there in Berlin, and three clerks from the Berlin Division of Propaganda.

Mr. Kassur assumed leadership of the Technical Commission of the Polish Red Cross. During conversations held on that day with Lieutenant Slovenzik, the following questions were raised:

1) the quarters for the members of the Technical Commission;
2) the spot of the work;
3) the means of communication for the members of the Commission;
4) the organization of the work of the Commission;
5) the preserving of documents;
6) the choice of a place for the new graves.

Because of the distance from Katyn to Smolensk (14 km.) and to the lack of means of communication, the members of the Commission were quartered in separate barracks in the village of Katyn, on the estate Borek, which was owned by a Pole, Mr. Lednicki, before World War I. This estate was 3.5 km. away from Kozy Gory. At this time the field hospital of Todt's organization was located there. The members of the Commission remained on this estate until May 20, and from May 21 to June 7, 1943 were quartered in the house attached to a village school near the station of Katyn. The members of the Committee were receiving food all day on the spot at the officers' mess of the Todt's organization. The rations were of the sort assigned to the nearby front detachment. It should be noticed that this food was sufficient.

Because of the lack of suitable accommodations in the forest, the work of taking out and examining the documents had by sheer necessity to be divided in such a way that the taking out of the documents and the reburial of the bodies was performed on the spot, i.e., in the forest of Katyn. A preliminary examination of the documents was carried on at the headquarters of the Secretariat of the Secret Police, a few kilometers away from the forest of Katyn in the direction of Smolensk.

Lieutenant Slovenzik expressed his opinion that the Polish Red Cross should bring its own means of communication to Katyn. After the explanation that all the Polish Red Cross' automobiles were requisitioned long ago, this problem was solved in the following way:

a) in order to get from the quarters to the forest of Katyn and back [the members of the Polish Red Cross Commission] were allowed to stop the military and private cars on the highway;

b) a motorcycle was delivered to furnish transportation to the office of the Secretariat of the Field Police.

The work was divided in the following way:

a) one member for the exhumation of the bodies;

b) two members for searching the bodies and removing the documents;

c) one member for examining the successive numbers of the bodies, which were then taken away to fraternal graves;

d) one member for the burial of the bodies;

e) two to three members for reading the documents;

f) since April 28, i.e., from the very moment of the arrival of the rest of the members of the Commission, Messrs. Wodzinski Marian, Cupryjak Stefan, Mikolajczyk Jan, Krol Franciszek, Buczak Wladyslaw, Plonka Ferdynand, the doctor of forensic medicine Dr. Wodzinski and his assistants from the Krakow dissecting laboratory were performing examinations of the bodies not identified by means of documents.

The procedure of the operation was as follows:

a) the bodies were exhumed and laid upon the ground;

b) documents were removed;

c) a doctor performed an examination of the bodies which were not identified;

d) the bodies were buried.

The work used to last from 8 o'clock to 18 o'clock every day, with one and a half hour for lunch.

The Commission states that the exhumation of the bodies has met with great difficulties. The bodies were pressed, [having been] chaotically thrown into the pits. Some bodies had their hands bound behind. The heads of some bodies were wrapped in overcoats, which were bound about the neck with a string. The hands were also bound at the back, in such a manner that the string was attached to the string tightening the overcoat at the neck. The bodies bound in this way were found mainly in one special pit which was inundated by subterranean water. The victims were extracted from this pit exclusively by members of the Commission. The German military authorities, because of the difficult working conditions, intended to refill this pit with earth.

In one pit there were found about 600 bodies laid face downward in layers.

The lack of sufficient number of rubber gloves caused great difficulty [in the work].

The exhumation of the bodies was being performed by the local inhabitants, who were driven to work by the German authorities. the bodies carried out from the pits on the stretchers were laid one beside another. Then the work of searching for documents began, in such a way that each body was searched individually, in the presence of one of the members of the Polish Red Cross Commission. The workers unstitched all the pockets, pulled out their contents, and handed over all articles thus found to the member of the Polish Red Cross

Commission. The documents and the articles were placed in envelopes marked with a successive number. The same number was impressed on a small plate and fixed to the bodies. Boots and even linen were unstitched in order to search for documents in a more thorough manner.

(Translated by: Dr. Peter Sieflanowicz. Supervised by Dr. Vladimir Gsovski, Chief, Foreign Law Section, Law Library, Library of Congress, May 14, 1952.)

If no documents or souvenirs were found, monograms (if any) were cut from the clothing or underwear.

Members of the Commission charged with the collection of documents had no right to examine or separate them; their duty was limited to placing in envelopes the following objects:

a) wallets with their contents,
b) all loose papers,
c) [military] decorations and souvenirs,
d) religious medallions and crosses,
e) one epaulette [from each body]
f) change purses
g) all valuable objects.

They were instructed to remove loose Polish banknotes, papers, coins, tobacco pouches, cigarette paper, wooden or tin cigarette cases. These instructions were issued by the German authorities so as not to overload the envelopes. The envelopes so prepared were tied with string or wire, numbered consecutively, and placed on a special table. They were handed over to the German authorities, who sent them twice daily by motorcycle runner to the Military Police Secretariat. If an envelope could not hold all the documents, another with the same number was used.

At the office of the Military Police Secretariat documents brought in by the motorcycle runner were taken over by the German authorities. The preliminary investigations and the ascertaining of names were done jointly by three Germans and representatives of the Technical Commission of the Polish Red Cross. The envelopes were opened in the presence of Poles and Germans. Documents found on the bodies had to be carefully separated with small wooden sticks from dirt, rotted matter, and fat.

First, documents were sought which would establish beyond doubt the identity of the victim. Identity was established on the basis of identity tags, identity cards, service cards, mobilization cards, even inoculation certificates issued in Kozielsk. In the absence of these, other documents were examined such as correspondence, visiting cards, notebooks, notes, etc. Wallets and purses containing Polish National Bank banknotes and coins were burned, and foreign currency, except Russian, and all gold coins and objects were deposited in the envelopes. Names which had been established and the contents of the envelopes were described by one of the German on separate sheets of paper in German, and the original numeration was maintained. The Commission gives the following explanation why the initial lists were only in German. Namely, the German authorities declared that they would immediately dispatch lists of the names to the Polish Red Cross as well as the documents after they were used. The Commission saw no reason to prepare a second list, especially since in the initial stage the personnel of the Commission was very small. If there were difficulties in establishing personal data, the notation "not recognized" was entered under the corresponding number, and documents discovered were listed. Such documents were sent by the German authorities to a special chemical laboratory for a detailed examination. [There,] when a positive result was achieved, the name of the victim was noted under the same number but on a separate list. It must be stated, however, that corpses without documents or souvenirs were present among the victims also. These were also given a number and a notation of "not recognized" was entered.

After the contents of an envelope were noted on a sheet of paper, all documents and objects were put into a new envelope under the same number, on which its contents were noted. This was the duty of the German members. Envelopes examined, separated, and numbered in this way were put into packing cases. They were placed at the exclusive disposal of the German authorities. Lists, typed in German, could not be checked by the Commission with the manuscript because it was not at the Commission's disposal. This system was followed from number 0421 to number 0794 in the presence of Mr. Ludwig Rojkiewicz. During the identification of numbers from 0795 to 03900 Messrs. Stefan Cupryjak, Gracjan Jaworowski, and Jan Mikolajczyk were present. The working method of the above-mentioned was almost identical with this difference, however, that they prepared their lists in Polish, which as occasion arose were sent to the Headquarters of the Polish Red Cross. From number 03901 to 04243 Mr. Jerzy Wodzinowski was present, and the same procedure was maintained. Identification of bodies numbered 1 to 112 and 01 to 0420 was performed exclusively by Germans before the Polish Red Cross Commission arrived. The Commission states that during the examination of documents, diaries, army orders, some correspondence, etc., were removed by the German authorities for translation into German. The Commission is unable to state whether such documents were returned and placed in their corresponding envelopes.

During the work of the Technical Commission of the Polish Red Cross in the Katyn forest, in the period from April 15 to June 7, 1943, 4,243 bodies were exhumed. Of these, 4,233 were taken out of 7 excavations placed closely together, which were discovered by German Army authorities in March 1943.

The eighth grave was found on June 2, 1943, and only 10 bodies were removed from it. They were buried in the No. 6 grave, which was still open at that time. German authorities stopped exhumation work from the summer until September, and the eighth grave after the exhumation of the ten bodies was covered up again.

Careful soundings by the Germans in the entire area were made for they were anxious that there should be little discrepancy between the announced figure of 10,000 to 12,000 victims and the reality. It is reasonable to suppose, therefore, that no more graves will be discovered. In grave No. 8, judging by its dimensions, the number of bodies should not exceed a few hundred. Soundings in the area have discovered several mass graves containing Russian bodies in varying degrees of decomposition.

All 4,241 exhumed bodies were reburied in six new graves which were dug in the vicinity of the murder graves. The only exception was made for the bodies of two generals, who were buried in two separate graves. The ground on both sides of the new graves is low and wet but the graves themselves are in an elevated and sandy location. The size and depth of these graves are unequal owing to local and technical conditions encountered during the work. The bottoms of all graves are dry, and each grave contains, depending on its size and depth, several groups of bodies, each group placed in several layers. Upper layers were placed at least one meter below the surface so that after the graves were covered with a mound one meter above the ground, upper layers are covered with two meters of earth. All graves have a flat surface, sides covered with sod. On each grave a cross two and a half meters high was placed, under which some forest flowers were planted. On the surface of each grave a cross of sod was placed. The graves are numbered as they were made in order to maintain the order of the numbered bodies. Bodies were placed in the graves with heads towards the east, one close to the other, heads slightly elevated, hands crossed. Each layer of bodies was covered with 20 to 30 centimeters of earth. In graves No. 1, 2, 3, and 4 the bodies were placed starting from the right side as they were brought in from the left side. The list of bodies placed in each grave is enclosed with this report as well as a map of the burial site, which covers an area of 60 × 36 meters, i.e., 2,160 square meters.

On the day the last members of the Technical Commission of the Polish Red Cross left Katyn, they placed on the dominating cross of grave No. 4 a large metal wreath made from sheet iron and barbed wire by one of the members of the Commission. This wreath, although made by hand and under field conditions, is of esthetic form and painted black; there is a thorn crown of barbed wire in the center with an eagle badge of solid metal from an officer's cap affixed to the cross. After placing the wreath, the members of the Commission honored the memory of the victims, standing in silence and saying a prayer; then took leave of them in the name of the Nation, their families, and themselves. The Commission thanked Lt. Slovendzik, 2nd Lt. Voss of the German military police, noncoms, enlisted men, and Russian workers for two months of very heavy exhumation work.

The Commission summarized its findings as follows:

1. Bodies exhumed from the graves were in a state of decomposition, and direct identification was impossible. Uniforms, however, in particular all metal parts, badges of rank, decorations, eagle badges, buttons, etc. were in a good state of preservation.

2. Death was caused by a shot in the base of the skull.

3. From the documents found on the bodies it appears that the murders took place in the period from the end of March to the beginning of May 1940.

4. The work at Katyn was under the constant supervision of the German authorities, who always detailed a guard to each group of the Commission at work.

5. All work was performed by the members of the Technical Commission of the Polish Red Cross, the German authorities, and inhabitants of local villages, numbering 20 to 30 persons. Some 50 Soviet prisoners detailed daily were used exclusively to dig and cover the burial graves and in leveling the ground.

6. General working conditions were difficult and nerve racking. Decomposition of the bodies and the polluted air contributed to the difficulty of the work.

7. The frequent arrival of various delegations, the daily visits to the area by a considerable number of military personnel, dissection of the bodies by German doctors and the members of the various delegations, made the work still more difficult.

Dr. Hugo Kassur, the leader of the Technical Commission, was unable to return to Katyn after his departure on May 12, 1943, and his duties till the end of the work were taken over by Mr. Jerzy Wodzinowski.

The Commission states finally that the requirements of German propaganda were a serious obstacle in its work. As much as two days before the arrival of a more important delegation work was slowed, and only 7 to 10 workers were detailed, the official explanation being that local inhabitants had failed to appear in spite of orders issued.

When professors of medicine from Germany or other states co-operating with the Axis, were scheduled to come, the bodies of higher officers or bodies which in addition to the bullet marks bore also marks of bayoneting or had their hands tied were reserved for them. Numerous intercessions of the Commission's leader were not respected. No attention was paid to the task of the Commission, and during the burial of bodies in the second grave gaps occurred in the numeration of bodies. Dissection of bodies by foreign professors took place without being co-ordinated with the work of the Commission, which in some cases made identification difficult. In order to avoid major complications in its work, the Commission was forced quite often to disregard German instructions which reserved certain bodies for other purposes.

German troops from the central sector of the front received an order to visit Katyn. Hundreds of persons visited the site of the crime daily. Through the Commission's intervention visiting was limited to a few hours daily, and military police were detailed to maintain order.

A few words of explanation to this report:

I have already mentioned the fact of German supervision. On one occasion Mr. Cupryjak, a member of the Commission, was ordered to show notes made in his notebook while examining the documents.

An incident which occurred between Mr. Kassur and Lt. Slovenczik cannot be omitted. On one occasion he came to us and declared that German authorities were informed that some of the Polish officers were of German origin or "Volksdeutsche." He demanded that they should be buried separately or at least in a dominating position in burial graves. He was given the answer that all murder victims were Polish officers, that it was impossible to determine their nationality and that

*   *   *   *   *   *   *

(Translated by Dr. K. Grzybowski, Supervised by Dr. V. Gsovski, Chief Foreign Law Section Law Library, Library of Congress May 14, 1953).

Appendix 11

Chairman Ray J. Madden's Invitation to the Ambassador of Poland in Warsaw
of March 18, 1952
(to Participate in the Investigation)

House of Representatives,
Select Committee to Investigate
the Katyn Forest Massacre,
Washington, D.C., March 18,
1952

His Excellency the Ambassador of Poland.

My Dear Mr. Ambassador: The House of Representatives of the United States of America on September 18, 1951, unanimously passed House Resolution 390. A copy of this resolution is attached for your information.

This resolution authorizes and directs a committee of Congress to conduct a full and complete investigation and study of the facts, evidence, and extenuating circumstances both before and after the massacre of thousands of Polish officers buried in a mass grave in the Katyn Forest on the banks of the Dnieper in the vicinity of Smolensk, U.S.S.R.

This official committee of the United States Congress respectfully invites the Government of Poland to submit any evidence, documents, and witnesses it may desire on or before May 1, 1952, pertaining to the Katyn Forest massacre. The committee will be in Europe during the month of April to hear and consider any testimony which may be available.

These hearings and the taking of testimony from witnesses are being conducted in accordance with the rules and regulations of the House of Representatives of the United States of America.

Sincerely yours,
Ray J. Madden,

Chairman, Select Committee to Conduct an Investigation and Study of the Facts, Evidence, and Circumstances of the Katyn Forest Massacre.

314

Appendix 12

Poland Government in Warsaw Response to the American Embassy in Warsaw and Forwarded from the State Department to Chairman Ray J. Madden of March 31, 1952

Department of State
Washington, March 31, 1952

My Dear Mr. Chairman: The American Embassy in Warsaw has received a note from the Government of Poland, a translation of which is as follows:

"On March 24, 1952, the Embassy of the Republic of Poland in Washington received a note from the Department of State transmitting a communication from Mr. Madden, Member of the House of Representatives of the United States Congress, to the Polish Ambassador, in which as chairman of the Committee of the House of Representatives for Katyn affairs he invites the Polish Government to present documents and witnesses in this matter.

"The transmission of the above invitation of the chairman of the congressional committee of the United States who, contrary to binding international customs, usurps to himself the right to extend invitations to sovereign governments has no precedent in the history of international relations.

"The attitude of the Polish Government re the activities of this committee was expressed in a declaration of the Polish Government published on March 1, 1952, and the Polish Government does not intend to return to this matter again."

Sincerely yours,
Jack K. McFall,
Assistant Secretary,
(For the Secretary of State).

Hon. Ray J. Madden,
Chairman, Select Committee to Investigate the Katyn Forest Massacre, House of Representatives.

Bibliography

Abraham, David. The Collapse of the Weimar Republic. Princeton Press, 1981.

Anders, Wladeslaw, General. An Army in Exile, (The Story of the Second Polish Corps). London: MacMillan & Co. Ltd., 1949.

Biddle, Francis. In Brief Authority. Garden City, New York: Doubleday and Company, Inc., 1962.

Collier's World Atlas and Gazetteer, by P. F. Collier and Son Corporation, New York, New York: 1946.

Czapski, Josef. The Inhuman Land. Chatto and Windus, London, 1951. (Translated from the French by Gerard Hopkins).

Czapski, Josef. Memories of Starobielsk [Souvenirs de Starobielsk], Temoignages, 1945.

Curry, Jane Leftwich, translated and edited by. The Black Book of Polish Censorship. New York: Random House, 1984.

Davies, Norman. White Eagle Red Star—Polish-Soviet War, 1919–1920. New York: St. Martins Press, 1972.

Davies, Norman. God's Playground (A History of Poland), Volume I—the Origins to 1795. New York: Columbia University Press, 1982.

Davies, Norman. God's Playground (A History of Poland), Volume II—1795 to the Present. New York: Columbia University Press, 1982.

Dawidowicz, Lucy S. The War Against the Jews, 1933–1945. New York: Holt, Rinehart and Winston, 1975.

Ekart, Antoni. Vanished Without Trace: The Story of Seven Years in Soviet Russia. London: Max Parrish & Co. Ltd., 1954.

Erickson, John. The Soviet High Command; A Military-Political History, 1918–1941. New York: St. Martins Press, 1962.

Erickson, John. Stalin's War With Germany. New York: Harper and Row, (A Cass—Canfield Book), 1975

Fainsod, Merle. Smolensk Under Soviet Rule. Cambridge: Harvard University Press, 1958.

Fischer, Louis. The Road to Yalta, Foreign Service Relations, 1941–1945. Harper and Row, Publishers, New York, Evanston, San Francisco, London, 1972.

FitzGibbon, Louis. Katyn (A Crime Without Parallel). New York: Charles Scribner's Sons, 1971

FitzGibbon, Louis. Unpitied and Unknown: Katyn . . . Dergachi . . . Bologoye. Bachman and Turner, London, 1975.

FitzGibbon, Louis. The Katyn Cover-Up. Tom Stacy, London, 1972.

Gilbert, Martin. Atlas of the Holocaust. Macmillan Publishing Company, Inc., New York, 1982.

Hart, B. H. Liddell. History of the Second World War. A Paragon Book by G. H. Putnam's Sons. New York, 1979.

Hitler, Adolf. (1889–1945). Mein Kampf [My Battle]. Originally written while in prison in the early 1920s. Abridged and translated by E. T. S. Dugdale, Boston and New York: Houghton Mifflin Co., 1933. Also translated by Ralph Manheim. Boston: Houghton Mifflin Co., 1943.

Johnson, Paul. Modern Times: The World From the Twenties to the Eighties. Harper and Row, 1983.

Khrushchev, Nikita Sergeevich. Khrushchev Remembers, (1936–1953), Volume I. Boston: Little Brown, 1970.

Khrushchev, Nikita Sergeevich. Khrushchev Remembers, The Last Testement, (1953–   ), Volume II. Boston: Little Brown, 1974.

Kravchenko, Victor. I Chose Freedom. New York & London: Charles Scribner's Sons. 1946.

Lane, Arthur Bliss. I Saw Poland Betrayed; An American Ambassador Reports to the American People. Indianapolis: Bobbs-Merrill Co., 1948.

Lineberry, William P. Poland. New York: The H. W. Wilson Company, 1984.

Littlefield, Henry Wilson. Outline—History of Europe, 1500–1848. New York: Barnes & Noble, Inc., 1939.

LIFE Magazine Series, commencing November, 1970.

Mackiewicz, Joseph. The Katyn Wood Murders. London: Hollis and Carter, 1951.

Mikolajczyk, Stanislaw. The Pattern of Soviet Domination. London: Sampson, Low, Marston and Co. Ltd., 1948.

Muncie Star Newspaper, Wednesday, January 14, 1987. p. 24.

New York Times, Page One, Major Events 1920–1975, as Presented. New York: Arno Press, 1975.

Oaks, John B. The Edge of Freedom. New York: Harper and Brothers, 1961.

Persky, Stan and Flam, Henry. The Solidarity Sourcebook. New Star Books, Vancouver, 1982.

Polish Cultural Foundation. The Crime of Katyn: Facts and Documents. Caldra House, London, 1965. (Polish Edition: 1948).

Ross, Bill D. Iwo Jima: Legacy of Valor. New York: The Vanguard Press, 1985.

Seton-Watson, Hugh. The Decline of Imperial Russia, 1855–1914. New York: F. A. Praeger, 1952.

Smith, Adam. The Wealth of Nations, (An Inquiry Into The Nature And Causes Of The Wealth Of Nations), (first published in 1776), Random House, Inc., New York, 1937.

Sussman, Leonard R. Article: Press Freedom, Secrecy and Censors, Freedom At Issue, January-February, 1987. p. 9.

Thorndike-Barnhart Dictionary, Scott Foresman and Company, 1952, (also published in 1942 and 1935).

TIME Magazine. Death in the Forest. July 17, 1972. p. 31.

Tolstoy, Nikolai. Stalin's Secret War. Holt, Rinehart and Winston, Toronto, 1982.

Turner, Henry Ashby, Jr. German Big Business and the Rise of Hitler. Oxford University Press, New York, 1985.

U.S. Congressional Hearings Before the Select Committee to Conduct an Investigation of the Facts, Evidence and Circumstances of the Katyn Forest Massacre. Part I. Washington, D.C. October 11, 1951.

U.S. Congressional Hearings Before the Select Committee to Conduct an Investigation of the Facts, Evidence and Circumstances of the Katyn Forest Massacre. Part 2. Washington, D.C. February 4, 5, 6 and 7, 1952.

U.S. Congressional Hearings Before the Select Committee to Conduct an Investigation of the Facts, Evidence and Circumstances of the Katyn Forest Massacre. Part 3. Chicago, Illinois. March 13 and 14, 1952.

U.S. Congressional Hearings Before the Select Committee to Conduct an Investigation of the Facts, Evidence and Circumstances of the Katyn Forest Massacre. Part 4. London, England. April 16, 17, 18 and 19, 1952.

U.S. Congressional Hearings Before the Select Committee to Conduct an Investigation of the Facts, Evidence and Circumstances of the Katyn Forest Massacre. Part 5. Frankfort, Germany. April 21, 22, 23, 24, 25 and 26, 1952.

U.S. Congressional Hearings Before the Select Committee to Conduct an Investigation of the Facts, Evidence and Circumstances of the Katyn Forest Massacre. Part 6. Exhibits Presented to the Committee in London. (The Polish Government in Exile's "White Paper.")

U.S. Congressional Hearings Before the Select Committee to Conduct an Investigation of the Facts, Evidence and Circumstances of the Katyn Forest Massacre. Part 7. Washington, D.C. June 3 and 4 and November 11, 12, 13 and 14, 1952.

U.S. Congressional Interim Report of the Select Committee to Conduct an Investigation of the Facts, Evidence and Circumstances of the Katyn Forest Massacre. July 2, 1952.

U.S. Congressional Final Report of the Select Committee to Conduct an Investigation of the Facts, Evidence and Circumstances of the Katyn Forest Massacre. December 22, 1952 (including Press Conference). (In response to House Resolutions 390 and 539 of the 82 Congress.)

U.S. Congressman George A. Dondero Speech in the House of Representatives on July 7, 1949.

U.S. Congressman Ray J. Madden Speech in the House of Representatives on September 29, 1949.

U.S. Congressman Derwinski Speech in the House of Representatives on May 14, 1962.

Wall Street Journal, Wednesday January 14, 1987. p. 1.

Websters's Collegiate Dictionary, G. & C. Merrian Co., Publishers, Springfield, Massachusetts, 1946.

Weschler, Lawrence. Solidarity, Poland In The Season Of Its Passion. Simon and Schuster, New York, 1982.

Whitcomb, Edgar D. Escape From Corregidor. Chicago: Henry Regnery Company, 1958.

Wittlin, Thaddeus. A Reluctant Traveller in Russia. London: William Hodge & Company, (Translated from the Polish by Noel E. P. Clark), 1952.

Wittlin, Thaddeus. Time Stopped at 6:30. Indianapolis: The Bobbs-Merrill Co., Inc., 1965.

Wittlin, Thaddeus. Commissar, The Life and Death of Lavrenty Pavlovich Beria. New York: The Macmillan Co., London: Collier-Macmillan Ltd., 1972.

Winston Dictionary, The John C. Winston Co., Philadelphia, Pennsylvania, 1952, (also 1943 and 1935).

Wyman, David S. The Abandonment of the Jews: America and the Holocaust, 1941–1945, New York: Pantheon Books, 1984.

Zawodny, J. K. Death in the Forest, (The Story of the Katyn Forest Massacre). Notre Dame, Indiana: University of Notre Dame Press, 1962. (Reprinted 1965, 1972 and 1980.)

INDEX